The Roots of Ethnicity

University of Pennsylvania Press
THE ETHNOHISTORY SERIES

Lee V. Cassanelli, Juan A. Villamarin, and
Judith E. Villamarin, Editors

A complete list of the books in this series
appears at the back of this volume.

The Roots of Ethnicity

The Origins of the Acholi of Uganda Before 1800

Ronald R. Atkinson

University of Pennsylvania Press

Philadelphia

Copyright © 1994 by Ronald R. Atkinson
Printed in the United States of America

Library of Congress Cataloging-in-Publication Data
Atkinson, Ronald Raymond, 1944–
    The roots of ethnicity: the origins of the Acholi of Uganda
before 1800 / Ronald R. Atkinson.
        p.   cm. — (Ethnohistory series)
    Includes bibliographical references and index.
    ISBN 0-8122-3248-8
        1. Acoli (African people) — Origin.   2. Acoli (African people) —
History — Sources.   3. Acoli (African people) — Ethnic identity.
4. Ethnicity — Uganda.   5. Ethnohistory — Uganda.   6. Chiefdoms —
Uganda — History.   I. Title.   II. Series: Ethnohistory series
(Philadelphia, Pa.)
DT155.2.A35A85   1994
967.61'004965 — dc20   94-12548
                                                          CIP

For
MY MOTHER, VANDORA QUIST SLAGAL

And in Memory of
MY FATHER, KENNETH L. ATKINSON
and
MY BROTHER, KENNETH L. ATKINSON, JR.

Contents

Illustrations

Preface

In the spring of 1985, Ed Steinhart asked if I would participate on a panel on ethnohistory that he was organizing for the African Studies Association meeting the next November. As Ed explains in his introduction to the special 1989 issue of the journal *Ethnohistory* devoted to the panel papers, Africanists have typically embraced neither the term ethnohistory nor the (mainly Native Americanist) literature done under that rubric. But I was more than a little interested. When Ed called, I was nearing the end of my first year in a full-time position teaching African history at the University of South Carolina, after being mostly outside the profession (and the academy) for several years. I was ready to return to work on the precolonial history of Acholi in northern Uganda and to begin rethinking what I had done and what I had learned as an impressionable young graduate student in the early 1970s. Ed's invitation gave me a perfect opening to commence that process.[1]

The responsibilities of teaching and the opportunity to become involved in an exciting educational project in South Africa at a critical juncture in that country's history (as well as my writing style) have combined to make the process longer than I imagined that spring of eight years ago. But during those eight years, the central focus of my reconceptualization of early Acholi history — ethnicity — has taken center stage in contemporary world politics, from the former old Soviet Union to the formative new South Africa. Ethnicity has entered into popular consciousness as well, primarily as a result of the particular ferocity of ethnic conflict (or conflict perceived and represented as such) in what used to be Yugoslavia. To the typical tragedies of civil war, the breakup of Yugoslavia has added "ethnic cleansing," and both the term and its devastating consequences have become a part of late-twentieth-century consciousness in almost the only way that that is possible, by flickering across the world's television screens.

Meanwhile, in a not unrelated development, ethnicity has taken on a much more prominent role in academic and intellectual discourse, as schol-

---

1. See Steinhart (1989).

ars around the world acknowledge and struggle to understand the existence and the power of ethnic mobilization and consciousness (see introduction). One particularly striking manifestation of this process for me was a September 1992 conference in South Africa on ethnicity and conflict in Natal that I attended as I was beginning the final round of revisions for this book. The conference was a stimulating and high-powered academic endeavor that brought together an impressive array of scholars on South African history, society, and politics, as well as the noted Russian historian of Africa, Irena Filatova, and the eminent Nigerian scholar Claude Ake, who broadened the focus of the proceedings with his keynote address, "Ethnicity, Culture and Class in Africa."[2]

As a newcomer to and sojourner in Natal, I learned a great deal during the conference about the complexities of the contemporary violence plaguing the region and about the social and historical dynamics underlying it. It was clear that concepts and representations of ethnicity — and particularly its manipulation and misrepresentation by the state and its surrogates in the Inkatha Freedom Party — were at the center of those dynamics. And one of the main messages of the conference was that it was essential to acknowledge, recognize, and attempt to understand and deal with ethnicity as a powerful force in late-twentieth-century Natal, South Africa, Africa more generally, and indeed in much of the world — however ethnicity might be defined and to whatever extent it is "real" or "imagined."

But the conference proceedings also illustrated how difficult and elusive the concept of ethnicity can be. Early in the proceedings, Irena Filatova resisted the notion of trying to define ethnicity. Later she noted that the conference would not have taken place even two or three years before, and added that just three years previously a team of scholars at a conference in the Soviet Union were denounced for speaking of ethnicity as existing at all. Another participant, with seeming agreement from others, remarked that ethnicity was "culture gone bad." In the three days of papers and discussions that dealt with ethnicity from many perspectives and in many contexts, conference participants were clearly grappling not only with a profoundly important and disturbing aspect of contemporary Natal, but with a difficult, even daunting, intellectual challenge.[3]

2. Ake (1992). The conference was organized by the Project on Contemporary Political Conflict in Natal and was entitled "Ethnicity, Society and Conflict in Natal." Other papers of particular relevance to the present study included Guy (1992), J. Wright (1992), Hayes and Maré (1992), and Nuttall (1992).

3. Professor Filatova's reluctance to attempt a definition of ethnicity and the comment about ethnicity as "culture gone bad" are reminiscent — as is much of the current discourse on

This book is one response to that challenge. One of its main arguments and underlying premises is that the depth and power of ethnic consciousness so manifest in our late-twentieth-century world often cannot be understood within analytic frameworks limited to the current century. And as exciting as the burgeoning literature on ethnicity is, it has an overwhelmingly twentieth-century orientation. This study, in contrast, focuses on what I am calling the "roots" of ethnicity among the Acholi of northern Uganda, by investigating late-seventeenth- and especially eighteenth-century developments that produced a new sociopolitical order across north-central Uganda. This order was characterized most importantly by chiefly forms of organization, and the establishment of these chiefdoms gradually set the area apart from both its non-chiefly past and its non-chiefly neighbors. A new society, a new collective identity, was in the making. Even before 1800, I argue, the roots of ethnicity — in this case an Acholi ethnicity — had been set.

The introduction to this study develops this argument more fully, first by exploring ethnicity within the context of twentieth-century Uganda, then by looking briefly at the historical and intellectual development of ethnicity as a topic or field of study, and finally by asserting that the current discourse on ethnicity needs to be extended to take a longer temporal perspective.

The chapters that follow are organized into three parts. Part 1, consisting of Chapters 1 and 2, sets the stage for the remainder of the book. Chapter 1 discusses the basic assumptions, priorities, evidence, and methodology that have shaped this study, giving special attention to oral sources as historical evidence. Chapter 2 investigates the physical environment and climate of Acholi, the mixed-farming economy established there from an early date, and the social organization and dynamics present during the mid- to late seventeenth century, just prior to the early stages of the transformations that would create a new sociopolitical order in the area.

Part 2 is comprised of Chapters 3 and 4. Chapter 3 looks at the main features of the new social order and political culture that come to characterize Acholi over the late seventeenth and eighteenth centuries, including a discussion of the extensive language shift that made Acholi a predominantly Luo-speaking area. Chapter 4 focuses on the initial, halting establishment of that new order during the late seventeenth and early eighteenth centuries, characterized by the emergence of the earliest Acholi chiefdoms.

---

ethnicity — of points made by Anderson regarding nationalism; see Anderson (1991, esp. introduction).

The core of the book is Part 3. Consisting of Chapters 5 through 8, this section examines the much more extensive establishment and consolidation of the new order from about 1725 to 1790, over virtually the whole of what became Acholi. This occurred in a context of unrest, hardship, and sometimes desperation in the region following a great drought and famine that probably struck during the 1720s. The drought radically altered material conditions and disrupted the social landscape, creating fertile ground for the development of chiefdoms in north-central Uganda on an unprecedented scale. The limits of this chiefdom formation, with all of its related political, social, and economic changes, began to mark out boundaries not present before, within which more and more people began to speak Luo, a language formerly used by only a small minority.

By the end of this period, people in Acholi shared a broadly common social order, political culture, historical experience, and language across north-central Uganda. The epilogue looks briefly at ways in which an Acholi society and identity continued to evolve during the nineteenth century, growing from its eighteenth-century roots.

Acknowledgments

I would like to thank, first of all, the many people in Acholi who over the years have agreed to share their knowledge and ideas of the Acholi past with researchers, both Acholi and outsiders. As the references attest, their numbers are many. I count myself lucky to have been among the researchers so entrusted and enriched.

I would also like to thank my assistants and interpreters, especially J. B. Okot, who worked with me on most of the interviews that I conducted and who consistently demonstrated skill, tact, and care in his work. He was also a good friend. Jackson Odong, Christopher Opio, and Marcellino Alum also helped at various times with interviews, transcriptions, or translations.

Colleagues in the History of Uganda Project who shared ideas, information, and enthusiasm about our collaborative endeavors included Bertin Webster, Ralph Herring, Maura Garry, Ade Adefuye, David W. Cohen, Keith Rennie, Paul Owot, Aidan Southall, John Lamphear, Randall Packard, and F. K. Uma. At Northwestern University, where I completed a Ph.D. dissertation on western Acholi in 1978, I have benefited over the years from the intellectual exchanges and friendships of Larry Yarak, Ivor Wilks, and especially John Rowe. John played a major role in making it possible for me to join the History of Uganda Project in the first place, was primarily responsible for obtaining a modest but essential Northwestern University Program of African Studies Special Grant that helped finance my research, supervised my dissertation, and made me feel welcome in his home for what is now more than twenty years.

Since I began to revisit and reconceptualize my work in Acholi following my full-time return to the academy in 1984, and especially since Ed Steinhart invited me to present a paper on his panel entitled "Ethnohistory and Africa" at the 1985 African Studies Association annual meeting, I have benefited from discussions with and critical readings of my evolving ideas from the following: Ed Steinhart, Ken Perkins, Terry Ranger, Carol Myers-Scotten, Ronald Robinson, Greta Little, Peter Becker, Ken Menkhaus, Abdullahi Aden, Ciraj Rasool, Patrick Harries (whose 1988 article provided me, at first without conscious awareness, the main title for this book), Andrew Spiegal, Yonah Seleti, Larry Glickman, and a group of particularly astute and harsh critics in one of my Honors College history courses at the University of South Carolina — Marty Clifford, Andrew Delfos, Patrick Doyle, Karla Fulmer, Heather Garris, Mary Hurteau, Victor Jenkinson, Lori King, Patrick Quattlebaum, Steven Qunell, Townsend Smith, Jenny Smoak, Carrie Stepp, and Shawna Wilson. I would also like to thank Julie Eyerman and the Humanities and Social Sciences Computer Lab at the University of South Carolina for skilled assistance in helping me prepare the maps for this book, Bobbie Reitt for her professional help in editing, Jennifer Mann for her careful help in proofing the galleys, and Bernie and Anne Harris and Merlyn Mehl for their sustaining support.

Finally, I would like to thank my wife Judy Wyatt, who has not only contributed in immeasurable ways to bringing this long project to a conclusion but who has made the journey along the way far more interesting, exciting, and enjoyable than anyone would have a right to expect.

Glossary and Pronunciation Guide

In Acholi Luo, the sound represented by the written vowel *a* is a short *a* sound (ă) like the *a* in about; *e* is a long *a* sound (ā) as in say or day; *i* is a long *e* sound (ē) as in bee; *o* is pronounced as a long *o* (ō) as in go, as the sound in out or about (ô), or as a short *o* (ŏ) as in song; and *u* is either a short *u* (ŭ) as in ultra, or a long *u* (ū) as in unit. With respect to consonants, *c* is always pronounced as *ch* in church (or Acholi); *g* is always a hard *g* as in game; *ng* is pronounced as the *ng* in song; and *r* at the end of words is virtually silent, as in *ker* (kāā) below. For a more comprehensive and linguistically precise guide, the standard reference is Crazzolara (1938).

abila (ă bē´ lă) shrine

ame (ă mā´) rainstones used for "rainmaking"

bul ker (bŭl kāā´) royal drum

bwola (bwō´ lă) special royal dance

dak ker (dăk kāā´) wife of the *rwot*ship

gang (găng) village

got (gôt) rock or mountain outcrop

gwelo (gwā´ lō) harvest ceremony

jago (jă´ gō) senior councilor of the *rwot;* evidence suggests that this term
    was rarely used before the twentieth century

jami ker (jă mē kāā´) royal regalia

jok (jôk) important "god" or "spirit"
    pl. *jogi* (jō gē´)

kaka (kă kă) lineage; other (supposed) patrilineal relatives elsewhere

kal (kăl) royal lineage; royal village or compound; place of the *rwot*

ker (kāā) royal authority or power

kom ker (kŏm kāā´) royal stools

kot (kôt) rain

kweri Madi (kwā rē mă´ dē) Madi hoes; special brideprice objects
    kweri tile (kwā rē tē´ lă) alternative for Madi hoes

ladit kaka (lă dēt´ kă kă) elder of the lineage
    pl. *lodito kaka* (lō dē´ tō kă kă)

ladit-pa-rwot   (lă dēt´ - pă - rwôt) elder of the *rwot*
 pl. *lodito-pa-rwot* (lō dē´ tō - pă - rwôt)
lakwena   (lă kwā´ nă) messenger of the *rwot*
 pl. *lukwena* (lū kwā´ nă); also sometimes the collective assembly of the
 rwot's councillors
lobong   (lō bŏng´) subordinate or subject lineage
loka   (lō kă´) land beyond the river
 Loka (lō kă´) Paluo; land beyond the Nile River
 lo-loka (lō - lō kă´) people from Paluo
luk   (lūk) illicit sexual intercourse
lwak   (lwăk) subordinate or subject lineages; also herd, group, crowd,
 multitude
mwoc   (mwŏch) lineage praise calls
ongon   (ō ngŏn´) legal norms or old precedents
Paluo   (pă lwō´) area and people in northern Bunyoro just south of
 Acholi
rwot   (rwôt) chief; ruler
 pl. *rwodi* (rwō´ dē)
tong ker   (tŏng kāā´) royal spears
tyer   (tyāā) tribute
twon   (twŏn) bull; a strong important person
won ngom   (wŏn ngŏm) father or "owner" of the soil
 pl. *wegi ngom* (wā gē ngŏm)

Introduction: Ethnicity in Perspective

The main argument underlying this book is that we cannot account for the strength and depth of ethnic consciousness in Uganda — or indeed in the rest of Africa and beyond — by looking only at the colonial and post-colonial eras. To be sure, colonial rule and its aftermath have played a major role in shaping the particular nature and manifestations of modern ethnicity in Africa. At the same time, many current expressions of ethnicity have roots that go much further back into the past than the last hundred years. These deeper roots need to be recognized and investigated. Only then can we begin to come to grips with one of the most complex and powerful social phenomena confronting and often confounding the late-twentieth-century world, from Africa to Asia to central and eastern Europe.

This book explores such long-term roots of ethnicity by examining the origins and establishment of a distinct social formation in northern Uganda and the early evolution there of a collective identity known since the later nineteenth century as "Acholi." Using primarily oral sources, I have reconstructed the ideological underpinnings and sociohistorical processes that contributed to the development of an "emergent Acholi" up to the late eighteenth century. This end date has been selected because by then a common social order and political culture had been established, and a common language had begun to be spoken, over almost all of what is now the Acholi District of Uganda — processes that laid fundamental foundations and set crucial parameters for the further evolution of Acholi societal formation and ethnic consciousness over the nineteenth and twentieth centuries.

This study, then, is far removed from the recent past. The history that unfolds here long precedes colonial rule, post-colonial politics, military coups, or the massive devastation that has dominated the past two decades of this small and beautiful country's history. But Uganda's recent and distant pasts do relate, in fairly direct if perverse ways. Many of the events and relationships characteristic of Uganda's recent history — including politics and political violence — have been intimately bound up with Ugandans' perceptions of their societal and ethnic identity. Of course, these perceptions are social constructions, "representations, rather than features, of the real world." Such representations, moreover, not only change over time but often distort and manipulate, particularly as part of a "discourse of domination" emanating from those in power in successive colonial and post-colonial regimes.[1]

But the colonial and post-colonial representations of ethnic identities in Uganda, however distorted or manipulative, have not been plucked from the air or created out of nothingness. Writing of the vast forest region of West-Central Africa, Jan Vansina notes that some ethnic identities there seem "to have existed only in the minds of French administrators." "On the other hand," he continues, "not all ethnic references are of colonial vintage." Indeed, I would argue that the ideological and sociohistorical forces involved in the construction and representation of ethnic identities in Africa are often, perhaps even usually, *not* confined solely to the colonial and post-colonial eras. In the present case, exploring the long-term roots of Acholi ethnicity takes us deep into the precolonial past, back to the early stages of the Acholi's always "unfinished process of coming to be." Before beginning that journey, however, it will be helpful to look briefly at ethnicity in the more familiar context of the twentieth century.[2]

Ethnicity in Twentieth-Century Uganda

Misrepresentations and manipulations of ethnicity were part of the very creation of Uganda by the British. At the center of that creation and the distortions of ethnicity accompanying it was the kingdom of Buganda (Map 1). Buganda was the largest, wealthiest, and most powerful state in nineteenth-century East Africa. It was also the state that Europeans of the time recognized as most similar to their own and thus worthy of some

1. Sharp (1988a, p. 6); he defines "discourse of domination" as comprising "a particular reading of a series of terms . . . (such as race, tribe and ethnic group) . . . which reveals the logic and serves the interests of those who wield power."
2. The Vansina quotations above are followed by the conclusion that "ethnic units must be abandoned as unanalyzed units for study." See Vansina (1990, pp. 19–20); I assume that "unanalyzed" is the crucial notion here, not the abandonment of studying ethnic groups generally. The "unfinished process" phrase is from Lonsdale (1977, p. 132), and is echoed, for example, by Ambler (1988, pp. 32, 157), Sollors (1989, p. xiv), Chapman et al. (1989, p. 9), and Vansina (1990, p. 19). Finally, the terrain of precolonial history explored in this book is not now a fashionable one. As David Henige trenchantly observes, "the early enthusiasm for precolonial history has not so much been tempered as virtually abandoned" (personal communication).

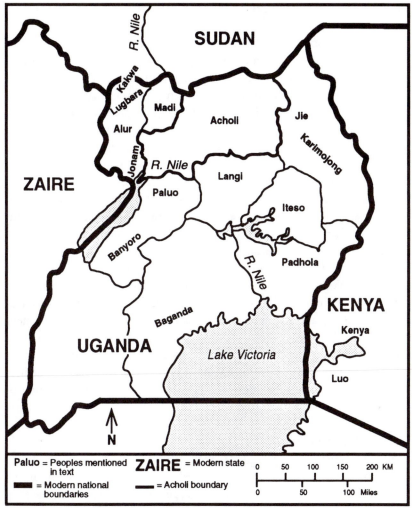

Map 1. Uganda and its peoples.

respect and recognition. Buganda became the focus of merchant, mission-ary, and other colonial activity in the region as the nineteenth century rushed into the twentieth and Europe "scrambled" for Africa.

And many Baganda, operating in a rapidly changing and intensely competitive and politicized society, saw potential advantage in allying themselves with the powerful new outsiders. Indeed, Buganda served as the bridgehead for extending British imperial rule into the rest of what became Uganda.[3]

Buganda also became the commercial and administrative center of the colony. Roads and schools and other infrastructural investments were concentrated there; so, too, was much of the new or expanded production for both local and distant markets. And though Europeans led in structuring these processes and gained most from them, powerful Baganda chiefs actively participated and benefited as well. All in all, the people of Buganda, particularly the powerful and wealthy, garnered a highly disproportionate share of the limited opportunities for social and material advancement available to "natives" in the colonial political economy.

In this context, both the Baganda and British elite emphasized, exaggerated, and sometimes invented ethnic distinctions. These distinctions were typically represented as age-old, fundamental, immutable, and "tribal"; they were also inextricably intertwined with the Eurocentrism and racism characteristic of European dealings with "the other" during this period. Ideologically, accentuating differences between the Baganda and others and representing such differences as inherently "tribal" served to justify the unequal distribution of capital and infrastructural development that marked the "special" relationship between the British and Baganda. In fact, the privileged access of Baganda (especially the elite) to social, economic, and political opportunities, and the very real material inequalities that ensued, helped create far greater differences and a greater awareness of difference than had ever existed before.[4]

ACHOLI UNDER COLONIAL RULE

Acholi, meanwhile, was marginal in many ways to early colonial rule. It was a dry and sparsely populated land located far to the north and of limited interest to those at the center of the colonial endeavor in Buganda (see Map 1). Acholi was also widely viewed as occupied by a tribe of a quite different and inferior order, on three main grounds. First, the Acholi were perceived to have little to contribute to the "development" of the colonial economy.

---

3. See the classic treatment of "Buganda sub-imperialism" by A. D. Roberts (1962); see also Michael Twaddle (1993) on one of the key figures in this sub-imperialism, Semakula Kakungulu.

4. A brief depiction of parallel processes in neighboring Kenya can be found in Ambler (1988, pp. 153–54). Please note that the term "tribe" and its derivatives (such as "tribal") are fundamentally imprecise and inaccurate; whenever they are used hereafter they should be envisioned as within quotation marks, though such markings will usually be omitted to avoid cluttering the page.

This opinion was due in part to the physical remoteness, sparse population, and limited productive capacity of the land, in part to the Acholi people's supposed "natural" laziness and aversion to work (the initial Acholi response to peasant cash cropping and labor migration was not enthusiastic). Second was the relatively small-scale and decentralized nature of Acholi political organization, which made the Acholi neither an especially feared enemy nor a valued ally. And third was Acholi social and cultural practices — especially the wearing of minimal clothing — which both the British and Baganda elite looked down upon as bizarre and primitive.

Marginal and inferior as they were considered, however, the Acholi were gradually incorporated into the colonial political economy. Through the 1890s, British activities in what became northern Uganda were sporadic and aimed at monitoring activities of the Belgians and French to the west and keeping them a safe distance from Buganda. During this period official British policy was to confine the protectorate to Buganda alone and limit dealings with other peoples to the maintenance of friendly relations.[5]

By 1902, policy had changed and Acholi was officially recognized as one of three districts in the Nile Province of a Uganda protectorate. Over the rest of the decade, a Buganda-style council of chiefs was established (largely to achieve what British administrator Charles Delme-Radcliffe called "the identification of the chiefs with the Administration and making them a part of the Government organisation"); firearms were increasingly registered; hut taxes were haltingly collected; and cotton was introduced and promoted as a cash crop. Firearms, meanwhile, continued to pour into Acholi as they had since the 1880s, making the district one of the most heavily armed in the protectorate. In late 1910 the British established their first administrative center in Acholi at Gulu; a second station was built farther east at Kitgum in 1914 (see Map 1).[6]

Far more intrusive intervention then ensued. Acholi firearms were confiscated and destroyed. Following this, many people were forced to move near roads built throughout the district, facilitating both communication and administrative control. Political authority in the district was also restructured. First, the imported Buganda-style council of chiefs, with a new "paramount" chief, was further entrenched. Second, many formerly

5. Dwyer (1972, pp. 60–68). Two typical examples of early colonial views of the Acholi, often erroneous and even more often disparaging, can be found in Sadler (1904/5) and in the memoirs of the first District Commissioner in Acholi, J. R. P. Postlethwaite (1947).

6. Dwyer (1972, pp. 102–29, 146–47); the Delme-Radcliffe quote is from Bere (1947, p. 8).

independent chiefdoms were amalgamated, thereby extending the authority of some chiefs over peoples they had never previously ruled while demoting or removing others. Third, even those chiefs remaining in office were controlled much more than before, with "their duties prescribed and their political activities strictly supervised." Finally, the administration "jettisoned [their policy of following] a rigid adherence to the Acholi law of succession in the appointment of chiefs" in favor of a much more ad hoc process. These changes produced winners as well as losers and were met with responses ranging from overt resistance (always scattered and localized, and almost always brutally suppressed) to active collaboration.[7]

Meanwhile, the administration increasingly promoted the production of cotton as a cash crop; indeed this became perhaps the fundamental goal of the government. The first Acholi District Commissioner, J. R. P. Postlethwaite, wrote that individual land tenure and cotton growing would create "a more stable society" and promote "the intellectual, moral and economic progress of the people." Cotton production also, of course, furthered two fundamental material objectives of colonial rule: the Acholi could use the money they earned both to pay taxes and to purchase the imported European consumer goods increasingly penetrating the colonial economy.[8]

If peasant production of cotton as a cash crop was Acholi's primary role in the colonial economy, its secondary role was to provide recruits for the colonial army or police and migrant labor to the more populous and "developed" south. Widely held British stereotypes about the Acholi made them attractive to security-force recruiters: one source, for example, refers to "their superior physique, habits of discipline, and unsophisticated outlook." By colonial East African standards, the total number and percentage of Acholi who entered the migrant labor force seems always relatively low, somewhere between 10 and 20 percent of adult males.[9]

Still, by the outbreak of World War II, a substantial number of Acholi were, or had been, members of the colonial army and police forces. Because

7. These developments are discussed in general in Dwyer (1972, pp. 130–88), which includes the quotation (on pp. 187–88) about chiefs being closely supervised. The "jettisoning" statement is from an entry Postlethwaite made in a 1915 District Record Book, quoted in Girling (1960, pp. 84, 175); I could not find this book in the Acholi District Archives in the early 1970s. The most extensive Acholi resistance occurred in Lamogi in 1911–12 in opposition to the government policy of weapons confiscation. See Adimola (1954); Dwyer (1972, pp. 130–59).

8. The quotation is from Postlethwaite (1947, p. 66); see also Girling (1960, pp. 175–76). Freund (1984, chap. 6) discusses the "penetration of capital" in colonial Africa.

9. See Girling (1960, pp. 178–81, 218).

cotton production and unskilled migrant labor yielded such low returns, many Acholi with army or police ties attempted to join the growing wartime forces. By the war's end, some 5,600 Acholi were serving in the army, roughly 20 percent of the male household heads then paying poll tax in the district. Demobilization after the war saw most of these men discharged, though enough Acholi remained to make them the Ugandan tribe with the highest number of soldiers.[10]

Meanwhile, the lines drawn on colonial maps and images in peoples' heads demarcating Acholi from neighboring tribes were increasingly operationalized, reinforced, and reified, in a pattern common to much of colonial Africa. On the basis of perceived (or presumed) common origins, political organization, language, and culture, Acholi was a designated tribe, and as such was administered as a discrete tribal unit. Politics was to be strictly limited and exclusively tribal. Individuals and social and political groups among the Acholi competed for power and influence within the context of their tribe, and the Acholi as a collective entity competed with other tribes for scarce social and economic investments and opportunities. All of this served the interests of those in power, who emphasized sharply differentiated and exclusivist tribal cultures and identities, and exaggerated and even invented differences among them. In this context, the Acholi and their neighbors increasingly saw themselves as different and distinct from each other, and acted as if this were so.

Missionaries also promoted a tribal consciousness in Acholi and neighboring areas, primarily by developing written vernacular languages and producing written accounts of local (or tribal) histories and customs. Both Protestant and Catholic missions played these roles in Acholi, but the most active were the remarkable J. P. Crazzolara and his fellow Verona Fathers. Together, missionaries helped create a powerful new idiom and new avenues for the expression of a consciously identified and clearly bounded ethnic (tribal) identity. They also produced a local educated elite who further developed and articulated this identity and propagated it to a much wider audience than the missionaries alone could have ever done.[11]

10. Ibid. High as the percentage of Acholi household heads in the wartime army was, Girling notes that it was only about one in every three who had tried to join; the majority had been rejected because they carried various disqualifying diseases.

11. Most collections of Acholi traditions made before the History of Uganda Project in the early 1970s were the product of missionaries or Acholi trained by them. The most extensive of these comprised much of the classic three-volume work on Luo-speaking peoples by Crazzolara (1950, 1951, 1954); see Chap. 1. The crucial role of missionaries in the creation of

ETHNIC POLITICS AND POST-COLONIAL UGANDA

By the late 1950s, as Uganda moved toward independence, many of the contradictions of colonial rule became obvious. Most important was the extremely privileged position of Buganda and, to a lesser degree, of the south in general. Disparities that had begun with the founding of the colony increased after World War II, when vastly greater resources than ever before were poured into the territory in a burst of activity that Lonsdale and Low have called a "second colonial occupation."[12]

When independence came in 1962, Buganda, followed by the rest of the south, had by far the greatest proportion of infrastructural development, capital investment, productive capacity, and social services (most notably in health care and education) in the country. And though others made marginal gains from all this, the primary beneficiaries were the mainly Western-educated, urban, and Baganda elite. Their numbers dominated the rapidly expanding civil service, and virtually monopolized its higher level positions as they were opened up to Africans.

For independent Uganda's first head of state, A. Milton Obote, and for the Uganda Peoples' Congress (UPC) Party that he led, redressing this imbalance was a priority. Of course, the imbalance was viewed differently by people in various strata of society and from various parts of the country, as was reflected by the four broad constituencies that provided the main support for Obote and the party.

The first consistency was the non-Bantu-speaking north. Support in this region was often expressed in ethnic terms. But it is significant to note that the most important level of identity invoked was regional rather than narrowly tribal. Obote was a northerner, from the Luo-speaking Lango ethnic group located just south of Acholi, and much of the regional enthusiasm for the UPC was based on the hope that fellow-northerner Obote would close the gap between their region and the south. So even though political discourse in the north had a distinctly ethnic tone, and was sometimes virulently anti-Baganda, the concerns were ultimately material. Most northern peasant farmers and their families hoped to catch up in such areas as income, consumer goods, health clinics, roads, and, especially, schools. The small but growing northern elite, on the other hand, seemed to look

---

new, or new kinds of ethnic identity in colonial southern Africa is analyzed by Vail (1989b, pp. 10–16), and is dealt with in specific contexts (again mostly in southern Africa) by Harries (1988, 1989); Ranger (1979, 1983, 1989); A. F. Roberts (1989); Vail (1981); Vail and White (1989). Much of this draws on the provocative work of Anderson (1983; 2nd ed. 1991).

12. Low and Lonsdale (1976).

forward primarily to obtaining positions and promotions in the party and in civil service.

The second major pro-Obote and pro-UPC constituency consisted of non-Baganda Bantu speakers who had much the same complaints about Buganda's domination that northerners had, and much the same hope for a change in their favor. The elite component of this second constituency was both larger and more important than that in the north.

A third constituency in the Obote camp came from the ranks of the urban working class, as well as politically conscious peasants and students attracted by the socialist strains in Obote's message. This was the one significant support group of Obote and the UPC that was not ethnically based and that cut across regional boundaries.

The fourth constituency in the early years of independence was the army. Initially this support was concentrated among the rank and file, many of whom were northerners. But it soon included more of the officer corps as well. For as the army grew larger and more powerful, receiving ever greater shares of the national budget, the officer ranks were transformed from a small number of mostly Europeans, Baganda, and other southern Ugandans to a much larger group increasingly from the north of the country. While short-lived, this army support and the attempts of Obote and his advisors to retain it played a crucial role in Ugandan politics.

The relationship between Obote and Acholi was equivocal. In Acholi as a whole, support for Obote and the UPC was lower than in most parts of the north for as long as opposition parties were legal. One reason was a strong Catholic mission presence and the adherence of many Catholics (encouraged by the missionaries) to the Democratic Party. The lukewarm reception to Obote in Acholi was matched by the relatively limited dispensation of government-controlled economic and social investments in the district. But there was one arena in which Acholi and Obote were strongly mutually supportive: the army.

The strong representation of Acholi in the colonial East African army following demobilization after World War II continued throughout the 1950s; about one thousand Acholi still served by the end of the decade. When colonial rule ended a few years later, the Acholi had more soldiers than any other Ugandan ethnic group, and their prominence in a Ugandan national army grew after independence. This was almost certainly due in part to the persistence of colonial manpower and recruitment patterns. But as Obote and those closest to him came to rely on the army as a crucial support group (eventually *the* crucial group), the number of Acholi in both the rank and file and officer corps grew even faster than the army as a whole. The only other ethnic group whose presence increased at a comparable pace, though it began from a much smaller base, was the Langi. To many, both in and outside the army, it seemed threatening that Obote was creating a security force made up more and more of fellow Luo-speaking "tribesmen" — in this case both Acholi and Langi.

This interpretation gained currency as Obote began to move against a growing array of opposing interests. In 1966 Obote called on the army to overthrow the king of Buganda and abolish that and other kingdoms recognized in the four-year-old constitution. Over the rest of the decade, Obote banned all opposition parties, pursued a seemingly serious move to the left that threatened both foreign and local capitalist interests (including those of many high level members of the party, civil service, and army), and also crossed swords with the man he had promoted from the ranks to head the army, Idi Amin. The combination of forces against him was too great to withstand, and in early 1971 Obote was overthrown in an Amin-led coup.

Despite the tendency of the Western press to depict Amin as an ignorant, relatively amiable if unpredictable buffoon, it was soon evident in Uganda that the Amin regime was not a joke. Politics under Amin quickly took on a harsh and even deadly form. It was a politics reduced to the most basic levels of acquiring and maintaining power and amassing the perks that resulted. Ideology was a totally cynical and instrumental tool used to gain support or throw opponents off balance. Anyone perceived as a threat was attacked. In pursuit of their ends, Amin and his supporters would seemingly stop at nothing. The regime not only terrorized and killed thousands of people; it destroyed Uganda's economy, institutions, and infrastructure. The toll is incalculable.

Amin's external support began with Israel and Britain (who each miscalculated strategic and commercial interests) and ended with Libya and other Middle Eastern states (primarily in response to Amin's belated emphasis on his Muslim background and promotion of the interests of the Muslim minority in Uganda). Internally, Amin's initial support was broad if not deep, consisting of many of those threatened by or opposed to Obote and his policies. But as the Amin regime's ruthless quest for power and constant attacks on those considered a threat went on, this support steadily narrowed. In the end the regime depended primarily on mercenaries from Sudan and Libya and soldiers from Amin's own small ethnic group, the Kakwa, located in the northwestern corner of Uganda and across the border in the southern Sudan (see Map 1).

With Amin's coup, Acholi's special access to the military turned into a deadly liability. From the coup's earliest stages, the Acholi and their Langi "relatives" were marked as enemies and, beginning with service personnel, bore a heavy share of the brutality and killing that Amin's men rained upon the country. After Amin's overthrow in 1979 (with Acholi soldiers playing a prominent role), Acholi ethnic identity throughout the 1980s alternatively offered opportunity or danger as one regime gave way to another in a spiral of political violence played out all too often in ethnic terms.[13]

Especially since 1971, then, little has mattered more to Acholi, individually and collectively, than ethnic identity. For many thousands of men, women, and children, being identified as Acholi has literally meant, depending upon chronology and circumstance, life or death.

Toward an Understanding of the Evolution of an Acholi Identity

What, though, has determined that some people in northern Uganda (and the southern Sudan) are called Acholi and others not? In what ways and to what extent are Acholi different from their neighbors? What sociohistorical structures, relationships, ideology, and processes of change contributed most to the differences? When did differentiation occur? What determined the geographical extent and boundaries of Acholi territory? In short, how did an Acholi society and collective identity develop? This study attempts to provide answers to these questions for the period up to the end of the eighteenth century. A follow-up volume, in preparation, will carry the story forward into the 1990s.[14]

Acholi would certainly continue to be marked by significant change over the nineteenth and twentieth centuries. But this change would take place upon foundations and within a framework already established. For example, the number and composition of the central sociopolitical units (chiefdoms) in emergent Acholi varied little from 1800 until well into the

13. For analyses of recent Uganda, see, for example, Hansen (1977); Mamdani (1976, 1983); Mazrui (1978); Nabudere (1980); and Hansen and Twaddle (1988a), especially the contributions by Wrigley, Southall, Low, Kanyeihamba, Edmonds, Obbo, Doornbos, Rowe, Mudoola, Nabudere, Twaddle (all 1988), and the introduction by Hansen and Twaddle (1988b).

14. In addition to the forthcoming book-length study, I discuss the evolution of an Acholi ethnic identity during the nineteenth century below in the epilogue and in Atkinson (1989).

twentieth century, when colonial rule became sufficiently entrenched to transform the political landscape. Second, the number of new lineages incorporated into these chiefdoms after 1800 would increase only slightly, after massive growth during the eighteenth century. Third, the common language that came to characterize Acholi, Luo, was already widely spoken in the area by 1800. And lastly, boundaries demarcating this emergent Acholi social order, political culture, and developing identity were already clearly discernable by 1800, beginning to mark Acholi off from divergently developing neighbors.

In short, Acholi society and ethnicity have roots that long predate the twentieth century, or even the nineteenth and twentieth centuries together. Importantly, this also seems true for many other parts of Africa and the wider world. Thus, if we are to understand the evolution of ethnicity, or the depth and power of ethnic consciousness and identity in the late-twentieth-century world, we cannot focus merely on the past two centuries, and certainly not on the colonial period alone, as the current literature on Africa tends to do.

This literature focuses on the creation of tribes and ethnic identities as a consequence of European rule and is both illuminating and exciting. It draws on the work of Fredrik Barth and those who have followed him to get beyond widely held stereotypes about ethnicity and tribes. But important as this recent work is, I would argue that we need to move beyond its narrow chronological focus.

SOME POPULAR BELIEFS AND STEREOTYPES ABOUT ETHNICITY AND TRIBES

Anthropologist Peter Skalnik has identified three notions of the term "tribe" that many if not most Americans and Europeans (and white South Africa, where Skalnik works) carry around inside their heads. One is the idea that people can be divided into two broad, almost universally applicable categories: those who are tribal and those who are not. "Implicit in this distinction is the idea that the former are *still* tribal: they represent an earlier stage in human social evolution when people belonged to 'tribes' rather than modern nations." The assumption that Africans "naturally" and necessarily belonged to tribes was a cardinal tenet in the beliefs of almost all involved in colonial rule in Africa; so too was the notion that Europeans did not.[15]

15. Skalnik (1989, p. 68). This notion of Skalnik's is discussed at some length by sociologists Ringer and Lawless (1989, pp. 1–27) in their chapter, "The 'We-They' Character of Race and Ethnicity"; it is also addressed in an anthropological context by Chapman et al.

Second, though Africans are all supposedly members of distinct units called tribes, it has proven very difficult to agree about what criteria might be used to identify these tribes. One idea is that they are primarily politically defined units. But, as in the case of Acholi, for example, the use of the term "tribe" persists in much popular thought "precisely because it implies significant additional dimensions such as culture, language, territory and even race."

A third common belief about "tribe" noted by Skalnik — and one particularly prone to manipulation by those in power in multi-ethnic societies — is that basic tribal identities are "regarded as ancient and powerful, and not open to amelioration, so that animosity and tension arise whenever and wherever members of different 'tribes' come into contact with each other."[16]

Until the late 1960s, "ethnic groups" were conventionally viewed by sociologists and anthropologists in ways that were little more useful than their views about tribes. In the same volume as Skalnik, John Sharp explains that ethnic groups were conceived essentially as

> simply cultural groups which had developed their distinctive features by virtue of their original (and enduring) isolation from each other. The common assumption was that when these groups were brought together in the modern era their boundaries were obvious and clear-cut. Moreover, these boundaries were, supposedly, the prime cause of the social problems of the "developing" world, because people were suddenly required to interact on a much larger scale than had hitherto been the case. People from different ethnic groups had difficulty in understanding and adapting to each others' ways and values. Hence, in the 1950s and 1960s, there was a rash of literature dealing with the supposed problems of "culture contact," "intercultural communication," and of fitting "old societies" into new states.[17]

In South Africa, apartheid ideologues drew upon such notions to create their grand delusion of ethnically based, "independent" Bantustans or homelands.

> The members of an ethnic group spoke one language, held to a distinctive set of practices, and shared a common system of beliefs. Because of these [sup-

---

(1989, pp. 12–20) as the "us and them duality" that has characterized notions of ethnicity "from early use." More broadly, see the "social identity approach" discussed by social psychologists Hogg and Abrams (1988).

16. Skalnik (1989, pp. 69–70. Skalnik goes on to point out how nineteenth- and twentieth-century anthropology has contributed to the hold that these notions have in the popular mind.

17. Sharp (1989b, pp. 79–80).

posedly] objective characteristics, it was argued, the members of the group shared common interests, and would naturally unite in order to propagate and defend their interests. . . . [A]ttempts to further common "ethnic" interests might well take the form of a striving for political autonomy from others. It was assumed that when this point was reached, the "ethnic group" in question had graduated to the more sophisticated stage of being a "nation."[18]

BARTH'S CONTRIBUTION TO THE STUDY OF ETHNICITY

The modern study of ethnic groups and identity was pioneered in the 1960s by anthropologist Fredrik Barth. His work was a major advance beyond the limited, static, and fundamentally erroneous ideas of ethnicity just described, and his working definition of an ethnic group is still one of the most useful available. For Barth an ethnic group was one based on "a membership which identifies itself, and is identified by others, as constituting a category distinguishable from other categories of the same order"; namely a category that "classifies a person in terms of his basic, most general identity, presumptively determined by his origin and background."[19]

The word "presumptively" is important here. Barth challenged the conventional view about ethnicity, a view based to a considerable degree on tribes in Africa as they had functioned and been represented during colonial rule. This view was that ethnic groups were fundamentally cultural groups that had virtually impermeable boundaries and "that had developed their

18. Ibid., p. 79. In large part because of the distortions and manipulations of notions of ethnicity by those in power in South Africa, it has been little explored by progressive scholars there until very recently. See Boonzaier and Sharp (1988); the clear call by Bonner and Lodge (1989) that ethnic cultures and identities "need to be confronted and understood, both as instruments of manipulation from above and as modes of accommodation and adjustment from below" (p. 11); and the papers from the 1992 "Conference on Ethnicity, Society and Conflict in Natal" cited in the preface and below in n. 22. Finally, for a broad critique of the assumption that ethnic groups almost naturally "graduate" into nations, which he identifies as "one of the fallacies of contemporary political thought," see Ra'anan (1990).

19. See Barth (1969, pp. 11, 14). Most attempts to define ethnicity or ethnic groups subsequent to Barth share much in common with his definition. For some representative examples, see Harik (1972, p. 303); Chazan, et al. (1988, p. 102); and J. Wright (1991), who writes that the construction of ethnicity is best conceived as a localized, sociohistorical process "by which people come to see themselves as belonging to a group (other than a kinship group) whose members share, or believe they share, a common historical origin and, therefore, a common culture, a common way of giving meaning to the world they live in" (p. 4). Many recent discussions of ethnicity, including some of the most thoughtful ones, take a highly questionable and large step beyond Barth's basic point that ethnic groups and boundaries only make sense in relational terms, as a result of social interaction rather than isolation. That step is to consider ethnicity primarily in the context of relationships within single polities, and particularly within modern states. For examples, see an especially insightful and nuanced article by John Comaroff (1987) and the previously cited Chapman et al. (1989) and Ringer and Lawless (1989). Anthropologist Richard Thompson (1989) takes the provocative stance that "Barth's contribution to ethnic theory has not been substantial" (p. 8).

distinctive features by virtue of their original (and enduring) isolation from each other." In contrast, Barth argued that ethnic boundaries result from social interaction, not isolation. As neatly summarized by Sharp, Barth's basic argument proceeded as follows:

> Ethnic boundaries are not sustained, moreover, because of traditional *cultural* differences, but because of political differences. Ethnicity is a political process by which people seek to form groups, and to differentiate one set of people from another, by appealing to the *idea* of ineluctable cultural difference. . . . [In fact] people can readily invent cultural differences if it is in their political interests to do so. Ethnicity is the pursuit of political goals — the acquisition or maintenance of power, the mobilisation of a following — through the idiom of cultural commonness and difference.[20]

Ethnic groups and ethnic identity, then, are not a necessary or natural outcome of cultural beliefs and practices, but a creation of politics and ideology.

This radically different and analytically more powerful approach to understanding ethnicity — or tribalism — led in turn to the crucial idea that such terms as "ethnic group" and "nation" are "fundamentally constructs of the human imagination rather than entities with a concrete, practical existence in the social world."[21]

THE RECENT STUDY OF ETHNICITY IN AFRICA

Beginning in the 1970s, and especially during the 1980s, a growing number of Africanist historians have drawn upon the work of Barth and his followers to explore the creation of ethnic identities and ideologies resulting from the imposition of European rule. Such creations were called "tribes," and many interests contributed to and were served by their invention.

For European colonial administrators in Africa, false historical assumptions about "naturally tribal" Africans combined comfortably with practical administrative convenience. For Africans, conversely, the changes

20. The passages quoted are from Sharp (1988b, pp. 79–80). The concept and use of the term "tribe" in anthropology has been widely debated and criticized since the late 1960s; similar self-scrutiny with respect to ethnicity followed from the late 1970s. See, for example, Fried (1966, 1975); Helm (1968); Southall (1970); Mafeje (1971); Godelier (1977b); Hansen (1977, pp. 15–35); R. Cohen (1978); Saul (1979); van den Burghe (1981); Young (1982); Horowitz (1985); A. P. Cohen (1985); Boyer (1987); Sharp (1980, 1988a, 1988b); Skalnik (1988); Thompson (1989).

21. Sharp (1989b, p. 80), relying especially on Anderson (1983; 2nd ed. 1991). It is striking that except for particular aspects and notions of sovereignty, virtually all of Anderson's general discussion and definition of nationalism in his introduction would apply to the current discourse on ethnicity. See also Comaroff (1987).

ushered in by colonial rule led both elites and the masses of peasant farmers and poor town dwellers to perceive advantages in belonging to tribal political units, cultural fraternities, and welfare associations. Such advantages ranged from political self-seeking to the desire for a sense of community in the new colonial towns. As John Iliffe has written of colonial Tanganyika, "The British wrongly believed that Tanganyikans belonged to tribes; Tanganyikans created tribes to function within the colonial framework." The creation of such new tribal entities and identities was accompanied by sharp and hard boundaries, and by divisions, rivalries, and attitudes of exclusiveness not present before, or at least not present in the same forms or to the same degree. And neither the new identities nor their consequences disappeared when colonial rule ended. Indeed, many of the particular characteristics commonly referred to as "tribalism" in independent Africa — and often presumed to be either primordial and unchanging on the one hand, or peculiar to independent Africa on the other — are most of all a colonial legacy.[22]

This recent work significantly advances our understanding of the role played by colonialism in the creation and transformation of ethnicity, or tribalism, in Africa. There is, moreover, intriguing parallel work in recent studies of Native Americans. In an interview in the news weekly *U.S. News and World Report*, historian Richard White notes that scholars are now finding that many Native American tribes

> were in fact the creation of European settlers, who herded disparate groups onto a reservation and required them to act as a single people. The Utes, as well as the Navajos, were originally scattered over a huge area with vastly divergent

22. The quote is from Iliffe (1979, p. 318). For investigations of the development of ethnic identity or "tribes" in East Africa, see Leys (1975, pp. 198–206); Ochieng (1975); Lonsdale (1977); Buchanan (1978); Iliffe (1979, esp. pp. 318–41); Ranger (1979, 1983); Ambler (1988); C. Newbury (1988); Atkinson (1989); Cohen and Odhiambo (1989); Spear and Waller (1993). Significantly, Buchanan and all five of the last sources cited include the precolonial period in their analyses. Even more extensive work has been done in southern Africa, concentrating mostly but not exclusively on the colonial period. See, for example, Marks and Atmore (1970); Vail (1981, 1989a, 1989b); Harries (1983, 1988, 1989); Hall (1984); Hamilton and Wright (1984); J. Wright (1986, 1992); Beinart (1987); Jewsiewicki (1989); Marks (1989); Papstein (1989); Ranger (1989); A. F. Roberts (1989); Guy (1992); Hayes and Maré (1992); Maré (1992); and Nuttall (1992). An awareness of the colonial creation of "tribes" has begun to make its way into survey history texts — see, for example, Davidson (1989, chap. 7). And from political science, see the arguments by Shaw (1986) that class and ethnicity coexist in a dialectical manner in contemporary Africa, that ethnicity is not only a political concept but a "contemporary economic response," and that ethnic sentiments and divisions are powerful structuring forces and need to be recognized as such; see also Smith (1981), Rothchild and Olorunsolo (1983), Horowitz (1985), Olzak and Nagel (1986), Chazan et al. (1988), Roosens (1989), Montville (1990), Wallerstein (1991), Kellas (1991).

cultures. The Cheyenne were a group of autonomous bands brought together out of necessity as clan members fell to smallpox. These groups often shared no previous political affiliation, and in some cases didn't even speak the same language, but "the whites needed to invent a tribe so someone could sign the treaties."[23]

Extending the Discourse: The Roots of Ethnicity

Rich and revealing as this recent literature is, it needs to be extended beyond its primarily twentieth-century focus. The dynamics of the colonial era and its aftermath cannot fully explain the phenomenon of ethnicity in Africa. However powerful the colonial experience was, it did not occur in an historical vacuum, and it neither erased nor totally overwhelmed all that had gone before. To overlook or underemphasize this basic reality limits our ability to understand ethnic identity and consciousness in either historical or contemporary Africa. It also inadvertently reinforces an old tendency, which is to divide sharply the precolonial and colonial eras of the African past and to focus overwhelmingly on the latter, rather than on the many patterns and processes of change that link and overlap the two periods. One of the most common and significant examples of such an overlap, I would argue, is the development of societal and ethnic identity.[24]

This is certainly the case with Acholi. The creation of an Acholi society and collective identity did not commence with colonial rule. The socio-historical developments that produced an "Acholi" entity and identity began hundreds of years before that; indeed, the social order and political culture that came essentially to define an emergent Acholi had become widely and firmly entrenched even before 1800. And because this order — based on lineages with an overlay of chiefly rule — is prevalent across East, Central, and Southern Africa, the investigation of its early evolution in Acholi will have relevance beyond the particular case in point.

23. *U.S. News and World Report* (21 May 1990, p. 62; special feature, "The Old West"); see also White (1983, 1991a, 1991b), Merrell (1989).

24. Thomas Spear makes a similar argument in the introduction to a recent work entitled *Being Maasai: Ethnicity and Identity in East Africa* (Spear and Waller [1993]). He notes that the contributors to the book do not simply dismiss ethnicity as a form of "false consciousness." For, he continues, "however derived, ethnicity remains a powerful ideology for identity formation and social action. That is precisely why leaders seek to invent and evoke it, and why followers are so often willing to kill and die for it" (Spear [1993, p. 16]). Conversely, for an exception to the general rule being proposed here, see Ranger (1989, esp. pp. 120–22, 141–44), who convincingly argues that many twentieth-century ethnic identities and divisions in Zimbabwe are not rooted in the precolonial past.

This book, then, is a study of the long-term roots of ethnicity among a people broadly representative of much of Africa. As such, it is an argument for extending the current literature on the historical development of ethnicity in Africa beyond the confines of the colonial period and even back beyond the nineteenth century.

Additional Issues Addressed

In addition to reconstructing and interpreting the evolution of an emergent Acholi society and collective identity before 1800, I address four other areas of fundamental significance in African history. In each, the Acholi (or Acholi in-the-making) serve as an especially useful case study.

The first is the growth of chiefship. Chiefdoms, as opposed to more centralized kingdoms or smaller-scale segmentary societies without chiefs, were the most common form of sociopolitical organization in precolonial East, Central, and Southern Africa. In north-central Uganda, moreover, the establishment and entrenchment of chiefdoms was the crucial development that provided a cluster of shared experiences, similar organization, and common ideology and political culture across Acholi. This complex process, occurring mainly over the eighteenth century, also created the objective and ideological differences that began to distinguish Acholi from neighboring areas and to furnish the bases for the development of a collective Acholi identity.

Second, I provide a detailed look at an early "frontier region" in East Africa. Anthropologist Igor Kopytoff argues that such frontier regions have played a central role in the creation and reproduction of African societies: "It is on such frontiers that most African polities and societies have, so to speak, been 'constructed' out of the bits and pieces — human and cultural — of existing societies." The frontier region in which an emergent Acholi developed lay just north of the large and sprawling kingdom of Bunyoro-Kitara. And, as we shall see, certain fundamental practices, structures, and ideologies derived from this kingdom provided the model upon which the Acholi chiefdoms were built.[25]

Third, I challenge one of the most common themes of East African historiography, which attributes the origins of kingship or chiefship

25. See Kopytoff (1986a, 1986b; the quote comes from the latter, p. 3); D. W. Cohen (1983).

throughout the region, including Acholi, to early Luo-speaking migrants from the southern Sudan circa 1500. I present a very different interpretation of the early Luo's role, of the processes by which chiefship was introduced and spread in north-central Uganda, and of the timing of these developments.

Finally, I provide an extended study in and argument for the use of oral sources for close and critical sociohistorical reconstruction and interpretation. Oral sources provide most of the evidence available about the precolonial Acholi past, and we are particularly fortunate that numerous researchers have been collecting and writing down these sources for over sixty years. Their endeavors have produced an extensive and diverse corpus of material that makes it possible to discover, reconstruct, and interpret the evolution of an Acholi society and collective identity back to their earliest stages in the late seventeenth and early eighteenth centuries. To conclude this chapter, I would like to quote an eloquent statement put forth many years ago on the use of oral sources by Jan Vansina, who pioneered their academic study in Africa:

> It is therefore no longer a question of whether oral traditions should be used. They are. It is not a question of whether they can be valid. How valid are they? This depends on the careful collection and analysis of the data. We must regret, along with many anthropologists and archaeologists, that much shoddy work is still being done. There is room for considerable improvement in our practices. . . . But one must not condemn the documentation because it is not well handled by some. Even as things stand, imperfect as they are, no one can imagine any longer a history of Africa reconstructed without any recourse to oral traditions. They have proved too valuable. That is why it is worth tackling the intricate problems involved in gathering and evaluating traditions. Much of what they have to say no other voice can tell.[26]

26. Vansina (1972, pp. 458, 464).

Part One

Setting the Stage

1. The Available Sources and Other Influences Shaping the Present Work

No historical reconstruction and interpretation is the product of a single operation or brief moment. Any rendering of the past derives instead from an extended and evolving discourse among at least four sets of influences: first, the assumptions, priorities, and training that the historian / researcher brings to the project; second, the ongoing influence of others' work; third, the nature of the sources — or traces of the past — available to the researcher; and fourth, the strategies and procedures that one employs to collect and analyze such traces. The purpose of this chapter is to explore these influences as they have shaped my understanding and presentation of the early evolution of the people now called Acholi.[1]

The Initial Primacy of the Political

When the History of Uganda Project began in the early 1970s, three powerful forces combined to produce an overwhelmingly political focus and framework for research: the preoccupations of Africanist history at the time, the dominant concerns of the Project, and the narrative traditions that were the principal sources available on Uganda's precolonial past.

Africanist history into the 1970s was, in Martin Klein's words, "political in focus, . . . occupied with chronology, and . . . concerned to refute those who sold Africa short." Historians of pre-twentieth-century Africa tended to emphasize the political, often by focusing on the political history of states, or at least societies with state-like institutions. The main reasons for this were obvious and practical. Written and oral sources tended to be

1. I would like to thank David W. Cohen and Bogumil Jewsiewicki for helpful comments on earlier drafts of this chapter. The term "traces" is adopted from Keith Jenkins's highly readable introduction to post-modernist approaches to history (1991); see especially his argument (pp. 47–50) that the term "evidence" properly applies only to traces of the past used to support an argument or interpretation.

richer and more accessible for states than for less centralized societies, and states had governmental institutions and political patterns familiar to scholars trained in the western tradition.[2]

A deeper ideological element also played a role, one that John Tosh described in the late 1970s as "seldom explicit but no less powerful for that." "Students of the African scene," he wrote, "have been much affected by the anti-colonial revolution which has taken place in their own lifetime. They have interpreted the emergence of independent African states as . . . the culmination of Africa's evolution over several centuries. Once this event is accepted as the grand climacteric, it follows that state-building and 'enlargement of scale' are the aspects of the past most worthy of attention."[3]

Under J. B. Webster, chair of the Department of History at Makerere University, the History of Uganda Project was firmly fixed in this scholarly mainstream, concentrating on such political issues as the enlargement of scale and development of state-like institutions. And with only minimal recourse to documented calendar dates, Project work also stressed the establishment of chronologies for the precolonial period that could be used across political and social boundaries. This emphasis reinforced the primacy of the political by focusing on well-known, mainly political personages and events, and especially on the collection of ruler lists and associated traditions.[4]

A political concentration was further promoted by the very nature of the most accessible sources on precolonial Uganda (and Acholi) — narrative traditions. These are a special case of the first of Marc Bloch's two types of historical sources: narrative accounts that "consciously intended to inform."[5]

Narrative traditions do not usually deal with complex social structures

2. Klein (1978, p. 277). My own graduate training was certainly within this tradition. This political emphasis has received substantial criticism, often from a materialist perspective. Probably the most comprehensive is by Caroline Neale (1985); see also Temu and Swai (1981). Shorter discussions include Wrigley (1971), Ranger (1976), Bernstein and Depelchin (1978–79), Lonsdale (1981), Crummey and Stewart (1981b), and Freund (1984, chap. 1). See also the special edition of *African Studies Review* (1987), guest edited by David Newbury.

3. Tosh (1978, pp. 4–5); see also Wrigley (1971), Stcinhart (1984), Jewsiewicki (1981b), and the references in n. 2. Stein (1980, pp. 259–60) discusses a similar phenomenon in Indian historiography. Recent studies of state formation and "enlargement of scale" — such as Corrigan and Sayer (1985) on early England — have reaffirmed the importance of such topics while also asking new questions and taking new directions. See also Braudel's comment (1984, pp. 50–51) on the return to fashion of the state in French historical studies.

4. Webster's concern with chronology can be seen, e.g., in Webster (1969, n.d. [1971], 1974, 1979); Webster and Odongo (1971, 1976a).

5. Bloch (1954, p. 61).

or social dynamics, except in abbreviated, idealized, or stereotypical ways. Nor do they focus on ordinary people or "material life," characterized by Braudel as the practical, repetitive, everyday considerations and transactions "there at the root of everything." Instead, they provide traces — again, often idealized or stereotypical — about politics, ideology, basic sociopolitical structures, notable rulers or other personages, and memorable events.[6]

This limited focus does not mean that conscious narrative traditions are unimportant. In the case of precolonial Acholi, they are not only the most abundant sources available, but often the only means by which change and movement in the Acholi past are revealed. Moreover, the historical traces contained in narrative traditions are essential, in lieu of written documents, for establishing and refining basic temporal, spatial, and structural frameworks — fundamental first steps in historical reconstruction.

As we shall see, Acholi traditions speak with many different voices. But the dominant voice of Acholi narrative traditions is heavily political in both tone and content. This dominant voice cannot be ignored. It deserves to be heard, though it no longer merits solo, or even primary, status.

Broadening the Scope of the Enquiry

All these emphases on the political influenced my expectations and priorities in Acholi. But other influences helped broaden this narrow orientation. First, not all Acholi traditions are of the conscious, narrative type. Some instead fit Bloch's second category of historical sources: the "evidence of witnesses in spite of themselves"; the "tracks which the past unwittingly leaves all along its trail." Two features of unconscious, non-narrative traditions give them special significance: (1) they tend not only to deal with different areas of the past than conscious narrative traditions but to be substantially independent of them; and (2) non-narrative traditions are far more likely to refer to actual human decisions and actions and are less prone to stereotypical, idealized, or normative representations of behavior and structure.[7]

Because my own interests in Acholi extended beyond the purely political, I collected non-narrative as well as narrative traditions from the outset.

6. See Braudel (1973, 1981; the quote is from 1973, p. xii). Tosh (1984, pp. 53–61) also discusses types of sources.

7. The quotation is from Bloch (1954, pp. 61–62); see also Cohen (1980, especially pp. 213–14) and Tosh (1984, pp. 53–61).

One such interest was anthropology, especially social anthropology, and I drew upon some of the insights of this discipline to explore such topics as authority, dominance, social stratification, sub-group identity and autonomy, the production and distribution of wealth, marriage patterns and procedures, ritual, and language—though unlike most social anthropology, I also focused on change over time in all these areas. Later, after I completed field research, materialist analyses pioneered by French Marxist anthropologists sharpened my understanding of lineage-based production, lineage ideology, and lineage leadership.[8]

In addition, I was aware that collecting and interpreting Acholi traditions effectively depended upon understanding Acholi society and culture. As Steven Feierman has written, oral traditions "are not strictly historical texts, but living social documents, [and] if we do not understand their social context and their social content, then we cannot understand our sources."[9]

As did most Africanists of the time, those of us in the History of Uganda Project in the early 1970s largely ignored social history, despite its increasing importance in the historical discipline as a whole. Africanists' isolation in this regard diminished in the late 1970s and especially during the 1980s, led by the revisionist, often materialist historiography that has dramatically reshaped the social and economic history of Southern Africa. In my own case, the opportunity to teach European, Russian, American, and African history in Ghana in the late 1970s and 1980s was crucial in introducing me to the social history being done in these fields.[10]

In an early essay in the field entitled "From Social History to the History of Society," E. J. Hobsbawm makes two points that have had a special impact on the present study. First, he asks for explicit discussions or assumptions, priorities, and methodologies, which is one of the main purposes of this first chapter. Second, he urges that social historians move beyond particular aspects of their field (such as demography, classes, and

8. See references below in Chap. 3, n. 3.

9. Feierman (1974, p. 4).

10. For criticisms of Africanists' tendency to ignore social history see Klein (1978, p. 277) and many of the sources in n. 2 above; also Clarence-Smith (1977). Important sources in reshaping South African historiography include Bundy (1979), Guy (1979), Marks and Atmore (1980), Peires (1982), Beinart (1982), van Onselen (1982), Marks and Rathbone (1982), Bonner (1983), Delius (1983), and Callinicos (1981, 1987). And with respect to African history more generally, David Newbury writes, "Recent research on Africa has been dominated by analytic paradigms associated with social history, and with good reason" (1991, pp. 9–10); the recent establishment of the Heinemann Social History of Africa Series supports Newbury's assertion.

social movements) to focus instead on the history of society, or societies, in the broadest sense. This is what I am trying to do in this book: to reconstruct and analyze the origins and early development of a particular society in north-central Uganda now called Acholi. And crucial to this socio-historical process was the evolution of a collective, eventually ethnic, Acholi identity, which I began to explore in a 1989 article in *Ethnohistory*.[11]

Historical Knowledge, Historical Sources, and Oral Traditions

Whether conservative, materialist, or post-modernist, all but the most empiricist and positivist historians would tend to agree that historical reconstruction and analysis depend, first, on assumptions and priorities, questions, methodologies, and models. As Werner Sombart has stated, "no theory, no history."[12]

Second, many would also agree that it is a chimera to claim to present the past as it "actually" was. Historians are always at least one step removed from what actually happened in the past. What is available to historians is not the past per se, but the "traces" or "remnants" of the past that "happen to survive into the present." Even in the most favorable of circumstances, these surviving traces are overwhelmingly fragmentary and incomplete. All that historians can do is to identify, organize, interrogate, and interpret the available traces "as signifying something about the past," and then use the results as "bases for drawing probabalistic inferences about what the past may have been like."[13]

Of course, this is neither a simple nor unrewarding set of tasks. In the best of circumstances the results can be elegant, sophisticated, and convincing. But history, like the other social and even physical sciences, can never prove anything, at least not beyond the trivial or tautologous. Historical "knowledge" is invariably incomplete, inferential, and a matter of probability rather than certainty. It is inherently limited by the inescapable dis-

---

11. Hobsbawm (1971); Atkinson (1989). An early East African example of the sort of historical reconstruction that Hobsbawm had in mind is d'Hertefelt (1971). See also Cohen's review of d'Hertefelt calling for more such work (1974d), what might be seen as his own response (Cohen, 1977), Stein's book (1980) on peasant state and society in medieval south India, and Vansina's (1978) on the Kuba of Zaire.

12. The Sombert quote comes from Braudel (1973, p. xi).

13. The term "remnants" and passages quoted are from Miller (1980b, p. 47); "traces" is from Jenkins (1991). See also n. 1 above.

tance between past and present, by the nature, quantity, and quality of the surviving traces of the past available for use by historians living in the present.[14]

When historians deal with the surviving remnants of the past from pre-literate (or recently and partially literate) societies, two special challenges present themselves. First, many of these remnants are oral sources. Second, in many instances no chronology based on documented calendar dates exists. These challenges do not preclude work on the pre-literate past. But they do require the recognition and use of oral sources as legitimate data for historical reconstruction and analysis. Space precludes a full discussion of such sources here, but those aspects of oral sources and their use that are particularly relevant to explicating the early evolution of Acholi will receive attention.

Oral sources are usually divided into two categories: (1) oral reminiscences or first-hand recollections, frequently referred to as oral history; and (2) oral traditions, defined broadly as "narratives and descriptions of people and events in the past which have been handed down by word of mouth over several generations."[15]

Both types of oral sources differ from written documents in many ways. One crucial distinction — and a key reason many historians are skeptical about oral sources — is that the interviewing necessary to generate texts makes the historian/recorder part of the texts' creation and not just their interpreter. Another important difference is the extent to which the past and present are blurred in oral sources. Most written documents not only refer to the past but can themselves be dated to a specific past time. Oral sources, in contrast, both refer to the past and exist in the present, as part of an ongoing social intelligence and discourse. In structuralist terminology, it thus becomes impossible to determine with certainty what part of, or to what extent, any oral source, especially oral tradition, is a past or present "sign." Some types and aspects of oral traditions are less susceptible to change over time than others and are thus likely to be more reliable or more

14. Note the first of Gregory Bateson's "basic presuppositions which all minds must share," namely that "science never proves anything" (1979, p. 27). Some would go so far as to argue that because of the inherent limits of historical enquiry, all such enquiries are essentially meaningless. One once-influential example is Hindess and Hirst (1975, pp. 308–23), whose approach was attacked by Thompson (1978, pp. 29–30) as idealist as any positivist historicism. See also, for example, Fischer (1970, p. 3); Hobsbawm (1971); Braudel (1970).

15. See Tosh (1984, p. 172). See also Cohen (1989, p. 9), who argues that overly formal and fixed definitions of "oral tradition" distort the complexity and richness of historical knowledge in societies such as Acholi.

genuine past signs. But without confirmation from independent sources we can never be sure.[16]

For some this uncertainty excludes traditions as legitimate source material. The blurring of past and present in traditions certainly adds difficulty to using them. But why should this one factor mark the division between evidence and non-evidence, history and non-history? Collingwood drew no such line. "Everything," he wrote, "is evidence which the historian can use as evidence." "It must," he continued,

> be something here and now perceptible to him: this written page, this spoken utterance, this building, this finger print. . . . The whole perceptible world, then, is potentially and in principle evidence to the historian. It becomes actual evidence in so far as he can use it. . . . The more historical knowledge we have, the more we can learn from any given piece of evidence; if we had none we could learn nothing. Evidence is evidence only when one contemplates it historically.[17]

Thus it is not the nature of the source that defines history, but the way that source is perceived and used as evidence. There is no valid reason to exclude oral traditions. They have proved too valuable in reconstructing the African past to ignore or condemn them, especially those collected with care and analyzed with skill. "That is why," to quote Jan Vansina again, "it is worth tackling the intricate problems involved in gathering and evaluating traditions. Much of what they have to say no other voice can tell."[18]

Traditions and Other Sources on the Acholi Past

Historical information about Acholi is contained in traditions that are not all alike and do not all speak with the same voice. Before exploring differences, however, it is important to note two significant commonalities. First, Acholi sources on the past are not maintained and transmitted by designated specialists. No figure in Acholi resembles the West African *griot*, or even the less specialized *bulaam* among the Kuba of Zaire. Second, with the

---

16. These issues are discussed in Miller (1980b).

17. Collingwood (1946, pp. 246–47, 279–81); Jenkins (1991, pp. 47–50). One of those who would exclude the use of traditions as legitimate source material for writing history is Clarence-Smith (1977); Vansina offers a critical retort (1978b).

18. Vansina (1971, pp. 458, 464).

exception of some songs and lineage praise calls (*mwoc*), historical information does not take the form of fixed or highly stylized texts.[19]

Instead, as David W. Cohen has written of the similarly organized Basoga farther south:

> To some extent everyone was involved in the preservation and transmission of historical information, though not necessarily consciously. . . . Traditions in Busoga were much less the arcane survivals of an oral past than the lively and ever-functioning intelligence upon which society and man rest. The transmission of historical information is not along orderly chains of transmission but across and through the complex networks of relationship, association, and contact that constitute social life.

Historical information in both Acholi and Busoga is thus transmitted through processes that "are not orderly, are not predictable, and are not reconstructible." Moreover, given the uniqueness of each historian/recorder's inquiry, the collection of this information proceeds as unpredictably as its transmission. Attempts to determine "original tradition" or clear chains of transmission are impossible. What *is* possible is not only to examine carefully Acholi traditions themselves, but to consider also the timing, methods, and approaches of the inquiries that led to their collection.[20]

Among the earliest to collect traditions in Acholi, beginning in the 1920s, was the Verona Father J. P. Crazzolara. His three-volume compendium, *The Lwoo*, was the single most important source on Acholi and neighboring areas when Project research began. Crazzolara claimed that the volumes were intended "to set down real history as a whole, in so far as I was able to reach 'documents' . . . [i.e.,] the traditions of the various Lwoo

---

19. On the *bulaam*, see Vansina (1978a, p. 17). I unfortunately did not realize the potential of songs as historical sources until late in my interviewing. Maura Garry did, and collected over five hundred songs, most written down over many years by Daniel Ongo from Pajule in east-central Acholi, who also often provided commentaries. See Garry (1972b, pp. xviii–xxxii), and the collected songs and commentaries (Ongo, 1971c); see also Okot p'Bitek (n.d. [a] and n.d. [b]).

20. The first quotation is from Cohen (1977, pp. 8–9), the others from Cohen (1980, p. 206); see also Cohen (1989). Such tasks as determining "original tradition" or "chains of transmission" were accorded great importance by Vansina in his pioneering *Oral Tradition* (1965), and subsequently by others such as Pender-Cudlip (1972, 1973). Hartwig (1974) and Cohen (1980, 1989) have commented critically on this issue, and more recently Vansina (1985) has given less importance to such matters. For other extended discussions of methodological issues involved in using oral sources, see Miller (1980a, 1980b), Irwin (1981), Spear (1981a, 1981b, 1982), Portelli (1981), Henige (1982), Tonkin (1982, 1986, 1992), and Tosh (1984, pp. 172–91).

tribes." These traditions, he continues, "allow us to trace a fairly clear picture of events of old—a picture which despite its rough outlines is nevertheless real and authentic."[21]

Although the above statement of purpose, method, and results is admirably clear and concise (if questionable), much of *The Lwoo* is not. Based on information collected over thirty years from throughout the southern Sudan and northern Uganda, *The Lwoo* is difficult to use. Focusing especially on Acholi, it is largely a compendium of place, individual, and group names, many simply arranged in lists or scattered without elaboration throughout an eclectic assortment of mostly narrative traditions and the author's interpolations. In addition, the volumes are disjointed; the translation from the German manuscript is uneven; and many points of approach, interpretation, and analysis can be doubted and debated. Still, as an encyclopedic reference and a broad historical reconstruction and synthesis, *The Lwoo* is invaluable.[22]

Father Crazzolara's work was motivated in large part by two related concerns: (1) that those who knew about the past were, literally, a dying breed; and (2) that such knowledge was important and needed to be preserved. These notions seem to have been widely held among both Acholi and others living and working in the area, from at least the 1930s. Numerous forces appeared increasingly to separate people of the "traditional," precolonial past from younger generations who had neither the same experiences nor the same knowledge. These forces included the entrenchment of a colonial system that increasingly dismantled and sup-

21. Crazzolara (1950, 1951, 1954; quote is from 1951, pp. 8–9).
22. Father Crazzolara's life and work were indeed remarkable. Born in Italy in 1884, he arrived in Khartoum, Sudan, as a young Verona Father in 1908 and was posted to northern Uganda in 1910. He came to Acholi in 1911, the year that foundations for Gulu town and the Roman Catholic mission in Acholi were established. When I left Acholi in December 1971, Father Crazzolara was still there, living in retirement at the Catholic mission in Gulu, following a lifelong series of postings throughout northern Uganda and the southern Sudan. He was an accomplished linguist in the Westermann mold, compiling not only the definitive Acholi *Grammar and Vocabulary* (1938) but similar works on the Nuer and Shilluk (both Western Nilotic languages), Lugbara (a Central Sudanic language), and most recently the Eastern Nilotic Akarimojong. He also collected traditions wherever he was stationed, providing the basis for *The Lwoo*. Father Crazzolara showed me his field notes. They were a scribbled, incomprehensible mixture of German, vernacular languages, and obsolete shorthand, impossible for use by anyone else. He assured me, however, that he had incorporated almost everything in the notes into *The Lwoo* and other writings; the way these read make me believe that he did just that. Most of this information comes from a series of interviews I had with Father Crazzolara, numbered A.H.T. 290–92, 295–96. After more than sixty years in East Africa, Father Crazzolara returned to Italy in 1975, where he died on 25 March 1976.

planted the Acholi polities, new economic patterns, and increasing mission activity (especially the extension of western education through mission schools).[23]

Such changes helped prompt many besides Crazzolara to collect Acholi traditions, though additional motives are also often apparent. Some, for example, glorified or at least emphasized certain chiefdoms at the expense of others; some seemed to be trying to stake out claims for themselves as experts on the past; and still others collected Acholi traditions to incorporate them into primary school textbooks for mission-run schools (though these texts dealt far more with the period after European and missionary contact than before). Nevertheless, the products of these efforts tended to be similar, whatever the authors' motives or whether they were Acholi or Europeans.[24]

As part of the History of Uganda Project, the Department of History at Makerere began to collect these sources, both published and unpublished, and translate into English the majority that were in Luo. Most were narrative traditional histories of Acholi chiefdoms, primarily in outline form. Many also included at least brief descriptions of "traditional" sociocultural practices and sociopolitical structures, as well as purveying a number of mythical, stereotypical, or ideological messages, such as those linking the origins of the Acholi (and many Acholi chiefdoms) with the early Luo and the Babiito dynasty of Bunyoro-Kitara. Although the quantity and range of detail in these histories varied considerably, almost all contained certain basic information: a list of remembered rulers for each chiefdom (called *rwodi* in Acholi Luo; singular, *rwot*); a narration of some of the notable events in the chiefdom's history (often structured in terms of the remembered sequence of *rwodi*); the identification of settlement sites associated with some *rwodi*; and a list of and sometimes additional details about constituent lineages. Conscious narrative history predominated. Sources of the unconscious, non-narrative type took a distinctly secondary place, though examples of such were indeed, to paraphrase Bloch, unwittingly left all along the way.[25]

---

23. Crazzolara (1951, p. 9, note) states his concern explicitly; Dwyer (1972) discusses some of these forces.

24. See References ("Traditions Collected Prior to the History of Uganda Project").

25. Material translated when I began fieldwork was limited to Okech (1953) and to parts of Anywar (1954) and of unpublished manuscripts by Canon A. O. Latigo (1970a, 1970b, 1970c). Eventually, translations of Anywar and Latigo were completed, along with that of two other published works in Luo: Malandra (1947), a scarce and long out-of-print collection of

Three other categories of information on Acholi were available when Project research began. The first consisted of late-nineteenth- and early-twentieth-century writings by European visitors to Acholi.[26] Next was a handful of secondary accounts of Acholi history, consisting mainly of brief articles, unpublished seminar papers, or passing references in sources on more general topics. Except for the most recent, these had a distinctly Eurocentric perspective.[27] Finally, there were ethnographic and anthropological investigations, some focused specifically on Acholi, others on different Luo or neighboring groups. The earlier were by missionaries and colonial officials; later studies included those by academically trained anthropologists, most importantly F. K. Girling's monograph on the Acholi and Aidan Southall's on the nearby and also Luo-speaking Alur.[28]

As I began field research, these sources were important in three ways. First, they provided the means to commence learning about Acholi society

---

traditions; and Pellegrini (1949; revised ed., 1963), a primary school text on Acholi history. The published vernacular histories were widely disseminated in Acholi and contributed to Acholi conceptions of their past, especially by reinforcing some of the stereotypical and ideological aspects of Acholi traditions discussed in this work. But these published sources never became authoritative; indeed, at the level of individual chiefdoms, details contained in these histories are just as often different from or even contradicted by later collections of traditions as they are corroborated.

In addition, a number of short manuscripts were collected in western Acholi and incorporated into the Acholi Historical Texts (A.H.T. 209, 210, 217, 220, 221, 289, and 306). Some longer manuscripts were also collected and translated, notably Olango's collection of traditions from the 1940s in Puranga (1970) and three long manuscripts by Daniel Ongo of Pajule (1971a, 1971b, and his collected "Songs of Eastern Acholi," 1971c). There was also an extraordinary and controversial manuscript written in English by J. Onyango-ku-Odongo on the early Luo (n.d. [1960s]), a revised version of which became the lead chapter in Webster and Odongo (1976). I remain deeply skeptical of Odongo's work. Finally, while still in Acholi I began corresponding with A. C. A. Wright, a government official in Acholi in the 1930s who had done research while posted there. I met Mr. Wright in England upon leaving Uganda and he kindly provided me with a series of outline narrative histories he had collected across Acholi in 1933–34 (Wright [1934]).

26. The most important are Speke (1863), Baker (1866, 1874), Emin Pasha (1888 and 1961–68 — extracts from his *Tagebucher*, ed. and trans. by J. M. Gray), Lloyd (1907), Tucker (1908), Kitching (1912), and Postlethwaite (1947).

27. Secondary sources on the late nineteenth and early twentieth centuries included R. Gray (1961), J. M. Gray (1948, 1951), Wild (1954), Adimola (1954), Bere (1946), Anywar (1948), I. F. Thomas (1963), and "Mengo Notes" — Extracts V (1948). The only sources on earlier Acholi history were two articles by Bere (1934b, 1947) and two seminar papers (Nyeko, n.d.; D. Newbury, 1969). Sources of general relevance to or with brief sections on Acholi included Crazzolara (1937, 1960, 1969), Wright (1949), Oliver (1963), Ogot (1964, 1967a), and Cohen (1968).

28. Many of these appeared in the *Uganda Journal*: Bere (1934a, 1934c), Boccassino (1939), Higgins (1966), Malandra (1939), Menzies (1954), Okot p'Bitek (1963, 1965), Usher-Wilson (1947), Wright (1936, 1940). Other sources included Westermann (1912), Grove (1919), Seligman and Seligman (1932), Butt (1952). Southall's monograph was published in 1956; Girling's in 1960.

and culture. Second, they made it possible to start building a tentative outline of Acholi history and, through the available ruler (*rwot*) lists, an initial chronological framework. Finally, these sources made clear how much we did *not* know. Contradictions, missing details, and huge gaps were apparent; certain groups and a wide range of problems received no attention whatsoever. Thus both a corpus of basic, though fragmentary, information was provided and a host of questions suggested, all of which helped guide subsequent field research.[29]

My fieldwork was part of a five-person team effort in Acholi under the auspices of the History of Uganda Project. Together, we collected by far the most extensive corpus of historical traditions ever gathered in the area. When this material is combined with earlier compilations of traditions and other relevant sources, the quantity, quality, and diversity of traces available on the Acholi past is substantial and impressive.[30]

The Collection and Analysis of Acholi Traditions

Field research in Uganda required clearance from several levels of government, from the National Research Council in Kampala, to the Acholi District Commissioner, to the county chiefs in the three westernmost counties of Acholi where I would work: Kilak, Aswa, and Omoro. Actual interviewing required the assistance of the next two levels down in the administrative hierarchy, the sub-county and local parish chiefs. These were usually local men who knew elders in their areas knowledgeable about the past. When I first began research, the cooperation of local chiefs in setting

29. I began field work almost immediately upon joining the History of Uganda Project in mid-1970, with no prior archival research in either the Gulu or Entebbe archives. Given the closing of research after Amin's January 1971 coup, this was a fortunate decision.

30. The other researchers were: (1) F. K. Uma, an undergraduate from Acholi who worked on the relationship between Acholi and northern traders during the second half of the nineteenth century. See Uma (1971) and his interview notes (Uma A.H.T 23–40, 54–62). (2) Paul Owot, another undergraduate who worked in and near his home area of Padibe in north-central Acholi. See Owot A.H.T. and Owot (1976). (3) Maura Garry, who did her M.A. field work in Pajule in east-central Acholi and Chua County in the northeast. See Garry (1971a, 1971b, 1972a, 1972b, 1976), and collected A.H.T. from Chua County, to be cited "Garry A.H.T." (4) J. B. Webster, who worked in Agago County in southeastern Acholi. Webster's field notes — cited "Webster A.H.T." — were generously made available to others in the Project; see also Webster's numerous writings listed in the References. Although the traditions collected by these colleagues are used extensively herein, my interpretations based on these traditions often vary considerably from those who collected them.

up meetings, explaining the project, and helping get elders to interviews was invaluable.[31]

Such an approach necessarily involved considerable contact with government. Though this was often helpful, there were also potential problems. In the intensely political climate of Acholi at the time, any association with government officials ran the risk of alienating elders who either distrusted government in general or might see me as allied with political opponents. To minimize such risks, it proved useful to emphasize to both chiefs and elders that I was not a government employee and that my research was sponsored by the university, an institution typically viewed not only as distinct from government but in a much more favorable light.[32]

A final benefit to utilizing government structures in organizing research was that modern sub-counties and parishes often reflect precolonial chiefdoms and lineages. Many even carry old chiefdom and lineage names. This frequent coincidence of precolonial groupings and modern administrative units meant that my wish to organize interviews in terms of the former was easily accommodated to working with local chiefs in the modern setup.[33]

EARLY INTERVIEWS

Most early interviews were with groups, where the primary purpose was to elicit basic information on each chiefdom and, when possible, on the chiefdom's constituent lineages. A secondary goal was to discover additional areas of knowledge possessed by the elders so that I could pursue enquiries in those areas, either then or later.

Group interviews were compatible with two essential features of Acholi knowledge of the past. First, as already noted, there are no designated specialists in Acholi responsible for transmitting historical information. Because of their positions, certain people might have special opportunities to acquire historical knowledge. Traditional rulers and lineage

31. Kilak County was divided into five sub-counties and thirty-six parishes; Aswa County into the Gulu municipal area, three sub-counties and thirty-one parishes; and Omoro into five sub-counties and thirty-seven parishes.

32. A similar research approach had earlier been used in Teso District southeast of Acholi. See Webster (n.d. [1969]); Webster, et al. (1973). For a good description of post-independence Acholi politics see Leys (1967); much of the partisan political activity he described had altered in detail by 1970 but continued to resonate in general ways, especially as promised parliamentary elections for early 1971 neared.

33. For example, eight of the thirteen sub-counties in which I worked carried old chiefdom names: Atyak, Pabo, Lamogi, Alero, Patiko, Koc, Paico, and Koro.

heads, or those close to them, are obvious examples. Yet it was soon clear that someone without position but with simply a special interest might well know more than these people. Early group interviews seemed an expedient way to find out who knew what. Second, Acholi knowledge of the past is fragmented in particular ways. Members of individual lineages within a chiefdom tended to possess historical information not known by others. The most effective way to begin tapping into this "separate group" knowledge (to use Feierman's phrase) was through group interviews that included members of several lineages.[34]

Indeed, collecting separate group, lineage-based traditions — most of it of the unconscious, non-narrative type — quickly became a primary focus of group interviews. In so doing, a significant problem often associated with group interviews was minimized: the problem of reducing the content of traditions collected in group situations to a single, limited, consensual core.[35]

Project interviews in Acholi were designated "Acholi Historical Texts" (A.H.T.) and given numbers. Those I did in western Acholi — numbered A.H.T. 201 through 310 — represent more than 200 hours of interviewing with some 150 interviewees. While a few of the final interviews were taped, most of the texts consist of as near to verbatim translations as possible of both my questions and elders' responses, with frequent renderings of Luo words and phrases.[36]

34. The phrase "separate group knowledge" comes from Feierman (1974, pp. 9–12). See also Cohen (1977, p. 9; 1989, pp. 10–13); the latter convincingly rejects David Henige's exclusion of such separate group knowledge from the realm of oral traditions. Finally, Webster's earlier use of group interviews in Teso and eastern Acholi influenced the way I set up early field research.

35. For a discussion of the tendency to reduce traditions in group interviews to a consensual minimum see Blount (1975); see also n. 40 below.

36. This interviewing method required the active cooperation of both elders and my assistant/interpreter. The former were required to break their narrative after every few sentences to allow for translation and transcription; the latter needed to listen to and interpret carefully even that which he felt repetitive or irrelevant. I had surprisingly little difficulty gaining the required cooperation of both.

I made minimal use of a tape recorder for several reasons. First, I was warned that it might inhibit openness and cooperation. Second, most information collected was not in fixed texts where exact textual renderings are essential. Third, reliance on a recorder would reduce the need for both me (with my limited Luo) and my research assistant/interpreter to monitor constantly what was being said, which was crucial for maintaining control of the interview. Finally, the cost in time and money to produce transcriptions and translations was prohibitive. For these reasons, the Project generally did not make extensive use of tape recordings. I did tape eight of the final interviews, all with elders I knew well. Two of these were in English and were the most successful of those taped (A.H.T. 270, 271). Of the other six (A.H.T. 299, 300, 302–3, 309–10), only the final two were under control throughout. In general, interviews done without a tape recorder were more satisfactory and effective than those done with them.

The types of historical information most frequently sought in early group interviews were these:

1. *A ruler* (rwot) *list, or lists, for each chiefdom investigated.* These lists were usually compiled by working backward from the last traditional *rwot*, checking remembered genealogical relationships in the process. Some elders, though, gave a list of *rwodi* from earliest to most recent, sometimes accompanied by brief, unsolicited narrative. Collected lists were compared with previously recorded versions, paying special attention to the number and order of remembered names and the degree of consistency among available lists. Soliciting a *rwot* list from a group of elders I had not previously met provided an initial indication of their historical knowledge, individually and collectively. In addition, a *rwot* list provided a basic framework within which many other traditions were set and from which a relative and tentative chronology could be established. It was crucial to elicit this framework whenever possible before going on to other traditions.[37]

2. *Stories of remembered events associated with each* rwot's *reign.* Some events were narrated without prompting in the course of presenting a list of *rwodi*. More often, I went back over lists and asked what was remembered about each *rwot* and the time in which he ruled. I also asked about certain types of events (numbers 3–8 below) and attempted to associate remembered occurrences with specific *rwodi*.

3. *Stories about remembered wars or battles.* In addition to the particular chiefdom being investigated, I originally hoped to obtain information about allied or rival groups as well, including the names of *rwodi* that could be used to establish chronological cross-references among groups. Unfortunately, such specific cross-references were rare.

37. Goody (1968, pp. 74–111) has argued that lists per se are mainly associated with literacy. He does acknowledge that some listing occurs in oral societies, the most obvious examples being the recital of genealogies (pp. 80, 92, 105, 108). But he also points out that lists and genealogical diagrams contained in written studies of oral cultures "have often been abstracted from a series of elicitations and enquiries" (p. 108). As this is what I did, "list" may not be precisely accurate to describe how the Acholi organized their recollections of *rwodi*. Still, *rwot* lists were produced, and I will continue to use the term. See Vansina's depiction of the Kuba fascination with lists, or with information readily reducible to lists (1978a, pp. 17–18, 22–27). In challenging the king "list" of Buganda and ruler lists in oral societies generally, Henige (1980) seems seriously to overstate Goody's arguments.

4. *Traditions of remembered droughts and famines.* The initial idea for collecting such traditions came from a list of historical famines in one of the Luo-language traditional histories. Although inaccurate, this list identified an important category of information potentially useful for chronological purposes, was soon developed and refined by Project researchers.[38]

5. *Information concerning settlement sites and movements for both chiefdoms and lineages.* The most basic information sought here was a sequence of specific place names of where groups had settled. I also asked why groups selected certain sites and made particular moves.

6. *Traditions of the origins of the constituent lineages of each polity.* Most frequently, these traditions named a general or specific geographical location from which the group was remembered to have come, which in turn often helped identify probable ethnolinguistic origins.

7. *Traditions relating the incorporation of constituent lineages into each polity.* These traditions, when available, usually provided the identity of the *rwot* remembered as ruling when the lineage was incorporated. Less frequently, they also identified the lineage head at the time and circumstances surrounding incorporation. In general, this proved to be a much more important category of source material than I first realized.

8. *Marriage and genealogical data on interviewees and their ancestors.* Initially collected mainly on *rwodi* and other royals, this information was eventually sought for other nineteenth- and early twentieth-century individuals as well. Again, this was an especially significant category of evidence.

9. *Information on religion and ritual, both lineage-based and polity-wide.*

10. *Personal information about the elders interviewed.* This included lineage affiliation, estimation of age, and sometimes marriage and genealogical data.

The traditions thus elicited represented both conscious narrative traditions and unconscious, non-narrative ones. Categories 1 through 3 are examples of the former; 4 through 10, the latter. This particular set of

38. The original source was Okech (1953, pp. 13–15); the first to see its potential was J. B. Webster. See also Atkinson (1978, pp. 79–98); and below, Chap. 3, n. 5 and Chap. 5, n. 1.

historical sources reflected my own interests and priorities at the time I conducted field research. As already noted, the process of generating oral data involves not merely the collection of sources but also their creation. Yet it must be emphasized that Acholi concerns were necessarily represented as well. Whatever my interests (at least without massive fabrication), the information obtained was available to be recovered only because it had been deemed important enough to have been remembered and passed down over time. Indeed, the practical considerations involved in the preservation of historical information in non-literate societies are crucial. As David W. Cohen writes:

> The capture of a leopard, or at least the specific elements of a hunt tradition, might be quickly forgotten, the rewards spread thin or fleeting (in a sense, nondurable). On the other hand the allocation of a political office and land to a particular person or lineage and the possibly related dispossession of another, were not likely to be forgotten by any of the principal participants in the affair, nor by their descendants. Their place in society and their rights to the office and land were preserved, and are preserved today, not in deeds, papers, or documentary titles of appointment, but in the corroborated memories of men and women around them.[39]

Most early group interviews tapped enough of such "corroborated memories" to elicit responses to my enquiries. Some such responses provided historical traces of great quantity and rich quality; a few produced disappointingly little. Clearly, highly complex group dynamics were operative, dynamics that not only varied from group to group but were often beyond my ability to influence or even comprehend. One factor that consistently affected interviews, however, was soon obvious. If the group being interviewed grew larger than five or six, one of two adverse patterns tended to develop. In the first, one or two elders, through personality, position, or sometimes even the extent of their knowledge, dominated the interview; the others, even those who later proved knowledgeable, were silent, restless, and seemed uninterested. A second pattern was equally likely, with elders impatient, interruptive, and frequently clamoring to speak at the same time.[40]

39. Cohen (1977, pp. 8–9); see also Feierman (1974, pp. 4, 9–12); Miller (1980b, p. 38).

40. Blount (1975) is an excellent account of the intricacies and dynamics of group interviews. It focuses on the complex processes by which groups of Luo in western Kenya reach consensual agreement on genealogies, including "the manipulation of information according to social relationships and cultural norms." Such manipulation, of course, makes these genealogies less than reliable for establishing chronology. Some analogous manipulation

In even the best circumstances, however (interviews where three or four informed elders cooperatively shared their knowledge), significant gaps showed. Furthermore, the number of elders who could relate appreciably more than basic information was relatively small. Finding one such elder in an early group interview was satisfying; finding more than one, a bonus.

FOLLOW-UP INTERVIEWS: INCREASING THE FOCUS ON NON-NARRATIVE TRADITIONS

After one or two introductory interviews on a chiefdom, I usually selected an individual or a small two- or three-person group for follow-up interviews of essentially two types. One concentrated on gathering more details about the history of the chiefdom as a whole or of its ruling group, often from members of the chiefdom's royal lineage (*kal*). Both narrative and unconscious, non-narrative historical traditions were sought, especially on the following topics: detailed genealogical and marriage information on the chiefdom's *rwodi*; succession preferences, practices, and ritual; details of other polity-wide ritual; and in-depth information on the structure and workings of government and politics. The second type of follow-up interview focused on lineage-based, unconscious, non-narrative traditions, usually from and about non-royal lineages (*lobong*). Here, I was mainly interested in obtaining further information on non-royal genealogies, historical marriages, patterns of migration and settlement, ritual practices, and, more broadly, historical trade and other economic practices and patterns.

Over time, I concentrated increasingly on lineage-based, non-narrative traditions for two main reasons. First, as already noted, such traditions are much more likely to refer to actual human decisions and actions in the past

---

must have occurred in producing *rwot* lists and associated genealogies in Acholi, but a number of differences exist between the situation described by Blount and that in Acholi. First, the Kenya Luo genealogies were detailed, extensive, and wide (if not deep), and were generally not associated with the holders of chiefly office. This makes them very different social constructs than the Acholi *rwot* lists and the mostly limited genealogies associated with them. Second, unlike the Kenya Luo genealogies, the Acholi *rwot* lists have been tied in to three major droughts and famines (c. 1725, 1790, and the mid-1830s) whose dates derive from such evidence as Nile-level data and neighboring Jie age-sets, completely independent of the *rwot* lists and genealogies themselves. See Chap. 2; Chap. 3, n. 5; Chap. 5, n. 1. Such independent evidence provides both a check on the relative reliability of the extant *rwot* lists and a means to establish a more reliable (if still tentative and imprecise) chronological framework. Finally, whatever internal dynamics have been involved in determining the extant Acholi *rwot* lists and associated genealogies, each such list is almost entirely independent of the others. Considered together, the extant *rwot* lists from the seventy or so Acholi chiefdoms are not the product of any group interview dynamic or consensual agreement.

than are consciously historical, narrative traditions, which tend to present past behavior, orientation, and structure in normative and even stereotypical terms. Thus, most of the limited sociological detail still recoverable in Acholi pertaining to the precolonial past will be found in unconscious, non-narrative traditions. Second, the localized lineage was the most important social and economic group in historical Acholi. It seemed logical to seek sociohistorical detail from and about this historically most important social unit. Moreover, despite the changes that lineages in Acholi have undergone in this century, they, unlike the chiefdoms, have continued to function as collective social and economic entities.

Two types of lineage-based, non-narrative traditions proved especially significant and surprising: remembered historical marriages and lineage incorporation into chiefdoms. In analyzing the village-lineage affiliation of nearly 450 nineteenth- and early-twentieth-century marriages, the most striking and unexpected pattern that emerged was their spatial distribution. Four quite distinct networks could be discerned, each geographically limited to a clearly defined portion of western Acholi and to the immediately contiguous non-Acholi area.

This prompted me to investigate whether other features of Acholi were similarly patterned. At least three were: trade, inter-polity cooperation and conflict, and the distribution of ethnolinguistic origins and twentieth-century dialects. Taken together, all of this revealed the existence of four distinct territorial areas or "zones" in western Acholi. Most interaction and cooperation, including the ties of marriage, occurred within these zones and not between them. Most hostilities, conversely, took place between groups occupying different zones.

Over the whole of Uganda Acholiland, eight such zones can be identified. And though they were neither formal nor named, these zones served as the only functionally meaningful groupings of people in Acholi beyond the individual chiefdoms until the second half of the nineteenth century. Moreover, just as modern parishes and sub-counties often reflect earlier lineages and chiefdoms, a rough relationship exists between present-day county boundaries and the old zones (Map 2).

These zones provide an important framework for understanding the complexity and subtle variations in chiefdom formation and subsequent developments in different parts of Acholi, as will be explored below. But two other points need to be made here. First, information on historical marriages revealed sociohistorical patterns that were extremely significant and completely absent from both conscious, narrative traditions and the

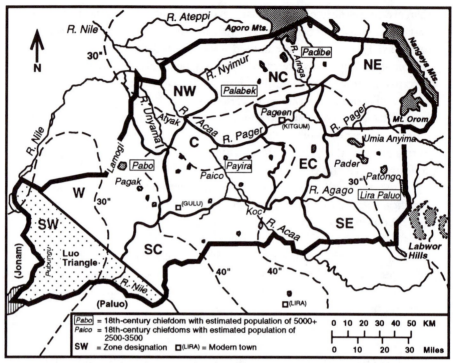

Map 2. Acholi zones and most populous eighteenth-century chiefdoms.

available literature. Second, this evidence was widely available. Unlike many topics of enquiry, where relatively few elders possessed detailed knowledge, most elders asked could provide details of their predecessors' marriages for at least two or three generations back, and sometimes further. The ties created and maintained by marriage obviously carried, and continue to carry, great significance. I regret that I did not begin to mine this rich source systematically until just before the Amin coup halted research.[41]

The second category of lineage-based, non-narrative traditions that produced unexpected results had to do with lineage incorporation into chiefdoms. Often, these traditions simply identify which *rwot* a particular lineage joined. In some cases, the traditions include such additional details

41. Just before Amin's coup, I had developed a questionnaire to collect systematically this marriage data. See Atkinson (1978, p. 73 and appendix 2).

as the name of the lineage leader at the time, the area from which the lineage had come, where the incorporation took place, and some of the circumstances surrounding incorporation. This sort of information, which before Project research had never been systematically collected or analyzed, suggested striking revisions in established ideas about the Acholi chiefdoms and their origins.[42]

The crucial indicator was chronology. In western Acholi where I first worked, almost all traditions dealing with the incorporation of specific lineages into chiefdoms indicate that this occurred no earlier than the late seventeenth century. Most point to an eighteenth-century date. The same proved true for the rest of Acholi. The implications were clear and profound: if the earliest lineages were incorporated into Acholi chiefdoms only in the late seventeenth and early eighteenth centuries, then the chiefdoms themselves were most likely creations of the same period. This was eventually corroborated by other sources. What was not corroborated was the widely accepted link between the origins of these polities and the earliest Luo, a link proclaimed in many Acholi narrative traditions (often supported by appropriately lengthy *rwot* lists) and in the standard histories of East Africa.

Traditions of lineage incorporation thus indicated a major change in the sociohistorical order in Acholi during the late seventeenth and early eighteenth centuries. Narrative Acholi traditions mask or deny such a change. Does this mean that some of these traditions are "true," others "false"? The situation is more complex than that. Despite appearances, the traditions in question are more than simply contradictory accounts of the same historical events. We are dealing instead with two sets of traditions that focus on separate aspects of the past and have separate social purposes in the present.[43]

One of these sets — based in and focused upon individual lineages — consists of unconscious, non-narrative, separate-group traditions. These

---

42. Crazzolara (1951 and 1954, passim) collected many traditions that conveyed information about the incorporation of lineages into Acholi chiefdoms; as with much else in *The Lwoo*, however, he did not do this systematically. J. B. Webster was the Project researcher who first began to collect information on lineage incorporation in Acholi.

43. Miller (1980b, pp. 37–39) points out that the existence of such discrete, sometimes even contradictory, bodies of tradition is a frequent characteristic of oral cultures. For a West African example, see Wilks (1978). Miller also argues that literate historians, unlike oral narrators bound by their oral methodology, can combine and compare these discrete sets of traditions in ways that can result in a better understanding of both the traditions involved and the past they depict. This is one of the goals of the present work.

traditions recount the remembered circumstances surrounding the incorporation of particular lineages into chiefdoms. Any connection between such traditions and the origins and development of chiefdoms is inferential, and incidental to the traditions in and of themselves. Considered in the aggregate, however, these lineage traditions present a compelling picture of the nature and chronology of chiefdom formation in Acholi. And given that non-narrative traditions are the main sources of past sociological detail, this picture cannot be easily dismissed.

The second set of traditions consists of conscious narrative traditions dealing with the origins of the Acholi chiefdoms. The basic theme of these traditions is that when the early Luo arrived from their homeland to the north, they brought the knowledge and accoutrements of chiefly authority. Many of these Luo, the traditions continue, soon asserted that authority by founding Acholi chiefdoms.

Although such traditions appear to account for a crucial sociohistorical development among the Acholi, the message they convey has more to do with ideology than with social change or history. These traditions link the Acholi — especially certain ruling Acholi lineages — with the early Luo, from whom the ruling Babiito dynasty of Bunyoro-Kitara and the founders of many other polities to the north and south claim descent. In asserting that link, the traditions depict the coming of the Luo as momentous, claim their primacy and special qualities, and explain both the origins of the Acholi sociopolitical order and the introduction of the Luo language.

On one level, narrative traditions thus associate the origins of many fundamental Acholi sociocultural practices and sociopolitical structures with the coming of the Luo. Looked at closely, however, these traditions present a much more complicated picture. In fact, details in these traditions contradict their thematic message and support instead the separate-group, non-narrative, lineage traditions.

Contradictions are revealed mainly through allusions to the fundamental concepts and structures of chiefly leadership — a particular type of chiefship, tribute, and royal drums. A few traditions make specific, if usually brief, references to the introduction of new chiefly institutions or practices. But this is rare. More often, indications of major change are suggested by a marked, abrupt shift in the tone and nature of narrative traditions. In case after case, these traditions suddenly begin to read differently at a particular point.

The likely timing of this shift ranges from the late seventeenth century into the eighteenth, and it is marked by such features as: (1) a noticeable increase in both the quality and quantity of detail; (2) mainly consistent *rwot* lists that contain names other than archetypal ones; and (3) *rwot* lists that are accompanied by generally realistic stories of activities and relation-ships and by sociological detail not present for earlier figures. It is also often at this point that references to tribute and royal drums first appear in the traditions, though there is typically no acknowledgment that these features were introduced at this time. Moreover, some chiefdoms even take their name from the person ruling at this juncture, despite an often long list of purported predecessors. Finally, to return to the separate-group traditions with which we began, outside village lineages have traditions of incorpora-tion only from this time.[44]

Aidan Southall has observed that it is a characteristic of both the Luo-speaking Alur and Kenya Luo "that their recollections of the past take on a quite different quality with reference to events which occurred before and after the moment when they passed some striking physical barrier or landmark and entered their present territory." In Acholi the landmark that marks a major change is not physical (though physical movement some-times accompanied the transition), but ideological and structural. Acholi traditions, even narrative traditions that often deny or ignore the very processes that transform them, speak with a different voice once they begin to relate that portion of the past when new ideas and structures of political leadership take hold and Acholi chiefdoms begin to emerge. It was this change of voice, this change in the nature of narrative traditions, that began to convince me of the extent of the transformation occurring in Acholi from the late seventeenth century on, despite indications to the contrary in the overt theme or message of those same traditions.[45]

44. All of the extant western Acholi *rwot* lists have been reproduced in Atkinson (1978, pp. 566–82). Archetypal Luo names are especially abundant among the early, pre-polity names in the Patiko and Payira ruler lists (two of the largest and most powerful of the Acholi polities), and in the ruler list of old "Tekidi" as presented in Odongo (1976). Southall (1972, pp. 9–10) discusses this problem, with special reference to the Patiko list. The third feature I note here represents one consequence of the distinction in oral societies between the "absent" and the "present" pasts. See Miller (1980b, p. 41) and Chap. 2 below.

45. Southall (1954, p. 148).

2. Social and Economic Life in Acholi Before the Late Seventeenth Century

The changes most crucial to the development of a distinctive Acholi society and collective identity began in the late seventeenth century and were played out against two interacting backdrops that are the focus of this chapter: (1) the physical environment and (2) the social and economic systems operative in north-central Uganda during the mid- to late seventeenth century. Together these not only provided the setting in which a common social order, political culture, and collective identity were created, but determined many parameters for those changes as well.

The Physical Environment

Modern Acholi District stretches along much of the northern border of Uganda. Situated on a plateau 3,000 to 4,000 feet (1,025–1,350 meters) above sea level, the district consists of nearly 11,000 square miles (28,400 square kilometers) of rolling savannah. The physical environment of this area is dominated by two fundamental features. The first is a lightly wooded savannah landscape of scattered trees, bushes, and thick, tough grass that can reach six feet in height; the second, a harsh climate marked by a long dry season and frequently late or unreliable rains.

Acholi's grasslands are broken up by streams and rivers that crisscross the area, and rock or mountain outcrops that rise sharply above the surrounding plains. The main river system of Acholi consists of the Acaa (Aswa on modern maps), Pager, Unyama, and their numerous tributaries, which flow northward to join the Nile. A second major system, in southeastern Acholi, is the Agago River and its tributaries (Map 3). Most Acholi rivers and streams are perennial; only in the worst years do any more than the smallest ones dry up. These rivers and their banks and valleys provide multiple benefits that have always made them attractive settlement sites:

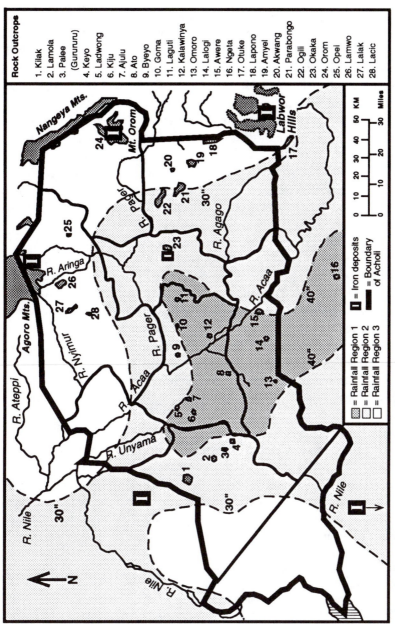

Rock Outcrops

1. Kilak
2. Lamola
3. Palee (Gurururu)
4. Keyo
5. Ladwong
6. Kiju
7. Ajulu
8. Ato
9. Byeyo
10. Goma
11. Laguti
12. Kalawinya
13. Omoro
14. Lalogi
15. Awere
16. Ngeta
17. Otuke
18. Lapono
19. Amyel
20. Akwang
21. Parabongo
22. Ogili
23. Okaka
24. Orom
25. Opei
26. Lamwo
27. Lalak
28. Lacic

□ = Iron deposits ▊ = Boundary of Acholi

▨ = Rainfall Region 1
☐ = Rainfall Region 2
☐ = Rainfall Region 3

Map 3. Rivers, rock outcrops, rainfall regions, and approximate location of iron deposits.

water and fish, better farmland, a greater number and variety of trees, and a protected flank against enemies. In addition, as prominent features of the landscape, rivers have frequently served as political boundaries.[1]

Such boundaries, however, were not barriers. Only the two branches of the Nile that mark portions of the western and southern boundaries of Acholi seem partial exceptions to this general rule. Yet even here, limited contact existed, and the major hindrance to greater interaction seems not the river, but the expansive tracts of largely uninhabited and sometimes inhospitable land separating the nearest Acholi settlements from those across the Nile.[2]

Rock or mountain outcrops (*got* in Acholi Luo) also played geopolitical roles in Acholi. Groups of various types and sizes seem to have long settled around Acholi's outcrops, almost surely because of the extra security they provided. In southeastern Acholi, for example, most people clustered around the slopes of the Ogili, Amyel, and Lapono mountain ranges until the nineteenth century. Farther west, *Got* Kilak served as home for many westernmost Acholi groups (see Map 3). In addition, the massive Agoro mountain range straddling the modern Uganda-Sudan border marked a significant boundary in earlier times as well. The changes that produced a common social order and political culture in Acholi south of Agoro did not extend north of the range, though a contiguous area of some four thousand square miles north of Agoro is also inhabited by people called Acholi. Finally, rock outcrops were also the homes of many of the important "spirits" (*jogi*; singular, *jok*) of the peoples of Acholi.[3]

CLIMATE AND RAINFALL

The overall climate of Acholi is determined primarily by a belt of low pressure. When this passes north over Uganda, usually during April or May, it draws the rain-bearing southeast trade winds after it; when it moves back south in October or November the rains cease. Specific features such as relief and secondary wind patterns then add their influence to create specific local rainfall patterns.[4]

---

1. See Langlands (1968), Webster (1976a, pp. 219–20), Crazzolara (1951, p. 176), and Ogot (1967a, p. 42, n. 8).
2. For nineteenth-century comments on the uninhabited land north of the Nile see Speke (1863, pp. 444–49), Baker (1866, v. 2, pp. 311–12), and Baker (1879, v. 2, pp. 130–31).
3. Although the Agoro range is cut by passes, the massiveness of the mountains may have helped keep northernmost Acholi distinct from Acholi south of Agoro. See Okeny (1982a, 1982b), Atkinson (1978, pp. 210–13), and the Patiko section in Chap. 4 below.
4. MacMaster (1962, p. 13); Jameson (1970, p. 12); Herring (1976a, p. 41).

Acholi's mean annual rainfall totals — according to twentieth-century figures — range from 30 to 60 inches (760–1,520 mm.), with most of Acholi averaging 45 inches (1,140 mm.). Most agricultural areas in Europe and the United States receive no more rain than this, and many get less. In East Africa, though, rainfall totals in themselves explain little, for the key issue is not just how much rain, but how dependable that rain is and when it falls. Map 3 demarcates three regions across Acholi reflecting 90 percent probability totals — that is, rainfall amounts that can be expected nine years of every ten. The contours of these regions correspond roughly with those marking mean annual rainfall figures, but the totals are reduced significantly: from sixty, forty, and thirty inches, respectively, to forty, thirty, and twenty.[5]

Region 1, receiving at least forty inches of rain nine years out of ten, covers much of central Acholi, including parts of the central Acaa River. This amount of dependable annual rain virtually assures a reasonable harvest from any of the long-established food crops in the area, including the preferred staples, eleusine millet and sesame. The largest of the Acholi chiefdoms (Payira), and seemingly some of Acholi's main population concentrations in earlier times as well, were situated in or near this most favorable rainfall region.

Much of the rest of Acholi receives a fairly dependable thirty to forty inches of annual rain. Here in Region 2, preferred crops can be grown with some confidence, especially near streams and rivers that help maintain reliable ground water. But more drought-resistant, less-popular crops are also often interplanted to provide a crucial extra margin of safety.

Region 3 is far worse off. There is not only less rain — only twenty inches in even the best nine of every ten years — but it is inconsistent and unreliable. Extra water from the Nile in the southwest and from some northern and eastern mountains assists the cultivation of eleusine and sesame in those parts of Region 3, but nowhere in the region can these crops be counted on. The more drought-resistant sorghum and bulrush millet (and, in modern times, cassava) supplement or even replace eleusine; shea butter from the *Butyrosperum* tree, common in much of Acholi, supplants sesame as the main food oil. Furthermore, stock rearing — especially

---

5. For overall average rainfall, see Thomas and Scott (1935, facing p. 113); *Atlas of Uganda* (1962, pp. 14–15; 1967, pp. 16–17); MacMaster (1962, pp. 13–14); Jameson (1970, p. 13). For the reduced reliable rainfall, see the East African Meteorological Department (1961), which Jameson (1970, p. 13) notes as "a better guide to agricultural planning" than maps of mean annual rainfall.

cattle — often takes on greater importance in this least-favored rainfall region than elsewhere in Acholi.[6]

Reliability and probability are only the first of a long list of concerns associated with rainfall in Acholi. The beginning or end of the rains can fluctuate widely, especially in Region 3, which can cause serious crop damage. Rain may fall only in localized showers, leaving nearby areas dry, or else pour down in such short, heavy bursts that it washes away great quantities of Acholi's light topsoil. Most importantly, the distribution of rainfall is highly unequal throughout the year. Nearly all of Acholi's rain comes in six to seven months from April or May to October. The remaining months stretch into a long and often difficult dry season, during which little or no agricultural work is possible. In addition, the lack of dry-season cloud cover contributes to a high rate of moisture loss from both plants and soil.[7]

This distribution of annual rainfall also determines the rhythm of everyday life. "During the rainy season," writes Girling,

> there is little intercommunication between different areas of Acholiland. The people are . . . fully occupied with agricultural work, but the long grass and the swollen swamps and streams [also] make travelling difficult. This periodic isolation and the ties of cooperation in work which are established between members of the same local communities seemed to have increased the internal cohesion of the village and the domain [chiefdom].

During the long dry season, in contrast, "travelling between different parts of the country is easier. Visiting between kinsfolk and friends takes place at this time; there are also funeral ceremonies, courtship dances and marriages which demand the attention of those living far apart. Large communal hunts are also organised."[8]

So the rains come and go. The grass grows green and high and then, as the dry season sets in, dies down and often burns, sometimes set by lightning, more often by human hunters and farmers. Wherever the land is cultivated, the grass cover gives way to cleared ground, then to crops, then stubble, and then, after two or three years, is left fallow to revert to grass again. Thus the succession of the seasons leads to ever-recurring cycles of

6. There is even evidence of early irrigation in the Aringa River valley of north-central Acholi. See Watson (1952); Owot (1976, p. 184). My understanding of the Acholi climate owes much to discussions with Ralph Herring and to his paper (1976a, esp. pp. 42–46). Information on crops comes from MacMaster (1962, pp. 49–59, 80–81), Jameson (1970, pp. 146, 149, 217, 237), and Herring (1976a, p. 39).

7. Herring (1976a, p. 42).

8. Girling (1960, pp. 14–15).

change in the natural environment, and to equally regular and repetitive cycles of labor and leisure for the farmers of the region.

THE ENVIRONMENT AND CHANGE

But everything changes, even the physical environment. In East Africa, evidence suggests that the climate was wetter and the landscape more forested up to about the third millennium B.C. But enough drying out had occurred by circa 1000 B.C. to produce a climate and landscape similar to today's. And it was only after this, historical linguistic analysis suggests, that Acholi began to be substantially settled.[9]

Even if the overall climate from circa 1000 B.C. seems to have been stable, shorter-term fluctuations in rainfall have greatly impacted the lives of Acholi's inhabitants. These fluctuations include seasonal ones (such as the early or late onset of a rainy season), two- or three-year failures of the rains leading to serious droughts, and longer cycles over decades of relatively abundant or deficient rainfall. All of these—and especially the second—have played an ongoing role in the historical development of many peoples in East Africa.

The primary means for placing such fluctuations in a chronological framework before documentary evidence in the late nineteenth century comes from hydrological data from Egypt. Annual measurements of the minimum and maximum flood levels of the Egyptian Nile have been recorded most years since A.D. 622. Maximum floods occur in August–September and represent mainly the input of the Ethiopian Nile. Minimum flood levels occur usually in May and are approximately two-thirds the result of water coming from the lakes region of East Africa. The precise relationship between rainfall in the East African lakes area and low flood levels as measured at Rodah is difficult to judge. One complicating factor is the intricate interdependence between the high and low flood levels, which makes it hard to separate out the input of the lakes region from that of Ethiopia. Another is the long-term silting of the river bed, which has altered Rodah's zero level. A third is the delay of water from East Africa reaching the Egyptian Nile because of the permanent, massive *Sudd* or great

9. Evidence indicating a wetter, more forested early East Africa is summarized by Kamau (1973) and Herring (1976a, p. 58); see also Ambrose (1982, pp. 137–38), David (1982, pp. 80–81), and Dale (1954, p. 26). Historical linguistic evidence and analysis is found in Ehret (1971, pp. 26–38; 1974b, chap. 1) and Ehret et al. (1974, pp. 89–92); see also Herring (1974b, pp. 32–34) and Lamphear (1986, pp. 232–35). For an example of regular human burning of wooded areas in Southern Africa, see Guy (1980, pp. 104–5).

swamp in the southern Sudan, causing run-off and evaporation before the water has the chance to reach Rodah.[10]

While acknowledging such difficulties, David W. Cohen has proposed one way of discerning the relationship. He begins by noting the pattern of low flood-level readings at Rodah for the years surrounding known rainfall deficiencies in the lakes region of East Africa in 1898–1900 and 1917–18. This pattern is a falling trend in the low flood levels lasting from three to ten years.[11]

More than thirty such falling trends appear in available Rodah records, including eighteenth- and nineteenth-century examples crucial for establishing a chronology in Acholi. Here, I want to concentrate on two earlier cases. The first suggests a series of five droughts during the late twelfth and early thirteenth centuries (1158, 1175–78, 1198–1200, 1226, and 1236); the second, another five probable droughts between 1424 and 1462. Such periods of repeated droughts, producing in turn a succession of crop shortfalls and probably famines, are examples of the sort of extreme circumstances that can place communities under such severe strain that significant upheaval and change occur. Are there any indications of such change during these two periods?[12]

In Egypt, recurring famine stalked the last twenty years of the twelfth century, beginning in 1180–82 when the Ethiopian (high) floods failed. Low flood levels in 1181–83 were also so low that they supposedly could not be measured, and people could walk from Cairo to the isle of Rodah. Subsequent famines struck in 1184, 1191–94, and 1201, with one-third of the population reportedly dying.[13]

Historical linguistic analysis provides clues that might link developments in East Africa to conditions in Egypt. Christopher Ehret calculates that the percentage of shared words in a standard two-hundred-word list between Shilluk (Northern Luo) and Central/Southern Luo is 72–75 percent. Drawing on archaeological and oral evidence from across East Africa, Ehret reckons that this percentage of word sharing indicates a division of the languages at about A.D. 1200–1300.[14]

10. See Tousson (1925). Herring was the first to use Rodah records compiled by Tousson to reconstruct the East African past (1974a, revised 1979a). Henige (1980) has been sharply critical of Herring's approach and skeptical about using the Nile records, a skepticism not shared by renowned historical climatologist H. H. Lamb (1982, p. 83).
11. Cohen (1974b).
12. See Tousson (1925); Cohen (1974b).
13. Herring (1979a, pp. 51–52), from Tousson (1925, pp. 458–74).
14. Ehret, personal communication. For a presentation of his method, see Ehret (1971, pp. 27–28 and appendices). This time scale shortens considerably that of Blount and Curley

Such linguistic divergence is consonant with a significant Luo migration southward, leading to Luo settlement in many parts of East Africa. Extreme climatic conditions, as suggested by the Rodah data for the late twelfth and early thirteenth centuries, could well have been a factor in both this linguistic division and population movement among the early Luo.[15]

The next period of probable recurring rainfall shortages in East Africa — in the early to mid-fifteenth century (1424–62) — was marked by extremely severe weather from Europe to China, especially during the 1430s. The early to mid-fifteenth century was also the period when Luo speakers first seem to have come to Acholi and neighboring areas, as indicated by three types of evidence. First, historical linguistic analysis suggests a separation between Southern Luo (Kenya Luo) and Central Luo (Acholi, Alur, Lango) during the period from about 1400 to 1450. This separation would have been accompanied, traditions suggest, by Luo settlement in Bunyoro and northern Uganda. Next, radiocarbon dating from the Bigo complex in Bunyoro, which was probably associated with the arrival of the early Luo, yields a late-fourteenth- or fifteenth-century date. Lastly, though less reliance can be placed on this, the standard Bunyoro-Kitara king list also suggests a fifteenth-century date for the establishment in Bunyoro of a new Luo Babiito dynasty.[16]

A final point about the Rodah records is that gaps do exist in the data. Unfortunately, some of these gaps fall in the late seventeenth and eighteenth centuries, the very period that is the main focus of the present work.[17]

(1970), whose analysis of five Luo languages suggests a split between proto-Northern Luo and proto-Central/Southern Luo c. A.D. 870 ± 200. Ehret's main criticism of Blount and Curley's estimate is that they fail to consider data from the Luo languages Jur, Padhola, and Anywak.

15. For alternative interpretations of Luo migrations, see Herring (1974b, pp. 1–171; 1979a, pp. 51–53); Webster (n.d. [1971], n.d. [a], 1979b); Odongo (1976). Cf. Atkinson (1978, pp. 112–15, 121).

16. Lamb (1982, pp. 178–200, 276–77) discusses the extreme weather worldwide during the late Middle Ages, noting especially the 1430s. Linguistic arguments are from Ehret (personal communication), who notes that the percentage of shared words between South and Central Luo languages in the standard two-hundred-word list is about 80 percent. This represents a divergence of South from Central Luo about five hundred to six hundred years ago, or about A.D. 1400–1500. Again the time scale suggested by Blount and Curley (1970), which puts the division at c. 1320 ± 150, is shortened; so are those suggested by Herring and Webster (see n. 15). On the Bigo complex see Shinnie (1960) and Posnansky (1966); Henige (1974a, pp. 44–45) and Twaddle (1975, pp. 156–68) question an association between Bigo and the Luo. Finally, see Nyakatura (1973) for the standard king list and Henige (1972; 1974a; 1974b, pp. 105–14) for challenges to the list.

17. Lamb (1982), however, does provide general climatological information for the seventeenth and eighteenth centuries.

The Economic Base: Material Life, Food Production, and Technology

"Material life," Fernand Braudel has written, "denotes repeated actions, empirical processes, old methods and solutions handed down from time immemorial." This material life, he continues, "is there at the root of everything." And at the root of material life, especially for peasants and members of pre-industrial societies, is food and food production.[18]

What can be discerned about material life in early Acholi? First, all the early inhabitants of Acholi, at least by the mid-seventeenth century and probably long before, lived similar lives, sharing essentially the same environment, technology, and agriculturally based material life. Second, archaeological evidence suggests that this agriculture was established throughout the eastern and central Sudan, of which Acholi is a part, during the first millennium B.C. (though none of this evidence comes specifically from Acholi). Third, historical linguistic research helps fill in the archaeological gap, as it both identifies Central Sudanic speakers as some of the earliest farmer-herders in the broader region and indicates that they were settled in Acholi by at least the last centuries of the first millennium B.C.[19]

Central Sudanic speakers thus seem the most likely people to have introduced agriculture into Acholi, or were at least among its earliest farmers. But John Lamphear sounds a cautionary note on this issue when he argues that it is not until the present millennium that we can even begin to be confident about linking particular technologies, cultural features, or way of life with a specific East African linguistic community. Before this, instead, "economic activity was typically multi-faceted, with distinctions between pastoralists, agriculturalists and hunter-gatherers/fisherman very blurred. It seems quite likely that in many areas circumstances which would have favoured bi- or multi-lingualism were present."[20]

FOOD CROPS IN ACHOLI

Some of the most important crops grown in Acholi today seem also among the oldest. These include eleusine millet (often called finger millet); sesame (called *simsim* in much of East Africa); and, especially in dryer areas,

---

18. Braudel (1973, p. xii).

19. Archaeological evidence is summarized by Phillipson (1977, chaps. 3 and 5, passim; pp. 218–20). Ehret's historical linguistic analysis (1974a, p. 92; 1974b) identifies Central Sudanic speakers as early agriculturalists. David (1982, pp. 80–82) provides the chronology.

20. See David (1983) and Lamphear (1986); the quote is from the latter (p. 235).

sorghum and bulrush millet. Most experts agree that East Africa was one of the centers of origin for eleusine and bulrush millet, that sesame is an indigenous crop of northeastern Africa, and that sorghum was first domesticated somewhere in Africa's savannah belt. Other crops grown in Acholi from an early date include the two pulses, pigeon peas and cowpeas, and many other leafy green vegetables.[21]

Food production always involves a balancing of individual and societal preferences and habits on the one hand, and technical, environmental, and cost considerations on the other. Eleusine millet is (and seemingly has long been) the preferred staple grain crop across northern Uganda and the southern Sudan. It is used both for food and making beer. Eaten usually with sauces or relishes made from subsidiary crops, eleusine provides a nourishing diet rich in vegetable protein. This versatile and nutritious grain is also less subject to bird and pest damage than sorghum, and it produces an expected yield almost double that of either sorghum or bulrush millet.

Such attractions, however, have had to be weighed against other considerations. Eleusine requires more fertile soil than sorghum or bulrush millet, and its shallow root system needs topsoil that remains moist long after planting. Hence eleusine is at great risk with any prolonged break in the rains. This hinders or even prohibits dependence on eleusine in the dryer areas of Region 3, and makes it somewhat risky in Region 2. In these areas, sorghum or bulrush millet must be sown along with, or must even replace, the preferred eleusine.[22]

Sesame demands somewhat less rain overall than eleusine, making it a relatively safe crop in both Regions 1 and 2. It cannot be depended upon in Region 3, however, mainly because it needs reliable rain early in its growth cycle. Where it can be grown, sesame is a valuable and valued source of oil and protein, and has long been considered worth its high labor costs and relatively low yields.[23]

21. On the antiquity of eleusine, sesame, bulrush millet, and sorghum, see MacMaster (1962, pp. 49, 55, 77); Stemler, Harlan, and Dewet (1975); Harlan et al. (1976, pp. 14, 417); Phillipson (1977, p. 218). Lamphear (1986, p. 256) notes that the wild progenitor of eleusine, "relatively rare in eastern Africa," existed in parts of Karamoja just east of Acholi. And on the seemingly long-established staple foods of Acholi, see, for example, MacMaster (1962, pp. 81–85); Jameson (1970, pp. 217–18, 243–46, 267–69); Parsons (1960b, pp. 2, 27–28, 32–34); A.H.T. 214, 222; Garry A.H.T., pp. 10, 33, 125; Webster A.H.T., p. 32.

22. Most information on eleusine comes from Jameson (1970, pp. 145–51); see also Herring (1976a, p. 39), MacMaster (1962, pp. 49–54), and Parsons (1960b, pp. 25–26). Jameson notes that eleusine makes much higher labor demands than the other cereals.

23. Jameson (1970, pp. 211, 237–39); Herring (1976a, p. 39); MacMaster (1962, pp. 77–81). Tosh (1978a, p. 428) notes that in 1940 under experimental conditions in Lango, just south of Acholi, sesame cultivation required sixty man-days per acre, per annum.

CATTLE IN ACHOLI

Although agriculture has apparently been primary wherever rainfall permits, farmers throughout the eastern and central Sudan seem to have almost always supplemented the cultivation of crops with the keeping of domestic animals. The roster of such animals common throughout Acholi — at least from the seventeenth century when the evidence becomes clearer — seems to have consisted only of chickens, goats, and some sheep. Cattle appear to have been important only in portions of the east and north.

This is surprising, first of all, because historical linguistics clearly indicates an early knowledge of cattle among Central Sudanic speakers, the most populous ethnolinguistic group in the western half of Acholi. Despite such knowledge, tsetse fly infestation in this part of Acholi might have always restricted cattle keeping there. The limited importance of cattle in Acholi is also surprising because of two related and widely held beliefs concerning the Luo: one, that Acholi has long been a Luo-settled and Luo-dominated area (discussed below); and two, that the Luo are prototypical cattle keepers.[24]

The strong link often asserted between the Luo and cattle keeping seems to flow from three dubious assumptions. First, cattle clearly play a central role among the Luo-speaking Shilluk and their Western Nilotic relatives, the Nuer and Dinka, in the Western Nilotic heartland in the southern Sudan. The assumption is that they must therefore be important to all Western Nilotic speakers, including other Luo. But this ignores several counterexamples. Cattle have been relatively unimportant not only in Acholi but among such Luo-speaking peoples as the Padhola of eastern Uganda and many Kenya Luo groups.

A second widely held assumption has been that all southward-migrating Luo were alike. Thus if some were associated with cattle — as was clearly the case — then all must have been. But this, too, overlooks diversity. Apart from the Shilluk, the Luo most clearly linked with cattle were those who moved through or settled in the dry, present-day Karamoja District of northeastern Uganda. The importance of cattle to these Luo can be attributed to a combination of a setting especially favorable to herding (and unfavorable to cultivation) and interaction with cattle-keeping Eastern Nilotic groups in the area. Members of this eastern wing of Luo migrants eventually settled in parts of Padhola and Busoga in eastern Uganda and

24. For historical-linguistic evidence see Ehret (1967, 1973, 1974a) and Ehret et al. (1974); for summaries of the traditional view of Luo "cattle culture," see Ocholla-Ayayo (1980, pp. 46–47) and Safholm (1973, pp. 22–23).

farther south in Kenya Luoland. But these same areas also witnessed the settlement of other Luo-speaking groups who arrived via more westerly routes that had brought them into contact with different environments and peoples. This western stream of Luo displayed a number of characteristics that distinguished them from the eastern wing, including a lack of emphasis on cattle keeping.[25]

Lastly, cattle were important, both practically and ritually, to the most renowned Luo migrant group in East Africa, the ruling Babiito dynasty of Bunyoro-Kitara. It has often been assumed that this close association with cattle was part of the Luo cultural baggage that the Babiito brought with them into Bunyoro. Two pieces of evidence make this unlikely: (1) Babiito beliefs and practices pertaining to cattle closely resemble those of both the earlier Bacwezi/Bahima rulers of Bunyoro-Kitara and later Bahima groups throughout East Africa; and (2) Babiito traditions specifically recount the group's adopting these beliefs and practices from the previous ruling dynasty.[26]

Wild Game and Other Resources

If the number of cattle and variety of domestic animals in Acholi were few, wild animals were not. Elephants, lions, leopards, water buffaloes, giraffes, rhinoceroses, hippopotamuses, hyenas, baboons, many varieties of antelope, and a large quantity and variety of monkeys and other smaller animals were all present. Although hunting was surely an ancient practice, the lack of archaeological work and the limitations of oral sources preclude our knowing how extensively these wild-animal resources were exploited by early peoples in Acholi. What we do know is that hunting was extremely important in the later Acholi chiefdoms as a social activity, a source of meat for people generally, and a source of tribute for *rwodi*. Acholi also contained many other non-domesticated food resources, including many species of fish; the leaves, shoots, stems, and fruits of numerous edible plants; shea butter; and honey from wild bees.[27]

Significantly, there were no local supplies of natural salt in Acholi and only widely scattered deposits of iron, both highly valued resources. In later

25. For discussions of the two main streams of early Luo migrants see Cohen (1974a); Herring, Cohen, and Ogot (1984); Cohen and Odhiambo (1989, pp. 15–22).

26. See, for example, Nyakatura (1973, p. 66).

27. For the importance of hunting and gathering by early inhabitants of East Africa and the persistence of these activities into our own era, see Lamphear (1986). For descriptions of later Acholi hunting practices see Baker (1866, v. 2, pp. 439–49), Usher-Wilson (1947), Bere (1934; 1960a; n.d. [c. 1978], pp. 144–63).

times at least, salt was sometimes imported from Bunyoro to the south. More commonly, a substitute was made from the ashes of certain kinds of grass. Iron was much more important and was mostly available either along or beyond what became the boundaries of Acholi (see Map 3). Within these boundaries, the only major source of iron was *Got* Orom in the extreme northeast; more limited deposits were found in and near the Agoro mountains in the north and near *Got* Okaka in the east-central zone. Mostly, the inhabitants of Acholi procured iron and iron objects from Central Sudanic areas to the immediate west, from the Labwor hills just southeast, or from more distant Bunyoro. The lack of salt and iron underscores a general absence of rare or precious resources in Acholi — at least until ivory took on new value during the later nineteenth century. This absence stimulated trade, especially in iron, creating networks that eventually facilitated the spread of the Luo language throughout Acholi (see Chapter 3).[28]

THE IMPLEMENTS AND ORGANIZATION OF PRODUCTION

Although no direct information exists on implements of production in early Acholi, three types of evidence from the region indicate that iron tools were used from an early date. First, traditions from all across northern Uganda identify Central Sudanic speakers — almost certainly among the first agriculturalists in Acholi — as early ironworkers. Second, archaeologist D. W. Phillipson suggests that Central Sudanic speakers may have passed on ironworking techniques to Bantu speakers living south of Acholi as early as 1000 B.C. Finally, Southern and Eastern Nilotes shared a word for "to forge iron." This means that ironworking must have been practiced before the two languages separated, or before the first half of the first millennium A.D.[29]

Two kinds of iron hoes were used in Acholi, both probably evolved from earlier wooden implements: one a straight, pointed, wooden stake and the other an angled digging stick, its two arms forming a sixty-degree angle. The latter was eventually converted into handles for heavy-socketed,

28. Information on sources of and trade for iron can be found in A.H.T. 213, 225, 232, 241, 246, 260, 265, 276, 278, 282; Webster A.H.T., pp. 25, 108, 125, 134, 161; Garry (1972b, pp. ix–x); Garry A.H.T., pp. 6, 11, 21a–22, 31, 42, 71, 76–77, 86, 99, 119, 124–25, 132, 146–47. See also Vansina (1990, pp. 60–61) for a discussion of the importance of iron for social and exchange purposes among early peoples in the rain forests of Central Africa.

29. On Central Sudanic speakers as early ironworkers, see, for example, Shiroya (1971, pp. 7–12; 1978, pp. 200–201); Lamphear (1971, p. 7) discusses early ironworking among Eastern Nilotic speakers but credits Central Sudanic peoples with the introduction of the practice throughout northern Uganda. See also Phillipson (1977, p. 227); Ehret (1971, pp. 39–40); Vansina (1990, p. 58).

roughly heart-shaped iron hoe blades, used in most of Acholi. In parts of eastern Acholi (and neighboring Lango and Karamoja) where the soil is lighter, a similarly shaped blade was often socketed or lashed to a straight handle five to ten feet long. This was used by standing upright and digging or weeding with a backward pull. Unlike the angled hoe, it was not suitable for deep cultivation or heavy soil.

Other iron implements included various types of knives (the most distinctive of which were cutting rings worn on the thumbs of both hands and used for harvesting), axes, spear blades, and arrow tips. Most men usually relied on either spears or bows and arrows as their main weapons, not both. And the preference seems clearly rooted in old sociocultural patterns: those of Central Sudanic origins tended to use bows and arrows; those originally Eastern Nilotic or Luo favored the spear.[30]

But the most important iron implement was the hoe, and the most important productive activity was agriculture. This was the case whatever the language spoken or culture practiced, whatever the changes over time, whatever the other economic activities. From probably the earliest stages of the Iron Age, if not before, the peoples of Acholi have been above all hoe agriculturalists. This means that they have shared in a means of production that is both ancient and widespread, extending in a broad belt around the world from pre-Columbian America, across Africa, to much of south and southeast Asia.[31]

This means of production, based on rudimentary tools and human energy, always requires much effort. Two features of agriculture in Acholi made labor demands there particularly intensive. First, both eleusine and sesame, the preferred staple crops, require extremely high labor inputs. Second, the short rainfall season means that great amounts of work must be done during the restricted periods in which clearing, sowing, and harvesting can successfully be carried out.

Because of the lack of archaeological work in Acholi, we do not know how early farmers there responded to these demands. But they probably adopted a strategy used by later cultivators in this and similar areas. This strategy, first of all, requires men to be an integral part of the work force. Technology, environment, climate, and the labor demands of the staple crops grown in savannah areas such as Acholi preclude reliance on the

---

30. On Acholi hoes, see Jameson (1970, p. 294), Parsons (1960, p. 22), and Girling (1960, pp. 59–60 with illustration). The most extensive treatment of the material culture of any Luo-speaking group is by Ocholla-Ayayo (1980, esp. pp. 92–114 and end figures 32–42).
31. See Braudel (1981, pp. 174–76 with map).

woman-based agriculture possible in more rainfall-abundant areas like Buganda. Second, many of the most arduous and time-restricted tasks on the land are performed by cooperative work groups. "Although they do not figure prominently in the ethnographic literature," writes John Tosh, "cooperative labour groups were and are common in those savannah regions of Africa where subsistence is based on grain crops." Such work groups in early Acholi were probably organized on the same basis as in the later chiefdoms: by village-lineage membership.[32]

Successful food production in Acholi required and still requires considerable effort. Although no one has done a quantitative analysis of food production and related activities in Acholi, anthropologist Stewart Marks has done so among a highly comparable farming, small stock keeping, and hunting people in Zambia. He calculates that the labor involved, directly or indirectly, in food production and preparation takes up approximately two-thirds of adults' total work time. Farming itself absorbs about a quarter of the time worked. This direct farm work, of course, is spaced very unevenly throughout the year; it is also shared by men and women, except for the heaviest field preparation tasks done by men alone. Building and repairing huts and granaries, tasks also shared by males and females, takes an additional 10 percent of annual work time.

The most time-consuming work of all is food and beer preparation. Including the collection of firewood, this takes up over 50 percent of annual hours worked. As all of these last-named tasks are "women's work," both where Marks worked and among the Acholi, the labor input of men in these societies should not be overemphasized. Men did (and do) essential and extensive agricultural work. So do women, who in addition put in more than half the total hours worked in the society. And this does not even consider women's role as primary child care providers. Women also contribute most of the labor for collecting wild vegetables, another 5 percent of total work time. Conversely, despite its high profile, the mainly male

32. The quotation is from Tosh (1978a, p. 420). Cooperative work groups in and near Acholi are discussed in Parsons (1960a, p. 23) on Teso, (1960b, p. 61) on Alur and Madi, (1960b, pp. 11–12, 15–16, and 1970, pp. 133–34) on Acholi and Lango; MacMaster (1962, p. 29) on Acholi and Lango; Safholm (1973, pp. 32–33) on Acholi and Lango; Lutara (1956) on Acholi; Girling (1960, pp. 17, 47–48, 59, 232–33) on Acholi; Bere (1955, pp. 54–55) on Acholi; Driberg (1923, pp. 97–98) on Lango; Curley (1971, chap. 3) on Lango; Middleton (1965, pp. 10, 12, 25) on Lugbara; and Catford (1951) on Central Sudanic Moru District in the southern Sudan. For other discussions see, for example, Mayer (1951, pp. 5–18), Gulliver (1971, pp. 188–215), Abrahams (1965, pp. 168–86), and Uchendu (1970).

domain of hunting (including trapping and fishing) occupies less than 4 percent of the total time spent in productive labor throughout the year.[33]

The object of all this labor, and its result, was to produce a normal surplus — despite the connotations of the label "subsistence," usually applied to this sort of economy. As William Allen explains, subsistence cultivators "tend to cultivate an area large enough to ensure the food supply in a season of poor yields. Otherwise the community would be exposed to frequent privation and grave risk of extermination or dispersal by famine, more especially in regions of uncertain or fluctuating rainfall."[34]

The Settlement Geography of Mid- to Late-Seventeenth-Century Acholi

Recent surveys of the archaeological and linguistic evidence suggest that Central Sudanic — or "proto-Central Sudanic" — speakers had expanded southward into Acholi by at least the end of the first millennium B.C., perhaps after climatic change made the region suitable for favored crops. Then, from early in the first millennium A.D., Eastern Nilotic — or "proto-Eastern Nilotic" — speakers, seemingly in extensive contact with Central Sudanic peoples, began to develop three main sub-communities and settle in or near eastern Acholi (see Figure 1).[35]

During the first half of the second millennium A.D., both Eastern and Western Nilotic groups made inroads into Central Sudanic areas that impinged on Acholi in three ways. The first was a series of Eastern Nilotic encroachments from about 1000 to 1600 into Central Sudanic-dominated areas north of Acholi. These seem to have set off a long, slow process of Central Sudanic moves from the affected areas into more southerly Central Sudanic territory, including Acholi. Second, during the same period numerous groups of the Teso-Karimojong (or Ateker) branch of Eastern

33. These are my calculations based on data contained in Stewart Marks (1976). On labor requirements for hoe agriculture in general, and comparisons with other types of productive systems, see Harris (1975, pp. 229–52 and sources therein). For child care practices and the sexual division of labor in Acholi see Apoko (1967).

34. Allen (1965, p. 38). Wilks (1978, p. 499) makes the same point about the Asante of Ghana.

35. Main sources for this paragraph are Lamphear (1986, pp. 233–35) and David (1982, pp. 80–82). Cf. Ehret et al. (1974, pp. 89–95); also Ehret (1967, pp. 1–3; 1968; 1971, pp. 26–38; 1974a; 1974b, chap. 1); Herring (1974b, pp. 32–35); Crazzolara (n.d.; 1954, passim).

Figure 1.
East African linguistic classification.

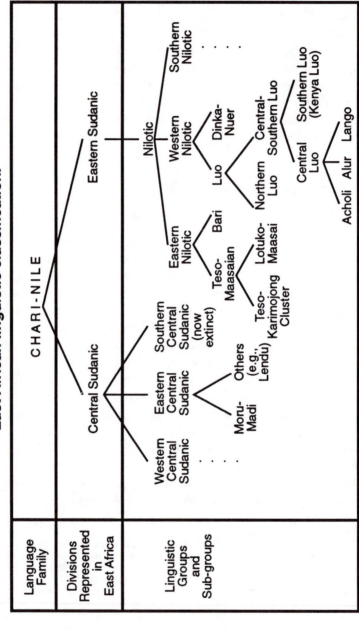

Adapted from Sutton (1974, pp. 82–83). Used by permission.

Nilotic speakers came into Acholi from the east. Most settled in eastern Acholi, but some made their way as far as the Kilak-Lamola region in the extreme west. Third, Western Nilotic Luo speakers made their first appearance in Acholi, probably during the early to mid-fifteenth century. Although these Luo were few and stayed mainly in border areas in the southwest and southeast, their arrival did add the third and final language group important in Acholi (see Figure 1).[36]

By the mid-seventeenth century, evidence is available to make the settlement pattern of the three language groups in Acholi clear. The earliest group — Central Sudanic speakers — remained the most numerous, especially in the west. A compilation of probable linguistic origins and approximate locations of all identifiable lineages in mid- to late-seventeenth-century western Acholi indicates that two-thirds of them (sixty-one of ninety-five) were Central Sudanic. Lesser concentrations of Central Sudanic lineages were present throughout the rest of Acholi as well.[37]

Eastern Nilotic Ateker were also numerous and settled throughout Acholi. Most were located in the eastern and central areas, with the eventual southeastern zone having probably the highest concentration. There, thirty-five of thirty-nine identifiable early lineages (90 percent) were Eastern Nilotic. In contrast, groups of likely Eastern Nilotic origin made up less than 20 percent of identifiable mid- to late-seventeenth-century lineages settled west of the Unyama River in westernmost Acholi (twelve of sixty-one).[38]

In essence, the settlement patterns of Central Sudanic and Eastern Nilotic groups in Acholi were mirror images of one another. The former were concentrated in the west, and especially in the northwest; the latter became progressively predominant the further south and southeast one went. Acholi in the mid- to late seventeenth century, as it had been for many generations before, was essentially a frontier region where Central Sudanic and Eastern Nilotic worlds met.

36. See Crazzolara (1954, pp. 325–89, esp. pp. 329–39 and 342–43, also 454–75); Ogot (1967a, p. 54); Shiroya (1970); Webster (1976a, pp. 224–25; n.d. [a]); Atkinson (1978, pp. 115–23, and references therein). Alternative chronologies to the above are presented by Lamphear (1971, pp. 8–9), Webster (n.d. [a]), and Herring (1974b, pp. 63–66, 84–87); and are argued against by Atkinson (1978, pp. 116–18).

37. For details of methodology and evidence used to determine the linguistic origins of mid- to late-seventeenth-century lineages in western Acholi, see Atkinson (1978, pp. 123–38). For evidence on southeastern and north-central Acholi, see Webster (1976a, pp. 222–26; 1976b, p. 300) and Owot (1976, pp. 177–78, 185–86).

38. For evidence on early lineages of probable Eastern Nilotic origins in southeastern Acholi see below, Chap. 4, nn. 58, 63, 65, 67, 69; Chaps. 5 and 6, passim. For evidence from westernmost Acholi, see Chap. 7 below and Atkinson (1978, pp. 123–38).

Conversely, Luo speakers in early Acholi were neither numerous nor widespread. Limited mainly to the southeastern and southwestern border regions until the late seventeenth or eighteenth centuries, the Luo played only a peripheral role in Acholi as a whole. Conversely, Acholi was then only a peripheral part of the Luo world.

The Pre-Polity Past: Problems of Reconstruction

Speakers of all three languages in early Acholi shared not only the same material life but similar sociopolitical organization, at least by the mid- to late seventeenth century. Even for this relatively late period, however, the evidence is scarce and difficult to interpret, mainly because the subsequent emergence of chiefdoms affected traditions of the pre-polity period in severely negative ways.

These chiefdoms, and the social order they helped shape, provided the framework within which traditions in Acholi have been maintained and transmitted. Surviving traditions thus concentrate on these chiefdoms, or at least on the portion of the past marked by their existence. Traditions of the pre-polity period, in contrast, tend to be few and sketchy. Joseph Miller has characterized distinctions such as those between pre- and post-polity traditions in Acholi as the difference between an "absent" and a "present" past. The time-depth of the latter extends back to "the origins of the components — or layers — of the present regime . . . the period that contributes to the reminders that fill the oral historians' present environment and thereby the recollection of the past. This present past corresponds to the more historical epochs of the oral traditions." In contrast, Miller writes,

> The establishment of a new dominant institution [such as chiefdoms in Acholi], or recognition of its establishment, casts loose from their moorings in the present all traditions about former times. Those stories then come to refer to what might be called the "past past," or the "absent past." It is in the absent past that historical traditions may become highly structured and most mythical in their phrasing. The traditions dealing with the absent past become fragmentary, and the remembered elements drift uncertainly as narrators varyingly attempt to link them to unrelated landmarks in the present past.[39]

Any reconstruction and analysis of the "absent past" is thus difficult, limited, and tentative. In Acholi an additional complication intrudes, as

39. Miller (1980b, p. 41).

many traditions mask or deny the emergence of the polities that determine the boundary between the absent and present pasts (see Chapter 1). Such traditions read as if the polities and their associated sociocultural practices, norms, and structures have existed from earliest times. This tendency in Acholi traditions has often gone unrecognized, contributing to a serious misreading of the early history of both the Acholi and, more generally, of the Luo. Traditions of Patiko, one of the larger and best researched of the Acholi chiefdoms, illustrate the problem.[40]

Available Patiko traditions provide numerous lists of *rwodi*, all of which include many names predating the actual founding of that chiefdom under *Rwot* Atiko in the late seventeenth century. These early names are presented as real ancestors of Luo origins from the north and real *rwodi*, and the existence of the polity is implied or even explicitly claimed. Aidan Southall is skeptical. "Patiko," he writes, "has been particularly influential in affecting the general account of Lwo history and migration, but the Patiko [royal] genealogy is extremely suspect. . . . The twelve names given by Crazzolara before Atiko are mostly archetypical names (Lwoo, Labongo, Cebami i.e. Kiyabambi, Olum, Kipir i.e. Nyipir, Kipfool) and none of them have any convincing historical content attaching to them."[41]

But Southall's skepticism is not typical. Most reconstructions of the Acholi past have accepted such traditions, and their implications of sociocultural continuity, with two crucial consequences. First, accepting all the names in Patiko's list as *rwodi* places the origins of the chiefdom much further back in time than its actual founding in the late seventeenth century. Indeed, acceptance of the entire list makes the founding of the chiefdom concurrent with the initial migration of the Luo into Acholi.

A second consequence flows from the first. If the first names in the Patiko list — and early names in the traditions of many other chiefdoms — are accepted as *rwodi*, then the early Luo must have brought ideas and institutions of centralized government with them when they came into Acholi. Here, the logic impels, lie the origins of the Acholi chiefdoms: they were established by the early Luo. Moreover, because traditions similar to

40. See Chap. 4 for my reconstruction of the founding of the Patiko polity; available versions of the Patiko *rwot* list have been collected in Atkinson (1978, pp. 573–74). Patiko is so well researched primarily due to the work of Father Crazzolara. His Patiko chapter (1951, pp. 223–55) provides the most extensive rendering of any Acholi chiefdom's narrative traditions yet compiled.

41. Southall (1972, p. 9). The point Southall is making is not precisely mine. He argues that history begins with Atiko, whereas I contend that the time of Atiko marks the beginnings of a new sociopolitical system, providing the dividing line between the "absent" and "present" pasts in Patiko traditions.

Patiko's are found in Luo-speaking and Luo-influenced groups throughout East Africa, the same line of reasoning has often been applied to these areas, and the same conclusion drawn. Thus has "state" formation all over East Africa been attributed to the early Luo.[42]

A close and critical reading of Acholi traditions, however, makes it clear that chiefdom formation there had nothing to do with the arrival of the early Luo in probably the early to mid-fifteenth century, but with completely different dynamics some two hundred to three hundred years later. Contrary to often-repeated assertions and assumptions, therefore, Acholi evidence, examined carefully, decouples the introduction of more centralized government from the early Luo.

The Pre-Polity Past: Sociopolitical Structures and Organization

Although evidence on the pre-polity or absent past of Acholi is limited, it does suggest strongly that no social or political structures incorporated large numbers of people. Most people appear to have lived in lineage-based, single-village political communities, with no formal political structures extending beyond this. Evidence on this issue is clearest and most abundant for the mid- to late seventeenth century (just prior to the establishment of the first polities) and has been most systematically assembled for western Acholi. This evidence indicates that nearly two-thirds of all identifiable lineages in western Acholi during this period belonged to such individual village communities.[43]

Specific information on these small sociopolitical units is lacking. Probably, however, their organization was similar to that of the village-lineages in the later chiefdoms, minus the overarching chiefly institutions and ideology (see Chapter 3). Indeed, attracting village-lineages into chiefdoms was almost certainly facilitated by the fact that incorporation required minimal diminution in the authority of existing village-lineage leadership and few changes in internal organization and practice. Such leadership and organization, moreover, appear broadly typical of non-centralized agricultural peoples across East and Central Africa.[44]

42. Examples of researchers accepting and arguing for the historical validity of the early portion of the Patiko *rwot* list and associated traditions are Webster (n.d. [1971], 1974, n.d. [a]); Webster and Odongo (1971). Cf. Cohen (1974c).

43. Atkinson (1978, pp. 140–43).

44. See, for example, the recent studies of small, village-based historical communities in

Although most inhabitants of mid- to late-seventeenth-century Acholi seem to have lived in single-village political communities, not all did. Sometimes, two to four villages joined together (temporarily, it appears) to form what might be called "multiple-village groupings." Scattered throughout Acholi, and probably also further south and east in Lango and Labwor, these groupings were often mixed in terms of the ethnolinguistic origins of their constituent village-lineages. Their leaders, too, came from lineages whose origins represented all three languages spoken in the area.[45]

Organization in these groupings seems to have been based on two adaptations of single-village community structure. The first is suggested by traditions from Patiko. The earliest multiple-village grouping indicated in these traditions included the eventual royal lineage of the Patiko chiefdom and the Panyagira village. The former was Luo-speaking in origin; the core group of the latter was Central Sudanic. Twentieth-century elders, influenced by the more stratified structures of the Patiko chiefdom, have sometimes characterized the early relationship between the two lineages as highly unequal; one account goes so far as to identify the Panyagira as the "purchased subjects (= slaves) of the royal clan."[46]

Other Patiko traditions, however, suggest a different picture. Here, the early Panyagira and "Patiko" are identified as "related," with no marriage allowed between them. In other words, it seems that the multiple-village grouping of "Patiko" and Panyagira was maintained, at least in part, by acting as if the members of the two lineages were a single descent group. Later, when more stratified structures and relationships evolved as part of the development of a Patiko chiefdom, this convention was no longer maintained and the two lineages were again regarded as separate (now, even unequal) descent groups. Unfortunately, such fictionalized relationships in the distant, absent past are only rarely remembered or even hinted at in the present. Thus there is no way to tell how prevalent these relationships were.[47]

---

central Kenya by Charles Ambler (1988, esp. pp. 14–30) and in the rain forests of Central Africa by Jan Vansina (1990, esp. pp. 73–100).

45. Evidence from Lango and the Labwor Hills is more inferential than conclusive. The multiple-village groupings discussed here share many similarities with later sociopolitical structures in Lango and Labwor, both the *etogo* and the small "*rwot*doms" found there. See, for example, Odyomo (n.d.); Herring (1974b, 1976b, 1979b). Western Acholi information comes from Atkinson (1978, pp. 141–44); on east-central Acholi see Garry (1972b, pp. 21–23, 43–51; 1976, pp. 322, 331) and Garry A.H.T., pp. 62–63, 68, 79, 86; on north-central Acholi, Owot (1976, pp. 184–85); and on the southeast, Webster (1976b, pp. 297–300) and Webster A.H.T., pp. 26–27, 32.

46. See Crazzolara (1951, pp. 225–26; 1954, p. 476).

47. On the eventual Patiko *kal* and Panyagira, see Crazzolara (1951, p. 226). A similar

A second adaptation of single-village organization in multiple-village groupings was based on each village within the grouping keeping its own head and control over most village affairs, while acknowledging the head of one village as "first among equals." This may have been because his village was the largest, most powerful, or longest-settled in the area; or perhaps because of his personal ability or charisma as a war leader or arbiter. Such leadership was unstable and could shift from the head of one village to another. The village composition of the groupings also seems to have changed with some frequency. Traditions of two groupings that eventually merged and then became part of the Palaro chiefdom in central Acholi illustrate this second adaptation, while including hints of the first as well.

The story begins with the arrival of a Central Sudanic–speaking group in the eventual central zone of Acholi sometime before the late seventeenth century. Arriving from the northwest, this group was made up of two lineages, one identified by the name of its remembered leader, Uma, the other called Larubi. The two are vaguely referred to as "brother" groups, but in central Acholi they established separate and apparently independent villages, perhaps indicating a fictitious brotherhood between the two lineages that was not maintained in their new location. In any case, another independent village called Lamogi was already settled on a neighboring hill, also with a Central Sudanic core lineage.[48]

Eventually, a fourth Central Sudanic lineage, Patwol, came into the area and joined Uma's group to form a multiple-village grouping of two. Traditions are clear that the two came into central Acholi at different times as core lineages of two distinct villages. Yet the Pauma and Patwol lineages "are considered akin today," and some even state that Uma was "the ancestor" of both the Pauma and Patwol. Once again, the first adaptation of single-village organization noted above seems operative.[49]

---

process may have occurred in the Pauma grouping, discussed below, and probably also among the Luo-speaking groups that became the royal lineages of Payira, Paico, and Paibona. See Anywar (1954, pp. 10–12); Okech (1953, pp. 31–32); A.H.T. 228, 231, 234–35, 237, 247; Atkinson (1978, pp. 225–31). Other possible examples come from east-central Acholi, see Crazzolara (1954, p. 537) and Garry (1972b, p. 43); from the northeast, see Garry A.H.T., pp. 119, 121–23; from *Got* Lapono in southeastern Acholi, see Webster (1976b, pp. 298–99); and perhaps from north-central Acholi, see Owot (1976, pp. 184–87).

48. The traditions read as if the entire process took place in the single generation before the founding of the Palaro chiefdom, i.e., the generation before c. 1695–1725. Because these traditions are part of Palaro's absent past, however, chronological moorings are suspect, and telescoping appears likely. Thus the beginnings of the events are left undated. Evidence for the Central Sudanic origins of the Pauma, Larubi, and Lamogi groups can be found in Crazzolara (1951, pp. 287–88, 294–95; 1954, pp. 459–73); and Wright (1934, p. 95).

49. Crazzolara (1951, p. 288).

Then the Lamogi village joined the Uma-led grouping. Following this, an Eastern Nilotic village-lineage entered the area from the Agoro mountains. Though it established contact with the Uma grouping, this Agoro group settled independently on a nearby hill, where it was, or became, the largest village in the area. Because of this, traditions report, the Agoro group and its leader became more "respected" than Uma — almost certainly meaning more powerful. In time, Lamogi and Patwol both withdrew from the Uma-led grouping and joined Agoro. Thus, one multiple-village community dissolved and another came into being. Uma reverted to being head of the Pauma village-lineage only, after which they joined the Agoro grouping as well. Larubi, the original village associated with Pauma, remained as a single-village community outside all of this maneuvering. Such was the situation at the end of the seventeenth or beginning of the eighteenth century, when the emergent Palaro chiefdom incorporated all of the above groups.[50]

These multiple-village groupings were a significant feature of mid- to late-seventeenth-century Acholi, and probably long before. They were also important to later developments. The chiefdoms that emerged in Acholi after around 1675 were organized around key ideas and symbols not present earlier, and they were typically larger, more structured, and more stable than multiple-village groupings. But similarities existed between the earlier groupings and later chiefdoms as well, especially bringing together a number of lineage-based villages under one leader. Chiefdoms were thus not totally alien structures. Some leaders of multiple-village groupings, in fact, appropriated the structures and ideology of rule introduced into Acholi from the south to become chiefs. Each of their groupings then usually became the core of the emergent new chiefdom. In other instances, member villages of a multiple-village grouping were all incorporated into polities as subordinate village-lineages, including those who had formerly led the grouping.[51] Limited evidence precludes knowing very much about these multiple-village groupings, including how long they had been in existence. *Rwot* lists and their associated genealogies and traditions, which

50. Ibid. (pp. 287–89). Here, too, the traditional narrative reads as if all took place in one generation, with the same person, Uma, leading the group for the entire period. Although possible, telescoping seems far more likely. Okech (1953, p. 65) does provide a series of names for those involved, with Uma placed in the middle of the list.

51. Atkinson (1978, pp. 142–43) includes western Acholi examples of both. For east-central Acholi examples, see Garry (1972b, pp. 21–23, 43–51; 1976); for southeastern Acholi examples, Webster (1976a, pp. 225, 227; 1976b, pp. 297–300); and Webster A.H.T., pp. 26–27, 32, 181–82; and for probable north-central examples, Owot (1976, pp. 184–85).

provide a means to establish a chronology for the polity period of Acholi history, are either absent or suspect for the pre-polity, absent past. And because traditions of multiple-village groupings are part of the absent past, they are more fragmentary and less reliable in general than those dealing with the chiefdoms. Even when evidence pertaining to multiple-village groupings has been retained in extant traditions, it focuses not on the groupings themselves but on the incorporation of the groupings' member lineages into later chiefdoms. One ramification of this highly selective process is that multiple-village groupings could well have been more numerous and widespread than extant evidence suggests.[52]

Conclusion: Fundamental Features of Pre-Polity Acholi

The limited evidence available on the pre-polity, absent past of Acholi suggests a number of fundamental features of social and economic life in the area before the late seventeenth century. These features both provide the setting within which the Acholi chiefdoms emerged and represent the essence of what can be recovered and reconstructed about the pre-polity past.

The evidence suggests, first of all, that the essential activities and organization of daily life were similar for all the residents of early Acholi, whether Central Sudanic, Eastern Nilotic, or Luo in origin. From at least the first millennium B.C., material life seems dominated by kinship-based communal agriculture, in which iron hoes were used to cultivate grain and other crops suited to the harsh savannah landscape and long, difficult, dry seasons. Social and political life seems to have been tied to kin-based structures as well. Politically independent single-village communities, each with a dominant core lineage, seem most common; impermanent groupings of two, three, or four villages provided a slightly larger-scale but less frequent and less stable form of sociopolitical organization.

Political independence for these small-scale communities did not mean that they were isolated. Common social and cultural beliefs and practices shared over wide areas, the need to marry women from outside one's own

52. For example, in two interviews with former members of the Paryanga grouping, the very existence of the grouping emerged only when I asked if the lineages being interviewed were living with anyone else when they joined Payira. It was then possible to collect information about the multiple-village grouping thus revealed. See A.H.T. 244–45.

lineage (and thus circulate the special goods required for bridewealth), and the periodic exigencies of warfare, drought, and famine must have all promoted ties extending beyond the small political entities. Details about such ties in pre-polity Acholi are no longer recoverable. But the situation in early Acholi was almost certainly similar to the area immediately south. The Central Sudanic- and Bantu-speaking peoples there, Ehret notes, should not be pictured as discrete or clearly definable tribes or ethnic groups. Instead, they "are best understood rather as loose collections of independent but mutually interacting communities sparsely inhabiting their various territories in comparison with later population densities."[53]

The "independent but mutually interacting communities" of early Acholi were made up of speakers of three major language groups: Central Sudanic, Eastern Nilotic, and Western Nilotic Luo. All these languages were maintained throughout the pre-polity period. Language differences seem to have been accompanied by certain cultural distinctions as well — for example in ritual, preferred weaponry, and forms of dress and adornment.[54]

But linguistic and cultural dissimilarities, to reemphasize, were not matched by similar differentiation in the economic, technical, social, or political spheres. Members of all three groups led similar lives. Indeed, the mixed composition of many identifiable multiple-village groupings, including the Agoro grouping described above, indicates that shared or similar structures and ways of doing things could outweigh differences of linguistic origins and culture — even at the very basic level of choosing where and with whom to live. Extant traditions significantly provide no clear indications, or even little hint, of culture-based or culture-generated conflict in early Acholi.

Finally, Acholi before the later seventeenth century was clearly much more a part of the Central Sudanic and Eastern Nilotic worlds than of the Luo. Before that time, there is no substantive evidence that Luo speakers in Acholi were numerous, widespread, or exceptional compared to their Central Sudanic and Eastern Nilotic neighbors. Nothing about their political, social, or economic organization seems to have set them apart or above.

53. Ehret (1973, p. 24). See also Southall's description (1956, chap. 7) of twentieth-century relationships among the non-centralized Central Sudanic Lendu and Okebu living west of Acholi in and near Alur.

54. For discussions of various traits associated with these three broad ethnolinguistic groups, see, for example, Webster (n.d. [a]); Atkinson (1978, pp. 41–50); Garry (1972b, pp. 52–53, 67–68, 94–99); A.H.T. 205, 215, 222, 233, 264, 284; Webster A.H.T., pp. 31, 54, 64, 163, 193.

And if the early Luo possessed any of the superior qualities attributed to them by some writers, no Acholi evidence exists to indicate that these had any significant effects on their neighbors.[55]

This emphasis on the historical and numerical preponderance of Central Sudanic and Eastern Nilotic peoples in Acholi does two things. First, it redresses an overemphasis on the Luo in the historical and ethnographic literature. Even more importantly, placing Central Sudanic and Eastern Nilotic speakers at center stage in terms of the origins and early history of Acholi's peoples brings historical perspective to the "tribal" rivalries and exclusiveness often characteristic of twentieth-century relations between Luo-speaking Acholi and their Central Sudanic and Eastern Nilotic neighbors. Such rivalries and attitudes — and their destructive consequences — are the products of later developments, especially those of the colonial and postcolonial eras, and not of earlier history.[56]

55. Evidence for ideas or institutions of centralized government among the early Luo is weak. For counterarguments in favor of the existence of such ideas and structures, see esp. Webster (n.d. [a]); Herring (1974b, pp. 132–37); Odongo (1976). For reconstructions of early Luo history and culture that do not assume such institutions, see Cohen (1974a); Herring, Cohen, and Ogot (1984); Atkinson (1974, 1978). Especially notable in attributing special qualities to the Luo in general are Crazzolara (1950, 1951, 1954) and Odongo (1976).

56. Although the history he has reconstructed and his approach to doing so are different from my own, the last point above is strongly echoed in the concluding section of Ambler's study of the nineteenth-century history of central Kenya (1988, p. 157).

Part Two

The Introduction of a New Sociopolitical Order and the Beginnings of an Acholi Society, c. 1675–1725

3. The New Order and Its Foundations

As late as the mid-seventeenth century, there was little to suggest that Acholi would ever be the home of a single society or collective ethnic identity. Situated north of the sprawling Bunyoro-Kitara kingdom, Acholi was a multicultural frontier region where Central Sudanic, Eastern Nilotic, and, though to a lesser degree, Luo languages and worlds met.

The speakers of these three languages did share essentially the same environment, technology, staple food crops, means of production, and small-scale, kinship-based sociopolitical institutions and ideology. The daily lives and social organization of the inhabitants of early Acholi were thus fundamentally the same. But these similarities in no way defined a single society, for they were widely shared among many other hoe agriculturalists across Africa. And no dynamics were discernible in Acholi by the mid-seventeenth century that might alter the status quo.

Beginning in the late seventeenth century, however, the situation began to change. Over the next 100 to 125 years, a new social order and political culture were established throughout Acholi, a process that began to transform the disparate inhabitants of the area into a single society with a developing collective and eventually ethnic identity. "Acholi" was in the making. What was this new order and what changes had set its creation in motion?

The New Order: An Overview

The first written descriptions of the sociopolitical order that began to be established in Acholi in the late seventeenth century date only from the 1860s. These sources tell us that the Acholi were then organized into numerous small polities or chiefdoms, each made up of a number of fenced villages. The villages were particularly striking, eliciting extensive comment in the early sources. Subsequently, an impressive array of social and historical research in the twentieth century has deepened our understanding of these villages and chiefdoms as both contemporary and historical institutions.[1]

By far the oldest of the two was the village (*gang*). Each village was named after the exogamous, patrilineal, patrilocal, and patriarchal lineage at its core (*kaka*). But there were always fluctuating numbers of other residents who were neither members of the patrilineage nor women married into it, especially in royal lineages (*kal*). Many of these were affinal relations, people related to the core lineage members through marriage. Others were informal and temporary clients or close friends of a village member. Some were refugees (who may have also fit into one of the above categories), war captives, or their descendants. Village-lineages seem to have averaged from about two hundred persons in the southeast to more than four hundred in the western and south-central portions of Acholi (see Appendix), though some villages were much larger. Separated from others in the chiefdom by a mile or more, each village-lineage had recognized rights to both agricultural and hunting land, and provided the setting for most of the day-to-day activities of its members.[2]

These activities included production, which was largely based on co-operative village-lineage labor, both on the farm and in the hunt. Fitting into what has been described as a "lineage mode of production" found across much of Africa, production and the relations of production in Acholi chiefdoms were organized and controlled by the head of each village-lineage, assisted by the lineage elders. These men also controlled the material means and ideological rules of marriage — and thus of reproduction — and were responsible for most of the social control exercised in Acholi.

1. The most important nineteenth-century sources are Speke (1863) and Baker (1866, 1874); see also Chaillee-Long (1877), Emin Pasha (1888, 1962, 1963), Schweinfurth et al. (1888). Twentieth-century sources are utilized and referenced throughout this study.
2. For descriptions of Acholi social structure see, for example, Crazzolara (1951, 1954), Girling (1960), Odongo and Webster (1976), and Atkinson (1976, 1978). See Appendix for estimates of average village-lineage numbers. The largest villages may have included several thousand people. See Langlands (1968, pp. 11–12), drawing on Ocaya (1959). Girling (1960, pp. 29, 36–40, 51–54, 62, 107–9, and 169–70) discusses the main categories of non-kin in village-lineages, the formal "adoption" procedures by which many were incorporated (often to an extent that the memory of their ever being "outsiders" was lost), and the numbers of such outsiders in two 1950s village-lineages (one royal and one non-royal). Clearly, patrilineal kinship was only one principle of affiliation and settlement operative in Acholi. Wilks (1978) shows that the same was true of matrilineality among the southern Akan of Ghana. And in a brilliant study, Cohen and Odhiambo (1989, esp. pp. 5, 12–15) argue that village membership among the Kenya Luo of Siaya was historically based even more on alliances and less on patrilineality than in Acholi. Cohen and Odhiambo also make clear that, like the Acholi, the Siaya did not fit the common depiction of Luo and other Western Nilotic peoples as a "classic, segmentary society."

Each head was chosen from an hereditary line of the core lineage of the village and was seen as the living representative of that lineage's recognized founder. By virtue of this, as well as special knowledge of his lineage's particular traditions and *ongon* (legal norms or old precedents), the head was also the person most responsible for conducting and interpreting village-lineage ritual. As Girling writes of the Acholi in the 1950s, "the village is a living reality, it is the social group into which they are born and spend the greater part of their lives, [and] it plays a major part in regulating their relations with other Acholi." Village-lineages (for convenience often referred to hereafter simply as "lineages") provided, in short, the economic, social, and ideological foundations of Acholi.[3]

The sociopolitical order that began to be established in the late seventeenth century was also, however, characterized by larger-scale sociopolitical structures superimposed over the lineages. These were the chiefdoms, which by the end of the eighteenth century numbered nearly seventy. The processes by which these chiefdoms were founded, as well as their fundamental institutions and ideology, were similar across Acholi. But there were important differences as well. For example, both the population of Acholi chiefdoms and the number of associated lineages in them varied widely — from one or two lineages in some chiefdoms up to almost forty, and from perhaps as few as five hundred people up to almost fifteen thousand (see Appendix). In addition, the highest density of interaction and shared experience among chiefdoms did not encompass all of Acholi but occurred within the eight fairly well-defined (if unnamed and informal) "zones" discussed above in Chapter 1.

The five largest chiefdoms in eighteenth-century Acholi seem to have had a population of about 5,000 or more by around 1790. These were Lira Paluo in the southeastern zone, Pabo in the western zone, Payira in the central zone, and Padibe and Palabek in the north-central zone. Another eight may have reached the 2,500 to 3,500 range, including representatives

---

3. The quotation is from Girling (1960, p. 56). The concept of a "lineage mode of production" has been developed and applied in Africa mainly by French Marxist anthropologists. See, for example, Meillassoux (1964, 1978a, 1978b, 1980), Terray (1972), Amin (1974), Coquery-Vidrovitch (1975), Rey (1975), Godelier (1977b). Four Africanist historians who explicitly use this approach are Bonner (1980), Jewsiewicki (1981a), Crummie and Stewart (1981a), and Guy (1987). Sacks (1982) and J. Wright (1986) focus on the place of women in such systems. Hammond-Tooke (1985) is critical. Two recent studies of precolonial regional social orders based on villages with lineages at their core are Ambler (1988) and Vansina (1990). Lastly, Andrew Spiegal (personal communication) has argued that the term "lineage" has such a restricted formal meaning that many anthropologists reject it, preferring the phrase "agnatic cluster"; I will respectfully stay with the more familiar term in this work.

from the southeastern, east-central, south-central, western, northwestern and central zones (see Map 2). Most Acholi chiefdoms, however, seem to have numbered from about 1,000 to 2,000 people, with a sizable minority of about twenty even smaller chiefdoms also scattered throughout Acholi (see Appendix). Some of the latter were eventually absorbed into larger polities; others, though retaining a formal independence, were closely tied to larger chiefdoms. But even without such ties, the power, influence, and independence of the smallest chiefdoms were always limited.

Each chiefdom, whatever its size and power, had its hereditary ruler or *rwot* (plural *rwodi*). The *rwot* was not only head of the chiefdom but of his own lineage, the royal lineage of the polity, *kal*. The *rwot* was the most important political, social, and economic personage in the chiefdom. But the degree of power available to *rwodi* was limited, as they shared both authority and decision making with the heads of the chiefdoms' constituent lineages. Indeed, social relations, production, and reproduction continued to be organized largely in terms of lineages, with lineage heads and elders occupying a prominent place in the sociopolitical order. Shared authority and a large degree of sub-group autonomy and identity merged in the Acholi chiefdoms with limited forms of centralization and stratification.

Such were the basic features that came to characterize Acholi society from the late seventeenth through the nineteenth century. This type of sociopolitical order — or something very similar — was widespread in East Africa, and one of the long-standing themes of East African historiography purports to explain its origins. The explanation runs as follows.

About A.D. 1500, cattle-keeping Luo-speakers began to migrate from their homeland along the Nile in the southern Sudan. These Luo spread throughout much of East Africa, establishing themselves, their culture, or their language as dominant almost everywhere they went. One reason they could do this, supposedly, was because they possessed the concepts and organization of kingship or chiefship. Numerous polities based on early Luo political culture then presumably developed throughout the region (including Bunyoro-Kitara and perhaps even Buganda) — many led by immigrant Luo groups and their descendants, others by non-Luo who had emulated the Luo model. In either case, the result was more centralized political organization for many of East Africa's peoples, including the Acholi.[4]

4. See, for example, Crazzolara (1937, 1951), Bere (1947), Southall (1956), Ogot (1967b), Cohen (1968), Oliver (1963), and textbooks by Were and Wilson (1968) and Fage (1978). Many Luo language histories of Acholi stereotypically associate both the origins of

When I joined the History of Uganda Project in the early 1970s, this was one of the basic departure points for research. As Project research advanced in Luo-speaking and Luo-influenced areas, however, evidence accumulated that did not fit the standard interpretation. In the Acholi case (as noted in Chapter 2), the early Luo seem neither a major presence nor major influence. Their numbers, language, and geographical extent all appear limited. They did not initiate changes leading to increased political scale or centralization, nor did they significantly influence or dominate the area's inhabitants. In short, the primary role commonly attributed to the early Luo in shaping Acholi history and society is not supported by evidence from Acholi. Conversely, the evidence indicates that peoples who originally spoke Central Sudanic and Eastern Nilotic languages were not only numerically preponderant, but played much more central sociohistorical roles in Acholi than generally recognized.

But if the migration and settlement of the early Luo did not lead to the spread of the Luo language throughout Acholi, then how and when did this happen? And if the early Luo were not associated with increases in centralization and political scale, then who or what was responsible for the similarly organized chiefdoms found in many areas, including Acholi, where Luo immigrants or influences are present? The short answer to these questions is that the establishment of a new, more centralized sociopolitical order in Acholi — and the subsequent spread of the Luo language there — resulted primarily from the introduction and spread of new chiefly institutions, ideology, and structures of relationship derived from Bunyoro-Kitara. The processes involved were long-term and complex, with especially slow and hesitant beginnings. For the first half-century from about 1675 to 1725, a mere eleven chiefdoms were successfully established in the whole of Acholi. Most of these were small and clustered in just two areas near the Acaa River in what becomes the central zone of Acholi and in the southeast.

Acholi and the beginnings of many Acholi chiefdoms with the early Luo and the ruling Babiito dynasty of Bunyoro; for example, Malandra (1947), Okech (1953), Anywar (1954), and Pellegrini (1963; orig. 1949). Butt (1952) and Ocholla-Ayayo (1980, pp. 46–47) overemphasize a Luo "cattle culture." The revisions in Oliver (1977, 1983) seem less perceptive concerning the early Luo than his pioneering 1963 chapter, perhaps because of his unfamiliarity with or unacceptance of History of Uganda Project work. Granted, the horrors of the Amin years, the collapse of a proposed History of Uganda series, and other factors have limited the accessibility and impact of Project research. Still, some have incorporated this research into their syntheses of early East African history. See, for example, Cohen (1974c, a revision of his 1968 chapter), Feierman in Curtin et al. (1978, esp. pp. 130–37), Alpers and Ehret (1975, esp. p. 473), and Odhiambo et al. (1977, esp. chaps. 4 and 5). For more recent and sophisticated discussions of Luo strategies of dominance, see Herring (1978) and Herring, Cohen, and Ogot (1984).

Over the remainder of the eighteenth century the situation would change dramatically. In about 1725, a great drought and famine struck north-central Uganda. The insecure and unsettled conditions caused by the drought increased the impetus to become part of larger-scale political structures and contributed to the establishment of many more chiefdoms, extending over a much wider area and incorporating many more lineages. By the time another major drought struck around 1790, the trend was clear: it had become virtually impossible for lineages to exist on their own, outside one of the chiefdoms. Such lineages had become increasingly isolated and exposed, until their only realistic alternatives seem to have been to join a chiefdom or leave the area.[5]

The sequence of change is crucial. First came the establishment of new, chiefly, sociopolitical institutions and ideology. This in turn forged new political entities and identities as well as wider social relations. Finally, a common social order and political culture developed, a new society and collective identity evolved, and a common language (Luo) spread.

Neither preexisting boundaries nor prior ethnolinguistic identities determined who accepted the new institutions and ideology. An original association did exist between the new order and Luo-speaking Paluo from northern Bunyoro, which may have inclined the minority of Luo-speaking lineages in Acholi to respond positively and become the ruling groups of new polities. But these Luo-speaking lineages were no more "Acholi" in the beginning than any others, and many non-Paluo and non-Luo-speaking lineages became the heads of chiefdoms as well.

It is important to emphasize here that even though the sociopolitical order that transformed Acholi originated outside, its establishment did not result from an "invasion" or any other large-scale movement of people. Some in-migration did occur, most importantly from Paluo in northern Bunyoro-Kitara. But the movement of ideas (or indeed, a system of ideas—

5. See Atkinson (1978, pp. 79–98). Here evidence independent of Acholi *rwot* lists and related genealogies is used to determine estimated dates for two major eighteenth-century droughts and another in the early nineteenth century. These dates are c. 1725, c. 1790, and c. 1833. The most important evidence comes from Nile level records at Rodah in Egypt (see Chap. 2). Western Acholi *rwodi* whose traditions associate them with these major droughts and famines were then "tied-in" to the externally determined dates. This provided the basis for calculating an average dynastic generation at just over thirty years. Other useful evidence comes from neighboring Jie, where Lamphear (1973, pp. 82–115; 1974; 1976, pp. 33–52) uses an innovative approach to establish a chronology without ruler lists. See also below, Chap. 5, n. 1; Cohen (1970), from whom the term "tie-in" has been borrowed; Henige (1974b, esp. pp. 17–26; 1981) for two negative assessments of using orally transmitted ruler lists for establishing reliable chronologies; and Miller (1982) on the effects of drought, disease, and famine in agriculturally marginal zones in West-Central Africa.

an ideology) along with political maneuvering and negotiation among many contesting groups, mostly from within the region, were more important to sociohistorical change in Acholi than the mere movement of people.

Thus the changes that produced a common social order and political culture, which in turn provided the bases for an Acholi societal and ethnic identity, began in the late seventeenth century and not with the initial arrival of the Luo some 250 years earlier. As Kopytoff notes, both this chronology and process appear broadly typical: "the formation of most African societies seldom dates back more than a few centuries. Rather than being exceptional, then, the ethnically 'ambiguous' society [or where ethnic and societal identity are in-the-making] is but another indicator of the general fluidity of ethnic identity in Africa, a fluidity that begins to reveal itself as soon as one brings history to one's investigation of ethnicity."[6]

The Paluo Factor in Acholi History

The institutions and ideology of chiefship crucial to the development of an Acholi society and identity were introduced into north-central Uganda via the Paluo. These Paluo were originally part of the same migrations that brought the first Luo to parts of Acholi and the new ruling Babiito dynasty to Bunyoro-Kitara. But unlike the latter, who moved on into the core area of Bunyoro and eventually adopted the Bantu language of the majority there, the Paluo settled in the very north of the kingdom and continued to speak Luo.

The Paluo were thus always at the periphery of Bunyoro-Kitara, geographically and linguistically. They were, nonetheless, a part of that kingdom, and their experiences and ideas of society and government were shaped by the Bunyoro-Kitara polity and their place in it. Three related aspects of this Paluo experience were vital to the development of a new social order and political culture in Acholi: (1) the basic Paluo concept of *rwot*, king or chief, as a hereditary ruler who enjoyed great prestige and respect; (2) organized tribute payments to rulers in recognition of their authority; and (3) their possession of royal regalia, most importantly royal drums, as symbols of their rule.

Once imported from Paluo, these features embodied the fundamental ideological elements and principal centralizing structures of the Acholi

6. Kopytoff (1986a, p. 7).

chiefdoms. This crucial combination of ideal and material components of political authority do not explain all sociopolitical change in late-seventeenth- and eighteenth-century Acholi. But they are among the most visible and significant markers of such change in the limited evidence available.

*Rwot*ship, Tribute, and Royal Drums in Bunyoro-Kitara

Shortly after they arrived in Bunyoro, their traditions assert, the Paluo joined the Bunyoro-Kitara kingdom. In so doing, the Paluo accepted the authority of the Bunyoro-Kitara king, whom the Paluo called *rwot*. This term, or a variant — for example, *reth* or *ruoth* — is common to nearly all Luo-speaking peoples, meaning king, chief, master, or some other leader. *Rwot* in Paluo meant not only the Bunyoro-Kitara king but also the heads of the Paluo chiefdoms (eventually seven in number). Each Paluo chief owed allegiance to the Bunyoro-Kitara king. Within his own chiefdom, however, a chief seems to have been a smaller-scale replica of the king. He received allegiance and respect; he collected tribute, keeping some and passing some on to the king; and he possessed royal regalia, originally conferred as gifts by Bunyoro-Kitara kings.[7]

Two points can be stressed. First, the Paluo concept of *rwot*ship referred to a cluster of general attributes of and attitudes toward political leadership. *Rwot* could be applied to whomever possessed these attributes, whether king of a sprawling polity like Bunyoro-Kitara or head of a tiny chiefdom in Paluoland. Second, if the concept of *rwot*ship was unrelated to polity size or population, practical matters such as the nature and extent of a *rwot*'s power and authority obviously were. The Acholi polities were closer in size to the Paluo chiefdoms than to the Bunyoro-Kitara kingdom. Thus, the power and authority of an Acholi *rwot*, even without an overlord, was more comparable to a Paluo *rwot* ("chief") than to the Bunyoro-Kitara *rwot* ("king").[8]

The relationship between *rwot*ship, tribute, and royal drums is made clear in Paluo traditions. In return for Paluo recognition, the Bacwezi ruling dynasty of Bunyoro-Kitara confirmed the existing Paluo leader as a

7. Much of our knowledge of the Paluo derives from Ade Adefuye's Ibadan Ph.D. thesis (1973). On the initial incorporation of the Paluo into Bunyoro-Kitara and the sociopolitical system then operative, see pp. 12–22, 30–36, 47–50; for changes in the later eighteenth and early nineteenth centuries, see pp. 57–70, 106 ff.

8. Ibid., p. 73. For a description of the similar figure of *ruoth* among the Kenya Luo, see Ocholla-Ayayo (1976, pp. 197–98, 201–16).

chief within the larger polity. The Bacwezi then provided drums and other regalia as symbols of authority and taught the new chief "how to organize . . . territory and to collect tribute." Some of this tribute was kept, some passed on to the Bacwezi king.

The surprising twist to these traditions is that the Paluo leader in question is remembered as a woman named Nyawir. How can this be explained, given that formal political leadership has almost always been the exclusive preserve of males, both among Luo groups and generally in the region? One interpretation is that Nyawir, whether she existed in fact or just in memory, was the result of what Victor Turner has called a "liminal" situation: a temporary condition where standard norms and roles are reversed. Perhaps the stresses of transition as the Paluo immigrants were incorporated into a new sociopolitical order under the Bacwezi produced such an extraordinary reversal.[9]

The royal regalia conferred on Nyawir included "drums, stools, spears, and beads." These then served as symbols of chiefly rule for Nyawir and her successors (who were male, as were all subsequent Paluo chiefs). When a second Paluo chiefdom, Pajao, was founded, its first ruler was given similar royal regalia by Bunyoro-Kitara's rulers, who by this time were no longer Bacwezi, but Babiito. In both instances, the most important regalia was the royal drum.[10]

Paluo and Bunyoro-Kitara court traditions agree on the fundamental place of royal drums in Bunyoro-Kitara political culture. They also agree that Bacwezi rule was crumbling when the Luo-speaking Babiito appeared on Bunyoro's northern frontier and that before withdrawing, the Bacwezi introduced the Babiito to many aspects of Bacwezi chiefly rule, taught the Babiito about the Bacwezi royal drums, and then left the drums for the new rulers. Court traditions add that Rukidi, the Babiito leader, would not even begin the installation ceremonies that would make him king until after he possessed the royal drums.[11]

9. See Adefuye (1973, p. 17); Turner (1969). Ken Menkhaus found traditions from the Jubba River valley in Somalia that recounted an equally anomalous early female leader at a time of traumatic change (personal communication, based on field research for Menkhaus [1989]).

10. Adefuye (1973, pp. 20–22, 36, 48). Adefuye does not accept that the Luo first learned about kingship from the Bacwezi rulers of Bunyoro-Kitara. But he does acknowledge that if such ideas were not new, "it is clear that it was the Bacwezi who first gave her [Nyawir] a drum and this instrument was likely new to her and her people" (p. 22).

11. The Paluo traditions are in ibid. (pp. 26–30); Bunyoro-Kitara narrative court traditions can be found in Nyakatura (1973, pp. 38–57). In two interviews, ex-*rwot* Jakayo Obunya recounted Paico traditions indicating that the early Luo did not possess royal drums before moving into Bunyoro-Kitara; see A.H.T. 231, 234.

There is no need to debate here whether these traditions relate actual historical events or structured stories of myth and symbolism. With respect to the place of royal drums in Bunyoro-Kitara political culture, it matters little whether Rukidi was a historical personage, or whether he actually waited to obtain the royal drums before beginning installation ceremonies. What does matter is that in the Bunyoro-Kitara context it was inconceivable even to contemplate kingship (*rwot*ship) without royal drums.[12]

Tribute and royal drums were thus always an integral part of the Luo experience of political authority in Bunyoro-Kitara. And traditions make clear that both the notion of *rwot*ship in Bunyoro-Kitara and the place occupied in that polity's political culture by tribute and royal drums did not derive from the incoming Luo, but were present before they appeared.[13]

Chiefdoms and Chiefship (*Rwot*ship) in Acholi

Bunyoro-Kitara political culture, as experienced by and filtered through the Paluo, served as the model for chiefdoms and chiefship in Acholi. One crucial characteristic of these chiefdoms was the limited power and authority of those at their head. Two such limits have already been indicated: the small size and population of the chiefdoms, and the *rwot*'s sharing of political power with constituent village-lineage heads. A third limit on the power of the *rwot* was the possibility for dissatisfied members of the chiefdom to migrate.

Low population density meant that land was always abundant and available. According to Uganda's last adequate census in 1969, Acholi District contained just over 465,000 people in an area of nearly 11,000 square miles (28,400 square kilometers), a density of only 43 persons per square mile (16.5 per square kilometer).[14] Eighteenth- and nineteenth-century population figures were probably only a third or a fourth of this (see Appendix). Another factor that made it possible to move away from an

12. For a structuralist analysis of these traditions, see Wrigley (1958, 1959, 1973). Buchanan (1969, 1973), conversely, uses traditions of this period to reconstruct history. See also Atkinson (1975) for a structuralist analysis of early court traditions in neighboring Buganda, and Vansina (1983) for a skeptical assessment of this approach.

13. Adefuye (1973, pp. 22, 26–30, 36, 48). The best discussions I have seen of Bacwezi-derived royal drums are by Karugire (1970; 1971, pp. 97–104). Though his focus is the kingdom of Nkore south of Bunyoro-Kitara, his work has relevance for the early Luo in Bunyoro.

14. The 1969 population figures come from Langlands (1971, pp. 2–3).

unpopular, abusive, or incompetent *rwot* was the wide social ties created by marriage links and patrilineal connections, real or fictitious.

In addition, three other features severely restricted the *rwot*'s coercive power. First, before firearms came into the area after 1850, the *rwot* had no access to special means of destruction. All the men were armed, with bows and arrows (especially in areas that were predominantly Central Sudanic in origin) or spears (an Eastern Nilotic preference). Second, the *rwot* had no access to any special fighting force. There was no army other than the whole body of able men in the chiefdom. And finally, although the *rwot* could call on these men and was ultimately responsible for organizing them for war, he did not monopolize the force they represented. This, too, was shared, usually with village-lineage heads who were also councilors of the *rwot*.[15]

CHIEFS AND SUBJECTS

Chiefs (*rwodi*) and royal lineages (*kal*) used many strategies to establish the new order and their leading place in it. Both *rwodi* and other members of *kal*, for example, frequently forged marriage alliances with potential or newly joined subordinate lineages. *Rwodi* recognized and even enhanced the position of the already established leadership within lineages. *Rwodi* used tribute from groups already incorporated to entice outsiders into the system with displays of wealth and generosity impossible for mere lineage heads or the heads of multiple-village groupings. Royal narrative traditions in particular recount many instances in which *rwodi* provided food to eat, a place to settle, or military protection or assistance for those in difficulty. *Rwodi*, moreover, seem to have demonstrated whenever they could one of the most significant contributions that they could make in the highly segmentary political environment of pre-polity Acholi: their ability to arbitrate disputes that individual lineage heads or the heads of multiple-village groupings could not. Similarly, *rwodi* represented themselves and were acknowledged by their followers as rainmakers — an especially attractive "power" in the dry and uncertain physical environment of Acholi. Finally, *rwodi* and their supporters might use violence or the threat of violence to pressure others to join (though traditions suggest that such coercive tactics were infrequent, this may reflect dominant ideology more than historical accuracy).

15. See Goody (1971). A new "military council" (*twon lok*) devoted strictly to military affairs may have been instituted in southeastern Acholi during the mid-nineteenth century; see Webster (1976c, p. 347).

Narrative traditions are corroborated by the separate-group, non-narrative traditions of those who became part of the new order as subordinate or subject lineages (*lobong* or *lwak*), which often emphasize incorporation during times of difficulty and dislocation. Drought, famine, and war could radically alter material conditions and promote such significant social change as joining a chiefdom. This is made most evident by the unprecedented levels of chiefdom formation and growth in Acholi following the great drought and famine of the 1720s. Positive enticements also brought lineages into chiefdoms, such as the continuing importance of existing lineage leadership, and the minimal interference with established internal lineage structures, relationships, and ideology that followed incorporation.[16]

Incorporation did require the recognition of a level of political authority above the lineage and beyond the leadership of multiple-village communities. This was no small matter. But each lineage continued to choose its own head, and he — with the assistance of his elders — also continued to organize lineage-based production, control the material means and ideological rules of marriage (and thus of reproduction), conduct and interpret most lineage ritual, settle most internal lineage disputes, and manage lineage affairs in general.

Most lineage heads, moreover, took on new roles in the chiefdoms in their capacities as the main advisors of the *rwot* and as spokesmen for their respective lineages within the polity. This was almost always true for the earliest and largest lineages in a chiefdom, and sometimes for all of them. The three most common titles used for lineage heads in their new roles were *ladit-pa-rwot* (elder of the *rwot*; plural *lodito-pa-rwot*), commonly used in western Acholi; *lakwena* (literally, messenger; plural *lukwena*), reported in many eastern Acholi texts; and most generic of all, *ladit kaka* (elder of the lineage; plural *lodito kaka*).[17]

One important new role for these lineage heads was working with their *rwot* to settle disputes between lineages within the chiefdom and between the chiefdom and outsiders. Lineage heads also helped determine and collect compensation for wrongs committed (again, both within the chiefdom and by outsiders), organized such major chiefdom-wide rituals as

16. Separate-group, non-narrative traditions of incorporation into the Acholi chiefdoms make up a crucial component of Chaps. 4–8 below.

17. The evidence is highly inconclusive, but a few Acholi polities may have had an additional layer of subordinate officeholders between the *rwot* and the village-lineage heads; see Webster (1976b).

the annual planting and harvest ceremonies, coordinated and supervised tribute collection and service, arranged funerals and burials when a *rwot* died, and helped select and install his successor.

Incorporated lineage heads also served new economic functions and received new economic benefits. In return for helping organize tribute, settle disputes, and arrange compensation, lineage heads were frequently rewarded with a portion of the proceeds. In addition, they played key roles in organizing polity-wide and multipolity hunts, which were among the largest cooperative ventures in precolonial Acholi. The benefits for the head of the lineage on whose hunting area a large hunt took place (in return for his taking primary responsibility for the spiritual and practical arrangements necessary for a successful hunt) could be especially worthwhile — as much as one leg from each animal killed.

The heads of older lineages in an area might have benefited most from this opportunity, as evidence suggests that they tended to control more or larger hunting areas than later arrivals. But other *lodito-pa-rwot* benefited as well. After the *rwot* received the leg due to him from every kill, he is remembered to have often passed some meat on to selected councilors. Finally, councilors also received goats, sheep, and other foodstuffs from the royal lineage for the part they played in installation, burial, and other ceremonies, and were among the primary beneficiaries when war booty was distributed.[18]

RELIGION AND RITUAL

In the important realm of religion and ritual, lineage heads also continued to provide leadership within their respective groups. Although there were many differences in specific religious beliefs and practices among lineages, almost all lineage ritual took place at the lineage's ancestral shrine and shared certain features. These shrines, *abila* in Acholi Luo, ranged from miniature thatched huts to small stone edifices. In most cases, the lineage head was the primary caretaker of his lineage's *abila* and led the group's

18. Accounts of the duties and benefits of lineage heads/councilors of the *rwot* can be found, for example, in Anywar (1954, pp. 133–35); Girling (1960, pp. 58, 63–64); Webster A.H.T., pp. 47–48, 82–83, 157–58, 171; Garry A.H.T., pp. 45–46, 80, 91–92; A.H.T. 213–14, 230, 241, 243, 246, 256, 266, 271, 285–87, 299–300, 302, 310. Dry-season hunts could involve thousands of people. The most common procedure was to encircle a large hunting area, burn the grass, and then close in with spears and nets. Lineage members hunted side by side and shared responsibility as a corporate group for covering designated sections. See Baker (1866, v. 2, pp. 439–49); Usher-Wilson (1947); Bere (1934, 1960a); and, for the most vivid and detailed account, Bere (n.d. [c. 1978], pp. 144–63). Girling (1960, p. 16) notes that a few of these hunts continued into the 1950s.

approaches to the ancestors. Such approaches occurred through various ceremonies (including small offerings of food and drink) and for many purposes (ranging from births to funerals). But whatever their specific purpose, the ceremonies almost always included requests to the ancestors that the lineage might prosper and grow and fostered lineage consciousness and unity.

Within most chiefdoms, lineage heads not only continued to play primary ritual roles in their lineages, but became key people in polity-wide ritual as well. Many took on specific chiefdom-wide and chiefdom-oriented ritual duties. Some, for example, oversaw maintenance of the royal regalia; some took care of their *rwot*'s *abila*; some kept the chiefdom's rainstones (*ame*) used for "rainmaking" in many chiefdoms; and some played special roles in installation and funeral ceremonies. And one lineage head in nearly every chiefdom, usually from the group acknowledged as oldest in the area, had his ritual position even further enhanced as he became ritual leader of the chiefdom as a whole.

Chiefdom-wide ritual focused on gods or spirits (*jogi*, singular *jok*) distinct from the ancestors. Because they are part of the belief systems of a wide range of contemporary Central Sudanic and Nilotic peoples, it is likely that the concept of such gods or spirits was an old one shared among all three ethnolinguistic groups in early Acholi. When chiefdoms developed, the concept seems to have been adapted so that certain *jogi* became the focus of polity-wide ritual. The *jogi* that filled this role tended to be those associated with the oldest lineages in their respective areas. Hence the special place in chiefdom-wide ritual accorded the lineage and lineage head—often called *won ngom*, "father of the soil"—responsible for dealing with these *jogi*. The combination of new political structures and leadership with old ritual ones may well reflect one of the most significant deals struck in the process of negotiating the new sociopolitical order. It reflected in concrete terms the interdependence of chiefdoms and lineages, politics and ritual, rulers and subjects.

The *rwot*'s position in chiefdom-wide ritual also reflected this interdependence. Many chiefdom ceremonies were held at *kal*, and the *rwot* almost always had a role to play. With the important exception of rainmaking, however, this role was most often a supportive one. The lead was usually taken by certain non-royal lineage heads; they and not the *rwot* oversaw and led ritual performance. The *rwot* (except within his own lineage) had little if any place in individual lineage ritual. Thus, preexisting ritual and the leading role played in such ritual by lineage heads were not threatened either by membership within a chiefdom or by that chiefdom's *rwot*.[19]

Fundamental respect for the religious practices of incorporated lineages and the resulting continuity of ritual beliefs and practices seems one reason why people generally — and not just lineage heads — might have decided to join a chiefdom. Another may have been the harsh and uncertain environment. Being part of a larger group offered potentially greater security, especially in times of drought or other danger. Membership in a chiefdom also meant a larger assemblage of associated village-lineages with which to exchange women, participate in trading expeditions, or hunt. And once the process of chiefdom formation began to accelerate after the 1720s drought, this created a momentum of its own. Vansina has described a similar momentum in Central Africa:

> Even the appearance of a single chiefdom broke the balance of power in the whole area. Its military potential exceeded that of neighboring, less well coordinated units. . . . For the sake of security [other] units were then ready to accept a chief. . . . Thus the creation of chieftaincy acted as a catalyst which transformed the basic [village- and lineage-based] institutions over a vast area.[20]

In sum, an array of sociohistorical forces and strategic tactics, considerations, and compromises promoted the development and spread of chiefdoms in Acholi, especially after the 1720s drought. A crucial feature of the process seems to have been the advantages or potential advantages offered to both subordinate lineages and their heads. Internal lineage affairs and practices remained under the control of the lineages themselves and of their heads and elders, including control of most production in what continued to be a lineage-based economy (indeed, a lineage mode of production). Conversely, the costs to incorporated lineages seem relatively few and minimal, with the option to migrate away if such costs did become too high.

19. For discussions of ritual and religion in Acholi, see esp. Seligman (1932, pp. 122–34), Wright (1936), Malandra (1939), Okot (1965, 1971), Garry (1971b; 1972b, esp. pp. 87–116); and Latigo Koro manuscript (1971). First pregnancy and birth ceremonies were the two main ceremonies not centered around the *abila*, taking place in the home. See Malandra (1939), Higgins (1966). The concept of interdependence between rulers and subjects in sociopolitical systems like the Acholi chiefdoms is noted by Kopytoff (1987, p. 17), and depicted convincingly among the Xhosa of South Africa by Peires (1982, chap. 4). Finally, because most women in Acholi lived outside their own lineages and with those of their husbands, there was a built-in excuse and rationale for limiting the role of women in lineage affairs and ritual.

20. Vansina (1990, p. 148).

ROYAL SUCCESSION

When asked about how succession to the *rwot*ship worked in Acholi, most elders suggested a system based on a variant of ultimogeniture. This variant identified the rightful successor as the youngest son of the wife who had undergone installation ceremonies with the former *rwot* (the *dak ker*, or wife of the *rwot*ship). Only slight probing, however, revealed that succession was based on consideration of a number of preferences and not a rigid, stereotypical rule. Qualities such as generosity, intelligence, and proper manners and behavior toward others seem to have counted far more than mere order of birth. Many discussions of succession with Acholi elders indicated that the son who best typified qualities such as these would be the most likely choice to succeed and that, given such qualities, this choice would be widely supported in both the royal lineage and chiefdom as a whole.[21]

The particular details of succession practices varied from polity to polity, including the identity of key participants. In most cases, village-lineage heads were prominent; elders of the royal lineage (*kal*) and the *dak ker* of both the former and succeeding *rwot* also often played important roles. In addition, four common features marked succession ritual in many chiefdoms.

First, royal regalia and other common symbols associated with *rwot*-ship were especially prominent in succession ceremonies. The royal drum (*bul ker*) would be played; royal spears (*tong ker*) and other regalia would be displayed; and the *rwot* and other primary participants would be seated on royal stools (*kom ker*) and draped in the leopard and lion skins always associated with *rwot*ship. Second, the *dak ker* of the chosen successor, often specially picked to be installed with him, had a role in the ceremonies second only to the new *rwot* himself (she was frequently a formidable figure afterward as well, especially where she was the caretaker of royal regalia). Third, in most chiefdoms, specific lineages and lineage heads had particular roles in the succession ceremonies. One lineage, for example, might be responsible for playing the royal drum. Others might provide councilors to

21. Goody (1966) has argued persuasively that a combination of succession preferences, rather than rules, governs succession to high office in nearly all political systems. Girling (1960, pp. 85–86) and most Acholi elders often concur, at least implicitly. See, for example, A.H.T. 204, 226, 229, 230, 234, 247, 261–62, 266; Webster A.H.T., pp. 13, 61, 74, 158–59; Garry A.H.T., p. 33. On criteria for leadership among the Kenya Luo, see Ocholla-Ayayo (1976, pp. 201–2). Finally, though no specific rule of ultimogeniture operated in Acholi succession, evidence indicates a preference for choosing younger rather than older men to succeed to the *rwot*ship; this may help account for the relatively long thirty-year dynastic generation calculated in Atkinson (1978, pp. 79–98) and used here.

be seated next to the succeeding *rwot* or *dak ker*, or someone to anoint the successor with oil. All such roles signified the special positions of these lineages and their heads within the chiefdom and provided a highly visible avenue for individual lineage participation and pride, while emphasizing the chiefdom as a whole and the person soon to be its new head. Finally, each succession ceremony marked a time when both the chiefdom and the person chosen to be its new head were in transition. The successor thus became a temporarily anomalous or "liminal" figure. As such, a number of conventions were momentarily turned upside down. In many chiefdoms the soon-to-be *rwot* was admonished, verbally abused, and even spat upon by members of the chiefdom — behaviors that would never occur after succession ceremonies were completed. All of these features marking the transition from one *rwot* to another — even the temporary aberrations — served the same purpose: to focus attention upon the person of the *rwot*-elect and in so doing to demonstrate the continuity of both *rwot*ship and the chiefdom.[22]

Succession conflicts are rare in extant Acholi traditions. In the southeastern zone, the first or second successions in a number of chiefdoms are remembered to have been marked by serious conflict resulting in five or six breakaway "brother" chiefdoms (see Chapter 5). But following this brief and localized flurry, few succession conflicts are reported until the second half of the nineteenth century. Only then did new, mainly economic circumstances provide the impetus and means for dissatisfied candidates to struggle actively against recognized successors. Before, while more competition and dispute almost certainly occurred than is retained in traditions, the picture of minimal conflict seems reasonable. The sons of *rwodi* had no political, economic, or military bases from which to contest a succession decision. They were not chiefs under the *rwot*, nor did they have any other means to attach to themselves either territory or large groups of people. Sons not chosen to succeed, therefore, had no special resources with which to oppose the decision, making active conflict over succession to the *rwot*-ship in Acholi difficult and, as traditions indicate, probably rare. Disappointed sons could usually do no more than move away.[23]

22. For some specifics, see A.H.T. 206, 215 (with information most at odds with the norms), 234, 247, 266, 308–10; Webster A.H.T., pp. 13, 19, 65; Garry A.H.T., p. 45; and Latigo manuscript (1970, pp. 87–94). See Turner (1969) on liminality.

23. The pattern of limited succession conflict in Acholi contrasts with Bunyoro-Kitara, where sons were territorial chiefs and often used their office and subjects as bases to fight for the throne when their father died. The position of Acholi royal sons also contrasts with Alur to the west. There, Southall notes (1954, 1956), "princes" who were disappointed with succession results often left home. They were then accorded almost automatic special status by those

The System of Tribute in Acholi

Tribute (in Luo, *tyer*) was paid to a *rwot* in recognition of that *rwot*'s authority. Recognition meant paying tribute; paying tribute symbolized recognition. This was true of the Paluo relationship to the Bunyoro-Kitara *rwot* and kingdom, within the Paluo chiefdoms, and within the chiefdoms of Acholi. When an individual or group in Acholi gave tribute to a *rwot*, they acknowledged him as their ruler and formed part of his chiefdom. As an elder from Labongo in east-central Acholi stated, "Mind you, this giving . . . [of tribute] is a payment, and when the people gave to the *rwot*, it showed that they recognized him as their chief."[24]

This same message was conveyed to Father Crazzolara when he was investigating the Payira polity's claim that it had sovereignty over other chiefdoms. Members of the latter retorted, "Ask people of Payiira to tell you whether people of other realms [chiefdoms], say Patiko, Palcoo, ever brought their *tyeer* (tribute) to the *Rwoot* of Payiira." Crazzolara continued, "Of course, even my informant of Payiira admitted that this was not the case. This all important fact of the symbolic offering by which a subject recognized his *Rwoot*, is decisive and excludes the superiority of Payiira over other realms, as people of Payiira know perfectly well."[25]

The theme was reiterated, with an interesting twist, in the western-zone chiefdom of Lamogi. I asked if the Koc lineage, upon joining the chiefdom, moved the ten miles or so from their home to resettle nearer the other Lamogi village-lineages. "No," I was told, "they did not move. But in case they killed some animals they took part of the meat to the [Lamogi] *rwot*." Thus the paying of tribute seemed to signify membership in a polity more conclusively than physical location.[26]

The symbolic significance of tribute was great. But its practical and material consequences were even more crucial. Tribute due an Acholi *rwot* was extracted in both kind and service. Tribute in kind included one leg of each large game animal killed, all leopard and lion skins (symbols of authority always due the *rwot*), and, in the later nineteenth century, one tusk of each slain elephant. Lineages with blacksmiths also provided spear-heads, arrows, hoe blades, and iron bracelets. Tribute service consisted

---

among whom they settled, becoming rulers of new polities and leading to a proliferation of "chieflets" or "segmentary states"; Ocholla-Ayayo (1976, pp. 210–11) notes a similar process among the Kenya Luo.

24. Garry A.H.T., p. 46.
25. Crazzolara (1954, p. 481).
26. A.H.T. 204.

mainly of collective village-lineage work days in the fields of the *rwot*'s wives during planting and harvesting seasons and at his compound to build and repair fences, granaries, and other structures. These services were at least as significant in economic terms as the more frequently noted tribute in kind — at least before ivory was collected. For example, grain planted and harvested with the assistance of tribute service was not only of immediate worth, it was storable for up to a year or more. Whether in kind or service, tribute production and collection were carried out within established village-lineage structures, and represented a crucial, if not transforming, addition to village-lineage-based relations of production.[27]

None of these forms of tribute was particularly burdensome (though they entailed real costs, especially in leaving one's own fields to work on those of the *rwot* during the limited period when successful clearing and harvesting was possible). But tribute payments and service did give the *rwot* significant material advantages over other members of society. These advantages, before the second half of the nineteenth century, did not take the form of an appreciable accumulation of wealth by *rwodi*. Instead, Acholi *rwodi* used tribute for social and political ends through a complex pattern of redistribution.[28]

For example, when chiefdom members worked in his wives' fields, the *rwot* feasted them and gave them large quantities of beer — made possible through earlier tribute. When a large hunt brought in much tribute, the *rwot* would use some of the meat to feast his subjects; he would also pass some on to selected lineage heads to reward their support, to recognize their position, or to try to gain their favor. And when a hunter brought the

27. Except for the special tribute for blacksmiths noted in Girling (1960, p. 96), these forms of tribute are almost universally agreed upon in available sources.

28. The concept of redistribution in the western social sciences developed out of a comparative study of the role of the "gift" (focusing especially on the notion of reciprocity) by French ethnologist Marcel Mauss (1954; orig. 1925). Malinowski (1922) drew on this work even before its publication, helping incorporate it into British social anthropology where it gradually became increasingly linked with the workings of chiefship and social stratification. Economic historian Karl Polanyi (1944; Polanyi et al. [1957]) carefully defined both reciprocity and redistribution and identified them as the first two levels of a three-tiered schema of socioeconomic behavior. During the 1960s, a group of anthropologists who can be termed "new evolutionists" developed probably the most integrated approach to redistribution and its relationship to chiefship and stratification. See, for example, Sahlins (1958, 1968), Fried (1967), and Harris (1973, chaps. 11 and 17). The society most like Acholi in which redistribution has been discussed in some depth is Alur; see Southall (1956). Girling does not address this issue to any degree in his monograph on Acholi (1960); he does, however, argue (pp. 36–44, 47–48) that the economic advantages of tribute and fines flowed downward from the *rwot* to other members of his lineage. Though probably true earlier to some degree, Girling's argument is based on twentieth-century examples that resulted largely from economic changes occurring only after 1850.

rwot a leopard or lion skin, he was given a goat or comparable gift in return, and would then go through prestigious ritual ceremonies that celebrated his bravery and skill.[29]

The *rwot* thus was the focal point in a redistribution of goods and services within the polity. In material terms, what the *rwot* received was balanced, or nearly so, by what he gave. But he did not necessarily redistribute equally. He could, for example, demonstrate extra generosity to newcomers, to lineage heads in general or the heads of older or larger lineages in particular, to others he wished to impress or influence or help, or to those who had been loyal or helpful to him in the past. He could also use some of the proceeds of his subjects' labor to marry extra wives. Such marriages were advantageous in many ways: they forged important social ties between a *rwot* and subject (or would-be subject) lineages and other chiefdoms; they symbolized the *rwot*'s wealth and status; and, through the wives' labor and reproductive power and the labor of others performing tribute service in the wives' fields, they generated more wealth as well.[30]

In a society in which generosity was highly valued and the means to acquire material wealth limited, the *rwot* could use his position as the most generous "giver" to build up a fund of social and political good will and support. As Marcel Mauss pointed out many years ago, such giving created dense webs of obligation and deference toward the giver. In the absence of any monopoly of force, this near monopoly of large-scale generosity served something of the same function: it could be used as a resource unavailable to others in the society to secure, maintain, and enhance support for both individual *rwodi* and *rwot*ship itself. Tribute made such generosity and its effects possible, and translated into real power over people.[31]

Ralph Herring indicates a final benefit of tribute when he notes that the moderate costs of tribute due an Acholi *rwot* "were all that was neces-

29. For a specific reference to *rwodi* passing on some proceeds of hunting tribute to lineage heads, see Garry A.H.T., p. 45. Fines were an important, though irregular, source of economic advantage to the *rwot*. The most frequently levied fines appear to have been goats (often she-goats) and chickens. These, and the offspring they produced, were used both to enlarge the *rwot*'s herds and flocks and to redistribute, especially as part of ritual ceremonies. Fines were levied for breaking such well-known codes of conduct as quarreling or fighting during times of planting and harvesting. As with tribute, fines were collected only within the boundaries of a chiefdom. See, for example, A.H.T. 222, 259, 270, 280, 299, 309; Garry A.H.T., pp. 45–46; Wright (1936).

30. Clignet (1970) discusses the relationship between polygyny and wealth and power; Peires (1982, pp. 27–44) depicts the use of chiefly redistribution for political ends among the Xhosa of South Africa.

31. See Mauss (1954 [1925]). For a different depiction of tribute in east-central Acholi, see Garry (1972b, pp. 49, 76–77).

sary" to join the chiefdom. "To this extent," he continues, "the presence of a central organ of government could not help but ease the process of incorporating new groups into the society. Furthermore, since the *rwot* was expected to mediate impartially any potentially dangerous quarrels within or among the clans [lineages], the strains attendant upon joining into the life of the society were also eased."[32]

The Royal Drum in Acholi

Just as tribute was an essential component of *rwot*ship in Acholi (as it was in Bunyoro-Kitara), so too was royal regalia. This was especially true of the royal drum, *bul ker*, which served as the primary symbol of authority within the chiefdom and of sovereignty in inter-polity relations. Chiefdoms and royal drums became so linked in Acholi that it became virtually impossible for people there to conceive of one without the other. When I asked Koc elder Layua Amal why the royal drum was so important, he answered that it was "because it was royal regalia [*jami ker*]. It showed you had *ker* [royal authority or power; *rwot*ship]. And in case someone came and took it away, then it showed you had no *ker* and you would have to look for it. . . . If you do not have your royal drums, then you do not have your *ker*."[33] Similarly, the elder responsible for the care of Patiko's remaining royal regalia once stated: "In other places there are crowns; here it is the drum. Without a *bul ker* you would not be called *rwot*."[34]

In Acholi, then, royal drums were symbols of both *rwot*ship and independence for the groups that possessed them. As such, they were treated with respect and care, marked by prescribed and ritualized behavior. For example, a royal drum was not removed from the compound of the *rwot* except in exceptional circumstances such as the funeral of a lineage head. Royal drums were also played only on special occasions (ones that usually emphasized the unity of the chiefdom), were attended by all the chiefdom's lineages, and were accompanied by a special dance called *bwola*. Examples of such occasions were installation and funeral ceremonies for *rwodi* and the

---

32. Herring (1973, p. 503).

33. A.H.T. 264. The term *ker* almost means the same as polity or chiefdom, which have no equivalents in Luo. But rather than describing polity or chiefdom per se, *ker* describes such aspects of the polity as royal authority, power, *rwot*ship.

34. The elder was Thomas Lakane in A.H.T. 308, one of Crazzolara's three main assistants in compiling *A Study of the Acooli Language* (1938, p. vi) and one of two principal informants named in Crazzolara's chapter on Patiko in *The Lwoo* (1951, p. 255n).

annual feast celebrating the harvesting of the first new crops of the year. And especially in eastern Acholi (if less so in the more rainfall-abundant west), royal drums were central to rainmaking ceremonies.[35]

In addition, a special mystique and code of etiquette surrounded all dealings with the drum. In most chiefdoms, only designated representatives from specific lineages were allowed to play, carry, or care for the drum. Failure to observe such prescribed behavior, it was believed, brought supernatural punishment. Lastly, in cases of disputed succession, or changes of dynasty, possession of the chiefdom's royal drum (and other royal regalia) was often a necessary but not sufficient element in a contending party's becoming legitimated.[36]

Early British colonial officials, who did not always grasp the complexities of Acholi society and politics, did seem to understand the relationship between possession of a royal drum and possession of sovereignty and authority. In establishing colonial rule in Acholi, the British confiscated the drums of many chiefdoms, especially from those placed under the authority of others in the new colonial set-up or those that the British considered troublesome. One Acholi chiefdom that lost its drum was Koc, and Koc elder Layua Amal had a clear explanation of what had happened. The British took the drum, Amal said, "to abolish all *ker*; to show that I have already defeated you."[37]

The colonial administration also eventually ruled that only *rwodi* who were also government chiefs could have their royal drums played. Others who had managed to keep their drums had to keep them silent. Layua Amal conveyed in vivid (if overstated) terms the sense of loss felt by the people of

35. See, for example, A.H.T. 215, 222, 233, 241, 310; Webster A.H.T., p. 46; Garry A.H.T., p. 91. Differences between east and west may have also been related to a stronger western presence of old Central Sudanic ritual practices, including rainmaking ritual that emphasized rainstones (*ame*) rather than royal drums. Eastern Acholi references to using royal drums in rainmaking include Webster A.H.T., pp. 3, 46, 56, 58–59, 69, 72, 82–83, 96, 101, 114–15, 165, 170; Garry A.H.T., pp. 21, 44, 65, 92; Garry (1972b, pp. 108–9); Webster (1976, p. 345) seems to minimize the royal drum's role. Drums were even used in rainmaking ritual among some mountain peoples of Karamoja further east; see Weatherby (1979).

36. See A.H.T. 204, 215, 222, 233, 264, 300, 308, 310; Webster A.H.T., pp. 14, 18, 40, 46, 67, 74, 96, 101, 114, 136, 140, 155; Garry A.H.T., pp. 80, 91; Latigo (1970, pp. 85–87); Garry (1971b, pp. 10–12; 1972b, pp. 45–48). That possession of the royal drum was not sufficient to confer legitimacy is indicated in traditions by such statements as the drum "did not like" or was "unhappy" with those who had (or sought to possess) it. See, for example, Webster A.H.T., pp. 103, 197 (n. 28).

37. Drums were taken from Pagak (A.H.T. 212), Parabongo (A.H.T. 218), Paomo (A.H.T. 207), Pawel (A.H.T. 226), Koc (A.H.T. 266), and perhaps Pamolo (Garry A.H.T., p. 10). A. C. A. Wright, an Assistant District Commissioner in Acholi in the early 1930s, remembered that taking royal drums was the act of individual officers and not formulated policy (personal communication). The Amal quotation is from A.H.T. 266.

Koc when the British took their royal drum: "If there had been no *mono* [foreigners]," he said, to restrain them, "the people would have just killed themselves when they took the drum away." Then, though it had been confiscated more than half a century before, Amal asked me if I could do anything to help get Koc's drum back.[38]

As with tribute, the royal drum both symbolized chiefly rule in general and enhanced individual *rwodi*'s ability to rule. Tribute strengthened the *rwot* mainly through its material socioeconomic and sociopolitical uses; the royal drum did so because of its central ritual position.

Together, the new type of chiefship (*rwot*ship), the new system of tribute, and the new royal drums represented the fundamental ideological components and principal centralizing structures of the polities that began to be established in Acholi from around 1675. Introduced into north-central Uganda from Bunyoro-Kitara, these crucial features of a new social order and political culture reflected not only the ideas of power in an emergent Acholi society, but also the power of ideas in such a place. As such, they shaped social, economic, and political relations in Acholi from the late seventeenth century on.[39]

The introduction and establishment of new chiefly institutions, ideology, and structures of relationship in north-central Uganda was a complex and long-term process. It was also of decisive importance. Those who accepted the new order, willingly or not, became part of a widening and deepening mainstream of sociocultural characteristics that gradually came to define "Acholi." In the process, those involved became distinguished from both their past and their neighbors. In other words, following upon the establishment of a new sociopolitical order, new societies, identities, and boundaries began to develop. And the modern map of much of northern Uganda and beyond began to take shape.

Language Change in Acholi

Another component crucial for the evolution of an Acholi society and ethnicity was a common language. By the 1860s, written sources tell us, the

38. See Wright (1936, p. 201); also Wright, personal communication. The Amal quote in this paragraph is from A.H.T. 264.

39. For an extended theoretical discussion, from a materialist perspective, of the relationship between ideology and power, see Therborn (1980); the title of his book, *The Ideology of Power and the Power of Ideology*, closely parallels the phrasing above.

people of emergent Acholi spoke Luo as at least one of their main languages. Yet as late as the mid-seventeenth century, Acholi had overwhelmingly Central Sudanic-speaking majorities west of the Acaa, Eastern Nilotic-speaking majorities to the east, and a combination of the two along the river where the two language frontiers overlapped (see Chapter 2). From the mid-seventeenth to the mid-nineteenth century then, language change (or language shift) had to have occurred on a massive scale.

The scarcity of evidence and complexity of the process make the discussion of language shift in Acholi both difficult and fraught with uncertainty. But it was such a crucial part of the evolution of an Acholi society and collective identity that it deserves discussion, even if that means little more than posing possibilities and problems.[40]

Language maintenance and language shift have been subjects of major interest in the field of sociolinguistics for more than two decades. Areas of particular interest have included: (1) the spread of major historical languages such as Latin, Greek, and Arabic; (2) the current spread of English in the U.S. and throughout the world; (3) detailed studies of either the maintenance of or shift away from such minority languages as Hungarian in Austria, Gaelic in Scotland, Albanian in Greece, Celtic Irish in Ireland, and numerous native American languages in Latin and North America; and (4) broad thematic symposia, programmatic syntheses, or theoretical treatments.[41]

"Yet," as Susan Gal writes in her study of language shift in Austria, "although language shift is geographically and historically widespread, there have been no ethnographic descriptions of it and, despite a large literature on the subject, the process by which it occurs is not understood." Working mainly with contemporary situations, linguists have identified numerous determinants — most of them social, economic, or political — that help to explain both the extensive changes involved in language shift and what determines the direction of that shift. But the way such determinants have interacted historically is often difficult to ascertain.[42]

40. This discussion of language change in Acholi is from Atkinson (1989, pp. 26–31, used by permission, Duke University Press); earlier attempts are Atkinson (1978, pp. 387–97; 1984, pp. 112–17). This and the 1989 account have benefited greatly from discussions with Gretta Little, Carol Scotten, and Ronald Robinson.

41. A key figure in developing this interest has been J. Fishman; see, for example, Fishman (1964, 1972a, 1972b, 1977, 1985). On the four identified topics, see (1) Brosnahan (1973); (2) Fishman (1977) and Veltman (1983); (3) Gal (1979), Dorian (1981), Tsitsipis (1983), Hechter (1975), Hill (1978), and Elmendorf (1981); and (4) the Fishman references above, as well as Gumperz (1982), Milroy (1980), Cooper (1982), and Lambert and Freed (1982).

42. Gal (1979, pp. 1–2).

At a broad level of generalization, widespread language change of any sort is fundamentally a reflection of changing social circumstances and most often involves peoples' changing the way they speak in order to identify with a group that possesses prestige or power. In cases where a socially more prestigious language gets used by increasing numbers of people in more and more circumstances, speakers immersed in this process will begin to lose the opportunity to practice their less prestigious language. Language shift occurs when languages "at the lower end of the prestige scale retreat . . . until there is nothing left for them appropriately to be used about."[43]

Historical linguistic research in East Africa indicates that language shift for a group settled among and interacting regularly with another takes at least three generations to complete — that is, at least seventy-five to one hundred years. After reviewing this research, Herring has suggested that language shift in northern Uganda has been determined by one or more of the following: (1) primacy of settlement; (2) economic advantage; (3) preponderance of numbers; (4) political preeminence.[44]

In the case of the establishment of Luo in Acholi, none of the first three factors apply. Luo speakers were the last of the three major linguistic groups to settle in Acholi; members of all three groups were primarily hoe agriculturalists, sharing the same means and mode of production; and the preponderance of numbers was overwhelmingly Central Sudanic speakers in the west of Acholi and Eastern Nilotic in the east.

That leaves political preeminence, and even here it was political preeminence of a specific type. Even after the establishment and spread of the new social order and political culture, originally Luo-speaking groups were a small minority everywhere in Acholi and were virtually absent from large portions of the area (especially in the west). This meant that political preeminence in Acholi was not linked to a particular group of people who always spoke a certain language but to the structures and ideology of a particular social order and political culture. The spread of Luo in Acholi was related first of all to the spread throughout the area of a prestigious Bunyoro/Paluo model of sociopolitical organization.

This new order had clear ties with the Luo language from its beginnings. First, its immediate source was Luo-speaking Paluoland in northern Bunyoro-Kitara. Second, those who first introduced the model were Luo speakers from either Paluoland or the "Luo triangle" area just to the north. Third, the earliest chiefdoms — those founded between about 1675 and the

43. Dennison (1977); also Gal (1979, chap. 1).
44. See Ehret (1971, pp. 26–27), Herring (1974b, pp. 30–31).

1720s—were almost all led by the Luo speakers just noted and would have been increasingly Luo-speaking from that period. Then, as the chiefly order was established and entrenched throughout emergent Acholi from about 1725–90, the political preeminence associated with this order seems to have promoted language shift toward the language with which the order was tied. That language was Luo.

This was even the case, as already noted, where there was almost no presence of originally Luo-speaking groups at all, as in Central Sudanic-dominated westernmost Acholi. The chiefdoms that developed in the far western zones were structured in the same ways, with the same ideological underpinnings as the Luo-speaking chiefdoms in the adjacent central zone. The originally Central Sudanic-speaking population of the chiefdoms of the far western zones, then, would have had increasingly more in common with their Luo-speaking neighbors to the east, and increasingly less with their Central Sudanic-speaking—but now differently organized—brothers and sisters to the west. In these circumstances, the eventual adoption of Luo in the westernmost chiefdoms both reflected changing relationships with their two sets of neighbors and stimulated the development of ties between these chiefdoms and those located farther east.

But this does not account for the means of shift. What processes facilitated people in chiefdoms without original Luo speakers to speak Luo? Certainly social contact with chiefdoms that were Luo-speaking—through political alliances, economic cooperation, and marriage ties—would have been one means. In addition, because new structures and activities associated with the chiefs were not present before, Luo words for many of these could well have been adopted by non-Luo speakers along with the new chiefly structures and activities themselves. This could have included not only specifically political terms but words associated, for example, with new forms of ritual such as polity-wide rainmaking and first-fruit ceremonies and economic activities associated with tribute.

But probably the most important means came through trade. Among the most important trade items in north-central Uganda were iron in either finished or unfinished form and the special iron bride-price objects called *kweri Madi* (Madi hoes) or *kweri tile* (Figure 2). These were large anchor-like objects necessary for finalizing bride-price payments throughout emergent Acholi (until the later nineteenth century, when they were largely replaced by cattle obtained in raids). In order to maintain their scarcity and prestige value, *kweri tile* were not produced by Acholi smiths but only in Central Sudanic-speaking areas just to the west of the developing boundary between Acholi and Madi or, some sources indicate, in Bunyoro-Kitara.

Figure 2. Madi hoe (*kweri Madi*).

Iron ore deposits were also scarce in Acholi. Except for relatively small deposits near *Got* Okaka in the east-central zone and near Agoro in the north-central zone, iron could be procured only from Orom in the extreme northeastern corner of Acholi, Labwor just beyond the southeastern boundary, Madi just to the west, or (less importantly) Bunyoro-Kitara to the south (see Map 3). Iron, in other words, was available mainly at or beyond the edges of emergent Acholi.

At the same time, in addition to locally produced tobacco and food-stuffs, two of the major articles traded for both iron and *kweri tile* were ostrich-egg beads and ostrich feathers. These could be obtained mainly from the dry plains east and north of Acholi. Trading activities in iron, then, involved travel patterns and networks that crisscrossed all of emergent Acholi, virtually from boundary to boundary. And at the very center of these networks were the earliest Luo-speaking chiefdoms of the central zone.[45]

Though trade seems the most likely mechanism for language contact, the main reasons behind language shift almost certainly had to do with notions of prestige attached to the new Bunyoro/Paluo sociopolitical order. There are numerous examples of peoples shifting their language to identify with a more powerful and prestigious sociopolitical system. Indeed, this is the main force behind the spread of Latin, Arabic, the modern European languages, and currently English.

One example of language shift in Europe seems particularly instructive for trying to understand the Acholi case: the spread of French in predominantly Dutch-speaking Flanders in the late eighteenth and early nineteenth centuries. During this period a new social, economic, and political order was created in the southern provinces of the Netherlands, including the creation in 1830 of a new state: Belgium. This new order was associated not only with French rule from 1795 to 1814 but with the beginnings of industrialization and the emergence of a new industrial elite. The creation of a new order was accompanied by the establishment of a new language: French. This was despite the fact that the vast majority of those who ended up speaking French in Flanders/Belgium were neither immigrants nor the descendants of immigrants. They were original Dutch speakers who chose to change their language.

Speaking or not speaking French became a means of defining those who belonged (or wished to belong) to the new order and those who did not. A language frontier was established, which defined and helped maintain a social boundary. When the new state of Belgium was founded as part of this process, three dominant characteristics set the new state off from its past: a more centralized political structure, a new monarchy symbolizing

45. The role of trade as a key catalyst in the process of language shift in emergent Acholi was first suggested to me by Ronald Robinson.

the new unity, and the speaking of French to symbolize the new nation and a new nationalism.[46]

The parallels of the Flanders/Belgium situation with that in Acholi seem clear and striking despite the slight difference in time and the vast differences in scale, technology, and material life represented by the two emergent societies. The polities of Acholi also represented a new social, political, and economic order. The adoption or non-adoption of Luo helped define who belonged to the new order and who did not, creating a new language frontier that helped delineate and maintain a new social boundary. Finally, the chiefdoms of Acholi also represented a more centralized political structure than had existed before; the unity of these polities was symbolized by their new "monarchies" (the chiefs or *rwodi*); and the population of the entire set of polities eventually all spoke Luo — ultimately a crucial determinant in defining a new society and ethnic group known as Acholi.

46. On the Flanders/Belgium case see Yarak (1974). My colleague Peter Becker has pointed out that earlier stages in the spread of French in present-day Belgium began as early as the sixteenth century.

4. The Emergence of the Earliest Acholi Chiefdoms

Paluo and Bunyoro-Kitara traditions both indicate that the central government first attempted to exert tight control over its northernmost domains around 1675. The remembered legacy of this policy in Paluoland was disruption, conflict, and, for some, emigration. Farther north, the effects included the establishment of the first chiefdoms in Acholi — chiefdoms based on the institutions and ideology of political leadership that Paluo carried with them. Significant as the Paluo were, however, they should not be overemphasized. Most emigrant Paluo settled in only three of the eventual eight zones of Acholi: the central, southeastern, and east-central. Elsewhere, the new chiefly order was established primarily through the activities of people already living there.[1]

From about 1675 to 1725, only eleven chiefdoms were successfully established in all of Acholi. Six became the earliest chiefdoms of an emergent central zone; four formed the basis for the southeastern zone; and one never left the area just north of Paluo. A close investigation of the traditions relating the establishment of these chiefdoms reveals far more than the first phase of individual chiefdom "histories." We also learn about the institutions and ideology underlying a new social order and political culture, about some of the processes involved in the establishment of these institutions and ideology, and about the nature of the evidence available to reconstruct and interpret these crucial sociohistorical dynamics.

Central-Zone Chiefdoms

Most chiefdoms established in the emergent central zone by about 1725 had ruling dynasties associated not only with Paluo but also with the adjacent "Luo triangle" (Map 4). Since the eighteenth century this area has been

---

1. Adefuye (1973, pp. 57–63), Webster (n.d.[b]). See also Buchanan (1973, p. 19), whose analysis of Bunyoro traditions "reveals that population movements, new ideas and institutional innovations did not usually occur simultaneously."

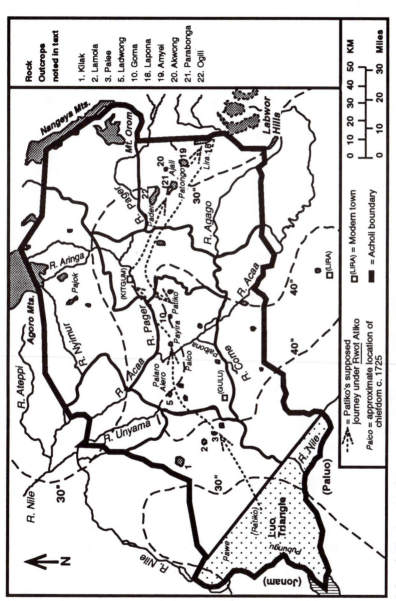

Map 4. Early chiefdoms in Acholi, c. 1675–1725.

peripheral to developments elsewhere in Acholi, mainly because it has been largely unpopulated (as the large portion of the area now set aside as Murchison Falls National Wildlife Park is still).[2]

Numerous traditions, however, suggest that the area once had more people, especially more Luo speakers. These traditions are part of an epic tale recounting a division of the early Luo at a place called Pubungu, usually identified as present-day Pakwac (see Map 4). Although the traditions in question are mainly mythical or stereotypical, their overall depiction of Luo migrations seems reasonable.[3]

One stream is remembered to have moved into the Luo triangle, and then south and east into eastern Uganda and Kenya Luoland from probably the fifteenth through seventeenth centuries. Their presence would have made the Luo triangle the area of modern Acholi with the largest number of Luo speakers during this period (hence the name) and also made it the area most similar to Paluo on the opposite side of the Nile.[4]

It was probably descendants of these Luo who moved north during the late seventeenth or early eighteenth century to establish five early Acholi chiefdoms — Alero, Patiko, Payira, Paico, and Paibona — which formed the core of an emergent central zone. The founder of the sixth early chiefdom in the zone, Palaro, was a Luo speaker from Paluo.

ALERO

Seven renditions of Alero traditions have been collected by five researchers, beginning in the 1930s. Individually and collectively, these traditions make clear the dividing line between Alero's "absent" and "present" pasts (see Chapter 2). That dividing line is the eponymous *Rwot* Alero, the first actual *rwot* of an Alero chiefdom. As with traditions of the absent past generally, those in Alero dealing with the pre-polity, pre-*Rwot* Alero period are limited, contradictory, and often mythical, stereotypical, or otherwise suspect.[5]

2. For nineteenth-century travelers' accounts of this unpopulated area, see Speke (1863, pp. 444–49) and Baker (1866, v. 2, pp. 311–12; 1879, v. 2, pp. 130–31).

3. The Pubungu story of a quarrel over a spear and a bead, resulting in a split of Luo "brothers," is well known. See Crazzolara (1950, pp. 59–66) for one lengthy version. Renditions from Acholi include those in A.H.T. 228, 247, 257, and Garry A.H.T., pp. 25–26, 32. With no recognition of their essential mythical and stereotypical quality, Odongo (1976, pp. 54–64) argues that the events usually associated with Pubungu occurred further east and earlier in the course of early Luo migrations.

4. See, for example, Ogot (1967a, pp. 46–62), Cohen (1972, pp. 124–54; 1974a), Webster (n.d. [a] and n.d. [b]), and Herring (1974c, section I, esp. pp. 57–58, 98–99).

5. None of the recorded pre-polity Alero traditions run more than a single page. See Wright (1934, p. 34), Crazzolara (1951, p. 256), Okech (1953, p. 67), Girling (1960, pp. 112, 221), and A.H.T. 208–10.

Three aspects of this absent past are especially revealing of pre-polity Acholi traditions. First, each extant Alero *rwot* list has a different list of remembered names preceding *Rwot* Alero, the first actual *rwot*. Second, available accounts identify different origins for Alero's eventual ruling lineage (designated in the pre-polity phase as "Alero"). Three versions begin in Paluo (or "Chope"); four take the group back to "Miciri" (literally Egypt, perhaps to be interpreted here as "far away to the north"). The last four also associate "Alero's" founder with the early Luo who journeyed to and then divided at Pubungu.[6]

This dichotomy may reflect no more than the remembered number of Alero's predecessors. The longer lists tend to associate "Alero" with Pubungu and farther north; the shorter lists, only with Paluo. In either case the ideological message of the traditions is clear: "Alero" is unequivocally a Luo group. In Acholi traditions the two most preferred and powerful claims possible for historical "Luoness" are links with Pubungu or Bunyoro/Paluo.[7]

Given the dubious historical reliability of pre-polity traditions (Chapter 2), as well as the pro-Luo orientation of the political culture that ultimately develops in Acholi, the accuracy of "Alero's" claim to Luo origins is hardly certain. But three factors suggest that the ruling lineage of Alero was at least Luo speaking by the time the polity was founded: first, the group's settlement by the time of *Rwot* Alero in the Luo triangle, where Luo seems to have been widely spoken; second, Alero's inclusion among those in Acholi who speak the most "standard" Acholi Luo; and finally, Alero's settlement near, and close ties with, other central-zone chiefdoms whose royal lineages have strong Luo claims.[8]

The final aspect of early "Alero" traditions to deal with here concerns the group's links with Paluo. Six accounts place "Alero" in Paluo some time during its history; one locates the group only in the Luo triangle. This variant version, collected by Crazzolara, cannot be simply dismissed, as it is the earliest and most extensive account of early "Alero" available. One or both of two interpretations might reconcile the apparent discrepancy: (1)

6. For the extant versions of the Alero *rwot* list, see the sources in n. 5 except A.H.T. 210. The Miciri version is in A.H.T. 208–10 and Crazzolara (1951, p. 256); the Chope version in Wright (1934, p. 34), Okech (1953, p. 67), and Girling (1960, pp. 112, 221).

7. None of the collected lists of Alero's predecessors is nearly long enough to support links with the early Luo in either location.

8. See the next paragraph on Alero's settlement in the Luo triangle; Crazzolara (1938, pp. xii–xiv) on Alero speaking "standard" Acholi Luo. On the basis of slim evidence and unconvincing argument, Crazzolara (1951, p. 256) posits a "Madi" (Central Sudanic) origin for Alero *kal*.

early "Alero" lived, at different times, in both the Luo triangle and Paluo; (2) the areas immediately north and immediately south of the Nile were not always clearly differentiated during this early period.[9]

When Alero traditions reach the figure of Alero, the quantity of information and the degree of consistency increase significantly; we are now in Alero's "present past." There is agreement on four important points. First, all accounts identify Alero's father and predecessor as Acic and his son and successor as Kirya, a sharp contrast to varying lists of preceding names. Accompanying narrative traditions also associate Kirya with a great drought and famine, almost certainly that of the 1720s. This allows Kirya's reign to be dated with some confidence to about 1710–40, and Alero's to about 1680–1710. Second, all accounts agree that Alero and his group were settled, by at least the end of his reign, in the Luo triangle. Third, no extant account of Alero traditions mentions a royal drum before the time of *Rwot* Alero; several note Alero's possession of such a drum. Finally, the name of the leader Alero also becomes the name of the polity. All of this indicates that, beginning with the figure of Alero, an Alero chiefdom began to develop.[10]

All available sources agree that the Pangora lineage was a part of the early chiefdom. One account includes other associated lineages as well, although the most extensive rendering of Alero traditions, with both narrative and non-narrative components, does not. On balance, early Alero was likely a very small chiefdom, consisting only of the royal lineage (*kal*) and the one associated lineage of Pangora.[11]

On the whole, traditions reveal that the small, fledgling chiefdom experienced difficult times. After leaving the Luo triangle to settle near the *Got* Lamola outcrop in what becomes western Acholi (see Map 4), Alero got into a series of conflicts. The first was with a group to the west identified simply as "Madi" (i.e., a Central Sudanic-speaking group). Trouble supposedly began after a wife of *Rwot* Alero's son Kirya ran away with the leader of the "Madi" group. Traditions do no more than blame Kirya's wife for what happened, providing an early example of a fairly common ten-

9. See references in n. 5; Crazzolara (1951, p. 256) is the variant version. While the other accounts all locate "Alero" in Paluo, they have the group leaving at different times.

10. A.H.T. 208–10, Crazzolara (1951, pp. 256–58, 266), Wright (1934, pp. 34–35), Okech (1953, p. 67), Girling (1960, pp. 112, 221). The reference to famine comes from Crazzolara (1951, p. 266); A.H.T. 208 and 209 mention epidemics of disease during Kirya's reign.

11. Crazzolara (1951, pp. 257, 277). A.H.T. 208 adds the Papuna and Palite lineages as early Alero *lobong*. The greater detail provided by a combination of narrative and non-narrative traditions in Crazzolara makes this version the preferred one. Okech (1953, p. 67) merely lists all of Alero's eventual *lobong* lineages as being always present.

dency in male-dominated Acholi traditions to make stereotypical scape-goats of women. What the episode seems actually to reveal is the inability of the two groups to settle a relatively common and minor problem without coming to blows. At least later, negotiation and compensation were much more typical. Perhaps conflict occurred here because the mediating role of *rwodi* was not yet firmly established or widely accepted; perhaps the conflict also reflected new complications in relations between groups on divergent sociopolitical trajectories. In any case, the Alero soon clashed with another Central Sudanic neighbor, the single-village community of Koyo. This was seemingly over a disputed hunting area—again, a common source of friction in later Acholi usually settled peacefully—though Koyo is also remembered to have been the home lineage of Kirya's errant wife.[12]

Alero traditions claim victory in both clashes. But some Koyo then forged a temporary alliance with a pre-polity, Central Sudanic "Pabo" group at *Got* Kilak. The two attacked and defeated the Alero. Then the Koyo struck again, this time in alliance with what was probably the emergent chiefdom of Palaro. Once more, the Alero were beaten. About this time *Rwot* Alero died and the troubled chiefdom under new *Rwot* Kirya left the Lamola area to "seek safety elsewhere."[13]

The Alero are remembered to have traveled eastward until they approached the Acaa River in the north of what becomes the central zone. There they met the already settled "Parabok" grouping, made up of the Pangu (or Parabok) and Paiwidi village-lineages, and petitioned them for food and protection. Guarded interaction followed while each side appraised the other. Eventually "Parabok" provided the Alero with land on which to establish villages and fields, and food crops until those fields could be planted and harvested.[14]

Since both the settled multiple-village grouping and incoming chiefdom were comprised of two lineages, neither had an obvious numerical advantage. Uprooted and battle-worn, the Alero seem likely to have been the weaker of the two. Yet somehow the Alero were able to turn the tables and attract their "Parabok" hosts and benefactors to join them as *lobong* (subject or non-royal groups).

Traditions provide three clues to help explain this turnaround. The

12. Crazzolara (1951, pp. 256–57), with support from A.H.T. 209.

13. Crazzolara (1951, pp. 256–57); A.H.T. 209 unconvincingly depicts these events as following Alero's death.

14. Crazzolara (1951, pp. 257–60), A.H.T. 208–9, Wright (1934, p. 35), and Okech (1953, p. 67). Crazzolara and A.H.T. 208–9 imply by their terminology that the "Parabok" leader was a *rwot* and thus "Parabok" a chiefdom. This is not supported by other evidence.

first is related to the system of tribute operative in the chiefdom. "Rwot Kirya," traditions recount, "even sent food, like game animals which [Alero] young men caught with ropes, and also other animals which were killed with spears, and gave them to his friend [the 'Parabok' leader]." This is the first reference to tribute in Alero traditions, and it shows how the *rwot* could have demonstrated wealth and generosity even after Alero's troubles and before they harvested the first crops in their new home. Second, Crazzolara suggests that the "Parabok" may have been impressed by Alero's royal drum(s). And third, as part of the negotiations that must have accompanied incorporation, the main "Parabok" lineage that joined Alero (the Pangu) became one of the two lineages in charge of the main chiefdom *jok* (*Jok* Labeja). This gave the Pangu and their head a lead role in much polity-wide ritual.[15]

Alero's larger size did not rid the chiefdom of the Koyo-Palaro threat. Two more surprise attacks resulted in a number of Alero deaths, and after extensive debate a decision was made to send a brother of *Rwot* Kirya to Bunyoro-Kitara (Paluo?) for assistance. Traditions imply that in response, the Bunyoro-Kitara king himself (though it seems likely to have been a lesser Paluo *rwot*) sent a contingent of "Lo-Loka" ("people from across the river," i.e., Paluo) to assess the situation and report back. They did, and soon a larger Paluo force, including the Bunyoro-Kitara *rwot*, was on its way to attack the Palaro and Koyo. After considerable fighting and many casualties, especially among the smaller Palaro-Koyo alliance, the Alero and their southern allies were victorious. The Koyo leader was killed, and the *rwot* of Palaro was either dead or taken away to Bunyoro.[16]

Alero traditions indicate that the presence of outsiders who had to be

---

15. The reference to tribute is in A.H.T. 209; the suggestion about the royal drum(s) comes from Crazzolara (1951, p. 258); and information about Pangu's ritual role is in both Crazzolara (1951, pp. 258, 277) and A.H.T. 208. A.H.T. 208–10 all claim that the Alero left their royal drum at Lamola when they moved away. The apparent contradiction may be resolvable. Traditions in Crazzolara note that the Alero had "come along with their royal drums — *bvuul tiimo*." But a *tiimo* drum is a "long, thin drum" (Crazzolara [1938, p. 396]), which is neither the typical shape of a royal drum nor its standard term (*bul ker*). Perhaps the Alero were temporarily using *bul tiimo* in lieu of their proper royal drum left behind at Lamola. A.H.T. 208 notes that the royal drum left behind was eventually replaced by a man from Parabok — hence, after the meeting of the two groups. A.H.T. 209 claims that the "Parabok" gave a small drum to Kirya, though this is not identified as a royal drum and probably indicates no more than "Parabok" acceptance of Alero rule.

16. Crazzolara (1951, pp. 261–66), A.H.T. 209. Both the advance expedition and the larger fighting force are identified throughout the Crazzolara narrative as "Lo-Loka," i.e., Paluo. And traditions from Pajule Paluo in the east-central zone also note that Paluo took part in the expedition. See Chap. 6; Garry (1972b, pp. 37–43; 1976, p. 323).

provisioned and the neglect of agriculture during fighting resulted in food shortages for Alero (and even worse for the defeated Koyo and Palaro). Then the rains failed—almost certainly during the 1720s—leading to drought and such severe famine that many Alero are remembered to have left the chiefdom to seek relief elsewhere.[17]

Alero traditions of the chiefdom's first two generations suggest two points about the early stages of the establishment of a new sociopolitical order in Acholi. First, adopting the new ideology and institutions of chiefship was no guarantee that a group would automatically increase its size or strength. Early Alero was unable to attract any more than a few outsiders or hold its own in battle against pre-polity adversaries such as Koyo and "Pabo." Yet, secondly, the small and often struggling chiefdom was able to attract and incorporate a multiple-village grouping as large as itself. Somehow the power, or potential power, of the new ideology and institutions of chiefship seems to have been perceptible. "True power," David W. Cohen once remarked, "has its own geography of forces."[18]

PATIKO

Just as Alero traditions take on a new tone from the time of *Rwot* Alero and the founding of an Alero chiefdom, so too do Patiko traditions once a Patiko polity emerges under *Rwot* Atiko. The limited nature of traditions associated with the pre-polity, pre-Atiko portion of the Patiko past have been noted above in Chapter 2. The most important ideological message of these traditions is to assert the Luoness of Patiko's ruling lineage in four ways: (1) by claiming that the group originated in a Luo-speaking area (identified unconvincingly as "Nywagi" or Anuak on the Ethiopia-Sudan border); (2) by associating the group with the famous Pubungu split of the southward-migrating early Luo; (3) by including stereotypical Luo names in a long list of supposed *rwodi*; and (4) by professing settlement in the Luo triangle from the time of Pubungu to the time of Atiko. Antithetically, the traditions also convey extensive interaction between "Patiko" and Central Sudanic areas and peoples. "Patiko's" remembered migration to Pubungu, for example, includes many and lengthy settlements in Central Sudanic areas north and west of Acholi. And after the Pubungu split, numerous

17. Crazzolara (1951, p. 266). Without specifically mentioning drought, A.H.T. 208 and 209 note that the earliest *lobong* lineage in the chiefdom, Pangora, moved away sometime during the rule of *Rwot* Kirya.

18. Personal communication.

references in traditions indicate long-term and ongoing interaction with Central Sudanic speakers in and near the Luo triangle.[19]

When traditions reach Atiko (ruled about 1680–1710), they move into Patiko's "present past" and improve dramatically in both quantity and quality. In the most extensive rendering of Patiko traditions, Crazzolara devotes seven pages to Atiko's period of rule in contrast to three for all twelve of his supposed predecessors. These traditions of Atiko can be divided into five narrative episodes, each warranting extensive rendering and comment.[20]

Episode 1 begins in the Luo triangle, where one of Atiko's wives, from "Baar," gave birth to twins. The proper celebration of such a special occasion required the sacrifice of a sheep to the lineage's *jok*. Atiko had no sheep of his own at hand (surprising for a *rwot*), so he requested one from his older brother Gicel. Contrary to custom and good manners, Gicel refused. Atiko then turned to a man from the now extinct Ometa village-lineage, and the proper ceremony was carried out. With the *jok* thus satisfied, the twins prospered and grew. They proved to be extraordinary. One of them (some versions say both) was magically not only human, but a lion cub as well! Eventually these twins began to hunt and provide much meat for Atiko. Because of Gicel's earlier behavior, Atiko did not share the meat with him in the customary manner. Gicel found out, and he and Atiko quarreled and then separated. Atiko moved away; Gicel stayed. Gicel's second son, Awel, is remembered eventually to have become the first head of the Pawel chiefdom.[21]

The first comment is to note the indication of Luo-Central Sudanic interaction. The origin of the twins' mother is identified as "Baar," which in Acholi traditions usually refers to a Central Sudanic area northwest of Acholi; the Ometa group that helped Atiko was also almost surely Central Sudanic in origin. Second, special ritual ceremonies after the birth of twins are practiced not only by twentieth-century Acholi but by other Luo groups as far away as the Kenya Luo. Whether mentioning such a ceremony here indicates cultural continuity or a reading back of more recent behavior cannot be determined. Third, the significance of the peculiar lion or part-

19. Patiko has the most extensive and standard rendition of narrative polity traditions of any Acholi chiefdom; see Crazzolara (1951, pp. 223–55). The early period is recounted on pp. 223–26, with a *"rwot"* list on p. 255; Atkinson (1978, pp. 197–204) discusses these early traditions in much greater detail than here.

20. Crazzolara (1951, pp. 226–33).

21. Ibid., pp. 226–27.

lion offspring is not developed here, but will be later. At this point their existence is entwined with the main theme, the separation of brothers following an argument and the subsequent founding of distinct but related groups—a common stereotypical device to account for the existence of different Luo communities. Finally, the brother is not always remembered as Gicel, but sometimes as Awel, Weli, or even Okumu. The point of the story is always the same, however: to identify Pawel and Patiko as "brother" groups.[22]

Episode 2 begins with Atiko and his followers moving from the Luo triangle to *Got* Palee (Guruguru on modern maps) in western Acholi. These followers are identified as the Panyagira-Pabala, Ometa (or Pometa), Paranga, Bura, Pagik, and Toro village-lineages. At *Got* Palee they met a group identified only by the name of its leader, Lee. Atiko asked Lee and his followers to accompany him on a journey eastward to "the end of the world." The invitation was declined, but Atiko and his group moved on, traveling east past *Got* Ladwong and then across the River Acaa to *Got* Goma, in the central zone of Acholi (see Map 4).[23]

Two comments are needed. First, the meeting between Atiko and Lee and his group (identified later as the Pugwenyi lineage) is the first instance recounted of contact between the new chiefdom and outsiders. It seems significant that Atiko could not convince the Pugwenyi to join. As with the early Alero, success in dealing with others was neither certain nor immediate. Second, separate-group, non-narrative lineage traditions make the list of *lobong* lineages given above highly suspect. Non-narrative evidence supports the inclusion of Panyagira-Pabala, Ometa, and Paranga in the young chiefdom. But it also indicates that Bura and Pagik were met only at *Got* Goma, and that the Toro were not a separate associated group but part of Atiko's own royal lineage.[24]

22. On the Central Sudanic identity of Pometa, see ibid., pp. 225–27, 231, 233; 1954, pp. 476–77; see also A.H.T. 224. For a depiction of twentieth-century Acholi twin rituals see Higgins (1966, pp. 178–81), Seligman (1932, pp. 120–21), and Anywar (1954, pp. 50–51); similar rituals among the Kenya Luo are presented, for example, in Hauge (1974, pp. 62–63). The Pawel "brother" of Atiko is identified as Gicel by Crazzolara (1951, p. 227; 1954, p. 453); as Weli or Awel by Okech (1953, pp. 47, 70), Okot (1971, p. 30), Wright (1934, p. 170), and A.H.T. 224 (text), 226–27; and as Okumu by Wright (1934, p. 171) and A.H.T. 224 (*rwot* list).

23. Crazzolara (1951, p. 227).

24. See Crazzolara (1951, pp. 225–27; 1954, pp. 476–77) and A.H.T. 224. In addition, (1) the Bura are widely considered an "aboriginal" group in the *Got* Goma area (see Crazzolara [1954, pp. 333–38, 491] and A.H.T. 241, 243); (2) the Pagik were part of the Lamwo grouping discussed below in Episode 3; and (3) see Episode 4 and n. 37 for more on Toro.

Episode 3 focuses on what happened at *Got* Goma. There the young chiefdom came into contact with a mixed group of lineages remembered collectively as Lamwo, seemingly organized into one or more multiple-village groupings. A man named Lapunu is identified as a leader of some sort, though it is clear that he was not a *rwot*. The villages included Pakwaca (Lapunu's lineage), Pailim (perhaps a branch of the former), Pagaya, Pailik, Pagik, Bura, and Pakwongo, some of whom were refugees from an emergent Pajok chiefdom whose establishment was part of an alternative process of polity formation north of the Agoro mountains.[25]

As Atiko and his group approached the villages around *Got* Goma, they stopped "in the open, *i tiim*," and "started beating the drum." At the sound, Lapunu ("the headman of the not too distant villages") came to greet the newcomers and invite them to stay among the Lamwo. Atiko declined, saying his people were too numerous. He added that any grain the Lamwo could spare would be appreciated and, in parting, gave Lapunu much meat. Lapunu, against customary procedure, did not share this meat with his people. He did, though, collect grain and bring it to Atiko, who thanked him, and invited him back the next day with all his people.

When Lapunu returned with just seven elders, Atiko was puzzled and insisted that a messenger be sent to gather the others. This was done, and all the people of the Lamwo villages came. Patiko served them as much meat as they could eat and gave them more to take home. Atiko asked them back the next day and repeated his lavish hospitality. He could do this, traditions explain, because his lion-twin "sons" hunted at night and provided their father with the proceeds of the kill. The Lamwo people, Crazzolara recounts, "commented on the new *Rwoot*, comparing him with their *Ladit* [elder]: 'This is a true *Rwoot*,' they said; 'we can hardly remember when our niggardly Lapfunu [Lapunu] provided us with food, while *Rwoot* Atiko chokes us with meat. *Rwoot* Atiko is a kind man who looks after his people; he ought to be our *Rwoot*.'"[26]

Lapunu made no attempt to fight against the tide, but told his elders to join the newcomer and "guard him well." He is remembered to have then given Patiko possession and care of the two protective *jogi* of Lamwo as well as "rights" to the nearby River Acaa. Thus the Lamwo grouping broke up. The Pagaya, Pakwaca, and some Pagik and Bura joined Patiko. The Pailim left with Lapunu as he returned toward Pajok but then broke away to join

25. Crazzolara (1951, pp. 227–31).
26. Ibid.

another chiefdom in central Acholi, Paico. The Pakwongo, Pailik, and sections of Pagik and Bura eventually joined yet another central Acholi polity, Payira.[27]

The first set of comments on this episode concerns the earlier history of many Lamwo village-lineages, including the Pakwaca and Pagaya who joined Patiko. These lineages are remembered to have moved south as a result of violence associated with the founding of a Pajok polity. The rulers of Pajok were Luo speakers from farther north, and both the process by which Pajok was established and certain of its structures distinguish this chiefdom and others in northernmost Acholi from chiefdoms to the south. Available information on the northernmost Acholi chiefdoms, divided in this century from the rest of Acholi by the border between Uganda and Sudan, is limited. For present purposes, however, a brief outline of developments is all that is needed.[28]

Like Uganda Acholiland, northernmost Acholi was settled by Central Sudanic, Eastern Nilotic, and Luo groups that were eventually brought into a common sociopolitical framework consisting of a number of similar, small chiefdoms. These chiefdoms were based on a model of sociopolitical organization derived from a Luo-dominated area, and Luo became the principal or even sole language. However, the Luo component in northernmost Acholi is not linked to Bunyoro-Kitara and Paluo, but to Shilluk and Anuak, Luo-speaking communities located hundreds of miles north of Acholi in the southern Sudan. Both Shilluk and Anuak feature prominently in the migration traditions of many northernmost Acholi groups. Social and political organization in the northernmost polities, moreover, was closer to that in Shilluk and Anuak than to the Acholi chiefdoms farther south. For example, the villages in northernmost Acholi chiefdoms were governed by sons of the *rwot* who set up residence in those villages, a pattern found in Shilluk and elsewhere to the north but not among the Acholi chiefdoms south of Agoro.[29]

27. Ibid.
28. For the little there is on northernmost Acholi, see Crazzolara (1951, pp. 169–78; 1954, pp. 396–99), Okeny (1982a, 1982b).
29. See Baker (1866, v. 1, pp. 319–20) for a nineteenth-century reference; Girling (1960, p. 100) for a twentieth-century one. Girling also suggests that Palabek and Atyak in the south may have also used the northernmost system, though he provides no evidence. Palabek traditions are conflicting, but some do suggest northernmost Acholi practices. See Crazzolara (1954, pp. 496–97); Owot A.H.T. 19–20; and Chap. 8 below. Conversely, no extant Atyak evidence indicates northernmost Acholi practices. For descriptions of Shilluk and Anuak society, see, for example, Westermann (1912), Seligman (1932, pp. 37–113), Evans-Pritchard (1940, 1948), Pumphrey (1941), Crazzolara (1951, pp. 122–52), and Butt (1952, pp. 45–80).

The chiefdom of Pajok provided the name for the northernmost region of Acholi and appears to have been the model for the alternative type of polity found there. Pajok traditions locate its founding in the second half of the seventeenth century, in the present-day Padibe area southeast of Pajok's eventual area of settlement (see Map 4).

These same traditions report a level of violence accompanying this process not present farther south. Entire villages are remembered to have been killed, and there is even a hint of cannibalism (although unlikely to be true, such allusions convey the extreme level of violence being portrayed, as nothing in Acholi traditions is more abhorrent than cannibalism). The traditions also suggest that incoming Luo from the north may have directed attacks specifically against an emergent polity based on the Bunyoro/Paluo model. If so, this may reveal a clash between two distinct political cultures, each being established at about the same time but derived from different Luo traditions and experiences — one essentially southern, the other northern.[30]

Patiko's connection with all this comes from those lineages or lineage segments that moved south to escape the violence, became part of the Lamwo grouping around *Got* Goma, and were then incorporated into Patiko. How do Patiko narrative traditions depict both the differences and the interactions between the Lamwo and the Patiko?

The traditions make clear first of all that Lapunu, head of the Lamwo (or part of Lamwo), was not a *rwot* and hence that his leadership and Atiko's were qualitatively different. The episode identifies two crucial ways in which this was so and why Atiko, but not Lapunu, was a "true" *rwot*. The first is Atiko's possession of a royal drum; the second is his central role in an organized tribute system. This episode contains the first references in Patiko traditions to these fundamental attributes of *rwot*ship, and the timing hardly seems coincidental. Atiko is not only a "true" *rwot*, but the first of an emergent Patiko chiefdom.

The mention of the royal drum is brief but occurs at the very outset of the episode. When the Patiko arrived in the *Got* Goma area, they initiated contact with the already settled Lamwo by "beating the drum." The royal drum announced not only the presence of a new group, but one of a particular and different sort.

---

30. See Crazzolara (1951, pp. 174–77), with a *rwot* list that suggests a late-seventeenth-century date for Pajok's founding that fits with Patiko movements. This would also have been before the chiefdoms of the later north-central zone were established, explaining both their absence from Pajok's traditions and vice-versa (see Chap. 8).

The treatment of tribute is both more extensive and less direct. The main message is Atiko's ability to provide the Lamwo with gifts of meat in a way that their leader could not. Atiko is depicted as being able to do this because of his supernatural, half-lion offspring. But the actual source of Atiko's largesse was surely tribute. As the Patiko were on the move, Atiko could have no opportunity to obtain tribute in the form of agricultural labor (which would explain Atiko's request for grain). What *would* have been available was tribute from the game animals killed by members of the chiefdom, providing the surplus that Atiko redistributed to such good effect. The Lamwo seem to have been impressed with both the practical and ideological advantages of this redistribution. Atiko's apparent ability to organize and mobilize his people made him appear a "true" *rwot*, which is sharply contrasted to the more limited capabilities of Lapunu.[31]

This episode is the first to relate the incorporation of outsiders into the new chiefdom. The *ker* of the chiefdom is defined largely in terms of drums and tribute, and Patiko's ability to incorporate others is attributed mainly to the power and attractiveness of the new institutions and the ideology that drums and tribute represented.

Episode 4 begins with Patiko still in the *Got* Goma region, where it came into contact with the Payira chiefdom, which had moved into the area from the east.

Atiko was not yet ready to remain in one place. He still wanted to travel to the "end of the world," and so once again led the chiefdom eastward. Not everyone liked this continual movement. For example, after Patiko came into the present-day Kitgum area of the east-central zone, a lineage there called the Pacijok apparently joined the chiefdom. But when Atiko moved on, the Pacijok refused to go. Undeterred, Atiko pressed ahead, and traveled another 150 miles southeastward until reaching *Got* Amyel or perhaps *Got* Lapono (see Map 4).

Here, because food was difficult to obtain, the Patiko stopped and turned back. They retraced their steps westward until settling near a small outcrop named Kirimo, where they once again came into contact with Payira. Located about ten miles away from their former home at *Got* Goma, *Got* Kirimo was the home of *Jok* Baka, one of the two *jogi* that Lapunu "gave" Patiko as the Lamwo grouping broke up (again, see Map 4).

At least two lineages are remembered not to have made the return

31. Crazzolara (1951, pp. 174–77); see also Malandra (1947, p. 2). For a somewhat similar story from Shambaa, though serving different purposes and structured as myth, see Feierman (1974, pp. 40–69).

journey. The Pabala remained in the southeastern zone and some Paranga continued eastward, eventually becoming an Eastern Nilotic-speaking Jie group known as the Panyingaro.[32]

The first comment concerns the two references to meeting Payira in the *Got* Goma region. Because Payira's own traditions of this period are so unclear (see below), these Patiko references are probably the best we have for locating Payira in the late seventeenth or early eighteenth century. Thus a passing comment in the traditions of one group proves to be extremely valuable information about another.

Second, Atiko's continuing desire to travel "to the end of the world" seems strange and the journey improbable. Yet extant traditions from the southeastern zone where *Got* Lapono and *Got* Amyel are located refer to migration into the zone by groups linked to Patiko and identify lineages still in the area that were supposedly part of that movement (see the Lira section below). Thus some sort of connection between Patiko and the southeastern zone seems likely.

Third, if the Patiko (or some of them) did in fact travel as far as the Amyel and Lapono outcrops, they *did* reach the end of their world. Beyond lay flat, dry plains even less suited to agriculture than eastern Acholi. Even today the series of outcrops of which Amyel and Lapono are a part mark the end of a world dominated by agriculture and the beginning of one that is mainly pastoralist. The same boundary also serves as a dividing line between two sets of processes that eventually produce a primarily agricultural Luo-speaking Acholi society on one side and the highly pastoralist Eastern Nilotic Jie and Karimojong on the other. And after returning from this "end" of their world, the Patiko settled in what was to become the very center of the world that such a chiefdom represented, the very center of what was to become Acholi.[33]

Episode 5, the final episode of Atiko traditions, focuses on the Pugwenyi lineage. Pugwenyi traditions claim that the group originated in Bunyoro and is related to both the Koc-Daca of the Acholi chiefdom of Lamogi and the Koc Ragem of Jonam, a small Luo-speaking people settled along the west bank of the Nile just north of Bunyoro. These separate-group, lineage traditions thus reaffirm Patiko narrative traditions concern-

32. Crazzolara (1951, p. 231). *Jok* Baka became one of the most important *jogi* in Patiko (with his "wife" *Jok* Alela playing a slightly less important role). See Okot (1971, pp. 60–73) and Atkinson (1978, pp. 217–19); the latter also looks at *Jok* Lawodomeke, a later chiefdom *jok* with roles and status comparable to *Jok* Baka.

33. The best discussion of historical developments among Eastern Nilotic peoples to the east of Acholi is Lamphear (1976).

ing Atiko's first meeting with the lineage (Episode 2 above), where under Lee's leadership the Pugwenyi declined Atiko's invitation to join the chiefdom. Some years later, Lee's son and successor, Ugwenyi, is remembered to have changed his mind and led a search for the departed *rwot*. Unsuccessful, the Pugwenyi met and reluctantly joined the Paico chiefdom. A serious quarrel eventually arose after the Paico *rwot* failed to arrange compensation for a Pugwenyi man murdered by another chiefdom member. Feeling betrayed and angry, the Pugwenyi left Paico to continue searching for Atiko. Some time later, while fishing in the River Acaa, the group met the Pagaya lineage of Patiko and learned that *Rwot* Atiko was living just across the river to the east. Pugwenyi then came and joined his chiefdom.[34]

This last Atiko episode ends with his death at *Got* Goma. Atiko is remembered to have had three brothers, identified as the ancestors of three distinct groups: Gicel, ancestor of Pawel *kal*; Ongu, ancestor of Pokumu; and Owiny-Amola, ancestor of the royal lineage of Toro.[35]

The first comment is that Pugwenyi's claims to Luoness seem much more ideologically than historically derived. Crazzolara dismisses the lineage's traditions of origin in Bunyoro as just one more example of a "lamentable tendency" or "prevailing fashion" among the Acholi, "which requires that every ancestor should have come from Bunyoro or . . . Pubungu." In fact, most Acholi lineages do not make such a claim, but whenever one does, the ideological message conveyed must always be kept in mind and the historical validity always questioned. Moreover, the story that purports to demonstrate Pugwenyi's relationship to Koc-Daca and Koc Ragem "is not too clear." No available Koc-Daca or Koc Ragem traditions even allude to Pugwenyi, and the name that links the two Koc genealogies, Daca, does not appear in Pugwenyi traditions. Instead, the eponymous "Ugwenyi" and "Koc" are identified as the two "sons" of Lee. Crazzolara's view, based on linguistic evidence, is that the Pugwenyi were "Lango" (Eastern Nilotic) in origin, and this interpretation is much more convincing than Pugwenyi's self-proclaimed Luoness.[36]

The purported relationship between Patiko and Pokumu also seems spurious. Primarily because of their strong ties with the clearly Eastern Nilotic lineages of Pailik and Patuda, the Pokumu (see Chapter 6) seem far

34. Crazzolara (1951, pp. 231–33). The most extended treatment of Jonam history is by Apecu (1972); see also Sargent (1976) and sharp criticisms of this essay, along with the rest of the volume in which it appears, by Henige (1980).

35. Crazzolara (1951, p. 233).

36. Ibid., p. 232; 1954, pp. 478–79; Apecu (1972, pp. 96–97); A.H.T. 203.

more likely to be Eastern Nilotic than a "brother" group of the Luo-speaking royal lineage of Patiko. The proclaimed link between the royal lineages of Patiko and Toro is also questionable — at least in the geographical context of Acholi. Toro's *mwoc*, or praise call, does include the name Owiny-Amola, the supposed name of Atiko's brother. But Toro traditions are clear in locating the chiefdom's royal lineage in Bunyoro-Kitara until the late eighteenth or early nineteenth century. Only then did the group move into western Acholi.[37]

On the other hand, a close relationship between the Patiko and Pawel royal lineages is so unanimously claimed in the traditions of both groups that alternative evidence, if any ever existed, has disappeared. It is possible, perhaps likely, that the chiefdoms of Patiko and Pawel *were* associated or even "brother" groups.[38]

Finally, the Pugwenyi reference to meeting Paico west of the River Acaa in the central zone fits well with Paico's traditions (see below), though the latter make no mention of Pugwenyi. Paico's silence could be because the Pugwenyi left Paico, or because of the generally negative story that the Pugwenyi traditions tell. If the Paico *rwot* could not settle an inter-lineage dispute within the chiefdom, he failed in one of his primary roles. This Pugwenyi story could be one more example (this time from non-narrative traditions) of difficulties experienced by emergent chiefdoms in dealing with others, both newly incorporated lineages and those still outside the chiefly order.

When Atiko died in around 1710, the polity he led seems the largest in Acholi at that time. With the addition of Pugwenyi, the chiefdom consisted of *kal* and eight *lobong* village-lineages. Atiko seems exceptionally successful in using both the practical and ideological attributes of *rwot*ship to attract new adherents. In contrast, during the period of rule of his son and successor, Okello-Woro (c. 1710–40), no new lineages are remembered to have joined. Perhaps a period of consolidation might have been needed

37. On the Eastern Nilotic origins of Pailik (and by association, Patuda), see Crazzolara (1951, pp. 229, 231, 294; 1954, p. 487); on Toro, see Crazzolara (1954, p. 474), Okech (1953, p. 54), A.H.T. 216.

38. Traditions asserting a relationship between Atiko and Pawel *kal* are Wright (1934, pp. 170–71), Crazzolara (1951, p. 227; 1954, p. 453), Okech (1953, pp. 47, 70), Okot (1971, p. 30), and A.H.T. 224, 226–27. All these sources agree that the two "brothers" quarreled and separated; most locate the split in the Luo triangle; and one source (Wright [1934, p. 171]) brings a royal drum into the story. Once the split occurred, Pawel is remembered to have remained in the Luo triangle until after the 1720s drought and to have never incorporated any *lobong* lineages. Okech (1953, pp. 53, 70) makes the contradictory claim, unsupported elsewhere, that the Pawel moved west into Central Sudanic Madi country. Because of limited evidence, Pawel will not be discussed further in this chapter.

following all the movement and incorporation of outsiders that characterized Atiko's time.[39]

PAYIRA, PAICO, AND PAIBONA

Traditions of Payira, Paico, and Paibona — and especially of their royal
lineages — indicate a close association among the three throughout their
history. Indeed, all three ruling lineages assert that one of their ancestors
was the famous Labongo, leader of the early Luo when they quarreled and
separated at Pubungu. Paico and Paibona traditions add that Ayira, Acoo,
and Abona were brothers, all sons of Labongo.[40]

These traditions serve dual ideological purposes. First, they proclaim
the royal lineages of the three chiefdoms as early Luo; then they link, from
early on, the smaller chiefdoms of Paico and Paibona with the eventually
large and powerful Payira. These purposes are so clear and are fulfilled so
well that any traces of "real" sociohistorical relationships embodied in the
traditions cannot be disentangled from the dominant ideological messages
being conveyed.[41]

For example, Paico and Paibona lived near Payira during the eighteenth and nineteenth centuries when Payira became the largest and most
powerful chiefdom in Acholi. As Payira came to overshadow and dominate
its neighbors, claims of "brotherhood" stretching back to the early Luo of
Pubungu would have been advantageous for Paico and Paibona, whatever
the historical realities.

Conversely, at least three considerations support the groups' claims to
have been part of the early Luo. First, as with Alero and Patiko, traditions of
the early period of the ruling lineages of Paico, Paibona, and Payira locate
these groups in the Luo triangle, one of the most prominent settlement sites

39. Though some ambiguity exists, Okello-Woro is the Patiko *rwot* most likely associated
with the 1720s drought and famine; see Crazzolara (1951, pp. 233–34). Patiko seems to have
remained in the central portion of the central zone throughout Okello-Woro's reign.

40. See Payira renditions in Crazzolara (1954, pp. 482–83), Anywar (1954, pp. 10–12),
Okech (1953, pp. 31–32), A.H.T. 247; Paico versions are in A.H.T. 228, 231, 234; Paibona's in
A.H.T. 235, 237. Okech (1953, pp. 42 and 72) merely identifies the father of Acoo and Abona
as Labongo. Some Payira traditions emphasize *Got* Kilak as a crucial site in their migrations
more than Pubungu.

41. The pre-polity portions of the three chiefdoms' *rwot* lists do not help. The sixteen
Payira *rwot* lists are so often inconsistent and contrived that almost no researcher has taken
them seriously. Paico and Paibona lists are not inconsistent, but have only one name prior to
their respective eponyms: the famous Labongo of Pubungu. As the estimated dates of rule of
Acoo work out to 1680–1710, and those of Abona to 1685–1715, they could not be the "sons"
of Labongo or anyone else associated with early Luo migrations except in the most figurative
sense. All extant variants of the three *rwot* lists are reproduced in Atkinson (1978, pp. 568–69,
576–78).

of the early Luo. Second (again, as with Alero and Patiko), Paico, Paibona, and Payira all settled in the central zone of Acholi where a higher percentage of royal lineages than anywhere else claim Luo origins and where people speak the dialect of Acholi Luo that is considered the "purest" and most "standard" in Acholi. Finally, despite Crazzolara's lament above, Acholi claims of ties to Pubungu are in fact relatively rare. Bunyoro/Paluo is invoked far more often than Pubungu to assert Luo origins, actual or imagined, with Shilluk the second most likely claim. The only Acholi groups whose traditions include references to Pubungu are the royal lineages of Alero, Patiko, Pawel, Koc, Bwobo, *and* Paico, Paibona, and Payira. Taking everything into consideration, no Acholi lineages are more likely to have been part of the earliest Luo settlements in northern Uganda than these.[42]

When we move on to early chiefdom histories, Payira's is the most difficult to reconstruct. The sixteen collected versions of Payira's *rwot* list are simply too varied and unreliable to provide a chronology or even a clear ordering of movements or events before *Rwot* Loni, who ruled circa 1780–1820. Fortunately, four other sources help fill the void.

First are the references in Patiko traditions noted above, which locate Payira in the *Got* Goma area of the central zone during Atiko's reign between about 1680 and 1710. Second, Lamogi lineage traditions assert that Lamogi was the first Payira *lobong*, incorporated in the *Got* Ogom area about ten miles southwest of *Got* Goma seemingly not long before the 1720s drought and famine. Thus Lamogi traditions place the young Payira chiefdom just where Patiko traditions indicate that it should be and just when it should be there.[43]

The two other sources that provide information on the early Payira chiefdom are Paico and Paibona traditions of migration into Acholi from the Luo triangle. Both indicate that the move occurred in conjunction with Payira at a time that can be dated from the Paico and Paibona *rwot* lists to around 1680–1710 or 1685–1715. At the end of this period, Paico and Paibona were settled just across the Acaa River from *Got* Ogom. And even though different versions of Payira traditions provide diverse migration

---

42. In a peculiar and unconvincing narrative on early Acholi in general, Odongo (1976) argues against Payira *kal*'s Luo origins and claims that it was not even Luo-speaking until the early nineteenth century. Given Payira's inclusion among those who speak the "purest," most standard Luo in Acholi (Crazzolara [1938, pp. xiii–xiv]), this last contention is especially untenable.

43. The Patiko reference is in Crazzolara (1951, p. 231); Lamogi lineage traditions come from A.H.T. 241.

details, almost all bring the chiefdom from the Luo triangle to the *Got* Ogom area one way or another before events almost certainly associated with the 1720s drought and famine.[44]

Available traditions of Payira's early chiefdom history are far more scarce and contradictory than Alero's and Patiko's. The primary problem is the lack of agreement concerning the identity, order, and number of early *rwodi*, which means that no coherent temporal framework exists to help order the early chiefdom's traditions.

The nature of the "absent past" in Acholi traditions makes the pre-polity portions of received *rwot* lists unreliable as chronological guides (see Chapter 2). In Payira's case this unreliability marks traditions of the early chiefdom period as well. This is atypical and seems due to Payira's particular pattern of growth and development. Payira remained a small chiefdom, with the Lamogi as its only *lobong* lineage from its founding during the late seventeenth century until after the 1720s drought. Then Payira began to experience a degree of growth unmatched anywhere else in Acholi. The chiefdom's central location, with many streams and rivers and the highest reliable rainfall in Acholi, placed it in an extremely advantageous position. This became especially important during and after the droughts occurring about 1790 and in the 1830s, when Payira came to exert unprecedented influence and dominance over other chiefdoms. And this is the period when the numerous versions of Payira's *rwot* list begin to show consistency, starting with *Rwot* Loni. Following this establishment of Payira's power and prominence came the long and distinguished reigns of just two *rwodi*, Rwotcamo (c. 1857–87) and Awic (1888–1946). All of these circum-stances seem to have produced Payira narrative traditions that concentrate on the late eighteenth century and beyond at the expense of the entire earlier period—both pre- and post-polity. It is as if the "absent" and "present" pasts are delimited differently in Payira traditions than elsewhere in Acholi.[45]

Paico's and Paibona's early chiefdom traditions are more coherent than Payira's, if no more extensive. Paico traditions indicate that the chiefdom under *Rwot* Acoo (c. 1680–1710) moved from the Luo triangle into the central zone, supposedly along with Payira. But the Paico, unlike the Payira,

44. Paico accounts are in Okech (1953, p. 31), A.H.T. 228, 231–32, 234; Paibona's in A.H.T. 235, 237. For Payira versions, see Anywar (1954, pp. 10–13); Crazzolara (1954, pp. 482–83), with some support from Webster A.H.T., pp. 64–65, 193n; Okech (1953, pp. 31–32); and A.H.T. 247.

45. Payira's history from c. 1790–1900 is most extensively rendered in Atkinson (1978, pp. 360–68, 476–87, 504–52).

did not cross the Acaa River, remaining instead near its western bank (see Map 4). There Paico was joined by its first *lobong*, the Pagaya. Though this Pagaya lineage does not claim to be related to the Pagaya incorporated by Patiko in the same zone and time period, it probably was. Both, indeed, were likely part of a widely dispersed old Pagaya group whose origins are unclear. Except for the temporary membership of Pugwenyi (see the Patiko section above), Pagaya seems the only lineage to have joined Paico before the 1720s drought. Thus, as with Payira, Paico before about 1725 seems to have remained a very small polity, consisting of *kal* and one or two associated lineages.[46]

Paico traditions provide evidence on only one more aspect of the chiefdom's early history, its royal drum. When I asked former *rwot* Jakayo Obunya what was remembered about *Rwot* Acoo and his time, he answered that Acoo had a brother named Juu who for unspecified reasons "took" Paico's royal drum to Bunyoro. Acoo followed Juu there, killed him, and brought the drum back to Paico. When asked about the origin of Paico's drum in a subsequent interview, Jakayo stated emphatically that there had been no royal drum before *Rwot* Acoo. Later still, he made the general observation that in the past, royal drums were obtained from Bunyoro, and then he provided a new twist to the Acoo-Juu story. In this version, Juu did not simply go off with the royal drum to Bunyoro but said he was going to do so. Acoo protested and when Juu took the drum anyway, Acoo killed him. "Then," the story concludes, "Acoo took the *dak ker* [wife of the *rwot*ship] of Juu and he succeeded."[47]

What can be made of all this? Some traditions suggest that Juu, the purported brother of *Rwot* Acoo, possessed the royal drum before Acoo did, that Acoo got the drum from Juu (after Juu tried to take it to Bunyoro), and even that Acoo got a *dak ker* from Juu. This makes Juu seem to be a *rwot*, even though he does not appear in any collected Paico *rwot* list. It is possible that Juu's name was dropped from the list because he was such a dramatic loser in the competition with Acoo to head the new chiefdom. Conversely, two strong indicators point to Acoo as the first Paico *rwot*. First, Acoo is specifically remembered as the first to have a royal drum; second, the name of the polity clearly derives from his name.[48]

46. On Paico's migration, see A.H.T. 228, 232; Okech (1953, p. 31). On the incorporation of Pagaya, A.H.T. 232. Crazzolara sometimes identifies Pagaya's origins as "early Lango," or Eastern Nilotic (1951, p. 294; 1954, pp. 456–57), sometimes as Luo (1951, pp. 115, 175–78, 229–30; 1954, pp. 477–78); Herring (1974b, pp. 93–94) accepts the latter.

47. See A.H.T. 228, 231, 234.

48. No Paico narrative traditions explicitly acknowledge that the origins of the chiefdom occurred with either Acoo or Juu. Instead, they allege origins dating from the first name in the

When we turn to Paibona, available traditions provide even fewer traces concerning its early chiefdom history than with Payira and Paico. The main message of extant traditions seems to be to assert Paibona's close relationship with Payira and Paico. The name of the chiefdom alone suggests that it was founded during the time of Abona, with estimated dates of rule from 1685 to 1715. Under Abona, traditions state, the chiefdom moved from the Luo triangle into the central zone of Acholi in association with Paico and Payira. There is no indication of any incorporation of outsiders.[49]

PALARO

The core of this final central-zone chiefdom to emerge before the 1720s drought was formed by the Agoro multiple-village grouping (see Chapter 2). At about the turn of the eighteenth century, this grouping consisted of the Agoro, Lamogi, Patwol, and Pauma village-lineages and was settled near the Acaa in the northwestern corner of the central zone. Palaro traditions recount that the Agoro leader, named Wiia, rendered a decision in a dispute over compensation for illicit sexual intercourse (*luk*). His decision placed the burden of payment on the Lamogi lineage of the woman. They refused to accept Wiia's judgment. The story continues with the arrival of a man from Paluo named Obura:

> He went about from group to group for a visit. He talked little but listened eagerly to what the people had to say. He heard of this case of *luk* and expressed his disagreement with the decision of 'Wiia. . . . In the next public assembly Obvura [Obura] rose to his feet and stated the *ongoon* [legal norm] that holds in Bunyoro: "The man has to pay for illegitimate intercourse, and the child belongs to him." The great majority of the assembly showed their satisfaction. In the end 'Wiia was persuaded to cede the *keer* (authority) to Obvura, because of his intelligence. Thus Obvura, from Loka [Paluo], became *Rwoot* of Palaaro.

Following this, Wiia and "his group" moved back to the Agoro mountains, leaving behind others of the Agoro grouping who then joined Obura. Obura thus "became the first, alas very unlucky, *Rwoot* of Palaaro."[50]

---

remembered *rwot* list, Labongo (supposedly the Labongo of Pubungu fame). Given this, one way to interpret the story of Juu and his "taking" the drum to "Bunyoro" is that it explains how Paico's drum — or the idea for the drum — came from Bunyoro-Kitara subsequent to the chiefdom's founding without having to admit its introduction at this time.

49. A.H.T. 235–36, Okech (1953, p. 72).

50. Crazzolara (1951, pp. 289–90); see a condensed form of the story in Okech (1953, p. 65). Palaro narrative traditions in Wright (1934, p. 95) identify the person who came from Bunyoro (specifically Bunyoro *kal*) not as Obura but his "father" Laro.

Palaro traditions, then, attribute the introduction of Bunyoro/ Paluo ideas and leadership to a single Paluo figure, Obura. Obura is depicted as having demonstrated some of the most fundamental and attractive qualities of *rwot*ship: intelligence, the ability to listen, the ability to speak persuasively, and, perhaps most importantly, the ability to mediate and arbitrate inter-lineage disputes better than the preexisting, pre-polity leader. He demonstrated these qualities so well, in fact, that he was accepted as the first *rwot* of Palaro. Former leader Wiia (who was clearly not a *rwot*) then moved peacefully away. Thus, Palaro traditions recount, the Agoro grouping came to its end and the Palaro chiefdom began.

These narrative traditions of the founding of the Palaro chiefdom are not altogether convincing. It makes no sense that Obura would have been accepted as *rwot* as an individual outsider without kinsmen or other supporters. And the displacement of Wiia and his type of leadership could well have been more complicated and conflictual than his simply ceding authority and moving away. But whatever the shortcomings of Palaro traditions, their portrayal of the crucial role played by Paluo ideas and Paluo leadership in the founding of the chiefdom is both persuasive and significant.

The seemingly peaceful introduction of this new sociopolitical order was completed in an episode of violence rare in Acholi traditions. As noted above, Palaro became allies of the Koyo lineage in a conflict with the young chiefdom of Alero, which the latter won with help from visiting Bunyoro/ Paluo forces. Many Palaro were killed, and *Rwot* Obura was either killed or taken away to Bunyoro by the victors.[51]

Both the overall sequence of events and much of the detail are similar in Alero and Palaro traditions, with three main exceptions. First, Palaro traditions blame the origins of the trouble on the Alero, whereas Alero traditions fault the Koyo and then joint Koyo and Palaro unprovoked attacks.[52]

Second, Palaro traditions claim that the Bunyoro-Kitara *rwot* who led the forces against Palaro (*Rwot* Olum or Olum Panya) was related to *Rwot* Obura and participated against Palaro because of old jealousies toward Obura. Alero traditions, in contrast, maintain that the Bunyoro-Kitara *rwot* agreed to help Alero because of the justice of Alero's case, without specifi-

<hr />

51. Palaro accounts have been collected by Crazzolara (1951, pp. 289–92), Wright (1934, pp. 95–96), and Okech (1953, pp. 65–66).

52. See the Alero section above; Palaro traditions in Crazzolara (1951, p. 290) suggest that the Koyo were a part of Palaro. This is not supported by Alero traditions or by Palaro traditions in Wright (1934, p. 95), which identify the Koyo as "friends of Palaro."

cally identifying the Bunyoro-Kitara *rwot* or noting a relationship between him and the *rwot* of Palaro.[53]

Third, both Palaro and Alero traditions relate similar stories about the ritualistic killing of an enemy leader by the victorious Bunyoro and Alero allies at the end of battle. In Palaro traditions this leader is *Rwot* Obura himself; in Alero's version the victim is the head of the Koyo lineage — the cause of conflict and focus of Alero enmity. Alero traditions add that *Rwot* Obura and his family were then taken away to Bunyoro. Palaro traditions claim that it was the dead Obura's son, Okello. In either case, significantly, Palaro was left temporarily without a *rwot*.[54]

Following military defeat and the loss of their *rwot*, the Palaro were confronted by famine, initially because fields had been neglected and destroyed during the fighting, then because of drought — surely that of the 1720s. The Palaro chiefdom thus ended its first generation of existence in a precarious state.[55]

Southeastern-Zone Chiefdoms

Four chiefdoms established themselves in the eventual southeastern zone of Acholi before the 1720s drought: Lira (later Lira Paluo), Ajali, Patongo, and Pader. When this process began in the late seventeenth century, the vast majority of lineages in the area were Eastern Nilotic. A few originally Central Sudanic lineages seem present as well, but almost no Luo ones (see Chapter 2). Nearly all of these lineages were settled near the string of outcrops from Ogili to Lapono that stretches diagonally across the zone from its northwestern corner. As the earliest chiefdoms emerged, they, too, clung close to the same hills and mountains (see Map 4).[56]

53. Obura is identified variously in Palaro traditions as (1) the son of *Rwot* (King) Olum Panya of Bunyoro (Crazzolara, 1951, p. 289); (2) the brother of Olum Panya (Okech, 1953, p. 65); and (3) simply a member of "*kal* Bunyoro" (Wright, 1934, p. 95). The traditions in Crazzolara also state that Obura was from "Loka Pawir" (i.e., Paluo), indicating that the Bunyoro *rwot* in question was more likely a Paluo chief than the Bunyoro-Kitara king. For a perspective from Pajule in the eventual east-central zone, see Garry (1972b, pp. 37–42).

54. See Crazzolara (1951, pp. 261–66 and 289–92); briefer accounts in Okech (1953, p. 65) and Wright (1934, p. 96) also identify Okello as the person taken to Bunyoro. Pellegrini (1963, p. 2) focuses on *Rwot* Obura's death at the hands of a jealous Olumpanya.

55. Remember that Alero traditions indicate that famine followed immediately upon the fighting. Palaro traditions in Wright (1934, p. 96) suggest drought only after the return of Okello from Bunyoro.

56. Webster (1976a, pp. 219–20; 1976c, pp. 297–98).

LIRA

Lira Paluo traditions provide an interesting twist to the Patiko traditions of travel to *Got* Amyel or Lapono. They recount that two brothers, Atiko and Lapono, vied for power while Patiko was still at *Got* Goma. Lapono proved unable to provide food for the people whereas Atiko was successful, thus gaining the adherence of the great majority. This caused Lapono to move away to the east with a small group of followers. They settled eventually at the foot of the mountain range that bears Lapono's name and they founded the Lira chiefdom.[57]

When Lapono arrived in the area, at least ten lineages, all Eastern Nilotic, are remembered to have been already settled there. They were organized into two identifiable multiple-village groupings led by the Adyang and Bukol lineages. Eventually, these lineages would provide the core of a Lira Paluo chiefdom, the largest in eastern Acholi. But the only groups incorporated into an earlier Lira chiefdom seem to have been three more recent arrivals: the Luo Gweng of "Loka" (Paluo) and the Kucure and Paimot of uncertain origins. All three are remembered to have joined Lira during the reign of *Rwot* Lapono (c. 1680–1710).[58]

It was not until after the 1720s drought that lineages of the Adyang and Bukol groupings were incorporated, putting Lira on solid footing. The *rwot* who they joined was Lapono's son, Lira (c. 1710–40), and the process is examined in the next chapter. For now, the important point is that prior to the 1720s drought the chiefdom seems small and fragile; even its name derives from the person ruling when the drought struck, Lira, and not his predecessor and first *rwot*, Lapono.[59]

AJALI

Ajali is widely credited with instituting many Bunyoro/Paluo ideas and institutions in the southeastern zone. Traditions from both Ajali and its neighbors variously claim that Ajali introduced into the area the Luo

---

57. Webster A.H.T., pp. 50–51; Webster (1976b, p. 298). Contrast two Lira Lapono interviews that note no relationship with Patiko; see Garry A.H.T., pp. 49–58. Scattered Lira Paluo references in Crazzolara (1954, pp. 483, 486, 548–50) also omit any Patiko connections, emphasizing instead links with Patiko's fellow central-zone chiefdom, Payira. Lastly, Lira Paluo traditions collected by Wright (1934, p. 99) begin only with a new dynasty established after the 1720s drought.

58. See Webster A.H.T., pp. 50, 70; Webster (1976b, pp. 298–99).

59. Webster (1976b, p. 299).

language, the royal drum, the special royal *bwola* dance, and even the specific type of royal drums that could help make rain.[60]

The main difficulty with these traditions is that no reliable chronological framework exists for Ajali before a *rwot* named Arumo Odwong in the later eighteenth century (c. 1765–95). Given this, no agreement exists on the identity of the Ajali *rwot* or *rwodi* responsible for introducing the Bunyoro/Palwo innovations. Even though his reign is clearly too late, the most common name mentioned is *Rwot* Arumo. His name has probably been substituted for earlier ones for two reasons: because it is the first included in all extant Ajali *rwot* lists; and because Arumo is the most famous of all Ajali *rwodi*, primarily because he is remembered to have sacrificed his life to end a severe drought and famine (almost certainly that occurring around 1790).[61]

The lack of a chronological framework severely limits what we can learn about the early Ajali chiefdom. It is clear that the original royal lineage was called "Loka" (i.e., Paluo). This particular Loka *kal* appear to have established themselves near *Got* Akwang, just north of *Got* Amyel (see Map 4). The only available royal genealogy identifies two generations of rulers from the time that the group's eponym, Loka, left Paluo (reportedly because of throne disputes) until a successor dynasty was established after the drought of the 1720s. This would suggest a founding of the chiefdom toward the end of the seventeenth century.[62]

Traditions also indicate that Loka *kal* had a royal drum (or drums) and other regalia, including rainstones for "making" rain. And before they lost power, Loka *kal* seems to have brought two *lobong* lineages into Ajali. The first was called Jonam, which a Jonam elder claims came from Paluo with the Loka. These Luo origins are possible, given present-day Jonam's location along the Nile just north of Paluo and west of the old Luo triangle. But two other texts identify the lineage as originally from the *Got* Lapono area in the southeastern zone, which would strongly indicate Eastern Nilotic origins. Whatever its origins, this first *lobong* lineage in Ajali was responsible, at least under the second dynasty, for the chiefdom-wide *jok*, *Jok* Omwony. The second associated lineage was the Daya, from Labwor to the southeast of Acholi. Seemingly bilingual (Eastern Nilotic and Luo) when

60. Webster A.H.T., pp. 14, 46, 149, 151–52, 165, 170; also Webster (1976c, p. 336).
61. Ajali *rwot* lists can be found in Webster A.H.T., pp. 8, 141–42, 145–46, 165; and Wright (1934, p. 26). Arumo's name appears in Webster A.H.T., pp. 142, 151, 165–66.
62. See Webster A.H.T., pp. 8, 143, 154–55, 167–68.

they left Labwor, the Daya joined *Rwot* Loka after his arrival in the eventual southeastern zone.[63]

PATONGO

Patongo was the chiefdom most closely associated with Ajali, and the nature of the relationship is agreed upon in the traditions of both groups. The Ajali were the cultural and sociopolitical innovators, introducing Bunyoro/Paluo institutions and ideology; the Patongo, already settled in the area, learned about and adopted these from Ajali. The transfer may have spanned several generations and not always have proceeded smoothly. In two Ajali interviews, elders remembered that after Patongo adopted the *bwola* dance from Ajali, fighting broke out between the two polities over the dance.[64]

The origins of the Patongo ruling lineage are not as agreed upon as the group's cultural borrowings from Ajali. Some traditions claim that the eventual Patongo *kal* came from "Bunyoro" (i.e., Paluo); one version, provided by the descendant of the last traditional Patongo *rwot*, stated that the group originated at *Got* Amyel and came from nowhere else. But the most convincing picture emerges from traditions that link the royal lineages of Adilang and Patongo and identify the origins of the two related *kal* as Eastern Nilotic, and not Luo from Bunyoro. Such origins might be inadvertently supported by one version of Patongo *kal*'s migration traditions, which takes the group from Bunyoro east to (Eastern Nilotic) Karamoja and then back west again to *Got* Amyel. The Karamoja reference may well be historically reliable while Bunyoro has been simply tacked on as an assertion of Luoness. The historian who collected all these traditions, J. B. Webster, comes resolutely down on the side of Eastern Nilotic origins.[65]

Although one or two predecessors are identified in several versions of the Patongo *rwot* list, the first actual *rwot* of a Patongo chiefdom was undoubtedly its eponym, Otongo. Given a brief reference to famine in traditions associated with Otongo, but even stronger indications during the time of his successor, Atego, their reigns can be divided by the approximate

63. Ibid., pp. 142–45, 153–55, 167–68.

64. See Webster A.H.T., pp. 151–53, 170, and his comments on p. 205, n. 24. The first Ajali *rwot* associated with the fighting was the famous Arumo Odwong; as noted in the Ajali section, this chronological reference cannot be relied upon. Traditions in Wright (1934, p. 159) state simply that Patongo met Ajali near Amyel and that "both were independent groups of Palwo and had their own drums."

65. Patongo accounts come from Webster A.H.T., pp. 7, 14, 16 (which includes the Karamoja reference), 38; Wright (1934, p. 159). Adilang and Ajali traditions come from Webster A.H.T., pp. 21–22, 28–32, 38, 40, 151–52, 170. Finally, see Webster (1976c, p. 336).

beginning of the 1720s drought. Thus, Otongo is estimated to have ruled from around 1695 to 1725, while Atego and his brother Lugenyi are reckoned to have shared the next thirty-year dynastic generation, from around 1725 to 1755.[66]

All extant traditions from both Patongo and outsiders agree that Patongo *kal* was settled at *Got* Amyel from at least the time of Otongo. Traditions also agree that many prior inhabitants were settled along the same slopes, with most sources identifying one or more "Madi" (Central Sudanic) lineages, a majority of Eastern Nilotic groups, and perhaps a smattering of Luo. At least two, and probably three, of these lineages joined the young Patongo chiefdom during the time of *Rwot* Otongo: the Eastern Nilotic Wangdyang; the Lakwar from the Labwor hills (Eastern Nilotic or possibly Luo in origin, and likely bilingual); and probably a remnant "Madi" group. One Lakwar elder recounted that the Lakwar first asked Otongo and his lineage to join them. But then the Patongo *kal* were "given the rwotship," or were accepted as rulers, "because they had a royal drum, and because they could make rain."[67]

The introduction of new sociopolitical ideas and institutions into the Amyel area may have sparked conflict. Some traditions suggest that just prior to Otongo's successful incorporation of Patongo's first *lobong* lineages, the "Madi" and the Eastern Nilotic lineages settled around Amyel fought. These hostilities are depicted as based upon cultural and even ethnic differences, and the remembered result was an overwhelming victory for the Eastern Nilotic "side." But could the fighting, even though presented in terms of twentieth-century ethnic identities and consciousness, have been related to differing responses to the new ideas and institutions being introduced into the area in this period?[68]

Whatever the cause or nature of the conflict, it is remembered to have ended by the time that Otongo, drawing upon the ideology and practice of neighboring Ajali, became the first *rwot* of a Patongo chiefdom. Patongo soon proved more adept at utilizing the concepts and structures of the new

66. See Webster A.H.T., pp. 11, 13–14, 23, 29–30, 147–49; Wright (1934, p. 159); Webster (1976c, p. 336).

67. On the settlement of Patongo *kal* at Amyel, see Webster A.H.T., pp. 7, 13–14, 16, 20, 22, 28–32, 38, 152. See pp. 3, 7, 9, 13–15, and 20 for comparable but not identical lists of early Amyel groups, including the three identified as joining early Patongo (the quote is from p. 3); see also Webster (1976c, p. 345). Additional information, especially on the Lakwar, can be found in Ajali interviews in Webster A.H.T., pp. 151–52, 165–66, 169–70. These Ajali texts claim that the Lakwar broke away from the first Ajali ruling lineage.

68. The narrative is in Webster A.H.T., pp. 151–52; other references to these early "Madi" are on pp. 13–15.

order than Ajali, incorporating probably six *lobong* lineages before the 1720s drought. In addition to the three lineages noted above, early Patongo *lobong* included the Pateng who are remembered to have accompanied Patongo *kal* to Amyel; the Parenga from Orom to the northeast; and the Okol from Didinga beyond Orom. Their incorporation made early Patongo the largest chiefdom in all of the emergent southeastern zone. Except for the Central Sudanic "Madi," these lineages seem clearly Eastern Nilotic. References to cultural and linguistic practices in the area clearly identify it as Eastern Nilotic-dominated. Even the Lakwar, from the bilingual Labwor hills area, are remembered to have spoken Eastern Nilotic Jie, and they and the Parenga (along with others who became part of Patongo) supposedly wore "Karimojong-type" headdresses. There is even a reference to the Lakwar performing age-set ceremonies, a practice that later in eastern Acholi was directly linked with neighboring Eastern Nilotic Jie.[69]

PADER

The fourth chiefdom that seems to have emerged before around 1725 in what becomes the southeastern zone was Pader, in the *Got* Parabongo area (see Map 4). Evidence about the chiefdom's early history is limited and contradictory. This is not surprising given the vast changes that Pader underwent after the drought occurring around 1790, when it left Ogili for the south-central zone and became involved in a confederation with two other small polities, Kilak and Paipir. It is not even possible to identify the origins of early Pader's ruling lineage. One source suggests, on thin evidence, that the origins may have been "Loka" (Paluo) because "the drums of the 'ker' are of Bunyoro shape." The available sources do indicate that the first *rwot* of the chiefdom was its eponym, Der, and that he probably ruled during the early eighteenth century.[70]

Pader, like the other early chiefdoms in the emergent southeastern zone (except Patongo), seems to have remained small up to the 1720s drought. Available traditions suggest that one *lobong* lineage, the Lamogi, may have been incorporated. If there were others, memory of them has been lost following the dramatic changes experienced by Pader after the next major drought occurring around 1790.[71]

---

69. Webster A.H.T., pp. 7, 9, 13–15, 151–52.
70. Wright (1934, p. 77) and Webster A.H.T., pp. 108, 111; these sources also identify Der's successor as his son, Lukweny Arata.
71. Webster A.H.T., pp. 110–11.

Conclusion

The 1720s drought ended the first phase of chiefdom formation and development of a common social order and political culture in north-central Uganda. This phase was marked by the initial establishment in the area of the fundamental institutions and ideology of sociopolitical organization that gradually came to characterize and help define an emergent Acholi. By the 1720s this process was still in its beginning stages, affecting only a small number of people in a few scattered locations. The next phase, from about 1725 to 1790, would see the process extended to include virtually all of Acholi and the peoples therein.

One distinctive characteristic of the first phase was that the ruling lineages of at least nine of the initial eleven chiefdoms were recent immigrants into north-central Uganda from Paluo or the adjacent Luo triangle. This correlation between Paluo/Luo-triangle origins and chiefly rule in Acholi continued in the southeastern and east-central zones but not others. In the northern and especially western Acholi zones, Paluo or other Luo-speaking lineages were rare. We can see a hint of what is to come in the example of Patongo. Its royal lineage did not consist of recent immigrants from Luo-speaking areas but an earlier, resident, Eastern Nilotic group. After the 1720s drought the number of non-Luo lineages among the ranks of royal lineages would rise significantly.

Something else that would increase after the 1720s drought is the role of separate-group, non-narrative traditions for understanding the emergence, growth, and functioning of chiefdoms in Acholi. In contrast, the way that narrative traditions depict the establishment of chiefdoms does not change. Narrative traditions often do not support a late-seventeenth- or eighteenth-century date for the founding of chiefdoms; instead, for ideological reasons, earlier origins are often indicated. Despite this dominant message of narrative traditions, however (during both the first and second phases of chiefdom formation in Acholi), actual chiefdom origins are revealed by a number of clues — sometimes from non-narrative traditions, often by initial references to tribute or royal drums, two of the fundamental attributes of the new polities (see Chapter 1).

Finally, the experience of these earliest chiefdoms demonstrates that the establishment of the new ideas and institutions in north-central Uganda was neither quick nor easy. In a period that extended approximately fifty years, only eleven chiefdoms seem to have been successfully established —

ten of them in just two of the eight zones of Acholi. And of the eleven, only Patiko in the emergent central zone and Patongo in the southeast incorporated more than three or four outside lineages during this period. Two appear to have incorporated none. The succeeding two generations will witness a remarkable deepening and broadening of this process in greatly altered material conditions following the 1720s drought.

Part Three

The Extension and
Entrenchment of the New
Order, c. 1725–90

5. The Southeastern Zone: The New Order Takes Hold

The first phase of chiefdom formation in north-central Uganda was brought to a close and the second phase set in motion by the 1720s drought. The resulting famine and related upheavals created conditions in which many more chiefdoms than before were established, and over a much wider area. All of the eventual eight zones of Acholi experienced the formation of new chiefdoms or the consolidation of old ones after the drought. With the exception of the old Luo triangle, which was excluded from this process and remains largely unpopulated today, the extension of the new sociopolitical order from about 1725 to 1790 marked out the geographical contours and boundaries of what would become Acholi.

The changes associated with this process were not only extended geographically after the 1720s drought, they were accelerated. Only eleven chiefdoms had been established during the approximately two generations before the drought. During the two generations after, almost sixty additional chiefdoms were founded. Furthermore, the vast majority of lineages in Acholi joined one of the chiefdoms, as opposed to the few incorporated before the drought.

The second phase of chiefdom formation and related social change produced a broadly common historical experience, social order, and political culture among virtually the entire population of north-central Uganda. These developments in turn established foundations for the evolution of an Acholi society and collective identity. No such foundations existed before about 1725. By the end of the century they had been firmly ensconced.

It is no mere coincidence that extraordinary sociohistorical change began with the severe drought of the 1720s. References to this drought or its effects are found in the traditions of many Acholi chiefdoms and beyond, most of which indicate extensive, even massive, hardship and disruption.[1]

---

1. Acholi references appear throughout this and later chapters. Lamphear (1971, pp. 15–17; 1973. pp. 82–115; 1974; 1976, pp. 33–52, 108–12) presents a methodology for using regularly spaced Jie generation sets for dating and argues for a 1720s date for this drought. Nile

The drought created vastly altered material conditions and social relations, providing fertile ground for a new social order and political leadership promising more security and stability. This is just what the new *rwodi* and their chiefdoms offered. In this context, more and more chiefdoms established themselves in Acholi over the eighteenth century, incorporating ever-greater numbers of lineages. As this occurred, the problems for lineages not yet part of a chiefdom multiplied; they were increasingly isolated, exposed, and out of step.

While post-drought conditions created pressures for people in Acholi to join larger political entities, the increase in scale was limited. Less than 25 percent of chiefdoms in Acholi by the end of the eighteenth century seem to have consisted of even 2,500 people, or more than ten village-lineages. Most were probably less than half that size (see Appendix). One probable reason for this was that the chiefdoms of emergent Acholi had no large polities to compete or fight against. The only truly large-scale polity in the vicinity was Bunyoro-Kitara. But despite providing the model for the new order in Acholi, Bunyoro-Kitara had minimal contact with and exerted virtually no political pressure on Acholi. Instead, its energies concentrated on internal affairs and relations with other large kingdoms farther south.

Even after people joined one of the chiefdoms in Acholi, they continued to function within an essentially face-to-face political culture. Becoming part of a chiefdom did not mean giving up the opportunity for personal interaction with those in authority. In fact, much that was central to political rule in the Acholi chiefdoms assumed such relations. This was how individuals and groups were integrated initially and maintained their sense of belonging, how disputes were arbitrated and resolved, and how tribute service and payments were rendered and redistributed.

The extension of the new order throughout Acholi did not mean that change proceeded everywhere in the same manner. In what becomes the southeastern zone, for example, eighteen new chiefdoms were founded between about 1725 and 1790, and two of the four already present had their dynasties replaced by new ones. In the neighboring east-central zone, fourteen chiefdoms developed. These two zones thus contained more than half the chiefdoms in all of Acholi by the end of the eighteenth century. In contrast, the northwestern and northeastern zones were home for no more than four or five chiefdoms between them.

---

level charts compiled by Tousson (1925) show a falling trend in low flood levels between 1722 and 1731; following Cohen (1974b), this trend indicates a rainfall shortage and probable drought in the East African lakes region c. 1723–25. Finally, see also Webster (1979b).

Three particular circumstances contributed to the establishment of so many chiefdoms in the southeastern and east-central zones. First, the line demarcating the poorest reliable rainfall region in Acholi passes through the southeastern zone and near the east-central zone. The 1720s drought undoubtedly hit the two zones hard, even as they were inundated by immigrants from even more devastated areas. Such conditions would have made the security and stability promised by the new chiefdoms especially attractive.

A second ingredient to so many chiefdoms being founded in the two zones was the nearness of the Labwor-Otuke hills, a key source of migrants after the 1720s drought. Before its inhabitants were scattered by the drought, the hills were a socially, politically, and linguistically mixed area that included a number of Paluo immigrants and chiefdoms based on the Bunyoro/Paluo model.

Third, the drought helped set in motion, just to the east of Acholi, the evolution of a contrasting society and identity called Jie. In what is now northern Karamoja District, Eastern Nilotic speakers began to develop a common social order and collective identity. This new order was not organized around agriculturally based chiefdoms, but a highly elaborated and structured age-generation organization closely tied to cattle herding. Over the eighteenth and nineteenth centuries, emergent Jie and Acholi social orders jostled against each other as they established their own identities, territorial claims, and ways of interacting with neighbors. In the process, significant complexity and sometimes hostility were generated. The areas of Acholi most affected by all this were the emergent southeastern and east-central zones.[2]

The Staging Areas for the New Order

The two principal staging areas for the establishment of the new sociopolitical order in what became the southeastern and east-central zones were the Labwor-Otuke hills just outside the southeastern zone and the *Got* Okaka area within the east-central zone (Map 5).

Although Labwor-Otuke receives only twenty to thirty inches of dependable rainfall per year, perennial springs and the extra margin of safety

2. On Jie history, see John Lamphear's work as part of the History of Uganda Project (e.g., 1970, 1971, 1972, 1973, 1976).

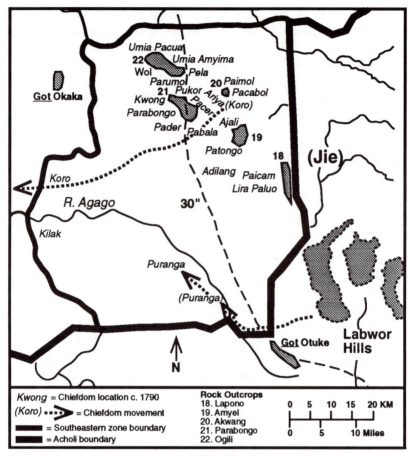

Map 5. Southeastern zone, c. 1725-90.

provided by the hills have made the area an attractive settlement site. "Like water into a catchment area," Herring writes, many groups

> have moved into the hills in search of food, water and protection. In the good years, when the rains were plentiful . . . the movement was slow. In those years when rainfall was poor or late in coming . . . the flow quickened and the . . . area became in these periods a melting pot where languages and customs joined and new ethnic groups were born. But then, in times of drought and famine, the inflow of people became a torrent which overwhelmed the re-sources of the hills and forced large numbers of hungry refugees south and west in search of food.

Beginning in probably the late fifteenth or sixteenth centuries, at least two or three major waves each of Eastern Nilotic- and Luo-speaking groups were included in the cycle Herring depicts, passing into Labwor-Otuke and then back out again.[3]

Evidence on the Labwor-Otuke hills before the seventeenth or eighteenth centuries is part of the area's "absent past" and is both scanty and suspect. It seems that early Luo-speaking migrants into the hills were part of two broader Luo movements, both of which extended as far south as eastern Uganda and western Kenya. One was an eastern stream that moved south through what is now Karamoja District, leaving small groups settled along the way, including Labwor-Otuke. The second stream was formed by Luo speakers who left northern Bunyoro and the Luo triangle to travel east, before branching both north and south. Some descendants of these early Luo eventually moved into Acholi, as purveyors of a new sociopolitical order and as ruling lineages of chiefdoms within it. But they had no such position in the Labwor-Otuke hills before the late seventeenth and early eighteenth centuries.[4]

Herring identifies the emergence during the seventeenth century of four broad, ethnolinguistically mixed communities in the hills area: (1) a "Labwor cluster" in and just north of the Labwor hills; (2) a "Lango cluster" in the eastern portion of present-day Lango District; (3) a "Miro cluster" in central Karamoja east and south of Labwor-Otuke; and (4) a "Bako cluster" in western Jie just northeast of the hills (Map 6). Each contained originally Eastern Nilotic, Luo, and smaller minority groups, and over the century most people in the region probably became bilingual, speaking Eastern Nilotic and Luo languages. All were grain agriculturalists, with small stock but few cattle.[5]

The limited extant traditions of these mixed communities give no hint of strife, either within or among them, until two new components were added. The first was the arrival in the late seventeenth century of Paluo groups and ideas. Their appearance "essentially divided the people between

3. The quote is from Herring (1976b, pp. 372–73); for pre-nineteenth-century developments, see Herring (1974b, section I; 1979b); Lamphear (1970; 1971; chaps. 3–5 of both 1973 and 1976); and Crazzolara (1960).

4. For discussions of both wings of Luo migrants, see Cohen (1974a); Herring (1974b, pp. 87–91, 97–103); Herring, Cohen, and Ogot (1984); Cohen and Odhiambo (1989, pp. 15–22). These sources and Ogot (1967a) suggest that these Luo began to arrive in eastern Uganda and western Kenya in the sixteenth century. See also Lamphear (1971, pp. 5–7); Herring (1979b, pp. 292–94); and Webster (n.d. [a]).

5. See Herring (1974b, pp. 109–23; 1979b, pp. 294–99). Both Lamphear (1976, pp. 99, 112) and Webster A.H.T., pp. 63, 152 provide support for bilingualism in Labwor-Otuke.

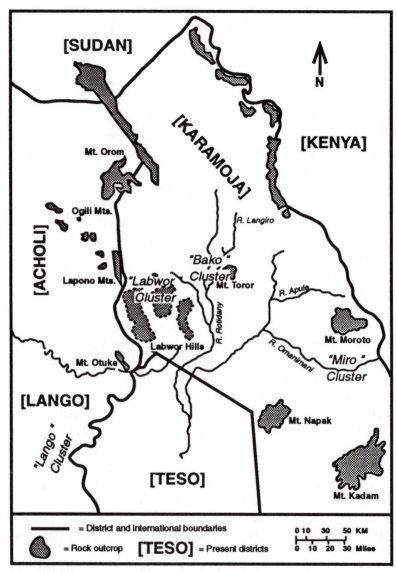

Map 6. Major communities in the Labwor-Otuke Hills and surrounding areas east and south of Acholi, c. 1700. Adapted from Herring (1974c, p. 14a). Used by permission of the author.

those who accepted the new leadership, those who maintained their autonomy but accepted their socio-political concepts, and those who rejected
both." These divisions affected every type of community in and around the
hills, though with their shared language, Luo-speaking groups seem to
have been somewhat more likely to follow the Paluo lead. But there was no
guarantee of a unified response even within individual lineages, and some
split up over this issue.[6]

No Acholi ruling lineage has traditions detailing their adoption in the
Labwor-Otuke hills of the sociopolitical order derived from Bunyoro/
Paluo. For example, when I asked Reverend A. O. Latigo about the origins
of the Koro royal drum, a key component of the new order, he knew no
specific stories. But, he added, "I know that when they came from Otuke
[after the 1720s drought] they had their royal drum."[7]

The advent of the Paluo and their institutions and ideology seem to
have upset the status quo and increased unrest in the hills area. But the
disruption remained minor until the 1720s drought. Communities in the
hills area had developed sophisticated agricultural techniques, but they
were still dependent on rainfall that was always limited and unpredictable.
When the rains failed repeatedly during the 1720s, one disaster followed
another. Severe famine, caused by both drought and locusts, intensified
divisions already generated by Paluo immigrants and ideas. The hills area
erupted into war, and many of the pre-1720s communities disintegrated.
Some groups eventually reformed; others contributed to new and different
communities in-the-making, including the Jie, Langi, Karimojong, Labwor, Nyakwai, Iteso, and Acholi.[8]

One favored destination for displaced Labwor-Otuke groups was the
Got Okaka area. *Got* Okaka and neighboring peaks are the most prominent
in all of east-central Acholi, providing a natural magnet for any groups
moving into the area. Many of the Labwor-Otuke migrants to Okaka
appear Luo or Paluo in origin; all seem to have spoken Luo as one of their
languages and to have had some experience of Bunyoro/Paluo institutions
and ideology. When they arrived at Okaka, they came into contact with
both older inhabitants and an influx of Paluo from northern Bunyoro
moving into the Okaka area at about the same time. Many of these migrants

6. See Herring (1974b, pp. 150–51); Webster (n.d. [a]) includes an account of the
many Paluo groups in the hills area.

7. A.H.T. 273.

8. Herring (1979b, pp. 294–99).

subsequently moved on, mostly to the north and east, providing the core, and often ruling lineages, of new chiefdoms.[9]

The Southeastern Zone

The influx of migrants from Labwor-Otuke and *Got* Okaka into the southeastern zone was important in three ways. Of initial importance were simply the numbers of migrants. At least thirty, and probably forty or more lineages came from Labwor-Otuke and Okaka after about 1725. Second, these migrants included the ruling lineages of twelve to sixteen new chiefdoms—the vast majority of new chiefdoms founded in the zone between about 1725 and 1790. Third, these Labwor-Otuke and Okaka immigrants spoke Luo as at least one of their languages, and their arrival marked the first time that Luo was widely spoken in the southeastern zone. All of these features helped create and nurture the dense social networks among the inhabitants of the area that led to its emergence as a definable southeastern zone.[10]

Important as they were, these Labwor-Otuke and Okaka migrants were only part of a complex mosaic of peoples in the zone—some long-settled residents, others recent immigrants uprooted by the drought or its after effects. This mix of peoples, speaking different languages and representing different social, cultural, and political backgrounds produced a volatile social climate. In this climate, eighteen chiefdoms were established in just two generations—more than in any zone in Acholi. The transformation even affected two of the four chiefdoms already present in the area, as the ruling lineages of both Lira and Ajali were replaced by new dynasties.

Most of the new chiefdoms developed along a range of mountains and hills stretching diagonally across the zone. The greatest concentration was near the peaks furthest northwest: the Ogili, Parabongo, and Akwang. Fourteen new chiefdoms clustered there, joining the earlier established Pader. Two other early chiefdoms, Patongo and Ajali, were located just to the southeast, near *Got* Amyel. The remainder of this chapter focuses on this small but intensive region of chiefdom formation (see Map 5).

---

9. The most extensive discussion of developments in the *Got* Okaka region is in Garry (1974b, pp. 1–51); see also Garry (1976, pp. 321–25).

10. Webster (1976a, p. 229); Webster's work on the southeastern zone in general is indispensable. See esp. 1976a, 1976b, 1976c, and his field texts (Webster A.H.T.). My reading of the texts and his, however, do not always agree.

Meanwhile, *Got* Lapono, the part of the range that is farthest southeast, became home for Paicam and Lira Paluo, the latter a successor to the older Lira polity. This entire range of hills and mountains provided both protection from possible enemies and a potentially significant margin of security during drought, with their perpetual springs and hardy, drought-resistant plants. Despite the attractions of the mountains, however, a few chiefdoms — Adilang, Puranga, and Kilak — ventured out onto the southeastern zone plains. These last five southeastern-zone polities, along with those of the neighboring east-central zone, are discussed in Chapter 6.[11]

The Ogili-Parabongo-Akwang Area

There are three probable explanations for the emergence of so many chiefdoms in the Ogili-Parabongo-Akwang region. First, these were the outcrops in the zone furthest removed from the sometimes unsettled and contested boundary being established with the divergently developing Jie. Second, they are the only peaks in the zone that can count on more than thirty inches of rainfall per year. And third, these are the outcrops nearest the *Got* Okaka region some thirty kimometers (twenty miles) due west. Of the fourteen new chiefdoms founded in the Ogili-Parabongo-Akwang area, the ruling lineages of nine have traditions linking them to Okaka. Eight of the nine and four others also have traditions of ties to Labwor-Otuke, as indicated in Figure 3.

Of these fifteen chiefdoms, Paimol and Umia Anyima have the most extensive traditions available on the eighteenth century. They are particularly rich in the non-narrative, separate-group traditions that can provide traces of historical social dynamics and social relations unobtainable from narrative traditions alone (see Chapter 1). These traces include (1) evidence on polity-wide ritual, particularly the two major ceremonies of the agricultural cycle, the planting and harvest ceremonies; (2) evidence on interactions and negotiations accompanying the incorporation of outsiders into chiefdoms; and (3) evidence on internal structuring within chiefdoms and on particular roles played by constituent village-lineages and their heads. Paimol and Umia Anyima traditions also reinforce the significance of the symbols, institutions, and ideology of chiefly rule at the core of the new social order and the political culture being established throughout Acholi.

11. See Webster (1976a, pp. 219–20).

FIGURE 3.   Traditions of Links with Okaka and Labwor-Otuke Among the
Ogili-Parabongo-Akwang Ruling Lineages.

Chiefdom	Traditions of Okaka Links	Traditions of Labwor-Otuke Links
Paimol	Yes	Yes
Pukor	Yes	Yes
Umia Anyima	Yes	Yes
Umia Pacua	Yes	Yes
Parabongo	Yes	Yes
Pabala	Yes	Yes
Kwong	Yes	Yes
Pacer	Yes	Yes
Wol	Yes	No
Parumo	No (?)	Yes
Pacabol	No	Yes
Koro	No	Yes
Ariya	No	Yes
Pela	No	No
The earlier-established Pader	No	No

Accordingly, these two polities will be the primary focus of this section,
with the other chiefdoms in the area being treated much more briefly.

PAIMOL AND ITS "BROTHER" CHIEFDOM, PUKOR

Paimol was established at the base of *Got* Akwang during the first generation following the 1720s drought. Sources agree that the chiefdom's first
rwot was its eponym, Omol (estimated dates of rule 1720–50), and that he
and his lineage came from Paluo via *Got* Okaka. Some versions add that
Omol was one of a set of royal brothers, sons of a Bunyoro/Paluo *rwot*.[12]

These same versions place Omol and his followers within a wider
movement of Paluo groups to the *Got* Okaka area. Many traditions bring
the associated Paluo groups to Okaka by way of Labwor-Otuke; others,
including the most explicit renditions of Paimol *kal*'s migration, depict a
more westerly route through central Acholi. Perhaps some Paimol *kal*
traditions ignore a sojourn in the predominantly Eastern Nilotic Labwor-

12. Omol's suggested dates of rule are extremely tentative because there is no agreed-
upon list of successors. *Rwot* lists and associated traditions from many southeastern- and east-
central-zone polities, however, point overwhelmingly to post-1720 origins for the chiefdoms
that emerged from the broad Paluo movements of which Paimol was a part; though see
alternative chronologies in Garry (1974b, pp. 12–15); Webster and Herring (1975); Webster
(n.d. [b]).

Otuke hills in order to assert a more direct connection with Paluoland and the institutions and ideology derived from there.[13]

However Omol's group reached Okaka, it is remembered to have included his "brother" Okor. The two are also remembered to have continued on together to the Ogili-Parabongo-Akwang range, where they and their respective followers separated. Most accounts indicate that the separation was originally amicable but turned hostile following the death of one or more children of Omol at the hands of Okor.[14]

This story may recount the first example of a southeastern zone chiefdom experiencing succession during its formative first or second generation. Whether secession actually occurred in this case is clouded by subsequent Pukor developments. Okor's line was displaced by another, which claims that Okor was not a "true" *rwot* (though the Pukor name alone suggests otherwise). Whether it had one ruling dynasty or two, Pukor was always "junior" to Paimol; it never emerged from under the shadow of its more prominent and powerful neighbor.[15]

When Omol and his followers reached *Got* Akwang, they met at least one and probably two lineages already settled there. The first was Taa, led by a man named Acut. Almost certainly Eastern Nilotic (one elder claimed that they were speaking "Lango Jie"), the Taa have no traditions of coming from anywhere else and are universally acknowledged as the earliest inhabitants of the area.[16]

13. See Crazzolara (1954, p. 521); Wright (1934, p. 132); Anywar (1954, pp. 100, 112); Garry (1974b, pp. 12–16a); Webster A.H.T., pp. 80, 88. Though I disagree with her chronology, Garry's reconstruction is the most comprehensive and convincing.

14. See Crazzolara (1954, p. 521); Wright (1934, p. 132); Anywar (1954, p. 112); Webster A.H.T. 88, 91–92. The first two do not discuss troubles between Omol and Okor and identify other "brothers" of Omol, including the founders of the Parabongo and Parumo chiefdoms.

15. On Pukor chiefdom traditions see Wright (1934, p. 166); Webster A.H.T., pp. 100–105. The latter discusses the change in dynasty and identifies the following lineages: (1) Awora (hunters and gatherers, perhaps Eastern Nilotic), (2) Okor (Paluo, the "brothers" of Paluo *kal* in Paimol), (3) Panmalo (new *kal*, claim to have come from Paluo via Payira), (4) Kaboye (Eastern Nilotic), (5) Pairom (Eastern Nilotic), (6) Karom (same as number 5?), and (7) Kapel (from Labwor, not clear whether Eastern Nilotic or Luo). Despite tracing their origins to Pajok in northernmost Acholi, the Pukor lineage in the chiefdom of Kilak (Chap. 6) claims to be so closely related to Panmalo *kal* that the two do not intermarry "even today"; see Webster A.H.T., p. 114.

16. See Wright (1934, p. 132); Anywar (1954, p. 113); and Webster A.H.T., pp. 80, 86, 93–94, 96–97. One source refers to the Taa as "owner of the place," or *wegi ngom*; see Webster A.H.T., p. 94. All agree that Omol and his followers met the Taa, and the Atura may have been present as well. In addition, Omol's followers may have included a lineage called Boi. See Webster A.H.T., pp. 80–81, 88, 196 (n. 11); Anywar (1954, p. 113). Neither Wright (1934, p. 135) nor Crazzolara (1954, p. 550) include Boi in their lists of Paimol lineages.

Three brief renditions of Omol's and Acut's meeting have been collected, over a thirty-five-year period:

1. "Acut had a little drum and a small spear but when he saw the drum . . . which Omol had brought from Loka [Paluo] and his Tong ker [royal spear] he said 'I have a man's blood on my hands. I cannot be chief. I will accept you as my lord.'"

2. "Omol found that the people of Acut were living on top of Mt. Akwang. . . . Later Omol ruled over these people as well as his own because he had a royal drum."

3. "Acut was the first clan to settle in Paimol before Omol came. . . . Omol brought the royal Palwo clan here. Acut was living when he arrived. Omol offered the royal drum and spear to Acut but he said that he did not know anything about such things. So Omol took over the rwotship."[17]

Though limited, these traditions convey two significant messages. First, all emphasize Omol's possession of a royal drum and indicate that this symbol of political leadership was a factor in Acut's acceptance of Omol as *rwot*. The claim in the first passage that Acut had a "small" drum and spear (unsupported by other traditions) serves to assert a degree of status for Acut as a leader—though he was clearly not a *rwot*. The second message is that the process of interaction between Omol and Acut was a peaceful one, with some sort of negotiations involved.

A likely component of those negotiations is intimated by the subsequent position of the Taa lineage and its head as the foremost ritual figures in the chiefdom, responsible for the main polity-wide *jok*, *Jok* Karaka. Located on *Got* Akwang, Karaka has been described as "the spirit of food, good health, hunting and production." Among the most important of the regular ceremonies associated with the *jok* was the annual harvest (*gwelo*) ceremony.[18]

Since harvest ceremonies were performed by most chiefdoms across Acholi, it is worth describing Paimol's in some detail here. First, Taa lineage elders would go throughout the chiefdom collecting small quantities of new millet. This would be presented to *Jok* Karaka and then brought to the *rwot*, who would "taste" the first fruits of the harvest. Next, lineage heads, in

17. Wright (1934, p. 133); Anywar (1954, p. 113); Webster A.H.T., p. 80.
18. See Webster A.H.T., pp. 82–83, 99; Anywar (1954, p. 135).

front of their respective ancestral shrines (*abila*), would sample the new millet crop. Only after this could others begin to eat it. Then the Taa lineage would call all the people to assemble before *Jok* Karaka. Every household was to bring cooked food made from the millet and other crops grown that year, a pot of millet beer, and, for the Taa lineage head, a portion of uncooked millet that one source said amounted "to about four baskets full." All people brought their weapons and hunting nets to be blessed as part of the ceremonies, and the *rwot* provided a he-goat to be sacrificed. A large and joyous feast of thanksgiving then ensued.[19]

Features of this Paimol harvest ceremony that are significant and widespread include the central role of the polity-wide *jok* and the non-royal lineage and lineage head responsible for it; the secondary but still important roles played by other lineage heads and the *rwot*; and the participation and celebration of all the people of the chiefdom.

The next lineage incorporated was Atura. All sources concur on their Eastern Nilotic origin and their close association with the Taa. But there is disagreement on whether the Atura were settled near the Taa at Akwang before *Rwot* Omol appeared. Outsiders say no; an Atura source insists that they were. The latter also suggests that the Atura were not as welcoming of Omol as were Acut and the Taa. The Atura did not overtly oppose Omol but are remembered to have resented the reduction of their sovereignty and independence when brought under his rule (symbolically represented by the supposed loss of a "small drum").

Just as the Taa played a central ritual role in the chiefdom, the Atura came to hold a key political position. The Atura head was what Paimol elders called the first *jago* of the chiefdom. This meant that he was the senior councilor of the *rwot*. He may have been given a small drum as a symbol of his position, and, once Paimol grew, he even seems to have been head of a territorial sub-grouping within the chiefdom.[20]

The third lineage to be incorporated was the Kudeng. Also Eastern Nilotic, the Kudeng are remembered to have been such a small group when they arrived at Akwang from Karamoja that they first settled with *Rwot* Omol and *kal*. One rendition of Kudeng traditions states that the group left Karamoja because of famine — almost certainly that of the 1720s. When the Kudeng settled with *kal*, their head was not only given the task of looking

19. Ibid.
20. See Wright (1934, p. 135); Anywar (1954, p. 113); Webster A.H.T., pp. 81, 93–96. The last notes that the Atura lost their position as *jago* when most lineage moved west after the drought of c. 1790.

after the royal *abila* (a prominent ritual role), he was also made *lakwena*. This term was typically used in the southeastern zone to mean one of the *rwot*'s councilors, while its plural (*lukwena*) described the collective assembly of councilors, or, as Webster often translated it, "council of the *rwot*."[21]

As caretakers of the royal *abila*, the Kudeng played an important role in the chiefdom-wide planting ceremony. This ceremony, like Paimol's harvest ceremony discussed above, was typical of those held in chiefdoms across Acholi. Its essential features included polity-wide participation and celebration, a propitiation of the ancestors of the *rwot* to help bring rain, and a major role for the *rwot* and his royal regalia in the proceedings while a non-royal lineage led the ritual performance per se.[22]

Paimol's particular planting ceremony proceeded as follows. Just before the time to plant, all the people of Paimol assembled at the royal *abila* located at the foot of *Got* Akwang. Each lineage brought a he-goat to be sacrificed at the *abila*. The contents of the goats' intestines were sprinkled around the *abila*, on the nearby graves of previous *rwodi*, and then on the chests of the people present, after which the goats were cooked and eaten as part of a large feast. The Kudeng prepared the *abila* and royal graves and helped in sacrificing the goats. There would also be dancing, both that day at the *abila* and the next at the *rwot*'s, where the royal drum would be played and the special *bwola* dance performed. The ceremony and celebration, especially the dancing, were to encourage rain.

The following day people were permitted to begin work in the fields, carrying with them seeds distributed by the *rwot* that had been mixed with soil from around the *abila*. They also carried with them the *rwot*'s strong admonition not to fight "with their neighbor or their wives." "If anyone did fight," Paimol traditions continue, "he had to pay one she-goat for the chief and one he-goat which was slaughtered for purifying the soil of the chief [at the royal *abila*]." The same traditions add that after working for about a

21. On the Kudeng, see Anywar (1954, p. 113); Webster A.H.T., pp. 81–82, 92–93, 97. On the harvest ceremony and the Kudeng role in it, see especially Anywar (1954, pp. 133–34). For briefer references to planting ceremonies, including minor differences from Anywar, see Webster A.H.T., pp. 83, 96, 99. For Crazzolara's definition of *lakwena*, see Crazzolara (1938, p. 276).

22. While the emphasis here is on the leading role of a non-royal lineage in planting-ceremony ritual, planting ceremonies also provided a crucial forum for the *rwot* to display his rainmaking prowess and regalia (often the royal drum). Especially in the context of the generation following the 1720s drought (when most Acholi chiefdoms were founded) such displays were almost surely an important determinant in the successful spread of the new chiefly order in Acholi.

week in their own fields, the lineages were called upon in turn to provide tribute labor to prepare the fields of the *rwot*.[23]

The last two lineages clearly incorporated by *Rwot* Omol were the Karuke and Loka. Each is remembered to have been large when it joined Paimol. The Karuke, as the others incorporated previously, were Eastern Nilotic in origin. The Loka, though, were surely an exception, as their name is a synonym for Paluo. As had their predecessors, both the Karuke and Loka received special places in the new chiefdom. The Karuke provided another councilor, or *lakwena*, to advise the *rwot*; the Loka lineage head became the chiefdom's second *jago*. Perhaps because of their size, the Karuke and Loka are remembered to have made up a territorial sub-grouping under the Loka *jago* (with the other comprised of *kal*, Taa, Atura, and Kudeng). Such sub-groupings were extremely rare in Acholi, and this case seems particularly puzzling given Paimol's few village-lineages. Perhaps the division did not occur until the six lineages noted above were joined by others in the nineteenth century.[24]

The limited evidence available on post-Omol developments in Paimol suggests that no additional lineages would join the chiefdom during the eighteenth century. The only references to events before the drought occurring around 1790 indicate fighting with nearby Pader and Pabala over hunting grounds and some Jie attacks to steal Paimol cattle.[25]

Considered together, the narrative and non-narrative traditions of Paimol's early chiefdom history provide important and representative examples of both the process of chiefdom formation in Acholi and the ways that extant traditions depict that process. These include:

1. the highlighting of the royal drum as a key symbol of the new sociopolitical order;

---

23. Anywar (1954, p. 134).

24. On the Karuke, see Webster A.H.T., pp. 81–82, 93, 98–100. On the Loka, see ibid., pp. 80–81, 85–87, 90–91, 93, 96, as well as Ajali references that identify the group as part of Ajali's original Paluo *kal* (pp. 143, 145, 154, 162, 167–68); see also two brief and suspect references in Anywar (1954, p. 113) and Wright (1934, p. 132). Two sets of elders suggested that Paimol *jagi* had councilors of their own who also sat on the *rwot*'s council, giving the Atura and Loka, in effect, double representation.

25. See Webster A.H.T., p. 94. This contrasts with Webster's first Paimol text (pp. 80–81), based on a large group interview, where every lineage was associated with the chiefdom's founder Omol. Alternative views only emerged in separate-group traditions. Evidence on post-Omol events comes from Wright (1934, p. 133). Ajali traditions claim that Paimol under *Rwot* Omol also fought with Ajali; see Webster A.H.T., p. 145.

2. the acknowledgement by the new rulers of the ritual primacy of the oldest lineage recognized in the area, and the extension of that lineage's ritual role to encompass the chiefdom as a whole;

3. the significance of chiefdom-wide ritual in such crucial realms as planting and harvesting, and the importance of both royal and non-royal lineages in such ritual;

4. the important role of the *rwot* (and in this instance the royal drum) in rainmaking; and

5. the negotiation and accommodation accompanying the incorporation of outsiders into the chiefdom (all the lineages to join Paimol in its formative stage negotiated for or were given special places in the structures of the chiefdom).

But not everything about Paimol was so typical. For example, political and ritual leadership in Paimol seems to have become remarkably fixed in this formative period. When other lineages, even large ones, were brought in after the drought occurring around 1790, they neither played special roles in polity-wide ritual nor provided councilors to the *rwot*. This virtual exclusion of later lineages and their heads from polity-wide positions of leadership was highly unusual. Even rarer was both the term *jago* and its eventual meaning in Paimol: the head of a distinct territorial sub-grouping within the chiefdom.[26]

Umia Anyima

Umia Anyima was one of five chiefdoms that developed near *Got* Ogili, some twenty to twenty-five kilometers (twelve to fifteen miles) northeast of Akwang. Its ruling lineage, like Paimol's, claims royal status in Paluoland and was part of the Paluo movement through the *Got* Okaka region. Just as *Rwot* Omol met and incorporated mainly Eastern Nilotic lineages at *Got* Akwang, so did Umia Anyima's first *rwot*, Otim, at *Got* Ogili. When *Rwot* Otim arrived, many other groups were living near Ogili as well, some organized as independent village-lineages, others as multiple-village group-

26. In both Lira Paluo and Ajali, Webster was told that the term *jago* was not used until the British introduced it; see Webster A.H.T., pp. 65, 157. Neither the term nor concept was common in central and western Acholi. Elders from five chiefdoms there reported that the term meant special or senior councilors; see A.H.T. 214, 226, 255, 285–86, and 309–10. No evidence exists that any central or western Acholi chiefdom of this period had territorial sub-divisions or functionaries like the *jagi* described above. The largest Acholi chiefdom, Payira, seems the most likely candidate, as Anywar (1954, pp. 491–92) suggests and Webster (1976b, pp. 295–96, 313) accepts. But the "small chieftainships" listed by Anywar within Payira turn out to be either branches of the Payira royal lineage or neighboring small chiefdoms.

ings, and some as the emergent chiefdoms of Umia Pacua, Wol, Pukor, and Pela.[27]

The earliest extant Umia Anyima traditions, collected by Father Crazzolara in the 1940s, have Otim (who ruled c. 1720–50) and his Paluo *kal* lineage traveling to the *Got* Okaka region, then to Loka Pel near Akwang. Two Eastern Nilotic lineages at Ogili, the Ngoliya (the earliest inhabitants in the area and *wegi ngom*) and the Paitook, heard that a "royal" was nearby. Having no *rwot* of their own, they sent a delegation to ask Otim to become their ruler. To entice Otim to Ogili, they pointed out that the Paitook had earlier moved away from Loka Pel because of drought. Persuaded, Otim and his people moved to Ogili and began the new chiefdom of Umia Anyima, with the Ngoliya and Paitook as the first *lobong*. The new chiefdom's name, Crazzolara adds, was derived in part from the fact that initially the incorporated lineages "spoke Lwoo language badly: *nyimi-nyimi.*" As a final point, Otim and his lineage are not presented in this account as larger or stronger but as the purveyors of a more prestigious and "advanced" culture.[28]

When Umia Anyima traditions were next collected, in the early 1970s, the Ngoliya had either died off or moved away. Memory of their role in the origin of the chiefdom had faded as well. The new version claims that when Otim and Paluo *kal* came to Ogili they met the multiple-village grouping of Mota, Melong, and Kanyum, as well as the separate Paitook and Kunledi lineages. None had a *rwot*. The oldest lineage at Ogili is now identified as the Mota, a status accorded them by elders from many lineages. The Mota are also acknowledged as having led their multiple-village grouping into the new chiefdom, a process that seems both symbolized and cemented by the marriage of *Rwot* Otim and a Mota woman. Each of the three lineage heads also became a councilor to the *rwot*.[29]

27. On the origins and migrations of Umia Anyima's ruling lineage see Crazzolara (1951, pp. 312–13) and Garry A.H.T., pp. 63, 79, 81. An Umia Anyima elder underscored the Eastern Nilotic origins of the area's lineages when he said that the early peoples of Ogili were "one" with the Eastern Nilotic-speaking Jie, Turkana, and Karimojong; see Garry A.H.T., pp. 84, 100A. This claim did not go unchallenged in light of the Luo ethnic consciousness characteristic of twentieth-century Acholi; one elder objected on the grounds that the "Jie and Turkana are Lango," or Eastern Nilotic; see ibid., p. 86. Lira Paluo traditions declare (in Webster A.H.T., p. 63) that people in such places as Paimol and Wol speak Luo differently because "[m]ost of them came from [Eastern Nilotic] Karamoja."

28. Crazzolara (1951, pp. 313–14). Garry A.H.T., p. 77, states that the Umia Anyima name came from the fact that the area was famous for its *nyim*, or sesame; Crazzolara's version was explicitly rejected.

29. Garry A.H.T.. pp. 62–63, 68, 80, 84, 100–101. For a brief version of the arrival of Paluo *kal*, including the identification of Mota as the earliest lineage, see Obol-Owit (1968, pp. 39–40).

Paitook lineage traditions collected in the 1970s also omit any reference to the Ngoliya. They do identify settlement at Loka Pel near *Got
Akwang*, as did Crazzolara's account. But the later, separate-group Paitook
traditions provide much additional detail. Before the Umia Anyima arrived
on the scene (how long before cannot be determined), the Paitook are
remembered to have come to Akwang from Karamoja. There they ended up
in conflict with the Taa, corroborating traditions from Paimol of early Taa
settlement at Akwang. The Paitook village was destroyed and the lineage
scattered. Some went to Ogili, where they settled on their own and prospered. Then the Kanyum arrived. Kanyum traditions claim that they led the
Paitook in what would have been a multiple-village grouping of two.
Paitook traditions give no hint of such Kanyum leadership but do recount
interaction culminating with fighting that left four Paitook dead. It was
after this that *Rwot* Otim arrived and the Paitook joined him. Once again,
traditions indicate that the new *rwot* married a woman from the newly
incorporated lineage and that the Paitook lineage head became one of the
rwot's councilors.[30]

Many of the available traditions of the early interactions between the
settled groups and *Rwot* Otim convey ideological messages common to the
new chiefdoms. Otim and Paluo *kal* were recognized as royals who asserted
their status and carried with them the familiar regalia; the earlier inhabitants are portrayed as fascinated by and ready to accept the claims and
accoutrements of royalty. The flavor of these traditions is provided in the
following passages:

1. "The Palwo came here as the kal . . . and got themselves accepted as
   the kal."
2. "The Palwo came with a drum which they were beating. The people
   here had no drum, so everyone went to dance with the Palwo and
   then the Palwo became the rwot."
3. "The Palwo came with jami ker [royal objects]. . . . That is why the
   Palwo became the rwot and are up to now."
4. "Before the Palwo came the . . . people had no rwot. Then the
   Palwo came from the big leader Kamraci in Bunyoro saying that
   they were rwodi."

30. Garry A.H.T., pp. 78–79 (on Paitook), 86 (on Kanyum). Obol-Owit (1968, p. 41)
identifies Kanyum origins as Eastern Nilotic Bira in the southern Sudan; from there the group
went to Labwor.

5. "There was only one drum in Omiya and that was in the home of Palwo."[31]

These traditions do not portray Otim, with only his own lineage accompanying him, as large or powerful. One text even declares that Otim and his lineage were "poor and destitute even without a wife." How and why, then, did Otim's lineage become accepted as *kal*? Perhaps the establishment of other chiefdoms around Ogili might have put increasing pressure on lineages to join in. In such circumstances, lineages that were skeptical about doing so may have perceived Otim a better option than others who seemed stronger and more established.[32]

Accommodation and negotiation do again seem to have been decisive ingredients in enticing *lobong* lineages to join the chiefdom. Marriage ties between Otim and two of the earliest *lobong* — the Mota and Paitook — have already been noted. Moreover, the heads of nearly all the lineages that joined Umia Anyima participated at the highest levels of decision making as *lukwena*.

Over the eighteenth century, Umia Anyima's *lobong* grew to include the Atinonyi, Loka, and Kupiir lineages. Like the earlier *lobong*, all were Eastern Nilotic (even the Loka, despite the Paluo connotations of their name). Atinonyi traditions remember that they joined *Rwot* Otim, after which they not only became part of the *lukwena*, but served as the primary caretakers of the royal drum and played (along with the *rwot*) a leading role in rainmaking. The Loka and Kupiir remember that famine drove them to Ogili, with Loka traditions adding that they arrived at about the same time as Paluo *kal*, suggesting strongly that the famine referred to was that which followed the 1720s drought.[33]

Two ambiguous groups sometimes identified as Umia Anyima lineages, but expressly excluded as *lukwena*, were the Atura and the Kunledi. The Eastern Nilotic Atura may not have been an independent village-lineage. When they came to Ogili from Paimol, they evidently settled with

31. Garry A.H.T., pp. 62–63, 68, 79, 81, 101.

32. See ibid., p. 101.

33. Ibid., pp. 80, 88, 91–92, 94 (on Atinonyi); pp. 62, 81, 94–95 (on Loka); 62, 80, 98–99 (on Kupiir). Crazzolara (1951, p. 314) lists these as Umia Anyima lineages and identifies Eastern Nilotic origins for them; Obol-Owit (1968, p. 40) also notes Eastern Nilotic origins for Loka. See also Crazzolara (1951, p. 314), Obol-Owit (1968, p. 40), and Garry's first Umia Anyima interview (Garry A.H.T., p. 62), where the name "Akobi" has been substituted for Atinonyi. Later Garry interviews indicate that "Akobi" identified a nineteenth-century cluster of lineages that included Atinonyi; see Garry, A.H.T., pp. 80–81, 88, 95.

the earlier incorporated Kanyum, perhaps even in the same village, and have always since remained associated with them. The Kunledi appear to have been a pre-Eastern Nilotic hunting and gathering group living near Ogili when the Umia Anyima were establishing themselves there. At first it entered into a symbiotic relationship with the chiefdom (exchanging meat for millet), which later may have led to incorporation. Some traditions include the Kunledi as an Umia Anyima lineage; others leave them out.[34]

THE OTHER *GOT* OGILI CHIEFDOMS

The other four chiefdoms that were established around *Got* Ogili were the Umia Pacua, Pela, Parumo, and Wol. Umia Pacua was the largest of these, eventually consisting of *kal* and an ethnolinguistic mix of seven or eight *lobong* — five probably Eastern Nilotic, one Luo, one Central Sudanic, and one of unknown origin. As the chiefdom's name implies, it is also the one most closely associated with Umia Anyima, though the precise relationship is not clear. The most credible migration traditions suggest that Umia Pacua *kal* was one of the Paluo groups that left Labwor-Otuke for the *Got* Okaka region after the 1720s drought; an alternative version claims origins in Jie to the east. The only traditions concerning the arrival of the royal lineage at Ogili under the chiefdom's eponym and first *rwot*, Umia (c. 1700–30), state that they "had their royal drum and spear."[35]

The Pela have often been referred to as an Umia Anyima lineage. But throughout her interviews in Umia Anyima, Maura Garry was told that Pela was a small, independent chiefdom with "their own drum." The likely origins of its ruling lineage was Eastern Nilotic. Available Pela traditions provide only one *rwot* list, with no associated traditions until the nineteenth century. All sources, whether Pela or Umia Anyima, agree that the Pela had only one *lobong* lineage: the Kanyum Pankele (or Panykele), related to the Eastern Nilotic Kanyum in Umia Anyima. One text added that Pela was the only chiefdom "that they know of who stayed so small and continued as a ker [independent chiefdom]."[36]

34. Garry A.H.T., pp. 62, 74–75, 80, 86 (on Atura); pp. 89, 94–95, 98, 100 (on Kunledi). On the persistence of hunting and gathering in this region generally, see Lamphear (1986).

35. Umia Pacua lineage information is in Webster A.H.T., pp. 129–32, 135. Wright (1934, p. 167) provides a somewhat confused reference to an Umia Pacua-Umia Anyima relationship. The credible migration traditions are in Crazzolara (1954, p. 521); a less believable account comes from Webster A.H.T., p. 129. The reference to the royal drum and spear and identification of *Rwot* Umia comes from Wright (1934, p. 167). Finally, the extant versions of Umia Pacua's *rwot* list are in Webster A.H.T., pp. 128–30, and Wright (1934, p. 167).

36. See Garry A.H.T., pp. 61–62, 80, 100; Crazzolara (1951, p. 314). A Taa lineage elder

Parumo was also small, though no list of Parumo *lobong* has ever been collected. Even the origins of its ruling lineage are obscure. One source identifies Eastern Nilotic Teso as Parumo *kal*'s original home, after which it passed through Labwor-Otuke before settling at Ogili. Another links the group with the broad Paluo movement through Labwor-Otuke and Okaka that also produced the ruling lineages of many other southeastern and east-central zone chiefdoms.[37]

The final Ogili chiefdom to be considered was Wol. Attempting to reconstruct Wol's eighteenth-century past is complicated by the fact that the chiefdom at some indeterminate point divided into successor polities (Rogo and Guda). Interviews in 1970 with Rogo and Guda elders produced confused and contradictory stories about both Wol and its two successors.[38]

Traditions from neighboring Umia Anyima are more helpful. After asserting their close relationship with Wol (and not Rogo or Guda), Umia Anyima elders stated that the ruling lineage of Wol, like their own, came from "Pajule"—the *Got* Okaka region. But, they added, Wol *kal* was not Paluo. Instead it was part of the originally Central Sudanic Pawidi lineage, long-time residents at Okaka who established themselves as an independent chiefdom there circa 1730–60 (see Chapter 6).[39]

Umia Anyima traditions add that Wol's "Pawidi" ruler came from Pajule "with his ker" and with the authority and accoutrements of *rwot*ship. This *ker* seems to have been recognized and accepted by six *lobong* lineages: the Kacua, Paryanga, Pawotokidi, Pabala, Kayana, and Katoro—all remembered as being from the *Got* Ogili area and thus almost certainly Eastern Nilotic in origin. The first three of these are recalled to have provided *lukwena* and the Pabala a *jago*, though the role that this *jago* played in the chiefdom is not clear. In addition, the Kacua were also responsible for the

---

from Paimol made the unlikely claim that Pela was founded by a "son" of Acut from Taa; see Webster A.H.T., p. 93. Pela's one extant *rwot* list comes from Garry A.H.T., p. 61. References to the Kanyum Pankele are from Garry A.H.T., pp. 63, 71, 73, 80–81, 86, 91.

37. Lira Paluo traditions comment on Parumo's small size as late as c. 1900; see Webster A.H.T., p. 76. Webster (1976a, p. 227) provides the origins and migration route of Parumo's ruling lineage and includes a Parumo *rwot* list attached to his mimeoed A.H.T., while Webster and Herring (1975, pp. 102, 106) claim Paluo origins for Parumo *kal*, though it is not made clear where any of this information comes from.

38. See Webster A.H.T., pp. 121–26.

39. See Garry A.H.T., pp. 81, 84, 86; Garry (1976, p. 324). Ogot (1967a, pp. 145–52) suggests early Luo origins for Pawidi; Crazzolara (1951, pp. 281–82) claims they are pre-Luo and "pre-Madi" (i.e., pre-Central Sudanic). But most evidence points to Central Sudanic. See Crazzolara (1951, pp. 258–61; 1954, pp. 442–43) and Garry (1974b, p. 36).

main *jok* of the chiefdom (*Jok* Mora) located on *Got* Mora about four miles west of Ogili.[40]

The available traditions of these last four Ogili chiefdoms are limited and the chiefdoms themselves small and seemingly unexceptional. Still, what little we can discern about them suggests that they shared the broad pattern of sociohistorical transformation that between about 1725 and 1790 began to create a new social order and political culture not only in the *Got* Ogili area but Acholi as a whole.

THE *GOT* PARABONGO CHIEFDOMS

Beginning about three miles south of *Got* Ogili and extending a similar distance southeast is a mountain range called *Got* Parabongo. Six small chiefdoms were settled there by the mid-eighteenth century, including the Pukor chiefdom that moved to the area after breaking from Paimol. The oldest was Pader, one of four chiefdoms established in the southeast before the 1720s drought. The unclear nature of earlier Pader traditions hardly improves for this later period. The three available *rwot* lists continue to be contradictory, with few accompanying traditions. Two of the three extant sources indicate that the group remained at *Got* Parabongo until after the drought occurring around 1790, with the Lamogi (originally Central Sudanic) as probably its only *lobong*.[41]

The eventual ruling lineage of Parabongo is linked with the broad Paluo movement through Labwor-Otuke and Okaka by a wide range of traditions, although those from Parabongo *kal* itself trace a more westerly route. These latter traditions have an obvious ideological purpose, which is to assert a relationship between this Parabongo and a second Parabongo chiefdom in western Acholi that extends back to initial moves into Acholi. This contention must be discounted because evidence from Parabongo West conclusively identifies its ruling lineage as one that broke away from Parabongo East only after the drought occurring around 1790.[42]

Parabongo East traditions identify their first *rwot* as Mingo (c. 1735–

40. The Umia Anyima traditions come from Garry A.H.T., p. 86; the rest from Webster A.H.T., pp. 122–24. Given their responsibility for the main chiefdom *jok*, the Kacua were probably one of the oldest groups in the area. There is no hint that the Pabala in Wol were related in any way to the Pabala chiefdom.

41. On Pader traditions, see Wright (1934, p. 77); Ongo (1971b, p. 1); Webster A.H.T., pp. 108–11. On the Central Sudanic origins of Lamogi, see Crazzolara (1954, pp. 459–61). On Pukor, see n. 15 above.

42. Parabongo traditions are in Webster A.H.T., pp. 135–36, 140. References linking them to other Paluo and to Okaka include Wright (1934, p. 132), Crazzolara (1954, pp. 520–21), Garry (1974b, pp. 14–15), and Garry A.H.T., pp. 5, 30, 33. For Parabongo West, see Chap. 7.

65), one of three sons of a Bunyoro/Paluo ruler who supposedly "sent his sons with drums to go to Acholi and rule where there were no kingdoms." *Rwot* Mingo is remembered to have "owned" three drums. One became the royal drum of Parabongo; the other two he supposedly gave out to the founders of fellow southeastern-zone chiefdoms of Ajali and Pabala. "This made Ajali, Pabala and Parabongo very closely related," one source asserts, and their drums "are all called Ladwol."[43]

One version of Parabongo traditions claims that when *Rwot* Mingo reached the *Got* Parabongo area he met four lineages, all of unknown origins: the Agum, Keti, Karyaka, and Lwala. The account intimates that the head of the Agum was a leader among the four, though it is expressly noted that he had no drum or, in other words, that he was not a *rwot*. All four joined Mingo, and the heads of all except the Lwala (because they were "too small") were given small drums to mark their positions as *lukwena*.

A second variant claims that Mingo met only the Agum and Karyaka, whereas the Keti are remembered to have joined Mingo's successor, Okutu Ti Madit (c. 1765–95), and no information is given on the incorporation of Lwala. Whenever they joined, all are remembered to have had special roles in the chiefdom; even the "too small" Lwala were accorded special duties related to the royal drum.[44]

Meanwhile, the three *Got* Parabongo chiefdoms of Pabala, Kwong, and Pacer were even smaller than the others already discussed. The Pabala chiefdom may have emerged out of the Pabala lineage that, according to Patiko narrative traditions, stayed behind in the east after Atiko's journey "to the end of the world." Alternatively, the only available Pabala *rwot* list identifies the chiefdom's first *rwot* and eponym, Bala, as a "son" of Labongo — a name frequently associated with the Paluo move through Okaka following the 1720s drought. This version would seem to be supported by traditions in Wright, which state that the Pabala assert "a relationship between them & Palwo origins." Whatever the particular origins of the Luo-speaking Pabala *kal*, they seem always to have been on their own; there are no traditions of any incorporated lineages.[45]

43. See Webster A.H.T., p. 136; a slightly different version is on p. 140. Ajali traditions do not identify their royal drum as named "Ladwong," but "Lapwony." See ibid., pp. 149, 154–55. Wright (1934, p. 165) concurs that Parabongo's royal drum name was Ladwol. The estimated dates for Mingo's rule are derived from two almost identical *rwot* lists in Webster A.H.T., pp. 135, 137, and Wright (1934, p. 165).

44. Webster A.H.T., p. 136, contains both versions. A Lwala lineage in Pacabol is identified along with the Taa as among the earliest inhabitants in the Akwang area, indicating Eastern Nilotic origins; see text and n. 48 below.

45. See Crazzolara (1951, p. 231); Webster A.H.T., p. 136; Wright (1934, p. 165);

The ruling lineage of Kwong is another group seemingly associated with the Paluo movement through the Labwor hills and Okaka after the 1720s drought. Supposedly descended "from either a son or grandson of Labongo," a Bunyoro/Paluo royal often associated with the trek north, Kwong *kal* settled near *Got* Parabongo from its founding. Only one *lobong* lineage is remembered to have joined: the probably Eastern Nilotic Kawotowic. And even they left in the aftermath of the 1830s drought.[46]

The final Parabongo chiefdom to discuss is Pacer. Almost all sources agree that the first *rwot* of Pacer was its eponym Acer, and that he was the brother of Omongo, founder of the Lira Paluo chiefdom (see Chapter 6). Contradictory claims are made about which was the elder brother and which had the larger royal drum. But there is consensus that the two brothers quarreled and separated in the vicinity of *Got* Lapono and that Acer then moved north with the smaller group of followers. Pacer always remained small, with only one known *lobong* lineage: the Central Sudanic Kakwor or Lukwor.[47]

THE *GOT* AKWANG CHIEFDOMS

The three chiefdoms of Pacabol, Koro, and Ariya all have distinct traditions of leaving Labwor-Otuke after the 1720s drought to settle at the southern edges of the Ogili-Parabongo-Akwang range. Only Pacabol remained until the late-eighteenth-century drought. Established near *Got* Akwang, Pacabol was almost always under the influence of neighboring and more powerful Paimol. Traditions indicate that its ruling lineage came from Paluo, moved through the Labwor-Otuke area, and eventually settled near Paimol around 1750. There they met and incorporated the Lwala lineage, acknowledged along with the Taa as the earliest inhabitants in the Akwang area and thus almost certainly Eastern Nilotic in origin. The Gweng and perhaps the Paracam, lineages of unclear origins from the mixed Eastern Nilotic-Luo

Webster and Herring (1975, p. 102). Ajali traditions add complicating and not very convincing details claiming that the Pabala broke off from Ajali; see Webster A.H.T., pp. 142, 156. Webster (pp. 202–3, notes 5 and 6) makes reference to a Pabala historical text (including a *rwot* list) not included in his mimeoed A.H.T.

46. Webster and Herring (1975, pp. 102–3, 106). A different and unsubstantiated interpretation of Kwong's origins is given in Webster (1976b, p. 294). The two extant Kwong *rwot* lists are in Webster A.H.T., pp. 137–40; Wright (1934, p. 165). Kawotowic traditions are in Webster A.H.T., pp. 137–38; Patongo references to Kawotowic are on pp. 14, 153.

47. See Webster A.H.T., pp. 43, 45, 52–53, 63–64, 77–79. Much in Pacer traditions is confused and contradictory, including two divergent *rwot* lists in the same interview; see ibid., pp. 77–79 and notes, pp. 194–95.

area to the south, also joined Pacabol before the drought occurring around 1790.[48]

Koro and Ariya seem to have traveled together from Labwor-Otuke to the *Got* Kalongo area near Akwang, probably arriving before Pacabol. Though it ended up as a non-royal lineage in the central-zone chiefdom of Payira, Koro traditions avow that Ariya left Labwor-Otuke and arrived at Kalongo as a fellow independent chiefdom. But there is no evidence that the Ariya ever attracted any *lobong* lineages.[49]

Koro was also small when it reached the Kalongo area, but it had incorporated two associated lineages: the originally Eastern Nilotic Ibakara and the Central Sudanic Pagaya. Most extant traditions link the eventual royal lineage of Koro with an eastern stream of early Luo migrants that passed south through present-day Karamoja and the Labwor-Otuke hills. One rendition, however, asserts Eastern Nilotic "Lango-Aje," or Jie, origins. Whatever its ultimate origins, the lineage was almost certainly bilingual before it left Labwor-Otuke and may have been so even before it settled there.[50]

Traditions indicate Koro *kal*'s adoption in Labwor-Otuke of the new sociopolitical order derived from Bunyoro/Paluo in three ways. First, Koro traditions attest numerous times that Koro *kal* possessed a royal drum when it left Labwor-Otuke. Second, Koro traditions make clear that the only two *lobong* lineages in the chiefdom during the eighteenth century (the Ibakara and Pagaya) were incorporated in the hills area. Finally, Ajali traditions note a person named "Okor" in Labwor-Otuke who founded a chiefdom there, a reference that Herring interprets "to represent the Koro people from the east."[51]

Koro's first *rwot* was most likely Tanyjuk (who ruled c. 1700–30). Traditions link his name firmly with Labwor-Otuke and with the onset of the drought and famine that eventually drove his son and successor, Tyeng (c. 1730–60), from the hills area. It was probably in the unsettled conditions of the drought that Ibakara and Pagaya joined the emergent chief-

---

48. Ibid., pp. 80, 94, 105–8; Anywar (1954, p. 140).

49. Ariya is mentioned briefly in Latigo (1970a, p. 36; 1970b, p. 3); A.H.T. 271, 307 — all dealing with the Koro chiefdom.

50. See Latigo (1970a, pp. 5, 14–15, 30, 34, 54, 66–67); Okech (1953, p. 50); Pellegrini (1963, p. 10); A.H.T. 272, 305, 307. Wright (1934, p. 87) does not mention movement through Karamoja, instead identifying Labwor-Otuke as Koro's first place of settlement. He does state that while at Labwor-Otuke "the people talked a language like the Karamojong."

51. Latigo (1970a, pp. 15, 54, 66–67; A.H.T. 272–73, 305, 307; Herring (1974b, p. 153).

dom. Koro traditions of the period corroborate Labwor memories: one Koro text supports the Labwor recollection that the devastation of locusts was added to that of drought; another recalls that Koro finally left Labwor-Otuke after people crowded in from the drier surrounding plains and overwhelmed the resources of the hills.[52]

After leaving Labwor-Otuke and moving to Kalongo, Koro and Ariya apparently remained closely associated, though Koro traditions allude to no interaction with other southeastern-zone chiefdoms. Internally, the Ibakara and Pagaya appear to have had equally important ritual and political roles.[53]

Small as it was, the Koro chiefdom epitomized the integrative potential of the new sociopolitical order. With one lineage probably Luo in origin, one Eastern Nilotic, and one Central Sudanic, Koro's example shows that those who embraced the order could accommodate differences as notable as diverse ethnolinguistic origins.

When *Rwot* Tyeng died (c. 1760), traditions recount that his son Okello Okiro was too young to assume the *rwot*ship. A caretaker or regent was selected, a not uncommon occurrence. What is exceptional in this case is the remembered identity of the man chosen to act in this role: Ociri, head of the non-royal Pagaya lineage. Except as a prelude to a change of dynasty, I know of no other instance where an identified regent was not a member of *kal*. Before he died, Tyeng had supposedly asked that Ociri be made regent because he had been "so cooperative" as lineage head and councilor. The unconventional nature of the request is underscored by the response: "First he met with opposition from his subjects, that since Ociri was a Madi [that is, of the Central Sudanic Pagaya lineage] it was not proper for him to rule at Koro." But the people eventually "gave way" and Ociri became the only non-royal regent expressly identified as such in extant Acholi traditions.[54]

Sometime during the regency of Ociri or reign of Okello Okiro, Koro left the Kalongo area and the protective string of outcrops of which it was a part to follow a small group of other chiefdoms (see Chapter 6) onto the southeastern-zone plains. By the time of the drought occurring around

---

52. See Latigo (1970a, pp. 5, 15, 54, 67; 1970b, p. 4); A.H.T. 268, 272, 305–7; Wright (1934, p. 87); Okech (1953, p. 50). Tanyjuk's name is explicitly linked to famine in A.H.T. 272 and 306. The latter also identifies the name of the famine as "Kec Bonyo" (famine of locusts), while A.H.T. 273 describes conditions in the hills after the famine. Labwor traditions are recounted in Herring (1979b, p. 295). A.H.T. 306 indicates two famines while Tyeng was at Kalongo, one of the few references to two possible mid-eighteenth-century droughts suggested by the Nile-level data. See Cohen (1974b, p. 19) and Herring (1979a, pp. 59–60), though they suggest slightly different dates.

53. Ibakara and Pagaya roles are noted in Latigo (1970a, p. 76).

54. Ibid., p. 15.

1790, under *Rwot* Okello Okiro, the chiefdom was settled some eighty kilometers (fifty miles) southwest of Kalongo at Apiri, just beyond the southeastern zone in the east-central zone (see Map 5).[55]

The Amyel Area

Even before the 1720s drought, *Got* Amyel, located not quite midway between the Parabongo and Lapono peaks, had become home for the Patongo and Ajali chiefdoms. No others would settle here during the eighteenth century, though by around 1750 Ajali's first ruling dynasty would have been replaced by a Paluo lineage from Labwor-Otuke.

PATONGO

Patongo, one of the two largest chiefdoms in north-central Uganda before the 1720s drought, continued to grow afterward. By the time of the drought, Patongo seems to have consisted of six *lobong* lineages and Patongo *kal*. Subsequently, as many as nine others of varied origins also joined, although traditions are vague about how many of these joined before the next major drought occurring around 1790. It is likely, though, that by the end of the eighteenth century, Patongo was second only to Lira Paluo in size and power in the southeastern zone (see Chapter 6).[56]

Few Patongo traditions, particularly of the separate-group, non-narrative type, have been collected to shed light on the chiefdom's internal structures, even at the basic level of determining which lineages provided councilors to the *rwot*. Two things at least are clear: (1) such councilors did exist and were important; and (2) the chiefdom had no territorial subdivisions before the advent of colonial rule.[57]

Two sets of Patongo narrative traditions, however, relate stories of succession disputes that go beneath the surface to provide rare glimpses into the dynamics surrounding the crucial process of succession to the *rwot*ship. The first involved two sons of the chiefdom's founder, Otongo.

---

55. A.H.T. 268, 272.

56. The lineages identified in Webster A.H.T., pp. 13–15, 20 are (1) Cobo (probably Central Sudanic in origin), (2) Kawotowic (Eastern Nilotic), (3) Kanyir (?), (4) Kalanga (Paluo), (5) Obong (?), (6) Pamolo or Kawatmolo (Central Sudanic), (7) Opi (?), (8) Otila (Eastern Nilotic), and (9) Omura (?). Traditions are not conclusive, but it appears that the Lakwar (see ibid., pp. 3, 7, 15) and then the Kawatowic (pp. 14, 153) were responsible for Patongo's main *jok*, *Jok* Amyel.

57. Ibid., pp. 6, 14; see also pp. 3, 7–9, 15, 152.

Atego succeeded his father at just about the time that the 1720s drought struck. Perhaps fueled by the resulting stresses, the Patongo clashed with emergent Jie during Atego's reign (c. 1725–?). One day as Patongo warriors returned from battle, they came suddenly upon Atego's son and preferred successor, Gwok, who had been out setting traps with a friend. Frightened, the boys began to run. Gwok fell, hit a rock, and died from the blow. "This apparent accident was believed to have been engineered by Lugeny, the brother of Atego, in order to enhance his own chances of securing the throne. Atego's wife, in sorrow, disgust and rage, threw the royal regalia out of the palace and persuaded her husband, the *rwot*, to abdicate." Atego went to live among his wife's village-lineage, Lugeny became *rwot*, "and thereafter his descendants, not Atego's provided the rwodi of Patongo."[58]

By most accounts Lugeny's son and successor was Ongia Otorongom (c. 1760–90), who apparently experienced both a smooth succession and an uneventful reign. But Ongia's death is remembered to have precipitated another round of intense competition among his sons, Okio and Pol:

> When Pol was made *rwot*, Okio buried the royal beads and grinding stone and went to Pukor. Constant drought followed [surely that of c. 1790] and the people sent a delegation to Okio to ask him to come back. Upon interrogation Okio said that all he wanted was power, his brother could have the cattle and wives of the inheritance. So the inheritance was divided in this way. Okio who was the youngest brother should have by custom inherited everything. But the dead *rwot*'s wives favoured Pol over Okio. The Councillors feared to force Okio upon the women and so they chose Pol as *rwot*. The women very much liked Pol especially because he used to share with them the game animals which he caught. Okio never did such a thing.[59]

It was argued above that actual conflict over the *rwot*ship appears to have been rare in the Acholi chiefdoms. The logic underlying this contention was the absence of material means for candidates to compete actively for the position or to dispute the choice once it was made. Even so, the *rwot*ship was a prize to win and eligible candidates must have regularly competed for it. The quotations above are significant primarily in their explicit revelation, absent in most traditions, of some of the dynamics involved in such competition.

58. Webster (1976c, p. 352). A virtually identical story is told in Webster A.H.T., p. 18, with a briefer allusion on p. 148. *Rwot* lists that identify Atego as Otongo's successor are in Webster A.H.T., pp. 7, 11, 16–17, and Wright (1934, p. 159).

59. Webster A.H.T., p. 19; also Webster (1976c, p. 352). Patongo traditions in Wright (1934, pp. 159–63) do not mention either dispute.

For example, royal wives probably often played important roles in succession, as they did in the two Patongo examples just recounted. It makes sense that women at *kal* (and especially the wives of *rwodi*), with their knowledge of and access to ritual, regalia, *and* the men involved in the formal decision making, influenced the process. That such influence is only rarely hinted at in traditions is almost certainly due, in large part, to the patriarchal nature of both lineage and chiefdom structures and to the gender biases that result. In addition, such female influence may only rarely come to light because most successions were less dramatic than those in Patongo and were thus forgotten, or, conversely, because the memories of such succession competition as Patongo's have been suppressed.

Three additional points can be made about Okio's succession dispute. First, the story affirms the importance of generosity in a *rwot*; Pol's munificence was what most recommended him to the royal women, while they rejected Okio because of his selfishness. Second, Okio's willingness to allow his brother Pol to inherit the cattle and wives of their father was unlikely to have been due to any awakening of generosity on Okio's part. He would surely have calculated that once he became *rwot* his access to tribute, fines, and war booty would provide compensatory wealth. And third, the reference to cattle in this story is one of the few from Acholi in this period. It is possible that this reference is merely a reading back of conditions that applied only after the mid-nineteenth century when Arabic-speaking traders from the north brought unprecedented numbers of cattle into Acholi. But the Patongo, by the late eighteenth century, may well have possessed more cattle than usual for two reasons: (1) they were settled in the worst rainfall region in Acholi, making reliance on agriculture alone especially risky; and (2) their close proximity to the emergent, cattle-keeping Jie would have given them greater access to cattle than most Acholi chiefdoms.

AJALI

Patongo's closest neighbor, Ajali, experienced even more upheaval with succession after the 1720s drought than Patongo. Patongo's ruling lineage, at least, emerged from its disputes intact; Ajali's Loka *kal* dynasty was displaced.

The small Ajali chiefdom, comprised of just Loka *kal* and the Jonam and Daya lineages, had been settled between the Akwang and Amyel peaks for a generation or two before the 1720s drought. After the Paimol came to nearby *Got* Akwang and began to establish itself there after the drought, Paimol and Ajali clashed — at least according to Ajali sources; Paimol traditions are silent on this matter. As a result, Ajali was driven off to the south, relocating nearer to *Got* Amyel.

Then a new Paluo lineage appeared on the scene. Subsequently called simply Paluo *kal*, it was part of the broader Paluo movement through Labwor-Otuke. Like many Paluo groups, traditions indicate that the reason they left Paluoland was troubles with a Bunyoro ruler, remembered in this case as "Silabambe." A group called Lyec accompanied Paluo *kal* on its migration, though whether it was an associated non-royal lineage or a branch of *kal* is not certain.[60]

Leaving Otuke after the 1720s drought, the Lyec and Paluo *kal* traveled north to settle eventually near Ajali. There the Paluo *kal* leader married the daughter of the Loka *rwot*. When the latter died, the *rwot*ship somehow passed from Loka to Paluo *kal*. One reason given for the transfer, by both Loka and Lyec elders, was that the Loka had taken on responsibility for an important *jok* as well, and the two jobs were incompatible. The Lyec elder then added a more convincing explanation: "The new group was large and the Loka clan felt that negotiations would be preferable to force. So Loka suggested a meeting." Another text notes that Paluo *kal*'s people "were now so numerous that they [Loka] could neither afford to lose them nor be above them."[61]

Ajali traditions provide a welter of additional and often differing detail. Some, for example, remember that the Loka transferred royal regalia, including the main royal drum, along with the *rwot*ship; others claim that the Loka had no drum (though evidence is overwhelming that they did). But one crucial detail missing is the identity of the Paluo *kal* leader involved in the transfer of power. Uncertainty and inconsistency, in fact, plague the Ajali *rwot* list until Arumo Odwong, whose death is firmly fixed in Ajali and neighboring chiefdoms' traditions because of his remembered heroic self-sacrifice to bring the drought occurring around 1790 to an end.[62]

Though it lost the *rwot*ship, Loka became the most important non-royal lineage in the reconstituted chiefdom and was accorded the status of both *wegi ngom* and senior *lakwena*. The Daya provided a second *lakwena*, and the Jonam were responsible for the main chiefdom *jok*. The Lyec, who

60. Webster A.H.T., p. 145, refers to the troubles with Paimol. On Paluo *kal*'s migration, see pp. 144–5, 151; participation in the broader Paluo movement and links with Parabongo *kal* are claimed in Parabongo traditions on pp. 136, 140 and in a Pacer text, p. 77. Contradictory Lyec evidence comes from pp. 143–44, 162–64. Finally, traditions in Wright (1934, p. 26) bring the group from Paluo, at the time of a leader named Atuno Gemo.

61. See Webster A.H.T., pp. 143, 154, 162, 167–68.

62. See ibid., pp. 143, 145, 154–55, 162, 167–68. The five extant versions of the Ajali *rwot* list are in ibid., pp. 8, 141–42, 145–46, 165, and Wright (1934, p. 26).

may have been a part of Paluo *kal* rather than a village-lineage on its own, had no special duties or privileges. It should be noted as a final point that Ajali elders contributed some of the most extensive and informative non-narrative traditions on the duties and rewards of councilors of the *rwot* available in Acholi (used above in Chapter 3).[63]

Conclusion

The southeastern zone, and particularly the Ogili-Parabongo-Akwang mountain range, provided the setting for the greatest proliferation of chiefdoms anywhere in emergent Acholi. The role of the 1720s drought was crucial in creating conditions favorable for chiefly growth. The southeastern zone has some of the worst reliable rainfall in Acholi, and would thus have been hit hard by the drought. At the same time, areas south and east of the zone are even drier and more marginal. Such circumstances would explain the large flow of immigrants into the zone following the drought, and would also make understandable the receptiveness of so many groups in the zone to new institutions and to a new ideology of leadership that promised greater security in highly unsettled times.

Both narrative and separate-group, non-narrative traditions have contributed to the reconstruction and interpretation offered in this chapter. Especially in the Paimol and Umia Anyima chiefdoms, non-narrative traditions provided revealing glimpses into the social dynamics involved in the establishment and workings of the new social order and political culture that was emerging throughout Acholi after the 1720s drought. Yet, much of the extant evidence (i.e., many of the remaining traces) available for sociohistorical reconstruction and analysis comes from narrative traditions. These traditions, emphasizing such features as the symbolism and ideology of royal drums, can be frustratingly narrow as explanations for or even descriptions of the fundamental changes characterizing the establishment of the new sociopolitical order. But together, non-narrative and narrative sources make it possible to build up a convincing and even extensive picture of the foundations — the roots — of this order as they were instituted in the Ogili-Parabongo-Akwang and Amyel areas between about 1720 and 1790, even if the brush strokes are sometimes broader or more muted than we would like.

---

63. See Webster A.H.T., pp. 153, 157–59, 162–63, 170–71; see also Chap. 3 above.

6. The Southeastern and East-Central Zones: The New Order Spreads

In terms of sheer numbers, the most dramatic explosion of chiefdom formation in Acholi occurred in the Ogili-Parabongo-Akwang mountain range following the 1720s drought. But this was not the only part of the emergent southeastern and east-central zones to experience the emergence of new chiefdoms or dramatic social and political change. This chapter looks at the other areas, first in the remainder of the southeastern zone, then in the east-central zone.

As in Chapter 5, separate group, non-narrative traditions will provide crucial source material for sociohistorical reconstruction and analysis. In addition, both narrative and non-narrative traditions concerning the *Got* Lapono chiefdom of Lira Paluo provide traces that reveal more than usual about both the politics of *rwot*ship within the chiefdom and the equally political realm of relations among neighbors.

The *Got* Lapono Area

About twelve miles (twenty kilometers) southeast of Amyel lies *Got* Lapono, the summit of the Lapono range (see Map 5). By about 1790 many chiefdoms were nestled among the more northerly slopes of the southeastern zone, but only Lira Paluo and Paicam made Lapono their home. Three influences seem to have produced this discrepancy. First, Lapono lay within a poorer rainfall region. Second, the Lapono range lay directly astride the contested and sometimes dangerous frontier between the emergent Acholi and Jie, each establishing their own identities and territorial claims. And third, Lira Paluo grew to be the largest southeastern-zone polity, and other chiefdoms may have wanted to keep some distance to maintain their independence.

THE LIRA AND PAICAM CHIEFDOMS

Long before Lira Paluo was founded, even before the 1720s drought, a predecessor polity had been established at Lapono. Most sources agree that when the drought struck, the *rwot* of this polity was its eponym Lira, who ruled from around 1720 to 1750 and was the son of the chiefdom's founder Lapono. The chiefdom may have taken on Lira's name because of what happened during his reign: following the drought, as many as twelve lineages (all probably Eastern Nilotic) joined the chiefdom, in contrast to the three *lobong* lineages that had previously joined Lapono.[1]

Traditions attribute the large influx of lineages to three causes. One was famine: "Lapono hills provided wild fruits — Acoge — and during famine hungry people . . . came to gather them and then stayed on and joined the Lira group." A second was military protection, especially important in unsettled conditions. And a third was the renown of Lira's rainmaker, most likely a *jok* at *Got* Lapono named Ayugi.[2]

Enough lineages are remembered to have joined Lira to make it one of the largest chiefdoms in emergent Acholi in the generation after the 1720s drought. Still, numerous lineages in the Lapono area remained outside the chiefdom. Many of these would later join the Lira Paluo polity that would supplant Lira after about 1750; others joined the first Paluo group to move into the area following the 1720s drought, the ruling lineage of the emergent chiefdom of Paicam.

Paicam's Paluo *kal* is remembered to have come to Lapono with a rainmaking royal drum, probably via Labwor-Otuke. The identity of emergent Paicam's *rwot* when the group reached Lapono is unclear, but the timing is not. All available traditions indicate that the chiefdom's royal lineage arrived before (but probably not long before) Lira Paluo *kal* appeared on the scene around 1750.[3]

---

1. See Chap. 4 and Webster A.H.T., pp. 50–51 and n. 18, p. 189; contrast with Webster A.H.T., p. 44 and Webster (1976b, p. 299). The nine new lineages that were almost certainly Eastern Nilotic were Katoro, Paner, Katugo, Agum, Bukol, Amyong, Adeng, Adyang, and Luyara. The other three lineages with probable Eastern Nilotic origins were Kaket (from the eventual northeastern zone of Acholi), Alano (from *Got* Kalongo in the southeastern zone), and Tenganywang (from the Agoro mountains). The overwhelming Eastern Nilotic presence at Lapono thus indicated does not accord well with Crazzolara's assertion (1954, p. 550) that the large majority of Lira Paluo "were to all appearances *Madi*," that is, Central Sudanic. His listing of supposed Lira Paluo lineages on pp. 549–50 is extremely confused.

2. One text, though, identifies Ayugi as one of *Rwot* Lira's wives, while another claims that the old Lira chiefdom had no "chief priest" (and thus no *jok*?) at Lapono, having left theirs back west at *Got* Bako. All references from Webster A.H.T., pp. 47, 51, 71, and n. 18, p. 189.

3. See Webster A.H.T., pp. 56–59, 68, and n. 29, p. 198. The royal drum was named "Ayenga," or "feeder," because when it was beaten, "rain would pour down and provide a rich harvest" (p. 56); the name of the drum is also provided by Wright (1934, p. 80).

In the interim, Paicam is remembered to have incorporated an ethno-linguistically mixed assortment of seven or eight Lapono lineages. Three of these — the Kalanga, Kadir, and Obia — provided the new chiefdom's *luk-wena*, while major portions of the others eventually left to join nearby Lira Paluo.[4]

We know little else about internal developments in Paicam before the drought of the 1830s when the chiefdom left the southeastern zone. Even the one topic that Paicam traditions of the eighteenth century address at some length — its relationship with neighboring Lira Paluo — is marked by a major contradiction. Traditions are clear that Paicam was overshadowed by and dependent upon its much larger and more powerful neighbor, especially in security and military matters. But there is disagreement concerning the nature of the dependency. Some texts indicate that Paicam was incorporated into the Lira Paluo chiefdom, primarily on the basis of claims that the Lira Paluo provided Paicam's first drum when it became a subordinate part of Lira Paluo or that they took Paicam's original royal drum away and replaced it with a drum of lesser status. Conversely, numerous other traditions attest that Paicam not only existed as a chiefdom with a royal drum before Lira Paluo came to Lapono but that Paicam retained this original royal drum into the 1970s. Paicam elders even pointed out with some pride that their royal drum was a powerful rainmaking drum, whereas Lira Paluo's was not. And though Paicam elders acknowledged Lira Paluo's ruler as a "senior *rwot*" (because of Lira Paluo's greater numbers), the implication is clear that he was not the only *rwot*. One text specifically asserts that Paicam provided no *lukwena* to the Lira Paluo *rwot* because "they resisted total incorporation." Finally, Paicam seems not only to have retained its royal drum but also not to have paid tribute to the Lira Paluo *rwot*, a definitive counter indication of direct political control.[5]

4. The seven lineages almost surely incorporated were the Eastern Nilotic Kalanga and Lapwor, the Kadir from Kumam and Okir from present-day Lango (either Eastern Nilotic or Luo), the Lamogi and Pagaya (Central Sudanic), and the Obia (of unclear origins from the Agoro mountains). On all but Pagaya, see Webster A.H.T., pp. 44, 54, 56–57, 66–67, with additional evidence on Lamogi in Crazzolara (1954, pp. 459–61), Wright (1934, p. 95), Garry (1972b, p. 20), and A.H.T. 202. Crazzolara (1954, pp. 399–400, 449–50, 549) identifies Central Sudanic origins for Pagaya; elsewhere (1951, p. 294; 1954, p. 456) he provides less convincing indications of Eastern Nilotic origins. The eighth lineage that may have joined was the Atek, of Eastern Nilotic or Luo origins from present-day Lango; see Webster A.H.T., pp. 44, 46. Webster A.H.T., pp. 56–57, 66 identifies Paicam's *lukwena*; pp. 46, 57, 66–67 provide information on Paicam's failure to add new lineages and the loss of substantial portions of the Lamogi, Padir, Obia, Okir, and Atek.

5. See Webster A.H.T., pp. 44–46, 48, 56–58; p. 63 includes traditions of a succession dispute between brothers, one or two generations after Paicam's founding; and pp. 138 and 193, n. 39 hint at a possible connection between Paicam and a sub-lineage of Kwong *kal*.

On balance, then, the evidence for Paicam's formal independence outweighs that against it. But Webster's comments on this issue are worth repeating:

> In theory, [chiefdoms such as Paicam] were as independent to determine their own behaviour as Lira Palwo itself. Modern elders are careful to emphasize this fact especially since the British subordinated the chiefdoms to the *rwot* of Lira Palwo in the early years of colonialism. However chiefdoms with populations of only one thousand people each were . . . dependent upon Lira Palwo for protection against neighbouring peoples, for arbitration in inter-chiefdom disputes and occasionally for support in difficult and touchy domestic disputes. . . . While the elders of the chiefdoms would totally reject the idea, it might be useful to look upon the chiefdoms as client states of Lira Palwo. It was the strong sense of chiefdom independence which presumably prevented expansionist tendencies within Lira Palwo and forestalled the conversion of client states into subordinate territorial units.[6]

The Establishment of Lira Paluo

The demise of the earlier Lira chiefdom and its replacement by Lira Paluo was set in motion by the arrival at Lapono (c. 1750) of a Paluo group led by a man named Omongo. Omongo is remembered to have come into the area with his royal drum, his brother Acer, and a large group of supporters. Traditions of Omongo emphasize his royal status in his original home in Paluo or the Luo triangle; they also indicate that he left after he lost a succession dispute with an older brother, after oppression by the Bunyoro-Kitara central government, or both.[7]

Migration traditions take the Omongo-led group through west and central Acholi to the *Got* Okaka area in the east-central zone and then to Lapono, with remembered links to several other groups that were part of the broad Paluo movement into the area after the 1720s drought. All of this seems both unremarkable and feasible. Much more problematic are proclaimed migration ties with the central-zone chiefdom of Payira, despite the fact that both Lira Paluo and Payira traditions assert that the two ruling lineages traveled together at least part of the time. The problem lies in

---

6. Webster (1976b, pp. 292–93); he argues (pp. 302–8) that Paicam did become a formal part of Lira Paluo.

7. The identification of Omongo and Acer as royal brothers and their split to form separate polities was noted in Chap. 5 and is widely agreed upon. See, for example, Webster A.H.T., pp. 43, 45, 51–53, 62–64, 77–79; Garry A.H.T., p. 49; Wright (1934, p. 99). Omongo's large group of supporters is reported in Webster A.H.T., pp. 43–44; Wright (1934, p. 103). Stories of succession disputes or oppression are in Webster A.H.T., pp. 43, 51, 62–63 and Wright (1934, p. 99).

timing. By the time of Omongo (who ruled c. 1750–80), Payira had already been settled in the central zone for some fifty to seventy-five years.

Three possible explanations could account for the dubious avowals of shared migrations. First, Payira's and Lira Paluo's royal lineages are remembered to have followed similar migration routes out of Paluo (or the Luo triangle) into or through central Acholi. Even with the time discrepancy, geographical correspondence alone could help explain the claimed migration links. Second, several later connections and similarities between the Lira Paluo and Payira chiefdoms could also have promoted the linking of the two as far back as their original migrations into Acholi. Payira and Lira Paluo were two of the largest and most powerful chiefdoms in Acholi; each claimed similar origins in Paluo (or the Luo triangle); they settled near one another in the mid-nineteenth century; and they established many social and political ties, especially between their respective *kal*. Finally, traditions identify an older "brother" of Omongo named Tira or Atira who separated from Omongo in the Luo triangle and whose descendants ended up as part of Payira. This connection could have provided both the means and an additional reason to claim an early association between the two groups.[8]

When Omongo and his followers reached the Lapono area, they were met with a mixed reception. They first came into contact with two or three lineages widely acknowledged as among the earliest at Lapono and thus almost certainly Eastern Nilotic in origin: the Aburu, Aywa, and perhaps Ameda. Before Omongo appeared, these three are remembered to have joined together with at least two others (the Padir and Pajimo) to form a protective alliance called "Agengo" or "I prevented" to avert defeat by enemies such as the emergent Jie. Traditions indicate that these Agengo lineages had joined neither Lira nor Paicam and that they "had no rwot" of their own. Traditions are also clear that the Agengo welcomed Omongo and his followers, invited them to settle nearby, helped them temporarily with food, and soon accepted Omongo as their *rwot*.[9]

---

8. See Webster A.H.T., pp. 43, 52, 62–65; Wright (1934, p. 99); and on Payira's migration traditions, see Crazzolara (1954, p. 483). Crazzolara (1954, p. 492) also identifies a Patira group in Payira. Lira Paluo's claimed connection with Payira, whose royal lineage is one of the most closely associated in traditions with the early Luo, is even accompanied by a brief version of the archetypal spear and bead story linked with the split of the early Luo at Pubungu (see references in Chap. 4, n. 3). This is the only such story in extant southeastern-zone traditions (also noted in Webster A.H.T., n. 25, p. 191).

9. See Webster A.H.T., pp. 44, 52, 56, 61–62 on the Agengo alliance and early settlement of all but the Pajimo (and contrast p. 53, which seems to mistake the reestablishment of the grouping in the nineteenth century with its origin). Conflicting evidence on the Pajimo (see pp. 52, 54, 74) seems to arise from there being two Pajimo groups in Lira Paluo, one early and

A number of other Lapono area lineages that had remained outside both the Lira and Paicam chiefdoms and the Agengo protective alliance seem also to have soon joined Omongo's polity. At least two of these, and perhaps three others as well, settled among the original Agengo lineages in one sub-grouping. Six or seven others formed another sub-grouping apparently settled near Paluo *kal*. The origins of many of these additional lineages cannot be ascertained, but they were clearly an ethnolinguistically diverse group.[10]

Not everyone around Lapono responded favorably to the dynamic new polity. The main opposition, not surprisingly, came from members of the previously established Lira chiefdom. With the non-royal Paimot lineage taking the lead, Lira is remembered to have been "prepared to fight Omongo and drive him away."[11]

But no actual fighting occurred. The members of the old Lira chiefdom "resisted but did not go so far as fighting although they wanted to." Two developments seem to have prevented overt hostilities. First, pro-Omongo forces outnumbered Lira's. The number of associated lineages in the new chiefdom seems quickly to have reached the mid- to upper teens, making it roughly equal in size to Lira. Omongo also received the backing of neighboring Paicam, tipping the scale decisively in his favor. And the support provided by this combination was more than nominal: "they even threatened to fight for him if necessary."[12]

If this imbalance of force was the stick that helped prevent overt hostility, Omongo is also remembered to have initiated a diplomatic move in the nature of the proverbial carrot. Omongo established four *lukwena*. Three of these came from the earliest lineages of the Agengo grouping to

---

one more recent; the existence of these two groups is explicitly claimed on p. 65, including the assertion that each provided a *lukwena*. The later Pajimo clearly came from the Paluo Pajimo of the east-central zone. Conversely the earlier Pajimo, seemingly settled early at Lapono, may have been related to the Eastern Nilotic Jimos clan of the Jie; see Lamphear (1976, p. 178). Finally, on the early and positive reception of Omongo by the Agengo, see Webster A.H.T., pp. 44–45, 58; Wright (1934, pp. 100, 103).

10. The lineages that seem to have joined the Agengo grouping were the Owiny (from Labwor, either Luo or Eastern Nilotic), as well as the Olung, Arwo, Acore, and perhaps the Karyeka (all of unclear origins). The sub-grouping that clustered around Omongo seems to have included the Pangwer and Bulobo (both "originated" at Lapono, so are probably Eastern Nilotic), Gule (Eastern Nilotic), Obia (unclear origins from Agoro), Lamogi (Central Sudanic), and Palingo (probably Luo, from Paluo or Kumam). The probably Eastern Nilotic Atule also seems to have joined Omongo, though which grouping it settled among is not clear. For basic information, see Webster A.H.T., pp. 44, 61–62, 73–74; see also p. 57 on the Obia; pp. 53, 74 on the Karyeka; and pp. 59–60, 73 on the Palingo (perhaps a sub-lineage of *kal*).

11. Ibid., pp. 45 (includes quotation), 50, 58, 64 (*mwoc*).

12. Ibid., pp. 58, 45.

welcome him: the Aburu, Aywa, and Ameda. The fourth went to the Paimot elder Owo Lwani. His acceptance of this position, it seems, blunted the hostility of both the Paimot and the larger Lira chiefdom and ended any united Lira opposition. Soon Lira's constituent lineages began defecting to Omongo's chiefdom, and the old Lira polity disappeared. The merging of the old Lira and the new Paluo-led chiefdom was symbolized in the name that the chiefdom took: Lira Paluo. But neither the fact of merger nor a symbolically inclusive new name ended all resentment and resistance from old Lira lineages. Indeed, vestiges of these were still discernible in interviews conducted in Lira Paluo in the 1970s.[13]

Still, Lira Paluo by the time of Omongo's death in about 1780 seems to have consisted of more than thirty lineages, a larger number than any other chiefdom in Acholi at the time. Perhaps because such size was so atypical, Lira Paluo traditions provide more clues than most concerning the chiefdom's establishment and growth. The dual motivation for the incorporation of old Lira lineages — the threat of greater numbers and the enticement of a position in Omongo's *lukwena* — as well as the familiar tactic of rewarding early supporters of a new *rwot* with political leadership have already been noted. In addition, one or two lineages from the old Lira grouping (the Kaket and perhaps Adyang) and one from Agengo (the Ameda) seem to have assumed primary ritual leadership within the polity, with each responsible for a *jok* on *Got* Lapono. Omongo also brought with him an impressive array of royal regalia (four drums, a royal spear, and special royal beads) and is credited with introducing into the area both an annual planting ceremony and the royal *bwola* dance. Then, in a passage that describes Omongo's attempts to join his earlier supporters with the more reluctant adherents of the former Lira chiefdom, he is portrayed as a successful soothsayer, arbiter, peacemaker, provider, and rainmaker — an impressive list:

> Soon after establishing himself Omongo asked the people of Lapono to see if it was possible for them all to live in peace together. Omongo brought two black cows and the hosts also brought a black goat and a black cow, they were killed and Omongo said that if the embryos within them were all of the same sex it would mean that they would all live in peace. The embryos proved of the same sex and the animals were eaten by all the people of both groups. . . . After some time Omongo began moving around the villages. People sitting idle were asked why they were so and if they said they had no hoe they were given or if

13. The co-opting of Paimot is indicated in ibid., pp. 45, 50. The resentment shows up again and again in Webster's interviews in Lira Paluo; see, for example, pp. 43–46, 48, 51.

no seed they were given by Omongo. At the beginning of each planting season Omongo beat the drum to call people to collect seeds and hoes. This helped to make people accept Omongo's rule. When there was drought he beat his drum and killed a he-goat to make rain.[14]

There are two final clues to Lira Paluo's exceptional growth. The first pertains to the politically effective way that *Rwot* Omongo redistributed the tribute his subjects provided him: "That rwot [Omongo] took the ker [rwotship] of the preceding people and joined them together. . . . He was giving meat to everybody and people were saying 'A[h], this should be the rwot.'" The second emphasizes the benefit of belonging to a large and powerful polity in the perilous location of *Got* Lapono, not far from the emergent Jie. As an elder from Paluo *kal* stated, "There were threats to security from Karamoja [the home of the Jie] and the . . . clans [lineages] at first negotiated for assistance and later joined Lira Palwo for greater and continuous protection."[15]

The Lira Paluo chiefdom thus became one of the largest and most powerful in Acholi. In the process, two fundamental structural developments occurred. First, three distinct territorial sub-groupings were recognized within the chiefdom. One consisted primarily of the fifteen or so lineages of the old Lira chiefdom. It was named by the others "Tenge," meaning "stay away," and as late as the 1970s, a number of Tenge elders exhibited the sort of animosity toward the wider Lira Paluo entity and its "traditional" Paluo leadership that must have prompted the sub-grouping name. The other two sub-units, in contrast, were as clearly in the royal camp as the Tenge were outside it. These were the "Agengo" (consisting of the original Agengo membership and five other lineages) and an "Omongo" grouping (named after the first Paluo *rwot* and also made up of about ten lineages). Although Lira Paluo traditions include a few references suggesting that there were officials designated to head these sub-units, the lineage identities, functions, and titles of these officials are left so unclear as to cast doubt on their very existence. Instead, traditions emphasize the lineage-based *lukwena*, or councilors of the *rwot*.[16]

14. Ibid., pp. 56, 59, 71 (on ritual leadership), 72 (quotation), and 74 (on regalia and introduction of planting ceremony and *bwola*).

15. The first quotation is from Garry A.H.T., p. 49; the second, from Webster A.H.T., p. 65.

16. On the three groupings, including their composition, see Webster A.H.T., p. 44 (also notes 9 and 10 above). For claims of Tenge political distance and examples of continuing resentment see Webster A.H.T., pp. 43–46, 48, 51. The only times that the terms *jago* or *jagi* are used in Lira Paluo is by elders from or in the context of a semi-independent Lira Lapono

The second structural development came concerned these *lukwena*. At some point the original group of four *lukwena* who advised Omongo was greatly increased. One text claimed that all Lira Paluo lineages sent councilors to the *rwot*. The same elders, however, then identified seventeen lineages as providing *lukwena*. To the extent that this list is accurate, it is striking that only one (as well as the original Paimot, which was not included in the list) came from the Tenge grouping. Such lack of representation seems to have both reflected and contributed to the Tenge isolation within the chiefdom. The identified councilors, meanwhile, came from seven Agengo lineages (including the three original *lukwena*), eight of ten remembered lineages in the Omongo sub-grouping, and the Atule lineage, whose sub-grouping has not been established.[17]

Three of four extant Lira Paluo *rwot* lists identify Omongo's successor as his son Cinga or Cing Alem. In what is remembered as a short time, estimated here as 1780–90, Cing Alem died. His brother and successor Odok also reigned briefly (estimated from 1790 to 1800), after which he was succeeded by yet a third son of Omongo named Ojwang (c. 1800–1820). This rapid succession of *rwodi* was set off when Jie came and poisoned Lira Paluo's wells during Cing Alem's reign, driving the chiefdom north to Ajali in the Amyel region where Cing became ill and died. Odok led the chiefdom back to Lapono but was killed when the Jie returned to attack them. Drought and famine — almost certainly that occurring around 1790 — struck in the midst of these traumas and may also have been their fundamental cause. Then, Ojwang (though some sources indicate that Odok was still *rwot*) led most of the chiefdom away from Lapono, first to present-day Lango and then to the south-central zone.[18]

Traditions recount that following the deaths of the two full brothers, Cing and Odok, their mother Nyagola was extremely upset. This senior

grouping established within the polity following their return from the west in the nineteenth century (see pp. 69–70); a Paicam elder uses the term once (p. 58). Against this, in an interview with elders from Lira Paluo *kal*, the statement was made that the "British substituted the term jago for lakwena" (p. 65).

17. Ibid., pp. 44, 65, identifies the sixteen lineages that provided *lukwena*; p. 65 also includes the same elders' claim that *lukwena* came from all Lira Paluo lineages. The list (with territorial sub-grouping): the Agum (Tenge); the Aburu, Ameda, Aywa, Karyeka, Owiny, one of the two Pajimo lineages, and probably Padir — "Odia" in the list, a name that appears nowhere else in extant Lira Paluo traditions (all of the Agengo sub-grouping); the Pangwer, Bulobo, Gule, Palingo, Lamogi, Obia, Wol, the second Pajimo lineage (all of the Omongo sub-grouping); and the Atule (sub-grouping not identified).

18. Lists of *rwodi* are in ibid., pp. 42–43, 52–53, 60–61; Wright (1934, p. 99). The story of the deaths of Cing and Odok is in Wright (1934, p. 100), which also includes references to famine (as does Webster A.H.T., pp. 60–61).

wife of Omongo feared a curse on her line (holding high office was always looked upon as high risk in terms of ritual danger) and insisted that the *rwot*ship pass from her family to that of junior wife Nyapat. This was done, and Nyapat's son Ojwang became the next *rwot*, establishing a new line of succession. The descendants of Nyagola's line have been taunted ever since for giving up their succession rights. Nyapat, on the other hand, is praised in the chiefdom's *mwoc* (praise-call) for producing many children; it is even metaphorically claimed that all the people in the chiefdom, even those from other lineages, "are her children." Once again, royal wives are identified as playing key roles in succession.[19]

THE SOUTHEASTERN-ZONE PLAINS

We have seen only one instance so far of a chiefdom leaving the southeastern-zone mountains to venture out onto the surrounding plains. But Koro's move (see Chapter 5) occurred a mere decade or so before the drought of circa 1790. By this time three other chiefdoms had established themselves on the southeastern-zone plains: Adilang, Puranga, and Kilak.

Adilang is a classic example of a successor chiefdom. Eighteen separate references in ten texts from Adilang and Patongo support the fundamental notion that the former was an offshoot of the latter. Both chiefdoms' traditions, moreover, invariably name Winymono as the first Adilang *rwot* and usually identify him as the son of Patongo's founder, Otongo. One of the reasons given for Winymono's leaving or being sent from Patongo's home at Amyel is that it became overpopulated.[20]

Overpopulation makes sense in only one situation in a region where land was always available and extra people were almost always welcomed: drought and famine. And the major drought of the 1720s fits into both Otongo's estimated dates of rule noted in Chapter 5 (c. 1690–1720) and Winymono's (c. 1720–55). In addition, two references in Adilang traditions note that Winymono's period of rule was marked by famine.[21]

Several Adilang and Patongo texts convey the sense that Winymono was "sent" by the Patongo *rwot* to the nearby plains in order to set up a new chiefdom. But the sources make clear that Winymono went as an indepen-

19. Webster A.H.T., pp. 59–60. For discussions of "cursing" in Acholi, see Okot (1971, pp. 145–53); A.H.T. 271.
20. See Webster A.H.T., pp. 8, 13, 18 (Patongo texts); 21–22, 28–32, 35, 38–40 (Adilang texts).
21. Ibid.; references to overpopulation are on pp. 13 (a Patongo text) and 32 (Adilang); references associating Winymono with famine are on pp. 21, 23. Adilang *rwot* lists and the associated traditions for estimating dates of rule are on pp. 11, 21, 23, 27–30, 34, 40–41, and Wright (1934, pp. 14–18).

dent if not a wholly equal *rwot*, and they note that he either took a royal drum with him or "made his own" once he left.[22]

Winymono seems to have moved to the plains with supporters from his own lineage and only one *lobong* group (the Kawotowiny, of probable Eastern Nilotic origins). Not far from Amyel, Winymono and his people met a cluster of Eastern Nilotic lineages organized as a multiple-village grouping. The grouping was headed by the Abunga, acknowledged as the earliest lineage to settle the area, and included the Otwil and Pagoya. These lineages soon joined Winymono and his earlier followers, and the core of the new Adilang chiefdom was established.[23]

Adilang's limited traditions about the incorporation of the Abunga-led lineages provide four traces of information. First, Winymono's followers, though they consisted of only two lineages, are remembered by the grouping they met as "a large crowd." Second, a brief passage describing the Abunga grouping's way of life (they both farmed and herded) begins by claiming that the Abunga were the only people found on the plains south of Amyel and ends with the terse declaration, "They lived in fear of fierce enemies." Given this, the "large crowd" of Winymono and his followers must have represented not only a potential threat, but a possible ally who could provide added security in a hostile environment and unsettled time. Third, the head of each lineage that joined the young Adilang chiefdom became a councilor of the *rwot*. Finally, the Pagoya (who seem to have previously played this role within the Abunga-led grouping) and perhaps the Kawotowiny became ritual leaders in the chiefdom.[24]

One more lineage has specific traditions of joining Winymono: the Kawotopio, a probable Central Sudanic group that moved into Adilang from the west. In addition, the Kawatopwor or Kapwor (of unclear origins) may also have joined the chiefdom during the eighteenth century.[25]

22. See Webster A.H.T., pp. 13, 18, 32, 34–35, 38, 40; p. 30 provides alternative notions about the origins of Adilang's original royal drum; p. 8 claims that Winymono was sent simply to gather shea nuts and that he then decided to stay and establish his own polity.

23. Ibid., pp. 25–26, 29–31, 34, 38–40, 169; also pp. 181, 183, notes 2 and 4; the latter suggests Abunga ties with the Otilang or Losilang of the Jie (see Lamphear [1976, passim]).

24. Webster A.H.T., pp. 26, 30, 38.

25. Ibid., pp. 25–26, 29–30, 34, 37–40. These sources also indicate that two other lineages, the Olube and Awila, joined Adilang in the nineteenth century, perhaps along with the Lwaala. Developments in Adilang after Winymono are very unclear, primarily because of confused and contradictory *rwot* lists. The four different *rwot* lists that exist are in Webster A.H.T., p. 11 (from Patongo); and pp. 21, 27–28, and Wright (1934, pp. 14–16) (from Adilang). References to famine during each of the three generations after Winymono exacerbate the confusion; see Webster A.H.T., pp. 21, 23, 30, 34.

The other chiefdom to venture onto the southeastern-zone plains not long after the 1720s drought was Puranga, from the Labwor-Otuke hills. The eventual royal lineage of Puranga appears to have come to Labwor-Otuke as part of the same eastern wing of early Luo migrants as was Koro *kal*. Numerous versions of Puranga traditions refer to the group's passing south through present-day Karamoja District before settling in Labwor-Otuke for what seems a number of generations. If they did not speak both Luo and Eastern Nilotic languages before, they would surely have become bilingual in the hills area.[26]

Extant traditions indicate only two things about the group's stay in Labwor-Otuke: first, they almost certainly adopted the Bunyoro/Paluo institutions and ideology introduced into the hills area after about 1675; and second, they left Labwor-Otuke in the aftermath of a serious drought and famine, surely that of the 1720s. One Labwor tradition specifically identifies famine as the cause that drove Puranga *kal* from the hills; other traditions blame the frequent conflicts that we know resulted from the drought. In either case, the texts convey the sense that within a few years of the drought, or by around 1730, Puranga *kal* had left their long-time home in Labwor-Otuke for good.[27]

One Labwor source remembers that the Puranga *kal* left the hills area "with a few people" only. Puranga traditions support this by indicating that no outside lineages were incorporated before their departure. The *rwot* who led the emergent, if small chiefdom away from Labwor-Otuke was either Cua Agoda or his son, Ogwang Omoro.[28]

26. On the eastern stream of early Luo migrants, see above, Chap. 5, n. 4. On Puranga traditions see A.H.T. 275, 280; Wright (1934, p. 137); Okech (1953, p. 44); Odongo (1976, p. 145); Pellegrini (1963, p. 10). The clearest indication of the group staying in Labwor-Otuke for some time comes from Patongo traditions; see Webster A.H.T., p. 16. For general discussion of bilingualism in the Labwor-Otuke area, see Herring (1974b, pp. 113–16; 1979b, pp. 294–99) and Lamphear (1976, pp. 99, 112). And two Eastern Acholi texts specifically identify Puranga as one of the bilingual groups in the hills area; see Webster A.H.T., pp. 63, 152.

27. As usual, there are no traditions of Puranga *kal* adopting the Bunyoro/Paluo model while in Labwor-Otuke; as noted below, however, traditions of the Lamur — the first lineage to join the group after it left the hills area — remember that it came with a royal drum. On reasons for the group's leaving the hills, see Herring (1974b, p. 118; 1979b, pp. 295–96); Olango (1970, p. 3).

28. The Labwor reference comes from Herring (1979b, p. 295). The Puranga traditions asserting that no other lineages joined in Labwor-Otuke include A.H.T. 275–76, 280; Odongo's claim (1976, pp. 145–46) to the contrary is contradicted by all other Puranga traditions. The traditions that name Cua Agoda as the *rwot* who led Puranga from Labwor-Otuke come from A.H.T. 280; the three accounts identifying Ogwang Omoro are in Wright (1934, p. 137), Okech (1953, p. 45), and Odongo (1976, p. 146). The first clear chronological

After leaving the Labwor-Otuke hills, Puranga *kal* seems to have moved slowly north and west, following the Agago River (see Map 5). Their first remembered settlement site was a place called Adodoi where they remained into the reign of Ogwang Omoro's son, Cua Omero (who ruled c. 1775–1805). It was there that the chiefdom managed to incorporate its first two *lobong* lineages. The first was the Lamur, probably Eastern Nilotic in origin and settled in the Adodoi area when Puranga *kal* appeared. The only detail in extant Lamur traditions concerning their incorporation is the recollection that Puranga *kal* came with a royal drum. Puranga's second *lobong* lineage was the Palaro, of unclear origins but with traditions of moving into the Adodoi area like Puranga *kal* from Labwor-Otuke. Then, still under *Rwot* Cua Omero, Puranga moved further west along the Agago to Orunya (see Map 5), though whether before or after the drought occurring around 1790 is not clear.[29]

The third chiefdom to have established itself on the southeastern-zone plains before the late eighteenth century was Kilak. Traditions present two versions of Kilak origins that are diametrically opposed and yet so equally plausible that I see no means to reconcile or choose between them. One variant—from a collection of drum songs and their interpretations compiled by Daniel Ongo—indicates that the origins of the chiefdom and its ruling lineage lay in Eastern Nilotic Turkana, east of Acholi. Two other sources, collected thirty-five years apart by A. C. A. Wright and J. B. Webster and his team, indicate just as clearly and convincingly an origin in the Central Sudanic area around *Got* Kilak in westernmost Acholi.[30]

The most likely explanation for the contradiction derives from Kilak's later history. After the late-eighteenth-century drought, internal conflicts led to a split of the chiefdom, after which its remaining members became junior partners in an ill-defined confederation of chiefdoms headed by

---

tie-ins are those linking Ogwang Omoro's son Cua Omero with both the drought of c. 1790 and events following the drought. This clarity is generally associated with much richer Puranga traditions as the chiefdom (under Cua Omero) moved into the south-central zone, added new *lobong* lineages, and became one of that zone's most prominent and powerful polities.

29. On the moves to Adodoi and Orunya, see Wright (1934, p. 137), Okech (1953, p. 45), Odongo (1976, p. 146), and A.H.T. 280. A.H.T. 276 and Olango (1970, pp. 2–3, 8) include information on the incorporation of Lamur at Adodoi; less convincingly, Odongo (1976, p. 145) claims this occurred at Labwor-Otuke. A.H.T. 275 and Olango (1970, p. 2) provide the Palaro information above; A.H.T. 280 adds that the group joined *Rwot* Cua Omero (seemingly before the drought of c. 1790). Conversely, Wright (1934, p. 153), Okech (1953, p. 44), and Odongo (1976, p. 146) all claim that this Palaro group came from the Palaro chiefdom to the west; though possible, eastern origins seem much more likely.

30. The first version comes from Ongo (1971b, pp. 19–23); the alternative from Wright (1934, p. 79) and Webster A.H.T., pp. 113–17.

Pader. These radical changes seem to have relegated Kilak's earlier history to its "absent past," and thus perhaps to the discrepancy in origins noted above.[31]

Kilak traditions do agree on some matters. All identify the ruler who led Kilak into the southeastern zone as the chiefdom's founder and eponym *Rwot* Kilak. Moreover, the next *rwot* identified is Okutu (or Okutu Twonjobi). The Webster and Wright sources add that he was *Rwot* Kilak's son, and Ongo and Webster link Okutu to a drought and famine that must have been that occurring around 1790. Placing the drought in the middle of an average thirty-year reign produces estimated dates of rule of 1775–1805 for *Rwot* Okutu and thus 1745–75 for *Rwot* Kilak.[32]

The Ongo and Webster versions part company again (and Wright is silent) in identifying Kilak's *lobong* lineages. The Ongo source names four Eastern Nilotic lineages from Turkana—Kilak *kal*, Ogole, Pagol, and Pajaa—while also hinting that the four may have been sub-groups of one lineage. Kilak elders interviewed by Webster provided a completely different list of four lineages remembered to have joined *Rwot* Kilak in the following order: (1) Laboye, from the predominantly Eastern Nilotic Parabongo area; (2) Wol Laroda, reportedly not related to the Ogili chiefdom of Wol but from the Central Sudanic *Got* Kilak area to the west; (3) Pukor, the same group as the Panmolo (of probable Luo origins), which provided the second dynasty of the Pukor chiefdom; and (4) Acuru, from the Lapono area and thus probably Eastern Nilotic.[33]

Here, at least, evidence exists to suggest a resolution to the conflicting traditions. The first clue comes from the Webster text when it recounts that "a number" of lineages left Kilak during the reign of *Rwot* Okutu. Although severe drought and famine was a contributing cause of this "dispersal," the precipitating event is remembered to have been the *rwot*'s "rude and savage" behavior in putting out the eye of his brother Too in a quarrel. Too and his supporters then left for "Pagol-Pajule," in the Okaka area of the east-central zone.[34]

The Ongo text provides a different twist to the story. Here, Too wanted to be *rwot* in place of his brother, and interfered with the chiefdom's royal drum. Okutu appealed to his brother to stop, and then enlisted the aid

31. See an interview with Paipir, which along with Pader and Kilak formed a Pader Paluo chiefdom or allied group of chiefdoms in the nineteenth century (Webster A.H.T., pp. 117–21); see also A.H.T. 279.

32. Ongo (1971b, pp. 19–20); Webster A.H.T., pp. 113–15; Wright (1934, p. 79).

33. Ongo (1971b, pp. 19–23); Webster A.H.T., pp. 113–16.

34. Webster A.H.T., pp. 113–16.

of the more powerful Pader chiefdom. When Too still refused to cooperate, the Pader assisted in punishing Too, resulting in his being blinded. Consequently, just as in the Webster text, several groups are remembered to have departed Kilak to go to Okaka. Ongo's narrative identifies those who left as Too and his Ogole lineage (or sub-lineage, if he was Okutu's "brother") along with the Pagol and Pajaa.[35]

The final evidence is included in traditions from Okaka, which also identify three lineages moving into the Okaka area from Kilak after the drought occurring around 1790: the Pagol, Pajaa, and Ogole. Taken together, the evidence suggests that the Kilak chiefdom by around 1790 — before the split following the Okutu-Too quarrel — consisted probably of *kal*, Ogole, Pagol, Pajaa (some or all of whom may have been related sublineages), Wol Laroda, Pukor, Laboye, and Acuru.[36]

The East-Central Zone

Political change in the east-central zone following the 1720s drought was concentrated in two areas. One was the *Got* Okaka region, a key staging area for the extension of the new order and, by around 1790, the home of nine small chiefdoms. The other was Labongo, located near the confluence of the Pager and Aringa rivers some eighteen to twenty miles (thirty kilometers) northwest of Okaka and named after a prominent figure associated with the Paluo movement through Okaka. Labongo was eventually the site of Kitgum, the second largest town and second most important administrative center after Gulu in twentieth-century Acholi. In the eighteenth century, five chiefdoms established themselves there, though one did not survive into the nineteenth (Map 7).

THE *GOT* OKAKA AREA

The *Got* Okaka area today is usually referred to as Pajule, from the name of the supposed ancestor of some of the oldest Okaka lineages. In the nineteenth century, Pajule also designated a confederation (or military alliance) of Okaka chiefdoms that developed after the drought occurring around 1790. Between about 1725 and 1790, however, no such confederation existed. Instead, as already noted, thirty or more Paluo lineages made the Okaka area their temporary home and a staging area for extending the new

---

35. Ongo (1971b, pp. 19–23).
36. The Okaka evidence comes from Garry (1972b, pp. 61–62; 1976, pp. 326, 332).

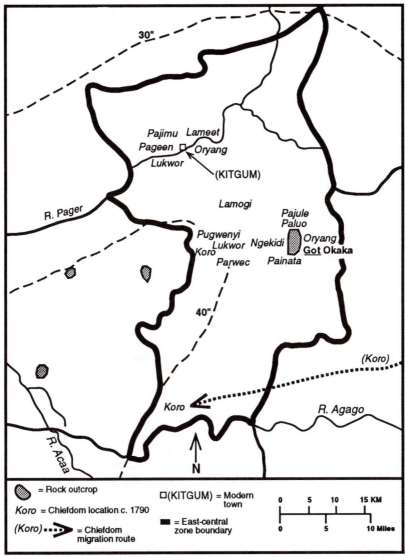

Map 7. East-central zone, c. 1725-90.

chiefly order to the east and north. In addition, nine small chiefdoms established themselves near Okaka as independent entities. Four clustered around Lukwor on the plains near Okaka: Lukwor itself (consisting probably of Lukwor *kal* and two *lobong* lineages), the Pugwenyi and the Parwec (with one associated lineage each), and the single-lineage polity of Koyo.

Four others were settled on Okaka's slopes: Pajule Paluo (with two *lobong* lineages), Ngekidi (with one *lobong* lineage), and the single-lineage polities of Painata and Oryang. Finally, another single-lineage polity, the Lamogi, settled on the plains but did not affiliate with either cluster.

Extant traditions indicate that the earliest Okaka lineages included the Palenga and Paranga (both claiming to be related to Puranga *kal*), and the Painata, Putuke, Paicano, Limule, and Paibony. Despite frequent claims that these "always lived" at Okaka, other renderings indicate probable origins to the east in Eastern Nilotic Karamoja or Jie. Painata traditions add that they followed their Palenga and Paranga "brothers" from Jie to Okaka via Labwor-Otuke. These lineages "formed the nucleus of Pajule, residing in pockets on the slopes of Okaka, with Palenga in a position of prestige if not of leadership."[37]

There is no way to tell how old this "nucleus of Pajule" lineages was or when others began to join them. By the early eighteenth century, however, many other lineages had settled in the Okaka area, a number of them clustered around the Lukwor. The originally Central Sudanic Lukwor and Koyo lineages seem to have met near Padibe or Pajok and then traveled south together to the Okaka plains. They may have left the Padibe/Pajok area in the late seventeenth century as a result of the violence accompanying the emergence of the northernmost Acholi chiefdom of Pajok (see Chapter 5). During their journey south, Lukwor and Koyo appear to have been joined by three other lineages under Lukwor's leadership: the Central Sudanic Pugwenyi (related to the Pugwenyi who joined Patiko), the Central Sudanic Pawidi, and the probably Eastern Nilotic Gem from the Agoro area (Crazzolara refers to these last as "original Lango of the north").[38]

The relationship among these lineages was complex. Garry writes that they were "never actually ruled by a Lukwor *rwot*" but simply looked to him for leadership. Koyo certainly seems an independent if closely associated lineage both before and after settlement in the Okaka area. Pugwenyi was

37. See Garry (1971a, pp. 2–3 and 19, nn. 4–17; 1972b, pp. 1–6); Crazzolara (1954, p. 488). The first of these sources includes the Limule and Paibony among the earliest Okaka lineages (Painata is identified as a "brother of Lenga"); the latter contains the quotation. Most of what we know of the east-central zone comes from Maura Garry's work, particularly her M.A. thesis on the Okaka area (1972b) and the Garry A.H.T. on Labongo. Crazzolara (1954, pp. 546–47) provides little more than a list of names, though he does identify Palenga as *wegi ngom* and the Painata as their "brother." Wright (1934, p. 81) also indicates that the Palenga were settled early at Okaka and were related to Puranga.

38. Garry (1972b, pp. 6–12, 27–36). This includes a critique of an earlier version of Odongo (1976), charging such blatant misuse of songs as historical evidence (including one referring to Lukwor and Koyo) that Odongo's work in general is suspect.

also unambiguously independent from early on, as indicated by the Eastern Nilotic Pateng lineage accepting the head of the Pugwenyi as *rwot* at about the time of the 1720s drought. Gem and Pawidi, on the other hand, seem to have acquired royal drums and other accoutrements of *rwot*ship only after the drought occurring around 1790. Before this, the only status for these two lineages that makes sense was to have been *lobong* under a Lukwor *rwot*. Finally, not long after Lukwor and the others settled on the Okaka plains, the Parwec and their *lobong* the Putuke (both of unclear origins) settled nearby and affiliated with the grouping.[39]

Within the first generation after the 1720s drought, then, the Lukwor-led grouping seems to have consisted of (1) Lukwor, a small chiefdom with Gem and Pawidi as *lobong* lineages; (2) Koyo, independent but with no *lobong* of its own; (3) Pugwenyi, with the Pateng as its only *lobong*; and (4) Parwec, with its associated lineage, the Putuke. A second center of chiefdom formation developed eventually around the grouping of lineages headed by the Palenga and settled higher up the Okaka slopes.

Before this, a host of new settlers and sojourners — many of them either Paluo or associated groups — made their way into the Okaka area after the 1720s drought. Most moved on, but the Oryang, Lukaci, and Lamogi stayed. Oryang traditions claim "Lango," or Eastern Nilotic, origins but also link the group with the "Cilibwami" movement of Paluo that came to Okaka by way of the Labwor-Otuke hills. Though the Oryang did not establish any leadership over other lineages once they arrived, they did apparently settle as a politically independent group near the also-independent and Eastern Nilotic Palenga and Painata.[40]

Along with the Oryang and Painata, the Lukaci and Lamogi also claim to have come to Okaka from Labwor-Otuke, most likely after the 1720s drought. When the Lukaci, originally from the mixed Eastern Nilotic-Luo region southeast of Acholi, reached Okaka they first settled on their own, though no evidence exists to suggest that they had a *rwot*, royal drum, or any other attributes associated with chiefdoms. The originally Central Sudanic Lamogi, in contrast, are clearly remembered to have brought a royal drum with them from Labwor-Otuke and to have established themselves as an independent, single-lineage chiefdom.[41]

---

39. Garry (1972b, pp. 18–19, 22, 36, 43–45). For more on the Parwec and their uncertain origins, see Atkinson (1978, pp. 422–23, n. 34).

40. Garry (1971a, pp. 8–9; 1972b, pp. 15–17). Garry (1976, p. 322) identifies the Oryang simply as a Paluo lineage that was part of the Labongo movement.

41. Garry (1972b, pp. 19–21).

The addition of permanently settled Paluo groups to the diverse and politically fragmented mix of peoples at Okaka is linked with the Bunyoro/Paluo military expedition against the young chiefdom of Palaro (see Chapter 5). When the army was about to reenter Paluo, traditions recount, a number of men rebelled and refused to return. Among them were Owiny Opok, a "son" of the Bunyoro/Paluo ruler who had led the campaign, and four of his "brothers" — Cunmor, Langote, Bagu, and Olano. All left with their supporters, eventually to settle at Okaka.

The most senior and prestigious among them was clearly Owiny Opok. Most accounts indicate that he came to Okaka with a royal drum, where he was joined by the Palenga and Lukaci as *lobong* lineages and by Cunmor and Langote and their followers as sub-lineages of *kal*. Palenga's close associate Painata, however, did not join the new Pajule Paluo chiefdom. Instead, it came to possess its own royal drum and was recognized as an independent though always single-lineage polity. Meanwhile, Olano and his followers settled on a nearby peak of Okaka while Bagu and his supporters joined the Gwara lineage to form the nucleus of yet another chiefdom, eventually called Ngekidi. This name was derived from the Luo word *kidi* (rock) supposedly because the Gwara first discovered Bagu alone, hiding behind a rock on Okaka's slopes.[42]

Soon after these Paluo groups established themselves, yet another Paluo element is remembered to have arrived on the scene led by Lagoro Aboga, another supposed "son" of the Bunyoro/Paluo *rwot* involved in the Palaro expedition. Traditions of Lagoro are difficult to interpret because long after his death he was "revealed" as a new chiefdom *jok* of Pajule Paluo. This was after the 1830s drought when Pajule Paluo was establishing leadership over a confederation of many of the small Okaka polities, and *Jok* Lagoro became a famous and powerful unifying symbol in the process. As a result, stories of Lagoro include much that is magical or supernatural. Still, we can find traces of early-eighteenth-century developments associated with a probably historical Lagoro.

Traditions begin with Lagoro's arrival at Okaka from Bunyoro or Paluo in search of his "brothers" Owiny and Olano. After finding them,

42. Ibid., pp. 37–41. See also Garry (1971a, pp. 9–10; 1976, p. 323); Ongo (1971a, p. 1); and a garbled summary version in Pellegrini (1963, pp. 1–2). Wright (1934, p. 81) identifies Owiny Opok as the first Paluo *rwot* in Pajule but provides no other details. Finally, no information is available on whether the early Okaka lineages of Paicano, Limule, and Paibony joined any eighteenth-century chiefdoms. Sometime after the drought of c. 1790, the Paicano joined the newly established Pawidi chiefdom, and the Limule and Paibony became part of the equally new Ibakara; see Garry (1971a, p. 22; 1976, pp. 332–33).

Lagoro settled with the Oryang who soon accepted him as their *rwot*. Though couched in supernatural terms, the Oryang response is remembered to have hinged on what is now a familiar theme: the ability of a "true" *rwot* to attract unaffiliated lineages with generosity made possible by tribute payments. The key passage reads "when Lagoro arrived at Okaka he impressed the clan [lineage] of Oryang by providing food."[43]

Lagoro is then remembered to have left Okaka to return to Bunyoro/Paluo) "to receive his father's blessing on his new kingdom [chiefdom] so that he could rule properly." On his way, however, he stopped in Paluo at the home of his sister Lamwoci and died. Garry relates three conflicting versions of what happened next: "One source says that the dying Lagoro directed that his royal regalia be taken to Owiny Opok," *rwot* of Pajule Paluo back at Okaka. The Oryang lineage, conversely, claims that Lagoro "bequeathed the regalia to them, since his daughter had married into their clan [lineage]." But then Owiny Opok wrested the regalia from the Oryang. A third version indicates that the Ngekidi also fought a losing battle with Owiny Opok's Pajule Paluo over the regalia, though fighting among all the groups is remembered to have been carried out with sticks and clubs only and not with more deadly spears. Such limited conflict suggests that the groups had or are remembered to have had close ties.[44]

All three of these accounts suggest that *Rwot* Lagoro was the source of the royal drum and other regalia of Owiny Opok and Pajule Paluo. Perhaps Owiny did not possess such regalia when he first came to Okaka, though some traditions assert that he did. Or perhaps he did confiscate the regalia of later Paluo immigrants to replace or add to what he had before—either to enhance his own prestige or reduce that of potential rivals. But a third possibility is that linking the origins of the drum and other regalia with Lagoro had nothing to do with the historical Lagoro but only with the powerful, unifying *Jok* Lagoro of the nineteenth century.

In any case, the Okaka area during the generation following the 1720s drought appears to have served not only as a temporary stop for many Paluo and other groups but as the more permanent home of nine small chiefdoms. Four of the latter were clustered on and near the Okaka slopes: Pajule Paluo, made up of Paluo *kal* and the *lobong* lineages of Palenga and Lukaci; the single-lineage Painata chiefdom; a Lagoro-Oryang polity; and the Ngekidi chiefdom, consisting of Bagu (and his lineage?) and the Gwara.

---

43. See Garry (1971a, p. 9; 1972b, pp. 41–42, 99–100; 1976, p. 323). Garry (1972b, pp. 99–116) provides an extended discussion of *Jok* Lagoro.

44. See references in n. 43.

On the surrounding plains were the four associated chiefdoms of the Lukwor-led grouping (Lukwor itself, Koyo, Pugwenyi, and Parwec) and the unaffiliated single-lineage Lamogi chiefdom.

Available traditions tell us little about the Okaka area during the eighteenth century apart from the sketchy information already recounted. One reference indicates that the eighteenth-century Okaka chiefdoms lived in peace with one another, "only broken by occasional Karimojong or Jiwe [Jie] raids."[45]

THE LABONGO AREA

Five chiefdoms were established near the confluence of the Pager and Aringa rivers between about 1725 and 1790, though one, Oryang, did not survive as an independent entity. The other four Labongo chiefdoms were Pageen (the largest east-central-zone chiefdom before around 1790, with eight *lobong* lineages, including the former Oryang *kal*); Lameet (with five *lobong* lineages); Pajimu (with three associated lineages); and Lukwor (related to the Lukwor of Okaka and also with three associated lineages). Oryang, Pageen, and Lameet are often presented as related, as part of the Paluo movement through Okaka (see Map 7).

Pageen, Oryang, and Lameet

Migration traditions of Pageen *kal* are the most extensive in the Labongo area and clearly link the group with the southward-migrating Luo who supposedly traveled to Pubungu before splitting up there. From Pubungu, the group out of which Pageen *kal* emerged is remembered to have moved northeast into present-day Lango District, to Otuke (where "they suffered from lack of water"), then to the Ogili-Parabongo mountains in the southeastern zone, then to the Okaka area, and finally to Labongo.[46]

Another set of broader and less detailed traditions recounts that the eventual royal lineages of Lameet and Oryang along with Pageen traveled from Paluo to Okaka where they became jointly known as "Twooro." Each

45. The quotation is from Wright (1934, p. 82). The three *rwot* lists are in Garry (1972b, p. 37; see also 1971a, p. 10; 1976, pp. 323–24); Ongo (1971a, p. 2); and Wright (1934, p. 82). The traditions collected by Wright claim that the Lamogi and Gem were incorporated into Paluo-led Pajule during this time; this does not agree with the more detailed accounts of Garry (especially 1972b), which indicate that such incorporation only took place in the nineteenth century.

46. Garry A.H.T., pp. 1–2, 5, 9, 20, 26, 28, 30; Crazzolara (1954, pp. 535–36); Wright (1934, p. 93); and Anywar (1954, pp. 100–101, 104) identify the relationship between Pageen, Lameet, and Oryang. The detailed Pageen *kal* migration information is from Crazzolara (1954, pp. 533–35).

includes the name Twooro in its traditions; the more extensive Lameet and Oryang royal genealogies also contain Labongo (and other stereotypical names indicating Luo origins). Traditions from Parabongo in the southeastern zone, meanwhile, claim that Parabongo *kal* is descended from a Bunyoro/Paluo founder (Labongo or "Silabwambe") who passed through Okaka and had among his sons someone named Tworo or Ototworo. This Tworo, moreover, is remembered to have become a *rwot* in "Labongo Kitgum" in general, or Lameet in particular.[47]

Is all this conclusive evidence of Luo or Paluo origins? Not according to Crazzolara. He noted that the migration traditions of the eventual Pageen *kal* begin only in the Agoro mountains and not further north in some Luo homeland. To Crazzolara this is a "very plain" indication of "Lango" (Eastern Nilotic) origins. He supports this assertion with a quote from one of his Pageen sources: "PaGeen with Pameet and Oryang are descendants of PaTwooro: they came from [the northern Agoro region of] Lango-Logire (although some of them say that they came from Loka [Paluo])." If this account is accepted, then all or most of the migration details given above can be seen as fabrications to buttress false claims of Luo/Paluo origins.[48]

However uncertain their origins, virtually all Pageen, Lameet, and Oryang traditions converge on Okaka. A host of sources identifies at least one and usually all three of these eventual ruling lineages with Okaka immediately before they moved to Labongo. Many add that the three, perhaps with others, stayed together at Okaka as a grouping known as "Twooro." One text even locates the original split of Pageen and Lameet there, with a stereotypical story accounting for Pageen *kal*'s emergence as the senior *rwot* and Lameet's as the junior.[49]

One way to make sense of these various traditions is to accept the existence of a Twooro grouping in the Okaka area that included the eventual royal lineages of Pageen, Lameet, and Oryang, but to assume neither the same origins for the three nor an earlier association. This interpretation accommodates Crazzolara's evidence and arguments for Pageen *kal*'s Eastern Nilotic origins from the Agoro region, as well as Garry's interpretation (above) of Oryang's origins as an Eastern Nilotic group from the south

47. Garry A.H.T., pp. 1, 5; Crazzolara (1954, p. 535); Webster A.H.T., pp. 135–36, 140; see also Pellegrini (1963, p. 9) for a compatible summary; and Anywar (1954, p. 100) and Wright (1934, p. 93) for less clear and less direct evidence.

48. Crazzolara (1954, p. 535).

49. Ibid.; Garry A.H.T., pp. 1–2, 5, 30.

that was part of the Labongo-Silabwambe portion of the Paluo movement into the Okaka area. Lameet *kal*, meanwhile, may well have been a Paluo group also associated with the Labongo movement and related to the royal lineage of Parabongo in the southeastern zone, as both Parabongo and Lameet traditions claim.

By most accounts, the first of the Twooro grouping to reach Labongo was Pageen *kal*. They are remembered to have arrived with a *rwot* and a "proper, large royal drum," and are widely acknowledged as ruling lineage of the senior, most important, and largest chiefdom in the area. Unfortunately, traditions about Pageen are limited and hampered by the absence of a Pageen *rwot* list. The chronology of the Paluo movements through Okaka with which Pageen *kal* and the other "Patwooro" groups are linked suggests strongly that the Pageen reached Labongo during the generation following the 1720s drought. They found there the Pacijok, Padong, Panyangor, Liba, and Lugwar lineages, none of which have clear traditions of origins or earlier settlements.[50]

Probably the first to join Pageen *kal* in Labongo were the Pacijok and Padong, each of which asserts earliest settlement in the area. The way in which Pageen *kal* chose between the two claims is suggested by a passage in Crazzolara. When Pageen *kal* came to Labongo, the Padong were "widely dispersed (in smaller groups)." If so, then Pageen *kal* might well have had more reason to deal and negotiate with the "fair sized" Pacijok. In any case, Pageen *kal* recognized Pacijok as *wegi ngom*.[51]

Other lineages incorporated into Pageen were the Lemo, the associated lineages of Keera and Paibwor, the Parakono, the Obem, and the former Oryang *kal*. Traditions imply that all these joined early, though the absence of a Pageen *rwot* list makes chronology unclear. The only real clue comes from Oryang traditions noting that the Oryang lost their royal drum and joined Pageen after coming to Labongo but before the first of two great famines that struck in successive generations — surely references to the droughts occurring around 1790 and in the 1830s. This suggests Oryang incorporation in the mid- to late eighteenth century. The only other reference to incorporation is an intriguing story about the Lemo, who, like Pageen *kal*, were also probably Eastern Nilotic in origin:

50. Garry A.H.T., pp. 23, 26, 28, 30, 33, 39, 40, 43–44; Crazzolara (1954, pp. 535, 537).
51. Crazzolara (1954, p. 535); p. 537 presents an interpretation of Pacijok's earlier history that does not fit with Crazzolara's Patiko chapter, other Patiko traditions, or Labongo traditions.

> When Lemo reached Guu [a prominent Labongo outcrop] they found the Cijook people as the wegi ngom, and the Pagen as rulers. . . . When Lemo reached this area the Pagen people tried to send them off again, because they were afraid that the newcomers would cause trouble by not accepting and obeying the laws in Pagen. Pagen, however, finally allowed them to stay, but only after a fight in which the Lemo stood their ground strongly.

When the elders were asked whether this was not unusual since most chiefdoms "would be glad to have their numbers increased," they replied that "long ago this was not so, and the settlement of strangers was not encouraged." While this atypical perspective may be only an aberration, it might represent a more common state of affairs than its almost total absence in traditions would suggest.[52]

No other Pageen *lobong* have extant traditions concerning their incorporation into the chiefdom. The Paibwor and Keera lineages seem to have shared both the same Eastern Nilotic origins as Pageen *kal* and the same original homeland just west of the northern Agoro mountains. But all we know of the Obem and Parakono (of unclear origins) is that they left Pageen to attach themselves to other Labongo chiefdoms established after the late-eighteenth-century drought.[53]

Oryang traditions focus on the lineage's history before settlement in Labongo. They include a long *rwot* list dominated by suspect, stereotypical Luo names and a remembered migration that took the group from "Cillu" (Luo-speaking Shilluk in the southern Sudan) to the Luo triangle and then to Okaka. All of this serves the same ideological end: to support claims of Luo origins. But Garry's evidence and arguments are convincing in their depiction of Oryang's Eastern Nilotic origins. She does see Oryang as having attached itself, in Labwor-Otuke or elsewhere in the south, to the Paluo movement into the Okaka area. Certainly, all extant Oryang sources link the lineage to Okaka; some add that the ruler there was "Twooro," whose "sons" included the founders of the chiefdoms of Oryang, Pageen, Lameet, Parabongo, and others.

The person remembered to have led the Oryang from Okaka to La-

---

52. Garry A.H.T., pp. 9, 23, 26, 30, 43; Crazzolara (1954, pp. 533–35, 537); Wright (1934, p. 93). The quote is from Garry A.H.T., p. 23.

53. On the Paibwor, see Crazzolara (1954, pp. 476, 491, 537–38) and A.H.T. 245; on the Keera, Garry A.H.T., p. 23 and Crazzolara (1954, pp. 537–38). The Obem became part of a small polity headed by the Panmolo; see Garry A.H.T., p. 9. And the Parakono joined the small Koc chiefdom established by a lineage from Paico; see Garry A.H.T., pp. 25–28, and Crazzolara (1954, p. 539).

bongo was the lineage's namesake, *Rwot* Oryang. Traditions recount that he possessed a royal drum and found the Pacijok already settled in the area, but they do not mention the Pageen or Lameet. Eventually, the Oryang somehow lost their royal drum, probably during the mid- to late eighteenth century, after which they joined the Pageen chiefdom.[54]

Traditions of Lameet *kal* assert Paluo origins, and particularly a relationship to the Paluo royal lineage of Parabongo in the southeastern zone. It was at Okaka, these traditions continue, that the Lameet and Pageen royal lineages separated from the "Twooro" grouping to become independent chiefdoms. It was also there that Lameet *kal* probably incorporated its first *lobong* lineage, the Lamola.[55]

Once Lameet *kal* and their Lamola *lobong* came to Labongo, four lineages that were already there joined them: (1) Liba, acknowledged as one of the earliest lineages to settle in Labongo, with one source identifying "Baar" (i.e., Central Sudanic) origins; (2) Pakor, associated with Liba but of unclear ethnolinguistic origins itself; (3) Bobi, with origins in the Eastern Nilotic area east of the northern Agoro mountains; and (4) Paibwoc, a lineage identified by Crazzolara as having Central Sudanic origins from "Baar." The only additional information in available Lameet traditions suggests that the Lameet continued to return to a *jok* in Okaka for many ritual ceremonies.[56]

Pajimu

Traditions identify the *rwot* who established Pajimo, the fourth chiefdom in Labongo, as Bilo (who ruled c. 1720–50). The traditions also assert that Pajimu *kal* came to Labongo from "Bunyoro" (surely Paluo) via a route west of Okaka through the central zone. Neither Pajimu nor other traditions indicate that Pajimu *kal* was connected with the "Twooro" grouping of royal lineages. Pajimu *kal*'s claim that they arrived in Labongo with a *rwot* and royal drum appears widely accepted, and Pajimu *kal* soon incorporated the Panyangor, Lugwar, and probably the Pamolo as *lobong* lineages. But a group interview with elders of Pajimu *kal* and the Panyangor and Lugwar

54. Garry A.H.T., pp. 5–6, 30; Wright (1934, p. 93).

55. See Garry A.H.T., pp. 1–2, 30, 32, 34 (which include some unconvincing suggestions that Lamola and Lameet *kal* were related).

56. See ibid., pp. 1–2, 31, 33, for information on the four lineages joining Lameet *kal*. Specific evidence on the Liba and Pakor comes from Garry A.H.T., pp. 2, 33, and Crazzolara (1954, p. 537); on the Bobi, Garry A.H.T., pp. 2, 33, Crazzolara (1954, pp. 397, 399, 537, 541–42, 547), A.H.T. 286–87; and on the Paibwoc, Crazzolara (1954, p. 537). Garry A.H.T., pp. 2–3, 6, suggests that the Lameet continued to go to a *jok* in Okaka (*Jok* Lagoro) for many ritual ceremonies.

lineages resulted in a series of highly charged rival claims that can be summarized as follows:

1. Panyangor and Lugwar elders began by saying that they were present, along with the Pacijok, when Pajimu *kal* arrived.
2. Pajimu *kal*, on the other hand, argued that Pajimu, Panyangor, and Lugwar came together from the central zone and met the Pacijok, and then even claimed that the Pajimu were present before Lugwar and Panyangor.
3. Then Panyangor elders claimed that they had a *rwot* when Pajimu came, with the Lugwar under them.
4. Lugwar elders reversed the story: they had the *rwot* and the Panyangor were under them.
5. Pajimu *kal* did not enter into that debate but did state that they came to Labongo with a royal drum and introduced it to Lugwar, who in turn "showed them the things of the Jok."
6. Lugwar elders countered with the assertion that Pajimu came to them and Lugwar showed them "the things of the *rwot*."
7. Panyangor elders said again that it was they who had the *rwot* and that Pajimu came from "Loka" (Paluo) and joined them.[57]

How can this welter of competing claims and counter-claims be resolved? The Panyangor and Lugwar assertion that they were settled in Labongo before Pajimu *kal* arrived is corroborated by traditions from other Labongo groups. Conversely, the evidence concerning the origins of the *rwot*ship and royal drum favors Pajimu *kal*, even when Panyangor elders attempt, in the following passage, to press their claims:

> Panyangor were the clan [lineage] with the *rwot*, and Pajimu came from Loka and joined them. The wife of Pajimu's *rwot* was dead and they went to Panyangor and said "Give us the royal drum so that we can have a funeral and mourn for our wife." They gave their royal drum to Pajimu, and they went with it. Then after some time Panyangor went to Pajimu saying that they wanted their royal drum returned, but Pajimu failed to return it. . . . The Panyangor were very sad about their royal drum, and they wanted it back.

57. Crazzolara (1954, p. 538) states that Pajimu *kal* came from Paluo with a royal drum and was joined by the others. Garry A.H.T., pp. 37–41, both corroborates this and includes the alternatives noted above. Garry A.H.T. also identifies Pamolo's probable Central Sudanic origins (p. 39) and provides an alternative version of the group's history from Pamolo elders, who argue that they were related to Pageen and Lameet *kal* before they broke away to form their own chiefdom (pp. 9–10).

Pajimu kept it, however, and eventually the Panyangor people came back to them.[58]

Two elements in this account totally undermine its ostensible contention. First, the central point — that the Panyangor would loan a royal drum to the Pajimu in the manner indicated — flies in the face of all other Acholi traditions and is totally untenable. And second, the narrative acknowledges the existence of a Pajimu *rwot* at the outset.

An even more conclusive assessment was given by an elder from the neighboring Pageen chiefdom, Bernard Odwar, when he was asked about disputed claims in Pajimu concerning the *rwot*ship:

> The Lugwar were in their place there [already in Labongo]. So they remained as the owners of the land. The Pajimu came from Bunyoro. They came with their drum and their chief. At that time the people from Chope [Paluo] were respected. . . . The people believed that the Chope had got rain [rainmaking powers], which we call "KOT." . . . They had drums and chiefs. So a man from there was respected and honoured . . . because of this kot. They saw you as a big man because rain is so important. We should also recognise, and this is important, that Pajimu came recently. Lugwar had no drum before Pajimu came. Panyangor had no drum. The people here had no chief, but these Banyoro [Paluo] they came with power, they came with their chiefs, with their leader, a man whom they respected . . . [so they] were immediately accepted as the rulers.[59]

Though overstated, Odwar in this passage locates the origins of the new order, in both the east-central zone and Acholi as a whole, and identifies some of its key components, particularly the symbolic role of royal drums and the powerful attraction of supposed rainmaking prowess. He also makes it clear that Pajimu *kal*, not the Lugwar or Panyangor, introduced this order with respect to the Pajimu chiefdom.

Lukwor

The final Labongo chiefdom to consider is Lukwor. Numerous sources state that a Lukwor chiefdom, related to the Lukwor of Okaka, was founded in Labongo under a *rwot* named Lacede (who ruled c. 1720–50). Traditions from the Lukwor at Okaka also identify a *Rwot* Lacede "who was exiled by his people, together with all his household" because of his cruelty.

---

58. Evidence on the early presence of Panyangor and Lugwar comes from Garry A.H.T., pp. 39–40, 43–44; Crazzolara (1954, p. 538); the quotation comes from Garry A.H.T., pp. 38–39.

59. Garry A.H.T., pp. 43–44.

Garry suggests that this occurred in the late seventeenth or early eighteenth century and that this Lacede then went to Labongo.[60]

Traditions also indicate that like Oryang, Lukwor is remembered to have eventually lost its rainmaking royal drum and its independence to become a *lobong* lineage in the Pageen chiefdom. When this occurred is not clear, but before it did, Lukwor's *lobong* lineages seem to have been the Anyara, Ayom, and Parapol. No information is available on the incorporation of these lineages or what happened to them subsequently, although the Anyara and Ayom have numerous branches scattered throughout Acholi and beyond, and, like Lukwor, were Central Sudanic in origin.[61]

Conclusion

The second phase of chiefdom formation in north-central Uganda, set off by the 1720s drought, saw a striking acceleration over the hesitant and scattered beginnings during the previous fifty years. Nowhere was this acceleration more marked than in the developing southeastern and east-central zones. The eighteen new chiefdoms founded in an emergent southeastern zone along with fourteen in the east-central zone (thirteen of which survived into the nineteenth century) represented more than half of all the chiefdoms established in Acholi between about 1725 and 1790.

The explosion of chiefdom formation and related social change in these two zones was due to a particular combination of circumstances. One was the influx after the 1720s drought of far larger numbers of Paluo lineages than anywhere else in Acholi. Many Paluo groups became the ruling lineages of new chiefdoms, and two set themselves up as new dynasties in already established ones. Before this, many of these Paluo lineages had lived along with numerous others in a dynamic and ethnolinguistically mixed center of settlement and activity: the Labwor-Otuke hills south and east of the southeastern zone. After the drought, numerous Paluo groups from both Labwor-Otuke and Paluoland itself flocked into the *Got* Okaka area in the east-central zone. In both Labwor-Otuke and Okaka, chiefly institutions and ideology derived from Bunyoro/Paluo percolated through

60. References to Lukwor's independence in Labongo come from ibid., pp. 13, 19–20, 30, 41, 44; Crazzolara (1954, p. 539). Other information comes from Garry A.H.T., pp. 19–20 and Garry (1972b, pp. 34–35).

61. Garry A.H.T., pp. 19–20; Crazzolara (1954, p. 539). The latter also provides additional evidence on the probable Central Sudanic origins of the Anyara (pp. 381, 383, 465, 483–84) and Ayom (pp. 397–99, 476, 492, 563).

mixed and closely settled clusters of people. Many groups that adopted the new institutions and ideology then moved on to establish themselves as ruling lineages of new chiefdoms, especially in the southeastern and east-central zones.

But this did not happen in a vacuum. Three contextual features stimulated the proliferation of chiefdoms in these two emergent zones. First, these were areas of low rainfall that would have been especially hard hit by the 1720s drought. The disruption, dislocation, and insecurity that followed created a highly receptive environment for new sociopolitical institutions and ideology, and a new political leadership promising greater security and stability. Second, the 1720s drought also set changes in motion just to the east of Acholi that were creating a new Jie society and ethnic group there. Inhabitants of the emergent east-central and, especially, southeastern zones were thus forced to contend with the added difficulties of coping with neighbors establishing their own identities and territorial claims — one more incentive to become part of the larger-scale chiefdoms. The same incentive probably explains the extremely atypical growth of the chiefdom located closest to the divergently developing Jie: Lira Paluo. Finally — and a point not to be underestimated — the numerous and strategically located mountains and outcrops of the two zones seem to have provided an extra measure of protection within which chiefdom formation and related social change could take firm hold.

Many of the above features were less prominent or were absent in the other zones that developed in Acholi, affecting the pattern of chiefdom formation in those zones. However, as we shall see in the next two chapters, both the processes by which these other chiefdoms were founded and the institutions and ideology upon which they were based shared much with developments in the southeastern and east-central zones.

7. The South-Central and Western Zones: The Continuing Extension of the New Order

The explosion of chiefdom formation that occurred between 1725 and 1790 in the southeastern and east-central zones — with more than thirty new chiefdoms founded and about 175 lineages incorporated — was not typical. Indeed, as we shall in this chapter and the next, the total of new chiefdoms established and lineages incorporated in all of the remaining six zones of Acholi during the same period did not equal the combined numbers of the southeastern and east-central zone.[1]

The South-Central Zone

The dissimilarity in numbers just noted was epitomized by the different trajectories of chiefdom formation in the neighboring south-central and southeastern zones. These two zones had no barriers or discernible markers separating them and each was comprised of overwhelmingly Eastern Nilotic lineages. Still, the eighteen new chiefdoms and up to 150 lineages incorporated in the southeastern zone contrasted sharply with the five chiefdoms founded in the south-central zone (one of which did not survive) and the no more than sixteen lineages that joined them (after which as many as seven left).

Why such disparities? One set of likely causes was linked to differences in rainfall. Unlike the dry southeastern zone, much of the south-central zone is part of the most abundant rainfall region of Acholi (Map 8). But as poor as rainfall in the southeastern zone was and as hard as it was hit by the 1720s drought, it was still better off than its neighbors to the east. Many

---

1. The lineages incorporated elsewhere do appear on average to have included greater numbers of people (see Appendix).

eastern migrants thus came into the zone, furthering already disrupted social relations and helping create the conditions that made attractive the extra security and stability promised by the new chiefdoms. Conversely, the more abundant rainfall enjoyed by the south-central zone did not set it apart from adjoining areas north, west, or south — all of which shared essentially the same advantage. And the high rainfall portion of the zone was relatively distant from both the hard-hit areas to the east of Acholi and even the concentrations of settlement and chiefdom formation in the south-eastern zone. There was thus no influx of settlers into the south-central zone in the troubled period following the drought.

Next, even before the 1720s drought, the southeastern zone was home for four chiefdoms organized on the Bunyoro/Paluo model, and more than twenty others with an experience of that model came into the zone in the drought's aftermath. In comparison, even after the drought, the south-central zone had only a handful of such lineages.

Finally, the emergent southeastern zone confronted during the eighteenth century a divergent and competing social order developing on its eastern frontier: the Jie. The south-central zone faced nothing comparable until after about 1790, when another devastating drought struck the region and an emergent Lango society and collective identity began to evolve in present-day Lango District just to the south. It was only then that chiefdom formation accelerated in the south-central zone and the new chiefly order became widely and deeply entrenched.[2]

In sum, the south-central zone in the eighteenth century was not marked by the influx and mix of people after the 1720s drought, including those with a knowledge and experience of the new chiefly order, that characterized the southeastern zone. Neither did it experience the degree of drought-induced disruption nor the existence of a contrasting and competing new social order developing on its doorstep to promote the wide-scale spread of that order. All of this contributed to changing the dynamic and limiting the extent of eighteenth-century chiefdom formation in the south-central zone.

Even though the scale was limited, the establishment of chiefdoms in the south-central zone was accompanied by new and different networks of

2. Although an emergent Lango Omiro only took hold in present-day Lango District during the nineteenth century, the area was not static before then. The 1720s drought seems to have contributed to an influx of settlers, considerable disruption, and even "relatively intense warfare." For information on Lango District in the eighteenth century, see Herring (1979b, pp. 295–99). Disruption and conflict may have spilled over into the adjacent south-central zone and contributed to the seemingly low eighteenth-century population of the zone.

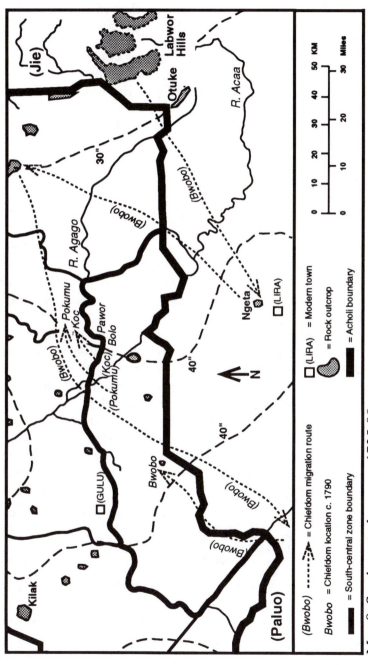

Map 8. South-central zone, c. 1725-90.

(Bwobo) ---->--- = Chiefdom migration route

Bwobo = Chiefdom location c. 1790

□(LIRA) = Modern town

▨ = Rock outcrop

■ = Acholi boundary

□ = South-central zone boundary

interaction. This interaction in turn served both to locate the area within the boundaries of a developing new social order and political culture, and to begin the creation of an identifiable "zone" within those broader boundaries. The royal lineages of four of the chiefdoms involved in establishing the new networks — Bolo, Pawor, Bwobo, and Pokumu — came from the Labwor-Otuke hills to the east. The traditions that provide the most illuminating glimpses into the emergent south-central zone's eighteenth-century past, however, come from the chiefdom of Koc, which arrived in the area from the west.

KOC AND POKUMU

Koc's origins are linked with Luo-speaking Jonam, located along the west bank of the Nile opposite the Luo triangle. Most traditions identify Koc *kal* as descended from early Luo who remained in the area after the split of the southward-migrating Luo at Pubungu. Some sources add that the group was part of the royal lineage of the Jonam chiefdom of Koc Ragem, whose origins and regalia were linked with Bunyoro/Paluo. Some further claim that an unsuccessful bid for succession in Jonam was the cause of Koc *kal's* trek eastward.[3]

Accompanying Koc *kal* on the trek, under either *Rwot* Latogo (c. 1735–75) or *Rwot* Olwa Kibira (c. 1705–35), was the Romo lineage. The small chiefdom made its way to the area of *Got* Palee (later usually called Guruguru) in westernmost Acholi, where it is remembered to have come into contact with the Pamuca lineage — early inhabitants of the area who later joined the Lamogi chiefdom. There also, according to one text that identified Olwa as *rwot* when Koc left Jonam, Olwa died.[4]

When most of the chiefdom decided to move on, a supposed "brother" of the *rwot* named Daca, along with a small group of relatives and followers,

3. Pubungu references or familiar Pubungu names in Koc traditions can be found in Crazzolara (1951, p. 304); Malandra (1947, p. 30); Okech (1953, p. 35); Wright (1934, p. 88); and A.H.T. 249, 257, 259, 261. Crazzolara and Malandra include information suggesting Central Sudanic ties, though Crazzolara (pp. 303–5) also includes Koc *kal* in his general argument that the Koc chiefdom was "Lango" (Eastern Nilotic) in origin. Koc ties with Koc Ragem and the latter's links with Bunyoro/Paluo are in Wright (1934, pp. 90, 92), Malandra (1947, p. 30), Crazzolara (1954, pp. 443–45), Apecu (1972, pp. 90–99), A.H.T. 261. References to a succession conflict leading to Koc's move from Jonam are in Okot (1971, p. 25), Okech (1953, p. 36), and A.H.T. 254.

4. Sources identifying Latogo are Crazzolara (1951, p. 305); Okot (1971, p. 25); Okech (1953, p. 36); A.H.T. 250, 254. Koc elder Layua Amal, who in nine interviews demonstrated exceptional knowledge, said in A.H.T. 249, 259, and 262 that it was Olwa Kibira. Malandra (1947, pp. 30–31) places the move several generations earlier than any of the other sources and, along with A.H.T. 259, notes contact with the Pamuca. The reference to Rwot Olwa's death in the Palee area is in A.H.T. 262.

remained behind. This group became the village-lineage known as "Koc" or "Koc-Daca," and like the Pamuca it eventually joined the Lamogi chiefdom. The fact that Koc traditions include references to Pamuca and Koc-Daca but fail to mention Lamogi suggests that Lamogi had not yet been established as a chiefdom when Koc was settled in the area, probably during or before the 1730s.[5]

Led by Latogo, the Koc traveled to the confluence of the Acaa and Agago rivers in the emergent south-central zone (see Map 8). Koc traditions identify this as a "Lango" area, which typically means Eastern Nilotic in general. Here, though, traditions distinguish the Eastern Nilotic "Lango" in the south-central zone from other Eastern Nilotic "Lango Omiro" farther south. Indeed, when the Koc arrived, the south-central zone "Lango" were under hostile pressure from their "Lango Omiro" neighbors. If we accept that the "Lango Omiro" name is a reading back of an identity that only took hold in the nineteenth century, this Koc depiction fits the general picture of disruption and conflict in the region after the 1720s drought. And these conditions, as we shall see, helped shape the response accorded Latogo and his small chiefdom.[6]

The first "Lango" lineages that Koc met in the south-central zone were the Pokumu and Patuda, already organized as a small chiefdom with Pokumu the royal lineage and Patuda its *lobong*. Both seem originally from Karamoja and then from the Labwor-Otuke hills, where they were probably exposed to and then adopted the institutions and ideology of chiefship and perhaps the Luo language as well.[7]

When the two small chiefdoms first encountered one another, Koc traditions portray the Pokumu and their *rwot* as more important than Koc: "Okumu surpassed us in importance . . . we were his visitors." But then the balance shifted. Pokumu remained a small two-lineage chiefdom, while Koc

5. See Crazzolara (1951, p. 305); Malandra (1947, p. 30); Okech (1953, p. 36); Okot (1971, p. 25); A.H.T. 250, 259, 303. In contrast, A.H.T. 201 and 203 from Lamogi indicate that the Koc-Daca did not travel with Koc to the Palee area but were there when the Koc arrived, and Crazzolara (1951, p. 305; 1954, p. 469) argues that the Koc-Daca were a "Lango" (Eastern Nilotic) lineage originally from the Palee area. His logic here is not clear because Palee seems so much a part of the Central Sudanic world that it is difficult to understand how any group "originally" from there would have been Eastern Nilotic.

6. Virtually all the sources in n. 5 include references to Koc's move into the emergent south-central zone. Malandra's version (1947, pp. 30–31) remains out of step with all other sources. Reference to Langi "pressure" and hostilities comes especially from Crazzolara (1951, p. 305), with briefer mention in A.H.T. 249.

7. See Crazzolara (1951, p. 305; 1954, pp. 487–88); Okech (1953, p. 35); Herring (1974b, p. 75, n. 37); A.H.T. 252, 259. These sources include passages that the two lineages were related and also identify Pokumu as part of an Eastern Nilotic Aceer multiple-village grouping in what becomes the central zone of Acholi.

grew. Eventually Koc so completely overshadowed its neighbor that Pokumu became in effect Koc's junior partner, though it always maintained its formal independence.[8]

Koc soon encountered other Eastern Nilotic lineages, including the Guna, Punok, and Dolo. Guna lineage traditions provide numerous details of that group's meeting with Koc and the conditions prevailing in the area during the mid-eighteenth century. These traditions also identify the area as "Lango" (Eastern Nilotic) while noting as well the nearby settlement of chiefdoms such as Pokumu, Bolo, and Bwobo, and the "Lango Omiro" farther south. This mixture of people suggests that, like neighboring Lango District, the area was bilingual, with both Luo and Eastern Nilotic languages being spoken.[9]

Strengthening the notion that the area was originally "Lango" is the widely accepted claim of the Eastern Nilotic Guna to be *wegi lobo*, an alternative designation for *wegi ngom* ("fathers or owners of the soil") and typically accorded the oldest or "original" inhabitants in a particular area. Guna traditions assert that when Latogo and his chiefdom first settled in the area, they symbolically acknowledged this Guna primacy by initially joining Guna rather than vice-versa, an interpretation reluctantly accepted by an especially knowledgeable elder from Koc *kal*, Layua Amal.[10]

Guna traditions then identify three major differences between the Koc chiefdom and Eastern Nilotic groups long settled in the area. First, their sociopolitical organization was fundamentally dissimilar. Guna elders emphasized that the Guna leader (named Otikori) who met *Rwot* Latogo was not a *rwot*. Instead, Otikori was called *twon* (bull; a strong, important person) and was a prominent war leader, widely acknowledged by the other Eastern Nilotic groups in the area. Koc narrative traditions add that Latogo was specifically told that the Eastern Nilotic lineages in the south-central zone had no *rwot*, but that "when circumstances required, they would select from among their ranks, a *Ladit me tong, me lweny*, 'chief of the spear, to lead the fight.'" Surely, Otikori was just such a leader.[11]

A second remembered difference between Koc and the Eastern Nilotic lineages centered on their weaponry. The latter fought with spear and shield, and Guna traditions both proclaim the advantages of doing so and

---

8. A.H.T. 252, 259, 303. Pokumu remained independent at least until the end of the nineteenth or beginning of the twentieth century.

9. A.H.T. 250, 258; interviews with the same Guna elder, Ocok Okwir.

10. A.H.T. 250, 254, 303.

11. A.H.T. 249–50, 254, 258; Crazzolara (1951, p. 395). This depiction of the *twon* or *ladit me tong* seems similar to later leaders among the Langi called *owitong*; see Odyomo (n.d.).

note with pride that the Guna were called upon by others to help them fight their enemies, sometimes from far away. Koc traditions, in contrast, emphasize bows and arrows and relate the following story:

> The new arrivals were not afraid of fighting and readily acceded to their request [from the south-central zone's Eastern Nilotic lineages] for armed assistance. The Jo-Koc . . . of those times used mainly the bow and arrow as their weapons (an indication of Madi [Central Sudanic] influence) and their arrows were provided with barbs. This proved a new and overpowering weapon. . . . The effect on the Lango-Omiru was deterrent: they ran away from these terrible weapons, and Koc and his [sic] new associates were left alone. The new association having been tested successfully, the old and the new groups joined together under Latogo.[12]

Lastly, Guna traditions suggest cultural distinctions between the incoming Koc and the settled Eastern Nilotic lineages. Contrasting hairstyles are particularly noted, perhaps because this was such a visible manifestation of differences or because it is one that can be observed today between Acholi and Eastern Nilotic neighbors.[13]

Despite the dissimilarities, Koc and three "Lango" lineages — the Guna, Punok, and Dolo — did "join together" to make up an expanded Koc chiefdom. Both narrative and separate-group, non-narrative traditions provide some now-familiar clues to help illuminate the processes and ideology of this "joining together."

First, joining (or, in Pokumu's case, allying) with Koc provided added security against "Lango Omiro" raids from the south, through both more effective weaponry and greater numbers. Related to this was Koc's size relative to other groups. As one Guna elder recounted, "If the Guna could be very many in number, then they could be the owners (*wegi*) of Koc. Then the Koc would have respected them very highly. But the Guna are much fewer in number; that is why they respect Koc."[14]

Second was the continued recognition and even the expanded role given to Guna ritual leadership within the Koc chiefdom. Not only did the Guna continue to be acknowledged as *wegi lobo* or *wegi ngom*, but their *jok*, Okome, became the main *jok* of the chiefdom. Both Guna elders and the Guna-lineage head were also given special roles to play in the funeral ceremonies when a *rwot* died and in helping select a successor.[15]

12. A.H.T. 250, 254, 258; quote is from Crazzolara (1951, p. 306).
13. A.H.T. 250.
14. A.H.T. 254.
15. A.H.T. 254–55, 260, 262, 266.

Third, when the Guna and others accepted the authority of *Rwot* Latogo, a ceremony was performed in which the *rwot* was "installed" with both a Guna and a Punok woman at his side. Since Latogo had been *rwot* for some time, this installation was evidently a reenactment for the benefit of the new members of the chiefdom. And although no details are available, the sense conveyed is that these women were subsequently special wives of the *rwot*, similar to *dako ker* (wives of the *rwot*ship). Along with the other negotiations entered into and the links established, the powerful ties of marriage between ruler and ruled were thus a fundamental part of the process of incorporation from early on.

A fourth factor facilitating incorporation was the way *Rwot* Latogo is remembered to have used the proceeds of tribute to attract outsiders. When the Koc first came into the south-central zone they had no fields. After borrowing millet for a time from Koc's Pokumu and Guna hosts, *Rwot* Latogo "invited" those groups (and perhaps the Punok and Dolo as well) to help the Koc dig fields of their own. In return, *Rwot* Latogo gave those who came a large feast, using dried meat previously provided to him through tribute. Traditions recall that such a great quantity of meat was prepared that the people could not eat it all and so took some home. People were impressed with the *rwot*'s generosity and contrasted it with what they had known: "our *rwot* [or leaders] didn't do things like this." The Guna and their *twon*, for example, are specifically remembered to have not shared meat; "they said that they did not like to, because they were *wegi tong* (owners of the spear)."[16]

Then a Guna hunter killed a leopard. In the chiefly order that Koc represented, leopard and lion skins were always due to the *rwot*. Since the Guna had no *rwot*, some Koc people demanded that the skin be given to Latogo. The Guna refused, with many determined to fight. But "they were advised not to," probably by their *twon* Otikori, who despite his reputation and prowess as a warrior is remembered to have encouraged cooperation with Koc from their arrival.

So the Guna assented to take the matter before the *rwot*. They argued that "our leopard skin should not be taken by force. We are the ones who killed the leopard." *Rwot* Latogo agreed and proposed that in return for the skin the Guna be given two goats: (1) a male to be slaughtered at the Guna *abila* to commemorate the bravery of the Guna hunter and propitiate the spirit of the formidable animal he had killed; and (2) a female to be kept by the lineage to produce offspring, which could be used for bride price and

16. Both of the above two paragraphs come from A.H.T. 258.

thus for the increase of the Guna themselves. "Then the people of Guna agreed to take the two goats, saying 'the rwot is good.' . . . From that time up to now the Guna people gave their leopard skins and [other tribute] to the rwot." Or, in other words, from that time the Guna (followed by the Punok and Dolo) became members of the Koc chiefdom.[17]

Finally, traditions indicate that the Eastern Nilotic lineages with whom Koc came into contact somehow responded to the symbols and ideology of the socio-political order that Koc represented. Two examples illustrate the point. First, Latogo "had brought with him only a *bvuul keer matedi* or a small royal drum, but since even this possession placed him in a higher position than anybody . . . he came across *Tè-Aweere* [the *Got* Aweere area of the south-central zone], they all agreed to recognize him as their *Rwoot*." Second, after emphasizing the importance of their leader Otikori and the recognition given him during early contact with Koc, Guna traditions present everything as suddenly shifting. Otikori "gave way" to Latogo, saying, "since you are the son of a *rwot*, if you want to become *rwot* [here] you can do so. . . . From that time they lived together [under the Koc *rwot*], even up to now."[18]

In the end, the complex equation of pressures and attractions that drew the Guna and other nearby lineages into the recently arrived Koc chiefdom outweighed those (including sociocultural differences) for remaining outside. But all such differences did not suddenly disappear. While hardly surprising, it is not often that extant Acholi traditions provide evidence concerning such matters. Once again, Guna lineage traditions are most illuminating. After the lineage's incorporation and not long after the death of the Guna *twon* Otikori, a man from either Guna or Punok supposedly impregnated a daughter of Latogo. In his anger Latogo blamed "the Lango" in general. In turn, because they were frightened or driven away, or perhaps because they refused to stay in light of Latogo's prejudice against them, a number of people from the Eastern Nilotic lineages left the chiefdom.[19]

17. A.H.T. 250, 259, 303 (the last claims that the Pokumu also killed a leopard and were involved in the negotiations about what should be done). For general discussions of this type of ceremony, widely practiced across Acholi, see Wright (1936) and Malandra (1939).

18. Crazzolara (1951, p. 306), A.H.T. 254. In A.H.T. 258 another Guna elder told a similar story about Guna's joining Latogo, though it was claimed that this did not occur until after the death of Otikori.

19. A.H.T. 250, 258. Was it mere chronological coincidence that these developments are remembered within the context of the death of Otikori? Otikori seems to have played a key role in the development of peaceful relations between Koc and the previously settled Eastern Nilotic lineages. His death may have removed a crucial tie that had bound the two together, allowing divisive tendencies to surface.

Sometime after this, Koc and Pokumu relocated north of the Agago River in the southern part of the east-central zone (see Map 8). One account states that "Lango Omiro" drove them to make this move. Here Latogo died. He was succeeded by his son Cong, who "did not live long." One source notes that a major drought, surely that occurring around 1790, struck immediately after Cong's death before his successor, Olwa, had time to go through official installation ceremonies. These details suggest that Cong had a short reign, estimated here as from 1775 to 1790.[20]

By about 1790, the Koc chiefdom was made up of five village-lineages: *kal*, Romo, Guna, Punok, and Dolo. In addition, the small but formally independent Pokumu polity, made up of Pokumu *kal* and Patuda, had followed Koc across the Acaa into the east-central zone. Thus Koc, one of the main foci of chiefdom formation in the emergent south-central zone between about 1725 and 1790—and one of the zone's largest nineteenth-century polities—ironically ended the eighteenth century settled outside of the zone.

BOLO, PAWOR, AND BWOBO

The ruling lineages of Bolo, the short-lived chiefdom of Pawor, and Bwobo all have traditions that bring them to Labwor-Otuke as part of the western stream of Luo migrants moving out of Paluo and the Luo triangle from the fifteenth through seventeenth centuries (see Chapter 2). It is impossible to know when they arrived in the hills area, but all seem present by at least the end of the seventeenth or beginning of the eighteenth century, forming part of the complex ethnolinguistic and sociopolitical mix described in Chapter 5. And each would leave Labwor-Otuke after the 1720s drought, carrying with them their experience of the institutions and ideology of chiefship introduced into the hills from Bunyoro/Paluo.[21]

Bolo *kal* traditions provide three references that almost certainly refer to the 1720s drought and Bolo's response. First, A.H.T. 278 claims that

20. See A.H.T. 252, 259, 262; Crazzolara (1951, p. 306), which includes the detail concerning the onset of drought before Olwa could go through initiation ceremonies. Malandra (1947, p. 31) mentions Cong's brief life.

21. For links between the eventual ruling lineage of Bolo and both the western stream of Luo migrants and Labwor-Otuke, see Olango (1970, pp. 8–9, 17); A.H.T. 277–78, 281; see also a vague reference in Wright (1934, p. 157) that "Bolo came from the east." On Pawor, see Olango (1970, pp. 3, 12–13). A.H.T. 275 and 280 indicate that the Pawor were originally Jonam, from just north of Bunyoro-Kitara. Again, Wright (1934, p. 158) states vaguely that an "Owo" led Pawor into the south-central zone from the east. Olango (1970, pp. 12–13) identifies "Wor" (an alternative for "Owo") as *rwot* when Pawor lived near Otuke and states that Pawor came to Labor-Otuke with the eventual Bwobo *kal*. For other references to Bwobo *kal*, including links with Labwor-Otuke, see Anywar (1954, p. 85), Crazzolara (1951, pp. 285–86), Okech (1953, p. 60), Herring (1974b, p. 118), and Garry (1972b, p. 58).

Bolo left Labwor-Otuke because of overcrowding and scarcity of food, both characteristics of the hills area during and after the 1720s drought. Second, traditions collected by Bolo elder A. Olango refer to another prominent feature of the drought: hostility among overcrowded and inadequately provisioned groups living in the hills. Third, Bolo traditions collected by Wright state that the Bolo left Otuke and moved west "ahead of Puranga," who likely migrated away not long after the 1720s drought.[22]

These sources concur that the person who led Bolo *kal* away from Labwor-Otuke was the group's eponym, Bolo or Obolo, with estimated dates of rule from 1710 to 1740. By explicitly linking Obolo with royal regalia — particularly royal drums — the sources also portray Obolo as the first *rwot* of a small Bolo chiefdom based on the Bunyoro/Paluo model (though no *lobong* lineages are noted). Certainly when Bolo encountered its first remembered outsiders (the Pawor) after leaving Labwor-Otuke, both groups' traditions depict Bolo as an established chiefdom.[23]

Pawor traditions provide two clues concerning that group's move away from Labwor-Otuke. The first refers to Pawor and the eventual Bwobo *kal* severing close ties in the hills area as a result of famine, after which each moved away. The second identifies the chiefdom's eponym, Wor or Owo(r), as *rwot* when the famine and subsequent move occurred, suggesting estimated dates of rule from 1710 to 1740.[24]

After leaving Labwor-Otuke, the Pawor are remembered to have moved west along the Agago River until settling in what becomes the south-central zone at a place called Yip (see Map 8). Extant Pawor traditions note contact with only two other groups during the course of this move. The first was almost certainly the same Eastern Nilotic Lamur lineage that became one of Puranga's first *lobong* (see Chapter 6); the second was the Paikat, of unclear origins from the mixed Eastern Nilotic-Luo area of present-day Lango District. Neither became formally associated with the Pawor, though both seem to have settled nearby in the emergent south-central zone.[25]

22. A.H.T. 278 (also 277, 281); Olango (1970, pp. 8–9, 14); Wright (1934, p. 157).

23. Ibid.

24. For references to the relationship between the *kal* of Pawor and Bwobo at Labwor-Otuke, see Olango (1970, pp. 1, 8, 12–13) and Anywar (1954, p. 92). The one extant Pawor *rwot* list is in Wright (1934, p. 158) and suggests that Owo's estimated dates of rule were 1710–40, which wrap neatly around the 1720s drought. A.H.T. 280 and Olango (1970, pp. 2, 4, 13) assert that the Pawor had their own *rwot* before incorporation into the Bolo chiefdom, a claim supported by the extant traditions from both groups.

25. Pawor narrative traditions in Olango (1970, pp. 12–13) claim that the Lamur and Paikat settled nearby soon after Pawor left Labwor-Otuke; separate-group Lamur and Paikat traditions indicate that the three became neighbors only in the south-central zone. The Lamur

Just as the Pawor were settling in, the young Bolo chiefdom appeared. The initial encounter between the two is remembered as a hostile one that communicated the very opposite of any "ethnic" affinity: "The Bolo considered the Pawor as strangers who must be killed," while "the people of Pawor also [wanted] to fight." Traditions do not relate whether actual fighting occurred, but they do indicate that the Pawor gave up "their royal spear and drum to the Bolo," provided land on which the Bolo settled, and became the Bolo chiefdom's first *lobong*. A Pawor elder notes one consideration that may have facilitated Pawor's incorporation: "In fact, the people of Pawor used the Bolo as their bodyguards against external attacks."[26]

When *Rwot* Obolo died (c. 1740) a succession struggle ensued that split Bolo *kal*. While various renditions of Bolo traditions provide different details, most identify competition over the chiefdom's main royal drum and incest by one of Obolo's sons as the main issues of contention. The two main sub-lineages that resulted from the split, Lamac and Pakena, remained in the area. Other sections moved at least temporarily away — south to Lango District and perhaps to Pader in the southeastern zone and Pawel in the west.[27]

All sources agree that leadership among the Lamac and Pakena, who maintain a distinction even today, resided with the Lamac because they had the main royal drum. The person who gained possession of the drum is remembered as a son of Obolo named Omac; hence, the sub-lineage name. Omac, however, does not appear in extant Bolo *rwot* lists: these name Obolo's successor as another son, Doli.[28]

---

version (in A.H.T. 276) names the south-central zone as Lamur's original home. Paikat traditions are in Olango (1970, p. 10) and state that the lineage moved into the south-central zone after the "Nyamdere" famine (almost certainly that of the 1720s), where they found the Lamur and Pawor. References to Lamur's origins are in Olango (1970, p. 12) and A.H.T. 276; to Paikat's in Olango (1970, p. 12). Olango (1970, p. 13) also asserts that the Pawor *rwot* when the group was "at the foot" of Otuke was "Wor"; Wright (1934, p. 158) notes that "Owo" led the group from "the East." Finally, additional lineages that do not appear in extant traditions were almost certainly settled in the south-central zone in the era of the 1720s drought. But they relocated and their earlier settlement in the zone has been forgotten following all of the dislocation and change of the eighteenth and nineteenth centuries.

26. The quotations are from Olango (1970, pp. 8 and 14); other material from A.H.T. 277–78, 280; Olango (1970, p. 8–9, 14); Wright (1934, p. 157).

27. A.H.T. 277–78, 281; Olango (1970, p. 8).

28. The main Pakena version is in A.H.T. 277; Lamac accounts are in A.H.T. 278 and 281. Omac and Doli are identified as sons of Obolo. Succession may have passed from one brother to the next, with Omac's name dropped because of the huge dispute associated with his name. Doli almost certainly belongs to the generation following Obolo, or c. 1740–70. See A.H.T. 281 (revising a rwot list in A.H.T. 278); Wright (1934, pp. 155, 157). A.H.T. 277 includes a less satisfactory list collected from a collateral line. Olango (1970, pp. 9–10) links Koco, Doli's probable son and successor, with the drought and famine of c. 1790.

The generation represented by Omac or Doli — or perhaps Omac and Doli together — has estimated dates of 1740–70. Nearly all extant traditions of Bolo's next *rwot*, identified as Doli's son Koco (c. 1770–1800), are related to a major drought that struck during his reign, surely the drought occurring around 1790. The unsettled conditions that followed caused another split of Bolo *kal*, led to grave trouble between Bolo and Pawor resulting in their disassociation, and ended in the death of *Rwot* Koco at the hands of emergent Lango Omiro warriors.[29]

An emergent Bwobo chiefdom, meanwhile, also seems to have left Labwor-Otuke following the 1720s drought. Like many others, the young chiefdom moved west and south rather than northwest into Acholi. After settling at Ngeta, some ten kilometers from modern Lira town in Lango District, Bwobo clashed with peoples developing along non-chiefly lines. Driven away, the Bwobo are remembered to have then traveled into southeastern Acholi where they continued to be harassed by "Lango Omiro" raiders (evidently people from present-day Lango District). As a result, Bwobo traditions continue, the chiefdom moved again, this time south all the way to "Bunyoro" — probably northern Bunyoro or Paluo (see Map 8).[30]

The *rwot* most often associated with these developments is the chiefdom's eponym, Obwogo (or Obogo). Different Bwobo *rwot* lists locate this name in generations ranging from around 1640–70 to around 1705–35. Support for the latest of these comes from Pawor traditions, which specifically place the Bwobo move away from Labwor-Otuke in the same generation as the Pawor eponym Wor or Owo(r), whose own, less uncertain estimated dates of rule are 1710–40.[31]

Obwogo is also the name in Bwobo traditions that is first linked with typical trappings of Acholi *rwodi* (in this case, leopard skins) and is most often associated with the chiefdom's initial incorporation of outsiders. The two *lobong* lineages clearly associated with Obwogo were the Palami and Koyo; some sources suggest that the Pailim, Poromo, Pakwaca, and Dolo may also have been temporary *lobong*. All of this, along with Obwogo's eponymous name, suggests strongly that he was the first, or at least a very

---

29. Extracted from A.H.T. 278, 281; Wright (1934, p. 157); and Olango (1970, pp. 9–10).

30. Olango (1970, p. 12). Discussions of movements from the Labwor-Otuke area into emergent Langi can be found in Herring (section I of 1974b, 1979b); Crazzolara (1960).

31. For the various versions of the Bwobo *rwot* list see Anywar (1954, pp. 85–87, 98–99), Crazzolara (1951, p. 286), Okech (1953, p. 60), and A.H.T. 223. The Pawor references are cited in note 24.

early *rwot* of a Bwobo chiefdom that emerged in the Labwor-Otuke area and was organized on the Bunyoro/Paluo model.[32]

But the stresses of the period appear to have been too great for the young chiefdom. If drought and famine, "Lango Omiro" harassment, and almost continual movement were not enough, Bwobo traditions report that *Rwot* Obwogo made the blatantly unreasonable demand that his subjects catch a leopard alive for the chiefdom's rainmaking ceremony. Whatever this story represents, all of the chiefdom's *lobong* and even some of the *kal* are remembered to have been outraged enough to leave the chiefdom. By the time Bwobo reached "Bunyoro" (certainly Paluo), it was small and struggling, consisting probably of only a reduced Bwobo *kal*.[33]

Traditions recall that Bwobo remained in "Bunyoro" until a good harvest, after which it began to move back north. Still under *Rwot* Obwogo, the beleaguered chiefdom eventually settled at the base of *Got* Omoro in the emergent south-central zone (see Map 8). There it remained into the nineteenth century, incorporating no new *lobong* lineages until after the drought of about 1790.[34]

The Western Zone

Stretching on a diagonal across the middle of the western zone of Acholi is a string of four prominent rock outcrops. The largest and farthest northwest is *Got* Kilak, rising to almost 1,400 meters (4,600 feet) from the surrounding plains some 1,000 meters below. The three smaller ones running away from Kilak toward the southeast are Lamola, Palee (or Guruguru), and Keyo (Map 9).

32. See esp. Anywar (1954, pp. 85–87). A.H.T. 223 links the first incorporation of Bwobo lineages to Obwogo's predecessor, Canya. Crazzolara's Bwobo *rwot* list begins with Obogo (1951, p. 286) and Okech's with Obwogo (1953, p. 60). Garry (1972b, p. 62) also places the events recounted here in the eighteenth century. The probably Eastern Nilotic Palami and Koyo are identified as Bwobo *lobong* in Anywar (1954, pp. 85–87), Crazzolara (1951, p. 286), and A.H.T. 223. The Pailim are noted as a part of Bwobo in Crazzolara (1951, p. 286) and A.H.T. 223; the Poromo and Pakwaca in A.H.T. 223. Anywar (1954, p. 85) includes the Pakwaca among the "Lango Omiro" that fought with the Bwobo. And traditions from the Dolo of Koc note that before they joined Koc they were a part of Bwobo, breaking away from the latter after fighting with them at *Got* Omoro; see A.H.T. 256.

33. Anywar (1954, p. 86), A.H.T. 223; see also brief references in Garry (1972b, pp. 58, 62), and a Bwobo song in Ongo (1971b, p. 42), lamenting Bwobo's meeting with the "Lango" and their continual movement.

34. Again, see Anywar (1954, pp. 86–87, 98) and A.H.T. 223. There are Bwobo *rwot* lists in these two sources and in Okech (1953, p. 60), and Crazzolara (1951, p. 286).

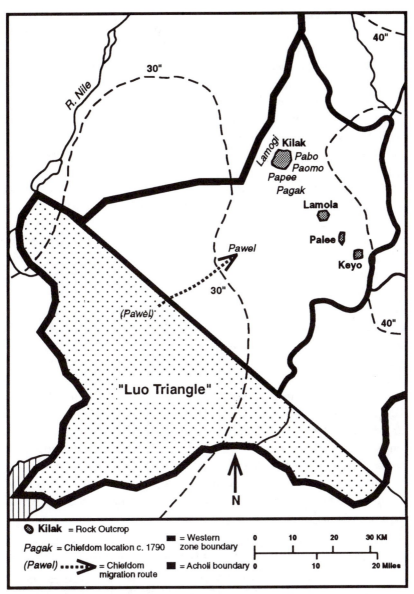

Map 9. Western zone and "Luo triangle" c. 1725-90.

The environs of these outcrops seem to have been among the most heavily populated areas of Acholi by at least the second half of the seventeenth century and probably long before then. Of the ninety-five identifiable lineages in the eventual western, northwestern, central, and south-central zones in the mid-seventeenth century, thirty-six (or more than a third) appear to have been located in the Kilak-Keyo region. One attraction of these outcrops was clearly protection: documents make it clear, for example, that the Lamogi chiefdom often relied on *Got* Palee (Guruguru) for defensive purposes during the late nineteenth and early twentieth centuries.[35]

Even more important in promoting a concentration of population was rainfall. Though located just outside the area of highest reliable rainfall, twentieth-century data indicate that Kilak and the smaller outcrops nearby are part of a small area (including modern Gulu town) that receives an average annual rainfall that is ten inches more than anywhere in Acholi. And earlier traditions, which emphasize the area as one that escaped drought and famine and attracted those fleeing such conditions elsewhere, support modern statistics. Indeed, though the droughts of the 1720s, about 1790, and the 1830s play a major role in the traditions and histories of peoples to the east, none of the extant traditions of the lineages and chiefdoms settled near *Got* Kilak indicate that these droughts struck their region.[36]

Traditions indicate that the Kilak area attracted settlers from both the western stream of Luo migrants and Eastern Nilotic speakers from regions far to the east. By the early eighteenth century, however, these early Luo had long since moved on and the originally Eastern Nilotic speakers had almost certainly abandoned their old language. Indeed by this time, the Kilak area, lying firmly within the Central Sudanic world, appears to have been one of the most homogeneous in language and culture in all of what would become Acholi.[37]

35. Early lineage information comes from Atkinson (1978, pp. 129–31). Delme-Radcliffe to Col. Coles (enclosure in Jackson to Lansdowne, dd. 23 Dec. 1901, Entebbe National Archives, File A.16.1) includes a graphic description of Lamogi using Guruguru for defensive purposes in the late nineteenth century, while Adimola (1954) and Dwyer (1972, pp. 130–59) provide lengthy descriptions of Lamogi retreating to Guruguru during their rebellion in 1911–12 against the colonial government's attempts to confiscate Acholi firearms.

36. For average twentieth-century rainfall figures see Thomas and Scott (1935, facing p. 113) and *Atlas of Uganda* (1962, pp. 14–15; 1967, pp. 16–17). For traditions emphasizing the Kilak-Lamola area as a haven in times of drought, see, for example, Wright (1934, p. 58), A.H.T. 205.

37. Atkinson (1978, pp. 129–31) indicates that eight of the thirty-six early identifiable Kilak-Lamola village-lineages were probably Eastern Nilotic in origin. A lingering Eastern

In this setting, five chiefdoms were established during the early to mid-eighteenth century: Pabo, Lamogi, Paomo, Pagak, and Papee. All were comprised of lineages that seem predominantly Central Sudanic in origin and entirely Central Sudanic in speech (see Map 9).[38]

The first three in particular, clustered around Kilak's slopes, were linked by dense patterns of intermarriage, collective activities such as joint dry-season hunts, and common cultural practices and ritual, all seemingly derived from their shared Central Sudanic background. Despite these similarities and ties, the three Kilak chiefdoms developed on very different scales. Pabo grew to include at least fifteen village-lineages and by the late eighteenth century was one of the three or four largest polities in all of Acholi. Lamogi was ultimately a medium-sized chiefdom of nine village-lineages. And Paomo, always overshadowed by nearby Pabo, never consisted of more than *kal* and one *lobong* lineage. Paomo's limited size and influence is paralleled by limited information, and it will not be discussed further here.[39]

PABO

Compared to Paomo's traditions, Pabo's are rich — having been collected by five different researchers over a thirty-five-year period. All versions provide substantial renderings of the origins of Pabo *kal* and lengthy *rwot* lists. Three of the five include the stereotypical, early-Luo settlement sites of Bunyoro and Pubungu in Pabo *kal*'s migration route, which support ideologically driven and dubious claims of Luo origins. But the Central Sudanic origins identified in the other two accounts are far more convincing. As

---

Nilotic influence is indicated by the persistence of a few Eastern Nilotic-derived words in the twentieth century: for example, *ateke(re)*, sometimes used as the term for lineage head (see Crazzolara [1954, p. 455] and A.H.T. 204, 214, 238); and *atiyang*, game animal (Crazzolara [1951, p. 232]).

38. There was also a sixth chiefdom located in or near the zone during most of the eighteenth century. This was Pawel, which did not fit in with the other chiefdoms of the eighteenth-century western zone any better that it had done among the earliest chiefdoms (as noted in Chap. 4). Evidence indicates that it remained a small, single-lineage polity; that it settled some twenty miles (thirty-five kilometers) from the *Got* Kilak chiefdoms; and that it had both positive and conflictual relations with its Central Sudanic neighbors (for example, "the Pawel are like the Madi"; "Madi groups attacked Pawel"). See Wright (1934, pp. 170–73); Okech (1953, pp. 70–71); A.H.T. 224, 226–27.

39. Evidence that Paomo was a polity separate from Pabo only became clear as a result of research in the 1970s. Even then, almost all that has come to light about Paomo is that (1) it was always small, consisting of the two Central Sudanic lineages of Paomo *kal* and Pakuma; (2) it had a royal drum; and (3) Pabo's long-time informal dominance over its smaller neighbor was institutionalized under colonial rule when Paomo was placed under the jurisdiction of the Pabo *rwot* — see A.H.T. 207; Crazzolara (1954, pp. 455–57); and Wright (1934, p. 58).

Crazzolara asserts, the Pabo *kal* "are confessedly Madi" — that is, Central Sudanic.[40]

The earliest names in the extant Pabo *rwot* lists are inconsistent from one account to the next, and the sparse traditions accompanying these names are confused, contradictory, or stereotypical. Clarity and consistency begin only with Ogwang, who lived five generations before a *Rwot* Loka who ruled between about 1875 and 1910. This gives Ogwang estimated dates of rule from 1725 to 1755. Two names, Okankweyo and Obyero, appear as Ogwang's immediate predecessors in three of five lists; a fourth reverses their order and adds a name between them. And one text adds that two or three lineages of probable Central Sudanic origins — the Padregu, Odree, and perhaps the Palwong — became associated with Pabo during the time of Okankweyo and Obyero.[41]

This information might be interpreted as indicating the emergence of a Pabo chiefdom during at least the generation or two before Ogwang. This is certainly the dominant message of Pabo narrative traditions, which contend that the chiefdom began with the earliest period recounted in traditions and with the earliest names in the remembered *rwot* lists (i.e., with Okankweyo, Obyero, or even before). Traditions also frequently link these first names in the list with the early Luo of Pubungu and Bunyoro.

But there are many clues that the first *rwot* of a Pabo chiefdom was Ogwang (c. 1725–55), which means that Okankweyo and Obyero were most likely the leaders — or somehow represent the leadership — of a three- or four-lineage, multiple-village grouping.

The strongest of these clues comes from both narrative and separate-group, non-narrative traditions, which indicate that ten to fourteen lineages joined Pabo during the time of Ogwang. All of these were almost certainly Central Sudanic speaking when they joined the new chiefdom, though it is likely that three had originally Eastern Nilotic roots. Whatever the precise number of the newly associated lineages, the growth they represented was striking. Clearly the period of Ogwang's rule was marked

40. The three collections of Pabo traditions that include Bunyoro, Pubungu, or both are Crazzolara (1954, p. 454), Malandra (1947, p. 8), and A.H.T. 205. The two narrative accounts that acknowledge Central Sudanic origins are Wright (1934, p. 58) and Okech (1953, p. 55). As the quotation indicates, Crazzolara does not accept the narrative traditions he collected (see 1954, p. 454; also p. 436.)

41. Okankweyo and Obyero are identified as Ogwang's immediate predecessors in Malandra (1947, p. 10), Crazzolara (1954, p. 454), and A.H.T. 205. Wright (1934, pp. 57–58) omits Obyero, and Okech (1953, p. 55) reverses the two names and interjects Ling between them. A.H.T. 205 provides the information on the Padregu, Odree, and Palwong.

by sociopolitical change on an unprecedented scale; clearly Pabo was now a chiefdom.[42]

Five other clues support the establishment of a Pabo chiefdom under Ogwang. First, Pabo's royal lineage is most often called P'Ogwang *kal*. As Crazzolara writes, the royal lineage is "characteristically called after this *Rwoot* [Ogwang]; did the preceding ones never exist or rule?" Second, in the one extant *rwot* list with related genealogical information, it is only from Ogwang that collateral lines or any relationships besides simple (purported) father-son succession have been maintained. Third, both the process of selecting a *dak ker* and her importance in the chiefdom "changed" during the time of Ogwang, which might be veiled references to the very origins of the position of *dak ker* accompanying the origins of a Pabo chiefdom. Fourth, the name Ogwang is even associated in one text with a major Pabo chiefdom *jok*.[43]

Finally, there is an intriguing story in Pabo narrative traditions concerning the sudden appearance of a mysterious stranger from "Bunyoro" (surely Paluo) who introduced rainmaking to *Rwot* Ogwang and Pabo.

> The person who brought rain to Rwot Ogwang of Pabo came from Bunyoro. His name was Okulaga. He had tied rain (*kot*) around his leg with bark cloth. The rain which he had tied around his leg was mistaken to be a very big wound, because all the time it was leaking and they thought that fluid was from a wound. He therefore sat apart from the other people at the rwot's *kal*. When the rwot saw him he called him to come and join them. But he refused, saying that he was smelly; therefore he could not come to where the rwot was. In reply the rwot said, I don't fear smelly things. Okulaga then came to where the rwot was.
>
> The rwot asked one of his wives to make porridge (*nyuka*) for Okulaga. . . . Okulaga refused, saying . . . he would spoil it with the fluid from his wound. But the rwot said, no, it doesn't matter. Then he took it.
>
> In the evening the rwot asked his wife again to warm some water for Okulaga to wash with. When the water was warmed it was taken behind the house so that Okulaga could wash. . . . The following morning [Ogwang's

---

42. In addition to the members of the multiple-village grouping posited above, the seven lineages that most clearly joined *Rwot* Ogwang were the Agoro, Pajinya, Paigwe, Cici, Pabiidi, Pagwedi, and Lapul. The Pagaya and Koyo, and perhaps the Pakedo and Pabwoc, may have also been incorporated. All were almost certainly Central Sudanic speaking when they joined the new chiefdom, though the origins of the Agoro, Pajinya, and Paigwe were probably Eastern Nilotic. Evidence on these lineages, including their probable origins, is assembled in Atkinson (1978, p. 130); A.H.T. 205 indicates that the lineages named joined Ogwang, with some corroboration in A.H.T. 206 and Wright (1934, p. 60).

43. On the first point see Crazzolara (1954, p. 458), A.H.T. 205–6; on the second, Wright (1934, p. 57); on the last two, A.H.T. 206.

wife] Nyokur again warmed water for Okulaga and took it behind the same house. But this time Okulaga decided not to go to wash. Instead he asked the rwot to bring out a new clean pot so that he could put in it what he had been tying around his leg. The reason he decided to do this, said Okulaga, was because he realized that he [Ogwang] was a good rwot. . . . Okulaga then told the rwot to get a black sheep to sacrifice (*tumo*). The main idea behind getting the black sheep was to make it possible for the rain in the pot to act so that when lightning from the skies threatened, the rain in the pot would attract that lightning. Then rain would come.[44]

How might this cryptic narrative support the introduction of chiefly rule in Pabo, at least inferentially? We know from numerous sources that rainmaking in the Pabo polity was done with both rainstones (*ame*, special stones kept in a pot at *kal* and used to help attract rain) and a rainmaking royal drum. The Okulaga story seems to recount the introduction of the former. But culturally this makes no sense. Rainstones are widely acknowledged as a Central Sudanic ritual preference with ancient origins. They would have been part of Pabo's Central Sudanic heritage, and not an eighteenth-century introduction from Bunyoro/Paluo, Okulaga's acknowledged home.

Conversely, the original source throughout Acholi of Pabo's other rainmaking regalia — royal drums — was indeed Bunyoro/Paluo. And royal drums were key components of the new chiefly order being established during the eighteenth century throughout Acholi, often appearing in traditions just when chiefdoms were being founded. Logically, Pabo's royal drum was most likely introduced with the founding of the chiefdom or, in other words, during the time of *Rwot* Ogwang. But how could this be acknowledged in the same Pabo *kal* narrative traditions that ardently proclaim that chiefship (and presumably its Bunyoro/Paluo accoutrements) had their origins long before? The obvious contradictions may have made doing so impossible. One way that traditions could have circumvented the issue was to make the Okulaga story seem to refer to the origins of the Central Sudanic-derived rainstone component of Pabo's rainmaking regalia, rather than the introduction of a Bunyoro/Paluo royal drum.[45]

Once the Pabo chiefdom passed through its first generation of dramatic transformation and growth under Ogwang, the pace of change ap-

44. A.H.T. 205. Wright (1934, p. 58) originally placed the Okulaga story under Ogwang, but then drew an arrow up to the earlier name "Bor." Okech (1953, p. 55) identifies the coming of Okulaga with the time of Ling, whom he places between Obyero and Okankweyo just before Ogwang.

45. See also very similar Lamogi traditions and interpretations of them below in this chapter.

pears to have slowed considerably. Traditions indicate that only one more lineage, the Central Sudanic Papolo, joined Ogwang's son and successor Ogol.[46]

Pabo traditions do not agree on Ogol's successor — the only time royal narrarive traditions are inconsistent from the time of Ogwang. Some sources list Ogol's successor as his son Opok; others name an anomalous figure called Ling. Ling is variously identified as (1) a son of Ogol; (2) a successor of Ogol but with no specified genealogical relationship; (3) a son of Ogol's son Opok (with no indication that he was ever a *rwot*); or (4) even a *rwot* before Ogwang, between the names Obyero and Okankweyo. This inconsistency suggests that Ling was somehow not a typical ruler. He may have been a regent; he may have been *rwot* so briefly that his place, or even inclusion, in the line of succession is uncertain; or something may have happened to erase or scramble the memory of him in Pabo traditions. There is no way to know; so Ling's place, if any, in the Pabo line of *rwodi* is problematic.[47]

What does seem clear about Pabo is that by the end of the eighteenth century it was a firmly established chiefdom settled along the eastern side of *Got* Kilak. Its twelve to sixteen village-lineages made it one of the largest chiefdoms in eighteenth-century Acholi. And it was almost certainly Central Sudanic-speaking, with no known Luo or Paluo groups present.

LAMOGI
Extant traditions of the Lamogi chiefdom's beginnings are not marked by the same spurious, ideologically generated claims of Luo origins found in Pabo. Instead, the problem lies with the Lamogi *rwot* lists, which are almost wholly inconsistent and lacking in associated traditions until a *rwot* named Wiira, who ruled during the mid- to late nineteenth century. Before this, it is difficult to ascertain even the most basic chronology. The only hints come from scattered cross-references in Lamogi and Pabo traditions suggesting that the founding of the Lamogi chiefdom occurred in the same general period as did that of Pabo.[48]

46. Ogol follows Ogwang in all extant Pabo *rwot* lists; A.H.T. 205 and Wright (1934, p. 57) identify Ogol as Ogwang's son. Papolo's incorporation by Ogol is indicated in Wright (1934, p. 61) and A.H.T. 205; its Central Sudanic origins are argued in Atkinson (1978, p. 130).

47. The various identifications of Ling noted above are in Malandra (1947, p. 10), Crazzolara (1954, p. 458), Wright (1934, p. 57), and Okech (1953, p. 55), respectively.

48. The extant Lamogi *rwot* lists are in Crazzolara (1954, p. 461; two versions), Okech (1953, p. 52), and A.H.T. 201–2, 204. The names that appear most often in these lists are Boro, Warom (Marom), Odoc, Wiira, and Yai, who was removed by the British in 1899.

One aspect of the Lamogi past is clear: its unequivocal ties with its Central Sudanic neighbors. This point, also often applied to Pabo and other chiefdoms in the western zone, was reiterated by many from both inside and outside the zone. For example, "*Paboo-Lamogi, wan aceel*: 'we are one people'; *Madi ominwa, wan aceel*: 'the Madi are our brothers, we are all one.' We dance Madi dances, and use *ateero k' atuum* (arrow and bow as weapons)."[49]

The name "Lamogi" is a common and seemingly old one, attached to numerous groups and many areas in and beyond Acholi. One of those areas, Crazzolara argues, was *Got* Kilak, from a time that long preceded the establishment of a Lamogi chiefdom or the arrival (sometime before the eighteenth century) of its eventual, Central Sudanic ruling lineage.[50]

Early lineages in the area included the Central Sudanic Pamuca and Pojwani, both widely acknowledged as among the "original" inhabitants of Kilak. They were responsible for approaching some of the old *jogi* whose shrines were located high on the mountain, and they later played primary ritual roles within the Lamogi chiefdom. The Koc (Koc-Daca) may also have been present in the area from early on, settled near *Got* Palee. Finally, some traditions claim that the Pailyec, Paingor, and Pokure lineages came with the eventual Lamogi *kal* to Kilak; more convincing versions indicate that the three were prior inhabitants. All six eventually joined the Lamogi chiefdom along with the Palema and Pucet-Pangira, whose locations before incorporation are unknown.[51]

The pre-polity relationship, if any, among these village-lineages cannot be ascertained from available sources. Nor is it clear from Lamogi evidence when or how a Lamogi chiefdom emerged or when its constituent lineages joined. Fortunately, traditions from and relating to neighboring Pabo provide helpful, if only inferential, information.[52]

49. The quotation is from Crazzolara (1954, p. 460); Central Sudanic origins for Lamogi *kal* and Lamogi's association in general with their Central Sudanic Madi neighbors are indicated in Crazzolara (1954, pp. 459–60), Okech (1953, p. 52); A.H.T. 202–3, 223; Adimola (1954, p. 166), and Delme-Radcliffe's reference at the turn of the century to the "Mogi clan of Madi" (Entebbe National Archives, File A.16.1, "Report on the Lango expedition," enclosure 16). Only A.H.T. 201 includes feeble claims of a "Shilluk" (i.e., Luo) origin.

50. Crazzolara (1954, pp. 459–61) discusses Lamogi as a term for a very old grouping of people which he terms "pre-Madi" (pre-Central Sudanic) or "Western Lango"; Atkinson (1978, p. 129) argues that this grouping was Central Sudanic.

51. See Crazzolara (1954, pp. 460–69); A.H.T. 201, 203–4; see also n. 5 above.

52. Links between Lamogi and Pabo are indicated in the traditions of both from the earliest portions of their respective traditions, long before the Lamogi or Pabo chiefdoms were established. See, for example, a Pabo reference in Wright (1934, p. 58) and a Lamogi one in Okech (1953, p. 52).

First, a Pabo source claims that the first Lamogi *rwot* came from the Pabo royal dynasty. This *rwot*, Odoc, is remembered to have been a "brother" of Ogwang's supposed father, Obyero. Lamogi traditions make the counter-assertion that one of their royal dynasty went to Pabo and took over its *rwot*ship. Without corroboration, we can be skeptical of both claims. What is useful is the indication that the Lamogi and Pabo chiefdoms were founded about the same time, which from Pabo traditions of its first *rwot*, Ogwang, was around 1725–55.[53]

Odoc's Pabo origins may be suspect, but there are hints that he might have been Lamogi's first *rwot*. His name appears more often than any other in extant Lamogi *rwot* lists prior to *Rwot* Wiira (five of six). Next, although Lamogi's royal lineage is most commonly called Boro *kal* (evidently derived from the Boro who appears before Odoc in four lists), one source does refer to P'Odoc *kal*. Another source identifies the sub-lineage of *kal* that provided Lamogi's *rwodi* as P'Odoc. And finally, Odoc is remembered to have been associated with a mysterious rainmaker from Loka similar to the one encountered earlier in Pabo traditions.[54]

In the version that includes Odoc, the rainmaker was incorporated into the ritually important Pojwani lineage and became responsible for the chiefdom's main *jogi*. Another account of the wandering rainmaker, however, directly links the founding of the Lamogi and Pabo chiefdoms. It is highly reminiscent of the Pabo story quoted above, though the name "Kalabara" is substituted for "Okulaga," and he is remembered as from "Loka" (Paluo), not Bunyoro in general. The names of nineteenth-century *rwodi* (Wiira of Lamogi and Ojoko of Pabo) have also been tentatively and unconvincingly brought into the story:

> *Kalabara* came from *Loka*. He had a carefully bandaged thick leg on account, he said, of a bad sore. . . . He came first to the *Rwoot* of Lamogi (Wiira?) and stopped with him. In the evening he asked for water to wash his sore and Wiira readily provided it. But the next day, at the same request, Wiira's wives became angry and declared that they failed to understand why they should wash the evil smelling sore of a stranger. Wiira felt sorry but could not help it. He therefore advised Kalabara to go to so and so (Ojoko?), *Rwoot* of PaBoo; which he did. Ojoko and his wives readily offered to prepare water for him,

---

53. The Pabo version is in A.H.T. 206; the Lamogi in A.H.T. 201. The fact that Lamogi and Pabo share many common ritual practices and beliefs, including similar royal installation ceremonies, is one more indication that the two polities may have been closely related from early on; see Crazzolara (1954, pp. 464–65; A.H.T. 201, 204, 206.

54. Sources for the four points made in the paragraph above are, respectively, A.H.T. 202, Crazzolara (1954, p. 467), A.H.T. 204, and Crazzolara (1954, p. 464).

whenever he wished and to wash his leg. When they brought water, he washed himself. As for the leg he just squeezed the thick bandage and plenty of rainwater came forth and covered the ground. His leg was not sore at all; Kalabara had hidden in his leg the rain he was endowed with. One day he asked the *Rwoot* to assist at the washing of his "sore". He removed the covering and showed his healthy leg and said that it was rain he had hidden in his leg. He was impressed by the kindness shown to him by the *Rwoot* and his wives and he, therefore, gave him the rain, i.e. the power to make rain and thus provide for the crops of his people. This explains rain-making of PaBoo.[55]

Two important points can be elicited from this tale. First, I interpreted the Okulaga story from Pabo as a highly stylized indication of the introduction of Bunyoro/Paluo-derived chiefly institutions and ideology — and the founding of a Pabo chiefdom — during the time of *Rwot* Ogwang, around 1725–55. This parallel tale links the rainmaker to both Lamogi and Pabo, suggesting that Lamogi was exposed to the same ideas at about the same time. The alternative identification in this version of nineteenth-century rulers Wiira and Ojoko is so obviously tentative that it presents no real problem. The Pabo version, clearly naming Ogwang as the Pabo *rwot*, is easily preferred.[56]

Second, this version indicates that Lamogi's opportunity to learn Kalabara's rainmaking secrets was lost to Pabo, with the Lamogi leader's selfish wives as the stereotypical scapegoats. If we accept that these "secrets" stand for the whole set of ideas and institutions of chiefly rule, what might this loss signify? It cannot mean that Lamogi lost the opportunity to "learn" the Bunyoro/Paluo-derived "secrets." An independent Lamogi chiefdom *was* established. A fragment of traditions from a Lamogi lineage in Pader in the southeastern zone might help. These traditions state that the lineage came to Pader from the Lamogi chiefdom in the west — making them the only Lamogi lineage in Acholi to claim ties with the Lamogi chiefdom. The lineage also makes the relatively common, if not usually convincing, claim to have brought with them a royal drum. The traditions add that this was not their "original drum," as both this and their rainstones had been "stolen by the Pabbo people." Perhaps, then, the transfer of Lamogi's "rain" to Pabo in the Kalabara story is a veiled account indicating that Lamogi somehow lost their initial rainmaking regalia — including the powerful symbol of the

---

55. Crazzolara (1954, p. 463).

56. The same basic story in A.H.T. 204 substitutes Yai, another late-nineteenth-century *rwot*, for Wiira and adds that Kalabara took the power to make rain to both Pabo and Atyak. Yet another version in Crazzolara (1954, p. 464) identifies the Pabo *rwot* as "Gol the son of Ogwang."

new order, their royal drum — to Pabo. Such a traumatic event might help explain the generally unclear traditions of the early Lamogi chiefdom, as well as provide another possible context for interpreting both the Kalabara and Okulaga stories.[57]

PAGAK AND PAPEE

The original ruling dynasties of the Pagak and Papee chiefdoms located just south of *Got* Kilak were each displaced by Paluo lineages. In Pagak this occurred during the first generation of the chiefdom's existence, or about 1720–50. And traditions of this dynastic change have two highly atypical features. First, descendants of both sides agree on a level of violence rare in extant Acholi traditions. Second, the two sides have maintained versions of the dynastic change that are among the most distinct and divergent in Acholi traditions.

The origins of the first ruling lineage of Pagak, which came into the Kilak area long before a Pagak chiefdom was founded in the early to mid-eighteenth century, lay clearly to the east. One account claims specifically that they came from present-day Lango District and spoke (Eastern Nilotic) "Lango." The first *rwot* of a Pagak chiefdom was its eponym, Gak. While many traditions list a number of Gak's predecessors, he was undoubtedly different from them. As one source states, "Gak was the son of Atwoka, who was an elder [*ladit*] but not chief [*rwot*]." Other traditions add that it was only during the time of Gak that other lineages joined Pagak, a telling sign of chiefdom formation.[58]

These lineages were Pojok, Pabel, Payugu, Pabwodo, and perhaps Papar and Palayer. As the Pojok took on primary responsibility for the polity-wide *jok* (*Jok* Longi), they were probably the longest settled in the area. In origin, the first four were likely Central Sudanic while Papar appears Eastern Nilotic and Palayer's cannot be determined. By the time the chiefdom was established, however, those not originally Central Sudanic speaking — Papar, Pagak *kal*, and perhaps Palayer — seem to have been settled long enough in the area to have probably adopted the language of the overwhelming Central Sudanic majority.[59]

Traditions contain no details concerning the founding of the chief-

57. The reference from the Lamogi lineage of Pader comes from Webster A.H.T., p. 111.
58. See Malandra (1947, p. 21); also A.H.T. 211–14.
59. See Atkinson (1978, p. 130) for evidence and arguments on the ethnolinguistic origins of the old Pagak lineages, with more on Pabwodo in Crazzolara (1954, pp. 453, 474). Pojok's ritual position is noted in A.H.T. 214; and A.H.T. 212, 214, and 215 all describe a chiefdom-wide harvest ceremony almost certainly based on old Central Sudanic ritual.

dom, almost certainly because of the traumatic dynastic change that soon followed and overshadowed previous developments. But the Pabel must have been an early or especially important *lobong* lineage, as its lineage head is remembered to have been a special *ladit pa rwot*.[60]

The most extensive information on the early Pagak chiefdom focuses on initial contacts with the Paluo lineage that would soon provide its second dynasty. This lineage, called "Pacunge," was led by Karakara (c. 1720–50). On their arrival, the Pacunge acknowledged the authority of the *rwot* of Pagak (usually identified as Gak) and became part of his chiefdom, even though they claimed to have been a royal lineage back in Paluo. All versions of extant traditions agree that Karakara came to Pagak with a royal drum, though all also agree that he gave this drum to Gak. One source adds that the Pacunge also began to "share game meat," or pay tribute to Gak, after which Gak responded in typical fashion by preparing a big feast for his subjects.[61]

In interviews conducted in 1970, descendants of both the original Pagak *kal* and the Pacunge agreed essentially on the basic points made thus far. But they differed about most subsequent details. The Pacunge version begins by asserting that when Karakara arrived, he "found" Gak, who was so frightened that he tried to hide. Karakara is remembered to have calmed Gak's fears and initiated good relations between the two groups. For example, on his own initiative, Karakara gave Gak a goat that the latter needed for ritual ceremonies to help his wives bear children. And while Gak is acknowledged as a *rwot*, this recognition is diluted by the claim that he did not have a royal drum — in other words, he was not a "real" *rwot*. Karakara and his lineage, meanwhile, are represented as having come with their *ker* (authority, *rwot*ship) and royal drum. Karakara is even depicted as submitting his drum to Gak voluntarily, not because the latter had more power or authority, but because Karakara's home was "close to the river" where the moisture could "spoil the drum." "It seems that your house is warm," Karakara said, "and can keep the drum well. . . . You can dance with it since I offer it to you because my house is very cold."[62]

The descendants of Gak turned almost all these stories around, to emphasize or favor Gak and Pagak *kal*. Instead of Karakara encountering a

60. A.H.T. 214.

61. See A.H.T. 212 and 213; the quotation is from the former. Karakara's involvement in a succession dispute in Paluo is indicated in Malandra (1947, p. 21). The extant Pagak *rwot* lists are in Malandra (1947, pp. 21–29), Okech (1953, p. 55), and A.H.T. 211–13.

62. A.H.T. 212

frightened Gak, it was the mother of Gak who found Karakara. Then Gak initiated interaction by inviting Karakara to visit him. The story of the goat was also changed. First, an elder from old Pagak *kal* claimed that it was Gak who gave a goat to Karakara. The objection to this was so strong, even by non-Pacunge elders, that the assertion was amended and the basic content of the Pacunge version accepted. But the explanation of what happened was altered. The elder from old Pagak *kal* claimed that Karakara did not give the goat for Gak's wives, but because it was needed for ritual purposes within the chiefdom as a whole. Karakara thus provided the goat because he was a "common man (*dano majwi*)" while Gak was the *rwot*, whose "goat was not supposed to be sacrificed." And it was at this point that the old Pagak *kal* elder made the assertion quoted above concerning the Pacunge's rendering of tribute to Gak.[63]

The two sides did agree that fighting accompanied the transfer of *rwot*ship from old Pagak *kal* to the Pacunge, and they also remembered the course and result of the conflict in similar ways. Trouble began after a large feast organized by Gak (suggesting that he was still *rwot*). On their return home, some of the Pacunge damaged the fields of Gak's wives. Gak angrily placed a curse on one of the Pacunge (who may have been Karakara's wife). When this person died, the Pacunge retaliated with an attack on Pagak *kal*. After a second battle, the Pagak *lobong* are remembered to have abandoned their *rwot* and fled, led by the Pabel lineage head. The Pacunge, acknowledged by all to have been the larger lineage, then killed many of the old Pagak *kal* and forced most of the rest, including Gak, to flee. The Pacunge regained their royal drum and took over as the new ruling lineage of Pagak. With the cessation of fighting, most of Pagak's old *lobong* returned and submitted to the authority of the new dynasty.[64]

The seemingly precipitous abandonment of old Pagak *kal* by their *lobong* is both puzzling and unprecedented in extant Acholi traditions. Fortunately, Malandra's compilation of Pagak traditions might help explain it. Here, Gak dies before the Pacunge came, leading to a disputed succession. Eventually a son of Gak named Bodo (mentioned nowhere else in Pagak traditions) reluctantly accepted the *rwot*ship, with apparently minimal support from the elders and people. Bodo was subsequently deposed and killed, and "anarchy followed." This was the situation when Karakara

---

63. Ibid.
64. A.H.T. 212–14. Only A.H.T. 213 had descendants solely from one side (Karakara's), and only here was the dubious claim made that fighting did not begin until after Gak had given up the *rwot*ship.

and the Pacunge arrived. A period of peaceful interaction and cooperation then ensued, after which "people started to give a part of the animals hunted to Karakara and thereafter made him their leader. This is how Karakara became chief [*rwot*] of Pagak."[65]

This version, which almost certainly derives from Pacunge elders, contradicts two fundamental elements of other accounts. First, it gives no indication that the Pacunge ever joined Pagak as subordinates before taking over the *rwot*ship; second, it locates all the violence *before* the Pacunge arrive. Given the richness and the ring of authenticity of the alternative traditions — from Pacunge and old Pagak *kal* elders — both of these aspects of Malandra's account seem untenable. But embedded in the dubious framework are crucial and believable details that are missing in other versions — particularly the depiction of dissension within Pagak prior to the collapse of old Pagak. Such divisiveness — even "anarchy" — would help to explain the Pacunge success in the conflict that is agreed upon in other sources, the desertion of old Pagak's *lobong* during the dynastic struggle, and their subsequent willingness to join the new rulers.

When the old Pagak *lobong* did return to join a reconstituted Pagak under *Rwot* Karakara and his Pacunge lineage, the head of the Pabel retained his position as special *ladit pa rwot*. The Pojok, however, lost their main role in chiefdom-wide ritual. Contrary to the usual practice in Acholi chiefdoms where ruling lineages had a subordinate place in most ritual, the Pacunge took over primary responsibility for the chiefdom's main *jok*, *Jok* Longi.[66]

Given the trauma of the dynastic change and its prominent place in Pagak traditions, it is not surprising that little is recounted of the period immediately following. Perhaps the remainder of Karakara's rule, as well as that of his son and successor Oceng (c. 1750–80), was as quiet as the silence of the traditions suggests.[67]

After Oceng died, however, another great conflict occurred. This was a dispute over the *rwot*ship between Oceng's sons, Adir and Veje, and their supporters. In this second dispute in Pagak, the memory of events maintained by the losing side (the descendants of Veje) is both more detailed

65. Malandra (1947, p. 21).

66. Pojok's loss of ritual preeminence in the new Pagak is noted in A.H.T. 214; the Pabel village-lineage head's continuing role as special *ladit pa rwot* is noted in both A.H.T. 214 and 215.

67. The identification of Oceng as son and successor of Karakara comes from Malandra (1947, p. 22) and A.H.T. 212 and 213.

and more widely accepted than anything available from the winners. Thus in the following summary, the "Veje version" is given priority, with "Adir version" alternatives relegated to footnotes.

When Oceng died, both Veje and his younger brother Adir wanted to succeed. When they could not reconcile their competing claims, they are remembered to have gone to *Loka* to submit their dispute to "Kamuraci" or "Kamrega"—stereotypical names that can denote either the Bunyoro-Kitara king or a lesser Paluo chief. This *Loka* ruler decided that Veje should succeed, and sent him back to his people as *rwot*, perhaps with new royal regalia. Adir, meanwhile, was kept behind as a prisoner because he had put forth "false" claims to the Pagak *rwot*ship.[68]

Veje was generally well received in Pagak and acknowledged as *rwot*. Eventually, his mother persuaded him to return to *Loka* and bring back her other son. But Adir was not allowed to stay at *kal*. Instead, Veje sent him to live in the village of their mother's brother, Palayer. Veje and his supporters clearly thought that Adir would be less of a threat away from the center of chiefly power. Before long, however, Adir managed to use his Palayer base to challenge his brother, in part by interrupting the flow of tribute: "When Adir settled in the new place his people began to send offerings of hunted animals to Weje [alternative spelling] as they had been arranged. But after three months few offerings were made because Adir instructed his people not to take animals to Weje. 'I am also the child of the chief [*rwot*] so why should you make offering to Weje?' "[69]

Veje could not allow such a flagrant challenge to his authority. After a failed attempt to resolve the impasse peacefully, Veje sent his followers to take "all that was in the possession of Adir." Adir and his followers resisted and fighting ensued, with one fatality remembered on each side. But even with the inconclusive battle, Adir and his adherents gained an important victory. In managing to hold out, they created, in effect, an alternative Pagak *rwot*ship alongside the established one. Veje was never able to re-establish his control or authority.[70]

In the meantime, the non-royal Payugu lineage decided that since there seemed to be no "true" (effective?) *rwot* of Pagak, they might as well rule themselves. Eventually both Payugu notions of independence and

68. A.H.T. 212.
69. Ibid.; Malandra (1947, p. 23), which includes the quotation.
70. Much of the detail is found only in Malandra (1947, p. 23), though the account is corroborated by a descendant of Veje and disputed by a descendant of Adir in A.H.T. 212.

Veje's claim to the *rwot*ship gave way to Adir, who somehow succeeded in gaining the support of most of the chiefdom, which survived into the twentieth century.[71]

Neighboring Papee did not survive. Following the drought of about 1790, a segment of the southeastern-zone chiefdom of Parabongo split off and made its way to the south of *Got* Kilak. There these Parabongo met, fought, defeated, and scattered Papee *kal* and their followers. The old Papee chiefdom never recovered. It disappeared, and a quite different Parabongo chiefdom took its place.

We do not even know the actual name of the chiefdom designated here as "Papee." The name comes from the man remembered as *rwot* when the Parabongo arrived in the late eighteenth or early nineteenth century. Given developments elsewhere in the Kilak region, a Papee chiefdom was probably established sometime during the generation after about 1720.

When the Parabongo arrived, Papee was located near a small hill called Odwede a few miles southwest of Kilak. The chiefdom had a royal drum that the Parabongo took after their military victory, and it seems to have consisted of *kal* as well as eight *lobong* lineages. This would have made Papee one of the larger eighteenth-century polities in Acholi. Like other chiefdoms in the western zone, Papee's lineages were predominantly Central Sudanic in origin (only *kal* and one *lobong* lineage, Gem, seem originally Eastern Nilotic) and, by the eighteenth century, they were almost certainly all Central Sudanic in speech. With Papee's defeat, its lineages fled either to Central Sudanic-speaking Madi or to western Acholi chiefdoms whose lineages were predominantly Central Sudanic.[72]

There is one final incident of significance remembered about Papee. This was a hunting dispute between Papee and nearby Pabo that escalated into warfare when widely accepted compensation and reconciliation procedures were not followed. The dispute began when both Papee and Pabo hunters claimed that they had killed a particular buffalo and thus deserved the meat from their kill. Papee traditions assert that the men from Papee were in the right, though the Pabo were just as adamant. A fight broke out, and a man from each chiefdom was speared. The Pabo man eventually died of his wounds, and the Papee braced themselves for a retaliatory attack. But no attack came.

---

71. A.H.T. 212 contains the Payugu story.
72. Parabongo traditions with material on the "Papee" are in A.H.T. 218–19, 221. Papee's probable *lobong* were the Gem, Orima, Pacega, Oruba, Pajaa, Lumunga, Ajebo, and Odree. Evidence and arguments on their ethnolinguistic origins is in Atkinson (1978, p. 131).

However, no compensation was ever paid nor were any formal reconciliation procedures arranged. The episode was thus neither settled nor forgotten. Some time later, a Papee man visiting Pabo was killed when he was caught having illicit sex with a Pabo woman. It was widely accepted that legitimate punishment for such a serious offense could end in death for the man, though this was neither inevitable nor even common. And to the Papee at the time, the harshness of the penalty seemed to have less to do with the offense than it did with the still-unresolved, earlier killing of the Pabo hunter. This, at least, is the way the incident is remembered in surviving Papee traditions, which also recount that the Papee felt they were in no position to retaliate or protest. Eventually, the still unresolved hostility was carried over to Papee's successor chiefdom and was a major factor in a nineteenth- century conflict between Pabo and Parabongo.[73]

The sort of incident that sparked this protracted enmity must have occurred often in the action and excitement of the hunt. What is unusual here is that compensation and reconciliation procedures were not carried out before things escalated as far as they did, and it was because of this escalation that memory of the original incident has been retained at all. Incentives for reaching agreement on compensation and reconciliation would have been especially great within chiefdoms and between neighboring polities that shared relatively dense patterns of interaction, as was true of those within the same zone. The low incidence of remembered warfare between such chiefdoms suggests strongly that "proper" procedures were in fact usually worked out.[74]

Conclusion

When eighteenth-century chiefdom formation in the south-central and western zones is compared with what occurred in the southeastern and east-central zones, there are both similarities and contrasts. The similarities were based on the common core of ideological, structural, and material foundations underlaying the process of chiefdom formation throughout emergent Acholi. The most striking contrasts had to do with the much smaller number of chiefdoms and lineages involved in this process in the south-central and western zones.

73. A.H.T. 219.
74. Discussions of compensation and reconciliation procedures, including accompanying ritual, can be found, for example, in Girling (1960, pp. 66–67) and A.H.T. 216, 243, 270.

Chiefdom formation in the western zone highlighted another contrast. The establishment of Pabo, Lamogi, Paomo, Pagak, and Papee in the neighborhood of *Got* Kilak marked the westernmost extension of the sociopolitical order that came to characterize Acholi. None of the five was founded by a ruling lineage that was originally Luo or Paluo. And except for the Paluo successor dynasties in Pagak and (after about 1790) Parabongo, as well as a temporary move into the zone by Pawel, there seem to have been no Luo-speaking lineages at all. Instead, western-zone lineages seem overwhelmingly Central Sudanic in origin and, at least by the eighteenth century, universally Central Sudanic in speech.

Yet these people gradually became more like the others in north-central Uganda now called Acholi, even shifting their language to become predominantly Luo-speaking. This complex transformation was set in motion by the process of chiefdom formation on the Bunyoro/Paluo model. Once the chiefdoms were established and succeeded in incorporating most of the village-lineages in the zone, the people there came increasingly to lead similar lives to those in the new chiefdoms — not only in the western zone but all across emergent Acholi. Conversely, they became less and less like their Central Sudanic neighbors who remained outside the chiefly order.

It is worth reemphasizing that neither the sociohistorical changes of chiefdom formation nor the eventual language shift that occurred separated the people of the western-zone chiefdoms in any sharp way from their Central Sudanic neighbors. A host of shared cultural practices (including much ritual), substantial trade, and frequent intermarriage continued to sustain important ties among them all.[75]

75. Cultural traits or practices in the later western-zone chiefdoms that can be clearly associated with earlier Central Sudanic ones include the use of bows and arrows as preferred weapons, the use of special "rainstones" (*ame*) for use in rainmaking ritual, and harvest and planting ceremonies that feature bringing soil from the place where sacrifices were made to the chiefdom-wide *jok* to be rubbed on the chests of the chiefdom's people; see, for example, A.H.T. 205–6, 212, 215, 222.

8. The Central and Northern Zones: The Consolidation of the New Order at the Center and Its Furthest Extension North

The introduction and spread of a new sociopolitical order in north-central Uganda had finite geographical limits. This chapter investigates those limits to the north, examining the extension of the new order into what become the northwestern, north-central, and northeastern zones. First, though, the chapter focuses on developments after the 1720s drought in one of the areas of Acholi where chiefdoms developed earliest: the central zone.

The Central Zone

By the time of the 1720s drought, six chiefdoms had established themselves in the central zone: Alero, Palaro, Patiko, Payira, Paico, and Paibona. All but Patiko were small and often struggling. Over the two generations after the 1720s drought, the central-zone chiefdoms—and the sociopolitical order that they represented—became much more firmly entrenched, with many more village-lineages incorporated. Payira in particular experienced explosive expansion, propelling it to become the largest chiefdom by far in all of Acholi.

PALARO AND ALERO

The 1720s drought could hardly have come at a worse time for Palaro, reeling from defeat at the hands of Alero and their Bunyoro/Paluo allies. The Palaro fields, neglected during the fighting and ravaged by the enemy, were in a state of disrepair. Their *rwot* Obura, moreover, had been killed, and the son widely favored as his successor, Okello, had been carried away to "Bunyoro" (probably Paluo).

Traditions associate Palaro's recovery with the return of Okello from captivity. The people of Palaro had never expected to see him again and had reluctantly chosen his brother Cua as *rwot*. But Okello somehow survived. After languishing as a hostage for some time, he went on a hunger strike in a bid to win his freedom. The strategy succeeded. The "Bunyoro" *rwot* holding him "thought the matter over and decided that it was to no purpose that Okello should die in his hands and that he had better set him free; which he did." And then, surprisingly, Okello's former captor virtually commissioned him to return to Palaro as the chiefdom's "proper" *rwot*. "You may go home," Okello was told, "and take the place of your father Obvura as *Rwoot* of Palaaro. Here are the insignia of your royal power, the *jami keer*: the *bvuul keer*, the *tong keer* (royal drum and spear), the *bvuul tiimo* (smaller drum), the *burjok* bead necklace and *ci-bara* (a magic medicine to protect the *keer*); go and be *Rwoot* of Palaro!"[1]

As Okello and his supporters approached Palaro on their return, they announced their presence by beating the new royal drum they had brought with them. The elders quickly consulted and decided to accept Okello back as their *rwot*. In one account the elders then "advised" Cua to leave; another uses the more forceful term "deposed." In either event, Cua gave way to Okello, and Palaro's fortunes began to change.[2]

First, the 1720s drought and ensuing famine ended; and Okello is remembered to have helped end it, since among the *jami ker* that he brought back with him were rainstones that he used to "make" rain and thus end the drought. This detail suggests that Okello became *rwot* around 1725, giving him estimated dates of rule from 1725 to 1755.[3]

The next steps in Palaro's recovery were a series of eastward moves, taking the chiefdom across the Acaa, deeper into the central zone, and near the area of highest reliable rainfall in Acholi. These moves continued during the time of Okello's son and successor Lagero (c. 1755–85) until the chiefdom was settled near *Got* Byeyo and Payira (Map 10). Traditions note "no fighting" during this time; and though details are lacking, sometime after the 1720s drought Palaro was joined by the Padanga, Baar, Larubi, Panyangilo, Jo-Lango, Paipeno, and Pagaya village-lineages. The first four of these were originally Central Sudanic, the last three probably Eastern Nilotic.[4]

1. Crazzolara (1951, p. 293), Wright (1934, p. 96), and Okech (1953, p. 66) also note Okello's return from Bunyoro/Paluo to become *rwot*.

2. Crazzolara (1951, p. 293) uses "advised"; Wright (1934, p. 96), "deposed." In both, Cua is remembered to have gone to Puranga with followers where they became (joined?) the Palaro lineage there.

3. Wright (1934, p. 96).

4. Most of the information comes from Wright (1934, pp. 95–96); corroborative detail is in Crazzolara (1951, pp. 287–88, 294–95) and Atkinson (1978, pp. 133–34).

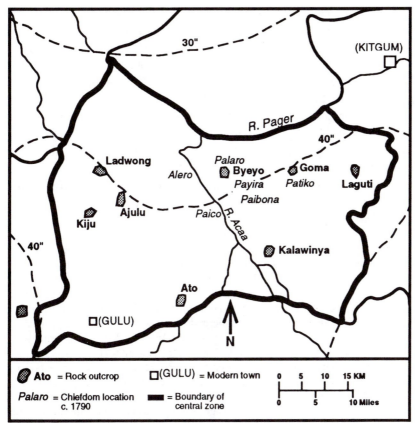

Map 10. Central zone, c. 1725-90.

By the time of the next major drought about 1790, Palaro was in a much stronger position than it had been when the 1720s drought occurred. Traditions indicate that the chiefdom and its royal line had experienced two generations of stability and peace. It had moved deeper into the zone of Acholi that received the most abundant rainfall and was most secure from raids by "outsiders" such as emergent Jie. It had also incorporated as many as seven additional village-lineages.

Meanwhile, Palaro's earlier adversary, Alero, also went through difficult and unsettled times. Whatever the fruits of their victory over Palaro, they were negated by the 1720s drought. Alero traditions remember the drought as devastating: "The spectre of a terrible famine stared at them all.

They were at a loss what to do to save their lives." Both the royal and *lobong* lineages of Alero split up, with people scattering in all directions.[5]

But some, both *kal* and *lobong*, "remained at home and managed to survive the famine." Among the *kal* identified as staying were *Rwot* Kirya, his wives, his son Koona, and a client or "slave" of the royal household named Kiyiino. Kiyiino is remembered to have been part of the expeditionary force from *Loka* that had fought with Alero against Palaro. But he fell ill and was left behind by his fellow soldiers. Eventually people from Alero found him and "offered him to Kiriya, who added him to his family, as his *lateen* or child."[6]

The role that Kiyiino subsequently played in Alero's history is recounted in traditions collected by Crazzolara in a sequence of events that he describes as "extraordinary and unaccountable":

> He gained the sympathy of everybody by his friendliness — *beere* — towards everybody. He becomes the favourite "son" of Kiriya, the favourite "brother" of Koona (Kiriya's son and heir presumptive) and he had, even more easily, won the heart of Amoono, the attractive widow of Kiriya and Koona's mother. At Kiriya's death [c. 1740] Kiyiino remained the beloved of everybody, prince Koona included. He [Kiriya] inherited Amoono, with the full approval of Koona. Oceng-Oyoo, the son of Kiyiino and Amoono, had like his father won the hearts of everybody. After Kiriya's death nobody was set up as his successor. . . . There seems to have been an interregnum. When Oceng-Oyoo had grown up, he, the son of Kiyiino, not Koona, the son of Kiriya, was set on the throne of Aleero and became its *Rwoot*. It was Koona who set him on the throne; and the old royal clan [lineage] simply and peacefully submitted to the new *Rwoot* and dynasty.[7]

This is indeed an extraordinary story. It may well camouflage change of a different sort than the passage suggests, perhaps a violent dynastic change or the takeover of the *rwot*ship by a Paluo group rather than by a single Paluo "slave" and his son, who had been "adopted" into the established *kal*. But the story may also be essentially accurate.

Every village in Acholi typically contained residents, both short- and long-term, who were neither members of the village's core lineage nor married to women of that lineage. The number and variety of such outsiders seems to have been substantially larger in royal lineages than in non-royal ones. Among them were war captives and others who were often

5. Crazzolara (1951, p. 266).
6. Ibid., pp. 266–68.
7. Ibid. A.H.T. 208 and 209 indicate that Kirya was succeeded by a brother, Oceng

described as "slaves." The social status of these captives and slaves was undoubtedly lower than others. But the difference was not necessarily a marked one, and it was always temporary. Slaves or their descendants were commonly incorporated into the lineage (or, in the case of adult females, were married into it).[8]

Kiyiino's initial status as a "slave" was thus not out of the ordinary. But two features of his circumstances were. The first is that Kiyiino's story has been retained in traditions at all. Only in special circumstances would the purposeful forgetfulness of such origins be overcome. Second, the case of Kiyiino and his son Oceng-Oyoo was not only special but extreme. Sons of slaves and clients of *rwodi* did not typically become *rwodi* themselves; there is only one known instance in extant traditions anywhere in Acholi of a similar situation—from the south-central-zone chiefdom of Puranga during the 1830s drought.

The extreme trauma of the 1720s drought might have made the implausible rise of Kiyiino and Oceng-Oyoo possible. The drought seems to have shaken Alero to its foundations, with many of its members and much of its leadership absent or weakened, disunited, and desperate. Traditions add that just after Kirya died, the favored successor Koona flew into a jealous rage when another favorite slave of his father received too much positive attention. Koona had the slave brutally killed. Since jealousy, uncontrolled anger, and brutality were not qualities that people looked for in their *rwodi*, Koona's candidacy was severely damaged. In such circumstances, perhaps the son of a former slave really did succeed to the *rwot*ship in Alero.[9]

A final point concerning Kiyiino is that in many respects he seems a variant version of Okello from Palaro. Okello was the son of a former *rwot* and a temporary captive who returned from Bunyoro/Paluo with new regalia to give the Palaro chiefdom a new beginning after difficult times. Kiyiino also came from Bunyoro/Paluo, was both a slave and then (adopted) "son" of the *rwot*, and through his son, Oceng Oyoo, provided the Alero chiefdom with a new beginning after times as difficult as Palaro's. The depiction of

---

Ladyang, before Oceng-Oyoo took over; Okech (1953, p. 68) states that Kirya's successor was his son Oceng, who was then followed by the Oceng of the successor dynasty. It is possible that a brother, or even a son, served as some sort of regent during the "interregnum."

8. See above, Chap. 3, n. 2. Girling (1960, p. 107) notes "how far removed" war captives or others such as Kirya were from the usual meaning of "slave": "In an economy in which the social division of labour was rudimentary, and where even the *Rwodi* worked in the fields, there was no place for slave-labour."

9. Crazzolara (1951, pp. 266–67).

these two figures in narrative Palaro and Alero traditions reads like classically structured myth, especially intriguing given the degree to which the histories (and traditions?) of the two polities are intertwined. But if these traditions *are* synchronically structured myth (rather than simply having the chance appearance as such), they are highly atypical for Acholi.[10]

In any case, Alero traditions indicate that after the installation of Oceng Oyoo (who ruled from about 1745 to 1775), the chiefdom moved nearer the Acaa and deeper into the central zone. Here, Alero appears to have regrouped. Some who had left during the worst of the drought are remembered to have returned, and three new lineages — the Lamoo, Payom, and Palite — also joined. As with Palaro, Alero by the mid-eighteenth century seems to have experienced a resurgence after trying times. And its resurgence likewise accompanied a move further into the center of Acholi.[11]

PAYIRA, PAICO, AND PAIBONA

For Payira, Paico, and Paibona, all settled near the largest river in Acholi and in the area of highest reliable rainfall, the two generations between the droughts of about 1725 and 1790 were eventful ones. Before the first drought, each consisted of only one or two village-lineages; by the end of the eighteenth century all had grown significantly, especially Payira.

Unfortunately, the reconstruction of Payira's developments during this period continues to be hampered by the absence of a clearly identifiable line of *rwodi*. It is almost certain that Loni was *rwot* when the drought of about 1790 struck and that he ruled for some time after the drought. Thirteen of the sixteen different collected Payira *rwot* lists identify Loni's immediate predecessor as his father, Onguka. Before Onguka there is mostly confusion.[12]

Despite the absence of consistent identification of *rwodi* before Onguka, Payira traditions do contain evidence that clearly refers to earlier times.

10. For an analysis of a set of traditions from the kingdom of Buganda as synchronically structured myth rather than the diachronically ordered history that the traditions purport to be, see Atkinson (1975); see also Vansina's skeptical response (1983).

11. See Crazzolara (1951, pp. 282–84), which also indicates Central Sudanic origins for the three new lineages. A.H.T. 208 and 209 provide an alternative chronology but lack the detail of the Crazzolara account.

12. See Anywar (1954, pp. 13, 38), Crazzolara (1954, p. 493). The sixteen collected Payira *rwot* lists are reproduced in Atkinson (1978, pp. 576–78, with accompanying notes). In both Anywar's and Crazzolara's accounts, Onguka is killed by a lion; Anywar's adds that he was very young at the time. Thus, Onguka has been assigned brief estimated dates of rule from 1770 to 1780 and Loni has been assigned a longer than average reign (c. 1780–1820).

The most dramatic of the earlier episodes is set in the context of severe drought and famine—surely that of the 1720s—and it narrates a crucial step in the expansion that would make Payira the largest chiefdom in all of Acholi by the end of the eighteenth century.

When the 1720s drought struck, affecting even the favored central zone, Payira seems to have been settled near the Acaa south of *Got* Byeyo (see Map 10) and to have consisted only of *kal* and the Lamogi village-lineage. But then, traditions from nearby Paibona tell us, Payira and Paibona "found" two, earlier-settled Central Sudanic lineages: Bura and Pangora. The former, *wegi ngom* of the Byeyo area, joined Payira; some Pangora did as well, with the others attaching themselves to Paibona.[13]

Some ten to fifteen miles east, another chiefdom named Pangang seems to have been in the process of establishing itself near *Got* Laguti. This chiefdom was made up of Pangang *kal* plus the Pakoo, Paciko, and probably Pakongo lineages. Traditions in Crazzolara indicate that some young men from *kal* committed two especially brutal murders of Pakoo women. When the Pangang *rwot* failed to settle the issue in a way that satisfied the Pakoo, they made two unsuccessful attempts to get the nearby Payira *rwot* to intervene.[14]

As the drought and famine continued, the Pakoo (and maybe other Pangang *lobong*) found another way to bring Payira into their affairs and gain revenge against their *rwot*. During the drought, certain foods continued to grow in the Pangang area that did not in Payira. Perhaps to maintain friendly relations, the Pangang *rwot* saw to it that some of these foods were provided to the Payira and their *rwot*. Here was a chance for the dissatisfied Pangang *lobong*. They sabotaged some of the food. Upon tasting this food, the Payira became angry, thinking that the Pangang must be attempting to poison their *rwot*. In retaliation, the Payira attacked the divided Pangang, with the assistance of the expanding Lira chiefdom of the southeastern zone and perhaps nearby Paibona as well. Pangang defeat was

13. Paibona traditions are in A.H.T. 236. A.H.T. 238, 247 and Crazzolara (1954, p. 491) identify Bura as *wegi ngom*; the probable Central Sudanic origins of Bura and Pangora are argued in Atkinson (1978, pp. 128–29, 132, 134).

14. Crazzolara (1954, pp. 483–87) provides the basic narrative; supporting details are in Anywar (1954, p. 13); Okot (1971, pp. 61–62); and A.H.T. 236, 239, 241. Some of these sources, including Crazzolara, refer to incidents or people that can be clearly identified with the drought of about 1790 rather than that of the 1720s. But the bulk of the evidence points to the earlier rather than the later drought; this includes references to Payira *rwodi* who precede the Payira *rwot* (*Rwot* Loni) who was ruling at the time of the 1790 drought. *Rwot* Onguka is identified in Crazzolara, Okot, and A.H.T. 236; *Rwot* Lyet in Anywar; and *Rwot* Lutwa in A.H.T. 241.

total. The polity was destroyed, its royal lineage scattered, its royal drum and other regalia taken. Afterward, major portions of each of the Pangang lineages, including the former Pangang *kal*, joined Payira. One of these, the Paciko, even provided one of Payira's six major *lodito pa rwot*.[15]

Following its victory and incorporation of the Pangang lineages, Payira became a chiefdom of eight village-lineages. Over the next two generations, although extant traditions provide almost no supportive details, as many as twenty or more additional lineages of both Central Sudanic and Eastern Nilotic origins joined Payira. Thus by the end of the eighteenth century, Payira seems to have been made up of at least twenty-five village-lineages and perhaps as many as thirty or more.[16]

By the end of the eighteenth century, only Pabo of the western zone seems to have approached Payira in terms of estimated population (though with far fewer lineages), and only the southeastern zone's Lira Paluo had a similar number of lineages, if a smaller population (see Appendix). Unfortunately, extant Payira traditions provide little information about its growth, for three main reasons. First, the chiefdom's confused and unreliable *rwot* lists before the late eighteenth century preclude a secure chronological framework. Second, Payira's *rwodi* from the late eighteenth century on—Loni, Lubwa, Rwotcomo, and Awic—were powerful rulers whose dominant place in Payira traditions overshadows all that went before. And third, a systematic collection of individual Payira village-lineage histories has never been undertaken.[17]

15. Crazzolara (1954, pp. 484–87) again provides the fundamental narrative and the emphasis on the role of the Pakoo; A.H.T. 236 (from Paibona) indicates that the Pangang *lobong* were involved in undermining their *rwot* and that Paibona and Paico, as well as Lira Paluo, helped Payira against Pangang.

16. The lineages with core groups of both Central Sudanic and Eastern Nilotic origin seem to have been the Pailim, Pakeyo, Patuda, Ariya, Pabit, Palami, Romo, Lamwo, Payom, Ywaya, Pailik, Pagik, Koyo, and members of the Paibwor grouping (the Paibwor, Paryanga, Pamaber, and Cobo). The Paibora, Pungole, Pagol, Puceng, Pugot, and Panyakotto may have joined as well. The Pailim lineage head was one of the *wegi ngom* of Payira, responsible for one of the main Payira *jogi*, *Jok* Kalawinya (a strong indication that the Pailim were part of Payira from early on). See Anywar (1954, p. 53), Girling (1960, pp. 29–35, 48–49), A.H.T. 238, and, on Pailim's likely Central Sudanic origins, Atkinson (1978, pp. 132–33). A.H.T. 247 lists the Pakeyo, Patuda, Ariya (a former southeastern-zone polity; see Chap. 5 above), Palami, Romo, Pabit, and the members of the Paibwor grouping as the earliest to join the chiefdom under *Rwot* Onguka. A.H.T. 245 includes additional information on the Paibwor grouping and its incorporation following a disastrous defeat at the hands of "Lango Omiro"; a partial identification of the mixed Central Sudanic and Eastern Nilotic origins of these lineages is in Atkinson (1978, p. 134). For scattered information on the remaining lineages, see Crazzolara (1954, pp. 491–93) and Atkinson (1978, pp. 134, 365–66).

17. A planned collection of such histories was interrupted by the Amin coup and the subsequent closing of Acholi to research. Before the coup, A.H.T. 241 (with Lamogi), 243 (Pangora), 244 (Cobo), and 245 (Paryanga) were completed.

It is possible to discern traces of Payira's internal eighteenth-century structuring. First, only the lineage heads from Lamogi, Paciko, Paibwor, Pakeyo, and Paibora seem to have held special *lodito pa rwot* positions. Evidence exists to suggest how four of the five might have obtained the office. Lamogi elders stated that their lineage head was a special *ladit pa rwot* because the Lamogi were the original *lobong* of the chiefdom. The Paciko may have gained a *ladit pa rwot* office in return for helping Payira to victory over Paciko's former Pangang rulers. The Paibwor *ladit pa rwot* was probably established as part of the process of bringing all four lineages of the Paibwor-led multiple-village grouping into the Payira fold. And Pakeyo's special *ladit pa rwot* position may have resulted from its being among the earliest remembered village-lineages to join Payira. Unfortunately, no information is available to explain Paibora's special *ladit pa rwot* (and a sixth *ladit pa rwot*, from Ongako, was probably created during the later nineteenth century). A second and related point is that available sources give no indication that eighteenth-century Payira had any formal territorial divisions or political functionaries above these special *lodito pa rwot*.[18]

Third, eighteenth-century Payira did seem to have had three *wegi ngom* ("fathers of the soil"; sing. *won ngom*), positions almost always held by the heads of village-lineages acknowledged as early or original inhabitants of particular areas. These were the Bura, Paryanga, and Pailim. Almost all chiefdoms in Acholi had only one *won ngom*; only Payira's remarkable growth can explain its having three.[19]

Three factors may help explain this growth. First, Payira was located near Acholi's largest river, the Acaa, and within the region of highest reliable rainfall. Payira was also both relatively distant and relatively insulated from the sometimes disruptive Jie to the east and, after the 1790s drought, from emergent Langi to the south. These advantages could have been powerful attractions for outside village-lineages. Second, once Payira's incorporation of others made it clearly more powerful than neighboring chiefdoms, something of a domino effect may have occurred. For nearby lineages not yet part of a chiefdom, Payira's exceptional growth might have

18. A.H.T. 238–39, 241, 243, and 246 all contain information on the special *lodito-pa-rwot*. Okech (1953, p. 35) and Anywar (1954, pp. 35–39) each list a number of "small chieftainships" (or groups with "small royal drums") in Payira, suggesting territorial subdivisions. But both lists consist solely of branches of the Payira royal lineage that became structurally and territorially differentiated only in the nineteenth century, or of groups such as Paibona and Gem that were in fact independent polities, even if dominated by their larger neighbor.

19. See Crazzolara (1954, p. 491), Girling (1960, pp. 29–35, 48–49), and A.H.T. 238, 245.

been an appeal in itself. In the political realm, growth can beget further growth. Finally, few Acholi traditions recount instances of the sort of extensive destruction that Pangang experienced at the hands of Payira. Such rare violence must have made a powerful impression on others in the region. Unattached lineages may well have decided to join Payira rather than risk being the object of its demonstrated willingness and ability to use force.

Nearby Paibona's first incorporation of outsiders seems to have been associated with Payira's early growth. Paibona traditions claim that Paibona was with Payira south of *Got* Byeyo when the two polities "found" and incorporated the Bura and Pangora. As noted, the Bura and some Pangora joined Payira while other Pangora joined Paibona. This first Paibona *lobong* and its head became responsible for the main chiefdom-wide *jok* of Paibona: *Jok* Adeca.[20]

Paibona's second outside lineage, the originally Eastern Nilotic Pabwodo, seems to have joined shortly after the first, and again the process was linked with Payira. The first step involved Paibona's fighting with Pabwodo's neighbor, the Paciko, who then "ran to Payira" and joined that chiefdom. This could have occurred as part of the more general Payira-Pangang conflict (a separate Paibona text indicates that the Paibona were a Payira ally in that conflict), or in the aftermath of the Pangang defeat, while Paciko was temporarily unaffiliated with either Pangang or Payira. In either case, it was after Paibona fought with Paciko that the Pabwodo were brought into the Paibona chiefdom — probably during the time of *Rwot* Lyek who ruled about 1715–45.[21]

Extant Paibona traditions recount nothing more about the time of Lyek or his son and successor, Cua (c. 1745–75). And most traditions of Cua's successor Obot (c. 1775–1805), including those about the addition of other lineages, almost certainly refer to the drought of about 1790 or after. With only two *lobong* lineages, Paibona thus remained a small chiefdom throughout most of the eighteenth century. Over the course of the century, it also seems to have become increasingly dominated by its larger and more powerful neighbor Payira, though it retained its formal independence.[22]

20. A.H.T. 236 (and see n. 13).

21. A.H.T. 236. There are only two extant Paibona *rwot* lists: Okech (1953, p. 72) and A.H.T. 235, with some additional details in A.H.T. 236–37; Lyek's estimated dates of rule are derived from A.H.T. 235.

22. Cua is included in both of the extant Paibona *rwot* lists (see n. 21). Confusion over Paibona's existence as an independent chiefdom may arise, at least in part, from Anywar (1954, pp. 35–39); see n. 18.

Paico meanwhile was settled just across the Acaa to the west. At the time of the 1720s drought, Paico was a small chiefdom like its neighbors. It had incorporated one *lobong* lineage of unclear origins — the Pagaya. Paico *rwot* lists indicate that Labora (c. 1710–40) was probably *rwot* when the 1720s drought occurred, though extant Paico traditions make no references to that drought. Labora's name *is* linked with Paico's first significant incorporation of outsiders. In my first interview in Paico, former *rwot* Jakayo Obunya said that all of Paico's lineages had joined while Labora was *rwot*. Even after providing later details that contradicted this sweeping generalization, when Jakayo was asked again about Labora he reiterated the general sense of the earlier message: "I told you about [L]Abora before. [L]Abora is the one who multiplied all the people here."[23]

Three lineages actually seem to have joined Paico during the time of Labora: the Parapul, Pangaya, and Pakwelo. The Pailim and Porogo then joined Labora's son and successor, Latege (c. 1740–70), completing the growth of this ethnolinguistically mixed chiefdom. Even after this growth, the head of Paico's first *lobong* (the Pagaya) continued to be acknowledged as a special *ladit-pa-rwot*.[24]

When Latege died, his son Lacora (c. 1770–85) was chosen as his successor over another son, Lajom, who also wanted to become *rwot*. Lajom then led a group of supporters away to the Labongo area of the east-central zone, where they eventually established the small Koc chiefdom (as corroborated by traditions from Labongo). Lacora left no living sons and was thus succeeded by his brother Owor (c. 1785–1800), who was *rwot* when the late-eighteenth-century drought struck.[25]

PATIKO

Patiko, the largest of the central zone's chiefdoms by the time of the 1720s drought (consisting of *kal* and eight *lobong* lineages), did not grow further during the remainder of the eighteenth century. The only story about the drought in extant Patiko traditions is an intriguing one involving its relations with the expanding power of Payira:

> forced by hunger a part of Patiko went over to Payiira. When they arrived there, they were not refused admittance but after some time, under the sup-

23. The quotation is from A.H.T. 228. Paico *rwot* lists, which are mainly consistent, can be found in Wright (1934, p. 9), Okech (1953, pp. 42–43), and A.H.T. 229.

24. A.H.T. 228, 230, 232, 234, 299–300, and, on ethnolinguistic origins, Atkinson (1978, pp. 132–33), and Okech (1953, p. 43).

25. A.H.T. 231, 234; Okech (1953, p. 42) identifies Owor as Lacora's successor but does not indicate that he was a brother. Information from the Koc chiefdom of Labongo on their Paico connection can be found in Garry Labongo A.H.T., p. 25.

position that they joined Payiira, their *Rwoot* . . . reminded the new arrivals of their duty to bring the customary *tyeer* (offering) to his residence. The people were alarmed, as they had never thought of joining Payiira as *lwak* (subjects). They reported the matter to their *Rwoot* at home. . . . The *Rwoot* of Patiko decided: "People who move on account of famine do not offer their *tyeer*" (to the *Rwoot* in whose territory they happened to sojourn). The *Rwoot* of Payiira agreed in principle with that decision, but with a distinction: "As for elder men, they shall not be requested to bring their *tyeer*, but younger men should."

The Patiko elders responded to this obvious Payira ruse with one of their own: "As hunger still sways us, we have to submit — in a way. Whenever a young man kills a large animal . . . (the young man) shall not blow his signal: an elder, his father shall do it. If one's father is not present, the latter's brother shall whistle. When small animals are killed (and no *tyeer* is exacted) then the young man may blow his whistle." The Payira *rwot*, the story concludes, could do no more than grumble. Thus even Payira, on its way to becoming the largest and most powerful chiefdom in Acholi, does not seem to have been able to enforce its wishes against another established chiefdom — even when the latter was disadvantaged because of drought and famine.[26]

The Patiko *rwot* most often associated with the 1720s drought is Okello-Woro (c. 1710–40). His successor was his son Ogol (c. 1740–70). Throughout both reigns the chiefdom remained settled to the east of the River Acaa well within the central zone (see Map 10). Some accounts suggest that another famine occurred during the time of Ogol, among the few hints in Acholi to a possible rainfall deficiency suggested by Nile level records for the 1750s or 1760s. But no other information about Ogol is available, and we also learn nothing about Ogol's son and successor Ajanto (c. 1770–1800) prior to the 1790s drought.[27]

The Three Northern Zones

Both the northwestern and northeastern flanks of the new sociopolitical order were marked by limited chiefdom formation. Atyak was the sole

26. Crazzolara (1951, pp. 233–34). The Payira *rwot* in the story is identified as Loni, not simply a random mistake. Loni *was* associated with a severe drought and famine, but it was c. 1790, not in the 1720s.

27. Ibid. The six extant Patiko *rwot* lists, highly consistent from the chiefdom's founding under *Rwot* Atiko forward, are in Wright (1934, pp. 2, 44), Malandra (1947, pp. 2–7), Crazzolara (1951, pp. 223–55), Okech (1953, pp. 56–58), Girling (1960, pp. 117, 220), and Okot (1971, p. 86).

representative of the new chiefly order in the northwestern zone. In the northeast, where we have limited sources available, two or three chiefdoms developed: Nam Okora (a small break-away polity from Patongo in the southeastern zone); Orom, nestled up against the iron-rich *Got* Orom; and perhaps a small chiefdom called Akara or Pajong. In contrast to these few outposts of the new order to the northeast and northwest, the emergent north-central zone experienced a much higher density of chiefdom formation. Probably eleven chiefdoms established themselves in the zone during the eighteenth century. Among these were Padibe and Palabek (seemingly two of the largest polities in eighteenth-century Acholi) and Cua-Bura (eventually the dominant chiefdom of the northeastern zone).

THE NORTHWESTERN ZONE

Located some twenty miles (thirty kilometers) north of *Got* Kilak near the Unyama River, Atyak represented the furthest extension northwest of the chiefly order derived from Bunyoro/Paluo (Map 11). As with the chiefdoms of the western zone that developed around Kilak, the constituent lineages of Atyak were overwhelmingly Central Sudanic.[28]

Atyak traditions have been collected by six researchers. Before a figure in Atyak's remembered *rwot* lists named Labongo Lawiarut (c. 1710–40), the six versions differ as to the names, number, and order of *rwodi*, as well as the traditions associated with each name. After Labongo the traditions consistently agree.[29]

Among all the variants in the early portions of traditions, two constants stand out. First, the lineage that eventually became *kal* of an Atyak chiefdom was clearly Central Sudanic in origin; second, this lineage seems long-settled to the west of the Nile in what is now Central Sudanic-speaking Madi. The group seems to have moved eastward across the Nile into the northwestern zone of Acholi several generations before Labongo Lawiarut, though pre-polity chronology is always speculative. Whenever the move occurred, it would not have been a major transition, for the new home of the eventual Atyak *kal* was like the old in terms of terrain, soils, and

28. Members of the Atyak chiefdom, moreover, would continue to speak Central Sudanic Madi as at least a co-equal language with Luo into the present century. See Okech (1953, p. 62); Crazzolara (1951, p. 297).

29. The lists, with associated traditions, are in Crazzolara (1951, pp. 297–301), Anywar (1954, pp. 105–11), Wright (1934, pp. 46–54), Okech (1953, pp. 62–63), Malandra (1947, pp. 17–21), and Girling (1960, pp. 225, 290). The name Labongo has strong connections with Paluo; see Webster and Herring (1975). The estimated dates for Labongo Lawiarut are based on average, thirty-year dynastic generations that were calculated back from a later *Rwot* Labongo who was firmly linked with the drought of about 1790; these dates substantially revise those in Atkinson (1978, pp. 246–51).

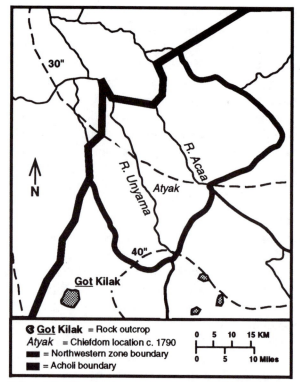

Map 11. Northwestern zone, c. 1725-90.

levels of expected annual rainfall. It was also just as thoroughly Central Sudanic.[30]

Each extant narrative of Atyak traditions reads as if Atyak were already a chiefdom by the time of the move. But other aspects of Atyak traditions provide a number of clues that an Atyak chiefdom was only established in the early eighteenth century during the time of Labongo Lawiarut. For example, Crazzolara's rendition includes a list of seven supposed predecessors of Labongo as *rwot*. Yet, as he reports, Labongo "is commonly called the ancestor of Atyak." Crazzolara's account then states that Labongo and

30. The sources in n. 29 above make the Central Sudanic origins of the eventual Atyak *kal* clear despite various attempts to claim Luo origins; see also Webster (1974, pp. 18–19). Atyak's crossing the Nile into the eventual northwestern zone of Acholi is placed four names before Labongo Lawiarut in Okech (1953, p. 62), three names before in Malandra (1947, p. 17), one name before in Crazzolara (1951, p. 297) and Anywar (1954, pp. 105–6), and during Labongo's generation in Wright (1934, p. 48).

his son Owiny quarreled, causing Owiny to leave Atyak to go to "Loka Pawir," or Paluo. Atyak traditions in Girling add that Owiny (though he is identified as a brother and not a son) "is said to have sent a present of a drum from Bunyoro, together with a Munyoro slave . . . to bear it."[31]

Atyak traditions as recounted by Wright also identify Owiny as a brother of Labongo who went to Bunyoro following a quarrel, and add that it was during the time of Labongo that Atyak incorporated its first *lobong* lineage, the Palobo. Anywar's collection of Atyak traditions corroborates an initial incorporation of outsiders during the time of Labongo (though the lineage named is the Batok or Patoko, not Palobo), and also identifies a prominent Atyak royal who traveled to Bunyoro in this period: *Rwot* Labongo himself.[32]

Taken together, these traces of evidence suggest that Labongo Lawiarut (c. 1710–40) was the first *rwot* of an Atyak chiefdom and that the chiefdom's origins were linked to contacts with Paluoland or Paluo ideas during Labongo's rule. These contacts were maintained over the next generation as well, though exactly who filled this generation as Atyak *rwot* is in question. Most accounts indicate that it was Labongo's son Onyamere; a few identify another son, Kwac.[33]

Kwac's position in Atyak *rwot* lists and traditions is analogous to Ling's in Pabo. In two renditions, Kwac is identified as the son and successor of Labongo; two others list him as Labongo's predecessor; a fifth combines the two names and presents them as a single figure, Labongokwac; and, finally, one *rwot* list omits his name altogether.[34]

One possible explanation for the confusion comes from Anywar's rendition of Kwac's succession. Here it is recounted that Kwac became *rwot* when his father, Labongo Lawiarut, left Atyak to go to Bunyoro. If this is what happened, then Kwac would have succeeded before his predecessor had died. These would have been most unusual circumstances, placing

31. See Crazzolara (1951, pp. 297–98), who reports some ambiguity concerning the people involved; see also Girling (1960, p. 38), which notes that "A drum of a type common in Bunyoro is in fact preserved among the regalia of the Attiak rulers."

32. Wright (1934, p. 48); Anywar (1954, pp. 106, 110). Anywar includes a different version of the quarrel cited in n. 31. And Malandra (1947, p. 17) presents a rendition of Atyak traditions that varies so from the others that I make no attempt to reconcile it here.

33. Wright (1934, p. 48), Crazzolara (1951, pp. 297–98), and Anywar (1954, pp. 106, 110) all suggest a renewal of Atyak ties with Paluo during the generation after Labongo Lawiarut.

34. Wright (1934, p. 48) and Anywar (1954, p. 106) identify Kwac as the son and successor of Labongo Lawiarut and as the brother of Onyamere; Crazzolara (1951, p. 297) and Malandra (1947, p. 17) indicate that he was Labongo's predecessor; Okech (1953, p. 62) combines the two names; and Girling (1960, pp. 90, 225) omits Kwac's name altogether.

Kwac in such an anomalous position that the legitimacy of his rule was open to doubt. This in turn could have led to the confused memory of that rule in Atyak traditions.[35]

Anywar's account also provides the only additional detail on Kwac's rule. This detail includes the recollection that Kwac "ruled a long time" and that he was *rwot* when the next of Atyak's *lobong* joined the chiefdom. These were the Koyo and a group of Cobo later known in Atyak as the Pocak. Like Atyak *kal* and the earlier-incorporated Patoko or Palobo, these lineages seem clearly Central Sudanic in origin.[36]

Kwac's successor was most likely his brother Onyamere, who probably ruled the shorter part of a dynastic generation estimated as 1740–70. Once again Anywar's account notes the incorporation of outsiders — in this case the Kibogi, Larube, Pakwec, Pacillo, and Pakor lineages. Since all seem to have been long-settled in the area, they were almost certainly Central Sudanic-speaking by the time they joined Atyak, though only the last was clearly Central Sudanic in origin. Their incorporation under Onyamere would have made Atyak a Central Sudanic-speaking chiefdom of at least ten village-lineages, one of the larger eighteenth-century chiefdoms in all of emergent Acholi.[37]

All extant traditions identify Onyamere's successor as his son Labongo (c. 1770–1800). During Labongo's rule Atyak *kal* began a process of structured segmentation that eventually produced a number of separate royal villages, each with a core membership made up of a particular sub-lineage of *kal*. Another Central Sudanic lineage in the vicinity, the Lupale, may have been incorporated. And finally, two versions of Atyak traditions — corroborating similar assertions in Pabo and Palabek sources — note contact during Labongo's time between Atyak and "Lango Omiro" raiders. The presence of emergent Langi from present-day Lango District so far north and west is plausible only in the context of the drought and famine of about 1790, providing an external chronological marker that fits well with Labongo's estimated dates of rule.[38]

---

35. Anywar (1954, p. 106).

36. Ibid., pp. 106, 110. Wright (1934, p. 54) indicates that Koyo only joined Atyak under *Rwot* Labongo (c. 1770–1800).

37. Anywar (1954, p. 110). Wright (1934, pp. 53–54) supports Anywar on the incorporation of the Pakwec and Pacillo but indicates that the Kibogi did not join until the time of Labongo. For evidence on probable origins of the lineages above, see Crazzolara (1951, pp. 298, 301–2; 1954, p. 522), Wright (1934, p. 54), and Anywar (1954, p. 110).

38. On the segmentation of Atyak *kal* see Anywar (1954, p. 106) and Girling (1960, p. 90). Anywar (p. 110) also includes information on the Lupale, while Wright (1934, p. 49) adds that the Kibogi and Koyo joined *Rwot* Labongo as well. The three references to Lango Omiro are in Anywar (p. 106), Wright (p. 49), and Malandra (1947, p. 18).

THE NORTH-CENTRAL ZONE

The primary focus of settlement and subsequently chiefdom formation in the north-central zone was a cone-shaped area formed by two forks of the Aringa River and capped by the southern slopes of the Agoro mountains. The buffer provided by Agoro along with the water of the Aringa (used to irrigate portions of the surrounding valley) may have been crucial in promoting a degree of chiefdom formation far surpassing that on its flanks in the northwestern and northeastern zones. As many as eleven eighteenth-century chiefdoms seem to have established themselves in the emergent north-central zone: Madi Kiloc (based on a predecessor polity named Parabok), Paloga, Lomura, Padibe, Palabek, Madi Opei, up to four small polities nestled up against the southern Agoro slopes (Logorone, Popoka, Lamogi, and Pobaar), and the eventual northeastern-zone chiefdom of Cua-Bura. An additional polity named Pocu emerged in the zone and then broke up before the end of the eighteenth century (Map 12).

Parabok-Madi Kiloc, Pocu, Paloga, and Lomura

A chiefdom organized on the Bunyoro/Paluo model may have begun to establish itself in the Aringa valley by the end of the seventeenth century, before being destroyed and scattered by the northernmost polity of Pajok temporarily settled in the area (see Chapter 4). But the first chiefdom with a lasting legacy in the zone seems to have been Parabok. Traditions indicate that its ruling lineage came from the originally Central Sudanic Parabok who had joined the young Alero chiefdom further south. Following difficulties in Alero, Bako (son of the Parabok eponym Abok) is remembered to have led a break-away remnant north. As Abok was a contemporary of *Rwot* Alero (c. 1680–1710), Bako and his followers probably arrived in the eventual north-central zone during the next generation, or between about 1710 and 1740. Once in the zone, the Parabok came into contact with the Oraba, Oceba, and Alarapii lineages, all similarly Central Sudanic in origin and perhaps members of a multiple-village grouping under the leadership of Oraba. In unspecified circumstances, the three accepted the immigrants as *kal* and became *lobong* in a Parabok chiefdom.[39]

The chiefdom seems only recently established when a Paluo lineage arrived from the Labongo area of the east-central zone. Traditions note that these Paluo came "with their *ker*"—using their royal drum and other royal regalia, their proclaimed rainmaking powers, and their strong relations with other Paluo ruling lineages further south to challenge the leadership of

---

39. Owot A.H.T. 1; also discussed in Owot (1976, pp. 186–87).

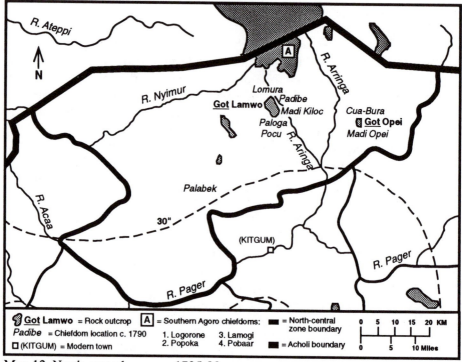

Map 12. North-central zone, c. 1725-90.

Parabok *kal*. Somehow the Paluo newcomers found allies among the Oraba and Oceba lineages who provided them with land on which to settle, despite Parabok *kal's* opposition. Not long after, the Oceba and Oraba began to give tribute to the Paluo immigrants. Then the Alarapii and even the former Parabok *kal* followed suit, though extant traditions provide no real clues as to how any of this occurred. The only thing clear about the transition from the Parabok chiefdom to its successor is that the Oceba lineage and its head took or kept the position as primary caretaker for the main chiefdom-wide *jok*, *Jok* Abayo. This is just what would be expected for some of the main supporters of the new royal lineage and the Madi Kiloc chiefdom that they led.[40]

Traditions identify only one other chiefdom, the Pocu, as being estab-

40. See Owot A.H.T. 1, 14. Owot (1976, pp. 185–86) seems slightly confused, especially in identifying Parabok as being responsible for the main chiefdom *jok* after the dynastic change, whereas Owot A.H.T. 1 is quite clear that it was Oceba.

lished in the north-central zone before its dominant chiefdom, Padibe. Pocu is remembered to have consisted of Pocu *kal* — variously identified as being originally Central Sudanic from the west, Eastern Nilotic from the east, or even an indigenous Aringa valley group who emerged from a hole in the ground — and five *lobong* lineages (two probably Central Sudanic and the others of unclear origins). Beyond this we know little, except that the chiefdom broke up and its lineages scattered, mostly within the emergent north-central zone. The best clue as to what happened comes from traditions in Pellegrini. They note that a "Lango" (Eastern Nilotic) group named Owolo came from the north to the *Got* Lamwo area. There they found the Pocu and another group, identified as Lomura. The Owolo attacked the others and "killed them all." Even if exaggerated, this episode might well recount the death of the Pocu chiefdom as an entity, if not of all the Pocu population.[41]

But who were the Owolo? The Pellegrini version of traditions identifies the leader of the incoming Owolo as Piko. An "Opiko" also shows up as the first name in the only available *rwot* list from Paloga, the *Got* Lamwo chiefdom that old Pocu *kal* joined after its polity was destroyed. And the third name in the Paloga *rwot* list is Owol, a variant of Owolo. Finally, in Crazzolara's listing of Paloga lineages he notes that one of the names of Paloga *kal* was "-Owoolo." These fragments suggest strongly that the Owolo in Pellegrini stands for an Owolo *kal* of a Paloga chiefdom. Assigning an average thirty-year generation to each name in the Paloga *rwot* list produces estimated dates of rule of 1740–70 for Owol/Owolo; this would place the establishment of a Paloga chiefdom and the demise of Pocu in the mid-eighteenth century. Paloga's likely composition included its royal lineage of probable Eastern Nilotic origin, the similarly Eastern Nilotic Gem and Itiba, the old Pocu *kal*, and the Bobi and perhaps Pabwor lineages of unclear origins.[42]

When the "Owolo" appeared at *Got* Lamwo, they are remembered to have fought and defeated not only Pocu but also another small chiefdom

41. Associated lineages included the Anyibi and seemingly a second branch of the Oraba (both probably Central Sudanic), as well as the Pocot, Paiwang, and Poture (all of unclear origins). See Owot A.H.T. 17; also Owot (1976, p. 185). Wright (1934, p. 164) and Crazzolara (1954, p. 502) add to the conflicting information concerning the origins of the old Pocu *kal*. Pellegrini (1963, p. 7) adds the material recounted in the last half of the paragraph.

42. See Wright (1934, p. 164), Crazzolara (1954, p. 502), and Owot A.H.T. 17. The *rwot* list is in Wright, with succession proceeding from father to son. For additional, often contradictory, evidence on the Bobi and Gem, each of which provides core lineages for many villages throughout Acholi and beyond, see Crazzolara (1951, p. 115; 1954, pp. 399, 488, 496, 507, 514, 539–42, 546, 558–60); A.H.T. 286–87.

called Lomura. Unlike Pocu, Lomura survived the Owolo attack. With a royal lineage identified as being originally from *Got* Lamwo, the Lomura continued as a chiefdom into the later nineteenth century when it became part of the Padibe, the dominant power in the region. Most of the limited information available on Lomura focuses on this late-nineteenth-century transition. The one extant Lomura *rwot* list is unadorned with any associated traditions, and the roll of supposed *lobong* includes the Palocire and Pawor (two probably Eastern Nilotic lineages from Agoro) as well as a lineage identified as Owolo (either a mistake or a group related to Owolo *kal* of Paloga).[43]

Padibe

The largest and most powerful north-central-zone chiefdoms were Padibe and Palabek. Each began its growth during the eighteenth century, but Padibe became especially dominant after the 1850s as a result of its close alliance with Arabic-speaking traders from the north. As with Payira, Padibe's prominence later in its history has surely contributed to the relative scarcity and uncertainty of information concerning its earlier past.

Ten different Padibe *rwot* lists have been collected. Many extend as far back as seventeen or eighteen purported generations before 1900 and are linked with "Rumbek" (the original Luo homeland), Shilluk (a well-known northern Luo group), or both. The early names in these lists are unconvincingly identified as *rwodi* of a Padibe chiefdom that was in existence from the beginning. Ancient Luo origins are thus avowed for both Padibe *kal* and the Padibe chiefdom.[44]

One thread of narrative traditions purports to explain the division of the Padibe royal lineage into two sub-groupings, the Patini and Pamot, following a succession quarrel between sons of the chiefdom's eponym and supposed first *rwot*, Dibe. The winner was the progenitor of the Patini and perhaps three "brother" groups: the Pabogo, Pagwer, and Polwal. The loser was Amot, founder of the Pamot sub-lineage, who left to become a "*rwot*" in "old Madiland" (Central Sudanic territory). After the split, Patini and

43. Most available evidence on Lomura comes from Owot A.H.T. 3, including a *rwot* list. Both Wright (1934, p. 127) and Crazzolara (1954, p. 500) include brief sections on Lomura as a Padibe lineage.

44. Of the ten collected *rwot* lists, Wright (1934, pp. 123–24), Girling (1960, p. 227), Latigo (1970c, pp. 6–9), and A.H.T. 7, 12, 15 include references to Rumbek/Shilluk origins; Crazzolara (1954, pp. 499–500), Anywar (1954, pp. 70–71, 83–84), and Owot A.H.T. 6 and 13 do not. A.H.T. 7 and 14 also take the Padibe ruling lineage back to Shilluk, as does Pellegrini (1963, p. 9) and Owot (1976, pp. 173–83).

the three others are depicted as moving slowly southward over several generations, until they reached the Aringa valley. Shortly after, the Pamot showed up as well. The latter's surprise appearance meant that the two long-separated sub-lineages were reunited, with the Pamot inexplicably taking the lead role as the new ruling dynasty of a now clearly historical Padibe chiefdom. The first Pamot *kal* ruler of this new or newly reconstituted polity was either Nyagwir (c. 1710–40) or perhaps Okoki (c. 1740–70).[45]

It is possible that the assertions of Luo origins made for the Patini and their "brother groups" — mainly via Shilluk — are historically accurate. But the ideological purpose of these claimed links with Shilluk are so clear and so pervasive (as they are made by as many as eight Padibe lineages, far more than in any other chiefdom in Acholi) that skepticism seems in order. One likely example of fabrication concerns the Pamot's supposed ties to Shilluk as "brothers" of Patini. The even greater emphasis in traditions on Pamot's ties with Central Sudanic Madiland, despite the lack of prestige associated with such ties, strongly suggests Central Sudanic rather than Luo origins.[46]

But if an early Pamot kinship with Patini is questionable, some sort of relationship does seem to have existed among the Patini, Pabogo, Pagwer, probably the Polwal, and perhaps another lineage called Koc before the Pamot arrived in the emergent north-central zone. This relationship is sometimes depicted as one of kinship, with some combination of the groups represented as "brother" sub-lineages. More convincingly, other traditions suggest an association among separate and unrelated lineages, most likely within the framework of an early eighteenth-century chiefdom with Patini as the ruling lineage. Elders from numerous lineages and in several texts identify Patini as the first or original *kal* of Padibe, with the others listed above as *lobong*.[47]

45. The version here is basically that given by Owot (1976, pp. 177–78, 181–84, 188–89), obviously drawing on parts of Owot A.H.T. 6, 13–15. A very confusing account of the change of dynasty is given on pp. 184, 189–90. And without necessarily noting such a dynastic change, Nyagwir is identified as the first Padibe *rwot* to settle in the north-central zone in Owot A.H.T. 6–7, 13; Okoki in Owot A.H.T. 12 and 15 and Anywar (1954, pp. 71, 83). Wright (1934, p. 124) and Crazzolara (1954, p. 499) identify earlier names in their lists.

46. The sources in n. 44, as well as Owot A.H.T. 4–5 claim Shilluk origins for the Padibe lineages of Patini, Pamot, Pabogo, Pagwer, Bobi, Polwal, Loi, and Lobi. Crazzolara (1954, p. 500) includes the statement about such references being an "additional modern fabrication."

47. Sources identifying Patini as the original *kal* of a Padibe chiefdom, with the other four (and sometimes others) listed as *lobong*, are Owot A.H.T. 6–7, 14. Conflicting views on the relationship among these lineages abound. Sources claiming that some or all (except Koc) were "brothers" include Owot A.H.T. 6, 13–15; Crazzolara (1954, p. 498); Anywar (1954, p. 72). Sources identifying them as separate lineages include Owot A.H.T. 5–7, 11–15; Wright

250 Extension and Entrenchment of the New Order

The Pamot then arrived from their Central Sudanic home to the west, led by either Nyagwir or his successor Okoki. Initially the Pamot seem to have established closest contact with the Polwal, perhaps an Aringa valley aboriginal group and member of the Patini-led chiefdom. As a Polwal elder recounts:

> When Pamot met Polwal out in a hunting area, the former asked the latter to give it food and allow them to stay together. The latter refused, but sent Pamot to Patini who were at Aringa. Patini refused to accept Pamot claiming that they were also hunters and they had no food to give to Pamot. So Pamot went back to Polwal who accepted them. Polwal did not know that Pamot had the royal drum, the royal spear and the royal knife together with the royal beads. These were all hidden by Pamot. When they had stayed together for a while, Pamot then gradually revealed its rwotship (ker). Polwal accepted this.[48]

The point about the Patini being hunters shows up in other texts as well. Indeed, Patini preoccupation with hunting is one reason given for their passing the *rwot*ship on to Pamot, as the responsibilities of rule unduly "obstructed their work as hunters." The apparent defection of lineages such as Polwal also surely contributed to Patini's abdication. And in one interview a Patini elder recounts the simple but powerful factor of numbers: "The Pamot were more in number than the Patini by then." As presented in traditions, the transition from Patini to Pamot rule was gradual and peaceful. As part of the process, the Patini took on the primary ritual role in the newly ordered chiefdom: being in charge of the main chiefdom-wide *jok*, *Jok* Kedi-Bul.[49]

Extant traditions are not clear about any lineages accompanying Pamot from old Madiland, though it is insinuated that a lineage named Loi may have done so. It is also unclear which lineages except the ones associated with Patini joined the new Pamot-led chiefdom. Three probably East-

---

(1934, p. 127). Pamot elders in Owot A.H.T. 7 acknowledge that the Patini "had its *rwot*ship" but add that they had no royal drum. This last remark about the drum may be a Pamot attempt to explain or justify the Pamot takeover by minimizing Patini's authority as "true" *rwodi*.

48. The quotation is from Owot A.H.T. 11. Polwal is identified as *wegi ngom* in Owot A.H.T. 11 and 13, and their role in easing Pamot's accession to power is noted in Owot A.H.T. 6 and 13. Alternative claims that Polwal came into the north-central zone with the Pamot (in Owot A.H.T. 7) or that Polwal only joined Padibe during the time of *Rwot* Anyalla in the mid-nineteenth century (in Wright [1934, p. 127]) are unconvincing given the weight of the alternative evidence.

49. Patini's supposed preference for hunting over chiefship is noted in Owot A.H.T. 6, 11, and (in a somewhat confused way) 13. The reference to Pamot's greater numbers comes from Owot A.H.T. 6 (which somehow gets turned around in Owot's chapter [1976, p. 189]). The gradual nature of Pamot's takeover is emphasized in Owot A.H.T. 7 and 11; and Owot A.H.T. 6 and 13 note Patini's primary responsibility for Padibe's main chiefdom-wide *jok*, *Jok* Kidi-Bul.

ern Nilotic lineages — the Pabwodo, Panyikwac, and Polar — seem to have been part of Padibe from early on, though no available traditions connect their incorporation with any particular *rwot*. One small group named Pa-dyang is remembered to have come north from Payira and become assimi-lated into Pamot *kal* during the time of *Rwot* Okoki.[50]

By the time of Okoki's death around 1770, Padibe appears to have been made up of seven to ten lineages of mixed ethnolinguistic origins. It was firmly established in the Aringa valley: one reference indicates that Okoki promoted agricultural production in the valley, including limited irriga-tion. Another source mentions raids from the east during Okoki's time but does not indicate that they were seriously threatening. Okoki's successor is most often identified as his son Otwal, whose reign was marked by a severe drought — surely that of about 1790 — and whose estimated dates of rule were 1770–1800.[51]

PALABEK

The other large chiefdom that developed in the eighteenth-century north-central zone was Palabek, and it has even more fragmentary and contradic-tory traditions of its early years than Padibe. The origins of the eventual Palabek *kal* were almost certainly Central Sudanic: the three oldest extant sources all link the group originally with the ancient Central Sudanic area of "Baar." In two of these sources the Luo place-name of Anuak (interestingly, not the more common Shilluk) is then added, a transparently ideological contrivance to signify Luo origins. By the time that the two most recent Palabek texts were collected thirty to forty years later, the process of shifting origins discernible in earlier sources was complete and invisible; the refer-ences to Baar had been dropped and the Luo names of Anuak and, now, Shilluk appear alone. This is certainly one instance where Crazzolara's comment about Shilluk origins as "additional modern fabrication" seems especially fitting.[52]

Clues concerning the possible establishment of this lineage as *kal* of a

50. Information on Loi is found in Owot A.H.T. 7 (with alternative views given in Owot A.H.T. 5, 14); on Pabwodo, Panyikwac, and Polar in Owot A.H.T. 6 and 14; and on Padyang in Owot A.H.T. 7.

51. The reference to Okoki and agriculture and irrigation comes from Owot A.H.T. 12, and is repeated in Owot (1976, p. 184). Wright (1934, p. 124) notes raids during Okoki's time; Otwol is identified as Okoki's successor in all the lists in n. 44 except Owot A.H.T. 6, Anywar (1954, pp. 71, 83), and Girling (1960, p. 227). Both Wright (1934, p. 124) and Owot (1976, p. 190) refer to famine during Otwol's reign.

52. See Wright (1934, p. 64), Pellegrini (1963, p. 3), Crazzolara (1954, p. 495), Owot A.H.T. 19–20. The first two have origins linked to both Baar and Anuak. The quote is from Crazzolara (1954, p. 500).

Palabek chiefdom are associated with two names in the available Palabek *rwot* lists. The first of these names is Kenyi, with estimated dates of rule ranging from 1650 to 1710. In the earliest collection of extant Palabek traditions by A. C. A. Wright, Kenyi is the fourth name in the remembered *rwot* list and the first to settle in the north-central zone. There he met a "Madi" lineage (perhaps later called the Ayu) led by a man named Anyang. The traditions ascribe to Anyang the typical attributes of leadership in the later Acholi polities: he "was a chief," with "cattle, goats and a drum," as well as rainstones for making rain. After meeting, the traditions continue, "Kenyi and Anyang joined as brothers." But then, despite all of Anyang's supposed leadership traits, Kenyi somehow became accepted as *rwot*, while Anyang and his line became special *lodito pa rwot* under Palabek *kal*.[53]

Other allusions to the establishment or perhaps the strengthening of a Bunyoro/Paluo-style chiefdom are associated with Kenyi's successor, Akanyo, and Akanyo's son Laro. Four of the five extant sources on Palabek, including Wright's, recount that Akanyo traveled to Bunyoro/Paluo for some reason (illness is most commonly given). Three add that when he returned, he brought royal objects back with him, including a royal drum. So far this sounds similar to other stylized accounts of the establishment of chiefdoms in Acholi. But then the traditions take a strange twist. The returning *rwot* was rejected by the Palabek people. They continued to support Akanyo's son Laro, who had been ruling in his absence and who did not want to relinquish the *rwot*ship. Most accounts then claim that Akanyo left Palabek in disgust, never to return, leaving his son as *rwot* with a new Bunyoro/Paluo royal drum and other regalia.[54]

Later in Laro's reign (which was probably from about 1710 to 1740), a man from Palabek is remembered to have killed the brother of the *rwot* of "Farajok"—the northernmost polity of Pajok. A battle between the two chiefdoms then ensued, leading to further deaths. This episode is significant for two reasons. First, it is one of the few incidents in extant traditions of

53. The story of Kenyi and the "Madi" comes from Wright (1934, p. 64). No other Palabek sources mention such a Madi lineage; Ayu was suggested as a possible alternative identification because Crazzolara (1954, p. 496) indicates that the Ayu-Alali lineage was from Baar or Madi and once had their own chief. Palabek *rwot* lists are in Wright (p. 64), Pellegrini (1963, p. 3), and Owot A.H.T. 19 and 20. A one-generation discrepancy in these lists necessitates the two-generation-wide estimated dates of rule given for Kenyi.

54. The four sources for the basic Akanyo story are Wright (1934, p. 65), Pellegrini (1963, p. 3), and Owot A.H.T. 19 and 20; of these, only Wright does not mention Akanyo's returning with a royal drum—perhaps because of the appearance of a drum in the story of his predecessor Kenyi. In the first draft of his recording of Palabek traditions, Wright (p. 68) has identified Akanyo as a brother of Kenyi; this is marked through and Akanyo is finally listed as Kenyi's son.

direct contact between northernmost Acholi chiefdoms and those further south before the late nineteenth century. Second, this contact may have been the means by which Palabek adopted the practice of sending members of *kal* to live with other lineages, or groups of lineages, and to rule over them on behalf of the *rwot*. Using royals in this way was one of the key features that distinguished northernmost Acholi from the more southerly Acholi chiefdoms. Palabek was the only chiefdom south of Agoro that did not fit this north/south distinction.[55]

Unfortunately, we can learn little about this chiefdom from the available sources. We do not even know, for example, which village-lineages were part of early Palabek, let alone when or how they were incorporated. Based on the contradictory evidence, it is likely that Palabek's *lobong* included at least the Ayu, Padwat, Logwar, Pabita, Pakala, Agoro, and Gem. The first five were probably Central Sudanic in origin; the last two, Eastern Nilotic. Only the first three have traditions clearly indicating incorporation before the 1790s drought.[56]

It is at least clear that the Palabek *rwot* at the time of the drought was Abi (c. 1770–1800), whose period of rule is associated with both a great famine and the same "Lango Omiro" raiders that appear in Pabo and Atyak traditions in the aftermath of the drought. Abi's most likely predecessor was Gimoro (c. 1740–70?), who was the probable son and successor of Laro. But this identification is most tentative, as available traditions neither agree about Gimoro's place in the Palabek *rwot* list nor provide additional information about him.[57]

Madi Opei, Cua-Bura, the Agoro Chiefdoms, and Unaffiliated Lineages
The remaining chiefdoms in the north-central zone all remained small throughout the eighteenth century. We know the most about Madi Opei. Three sets of traditions collected over more than thirty years agree that Madi Opei's ruling lineage came from "Madi" and was thus Central Sudanic. Conflict-ridden sojourns to both the north and south are remembered to have preceded settlement at an outcrop named Opei, fifteen

55. The reference to Palabek conflict with Pajok is in Wright (1934, p. 65). Information that Palabek used resident royals to help rule non-royal villages comes from Crazzolara (1954, pp. 496–97), Owot A.H.T. 19–20, and Girling (1960, p. 100). Girling also suggests that Atyak may have used this approach, though no supportive evidence has been found.

56. See Wright (1934, p. 67), Crazzolara (1954, pp. 496–97), Pellegrini (1963, p. 4), and Owot A.H.T. 19–20.

57. Sources for the various *rwot* lists are included in n. 41. The traditions associated with *Rwot* Abi come from Wright (1934, p. 65).

kilometers east of the Aringa River (see Map 12). The *rwot* who led the chiefdom into the north-central zone was Bang or Obang (c. 1750–80), after whom the royal lineage Pobango *kal* is usually called.[58]

When they arrived at Opei, the Pobango were clearly a proper *kal*, in possession of a royal drum, and probably accompanied by a *lobong* lineage. This lineage was Gem, a common lineage name with northern origins that were probably Eastern Nilotic. A Gem elder in Madi Opei claimed that his ancestors joined *Rwot* Obang in the Labongo area in the east-central zone and then came north with him. As the first *lobong* of Madi Opei, the Gem and its head had a special place in the chiefdom which included being responsible for the chiefdom-wide *jok*.[59]

Got Opei was not uninhabited when the Pobango and Gem arrived. Among the prior inhabitants were the Lamogi (also a common lineage name, this time with Central Sudanic origins). The Lamogi were acknowledged as the oldest inhabitants of the area; they seem to have had some sort of pre-Pobango leadership role at Opei; and they were incorporated into the incoming Madi Opei chiefdom as *wegi ngom*.[60]

Settled on the opposite (eastern or northeastern) side of *Got* Opei were Eastern Nilotic lineages from further north, collectively known as "Lawioduny." These included the Odya, Lotuko, and Locemedik, who seem to have retained their independence for some time before being incorporated into Madi Opei. Indeed, this incorporation may not have occurred until after the 1790s drought, when a number of other *lobong* lineages joined the chiefdom.[61]

A second chiefdom established near *Got* Opei between about 1725 and 1790 was the eventual northeastern-zone chiefdom of Cua-Bura. This polity experienced tremendous dislocation, disruption, and other change following the late-eighteenth- and early nineteenth-century droughts, and extant traditions focus on this post-eighteenth-century history.

The one area of consistent agreement in early Cua-Bura traditions is the Central Sudanic origins of the eventual Cua-Bura *kal*. The person most often identified as leading the group away from their original home in

58. The three sources are Wright (1934, p. 116), Crazzolara (1954, pp. 505–6), and Owot A.H.T. 16. The estimated dates of rule of Obang are based on Wright, which has the most complete genealogical and other information associated with his *rwot* list.

59. Information of the royal drum comes from Wright (1934, p. 117), and that on Gem comes from Owot A.H.T. 16; see n. 42 on Gem's unclear origins.

60. Most information on Lamogi is in Crazzolara (1954, p. 506); see also Wright (1934, p. 117) and Owot A.H.T. 16.

61. See Wright (1934, p. 119), Crazzolara (1954, p. 507), and Owot A.H.T. 16. Pellegrini (1963, p. 11) also contains a brief reference to Lawioduny, emphasizing its strong Eastern Nilotic character.

"Baar" is Waka (c. 1715–45), the remembered son and successor of the eponymous founder of the ruling dynasty, Bura. He is also noted to have been a proper *rwot* with a royal drum and other regalia. One source notes that Waka and his followers left Baar "looking for food," a possible reference to the 1720s drought which falls within Waka's estimated dates of rule. In any case, the Cua-Bura under Waka (or as one source indicates, under Waka and his successors) went from Baar through Pajok to *Got* Opei. There, Cua-Bura seems to have settled until some time during the later eighteenth or early nineteenth century when they continued eastward into the northeastern zone. As Crazzolara notes, traditions of this period are "incomplete and obscure," with the timing of Cua-Bura's moves, the name of Waka's son and successor, and the identity of *lobong* lineages (if any) all uncertain.[62]

Polities established in the Agoro mountains marked the furthest extension north of chiefdom formation on the Bunyoro/Paluo model. But their emergence did not lead to the same degree of social and cultural homogeneity in the mountains as in most parts of north-central Uganda. The reasons for this seem to have stemmed mainly from the physical nature of the Agoro range, the most massive and rugged in all of Acholi. Such terrain may explain the unusually high level of social isolation and independence, evidenced in two main ways. The first was the number of separate dialects, or even languages, spoken in the mountains into the present century, which are identified by Crazzolara as "ancient Lango" (Eastern Nilotic). The second was the existence of a number of Agoro lineages that seem to have always remained outside any polity.[63]

Four Agoro chiefdoms seem to have been established, though it is unclear when they were founded or even what they were called. Only one had a ruling lineage unambiguously identified as indigenous to the mountains. The most likely name of this chiefdom was Longorone (though Crazzolara uses the place-name Ngaaro, from a small perennial river in the area). Longorone *kal* are remembered to have been rainmakers and may have had as many as seven associated *lobong* lineages. The one *rwot* list collected for the chiefdom is obviously skeletal, containing only four names with no associated traditions.[64]

62. Central Sudanic origins for Cua-Bura *kal* are indicated in Wright (1934, p. 71), Crazzolara (1954, p. 522), and Pellegrini (1963, p. 6). The first two identify Waka as a "proper" *rwot* with a royal drum; the first also includes a reference to the poor soil and climate of their original home. Conflicting ruler lists, chronologies of settlement, and lists of *lobong* lineages are in Wright (1934, pp. 71–76); Crazzolara (1954, pp. 522–30); and Garry A.H.T., pp. 121, 123, 127, 133, and 137.

63. See Crazzolara (1954, pp. 508–15).

64. See Owot A.H.T. 18, which includes the list and the reference to rainmaking, and Crazzolara (1954, pp. 509–10).

A second Agoro chiefdom was Popoka, with two or three possible *lobong*. Two contradictory traditions of origins have been collected for Popoka *kal*. One identifies Central Sudanic origins from Baar; the other indicates origins in Agoro, from which the eventual ruling lineage went west to the Pajok area and then returned as *kal*. If the latter actually occurred, then at least one Agoro chiefdom would have had its roots in institutions and ideology derived not from Bunyoro/Paluo, but from the alternative political culture with northern-Luo origins that typified the northernmost Acholi chiefdoms.[65]

The royal lineage of the third Agoro chiefdom, usually referred to simply as Agoro, has uncontested traditions of Central Sudanic origins; it is even called Baar or Pobaar *kal*. Extant traditions of the chiefdom contain the only Agoro reference to a royal drum and the only Agoro *rwot* list of any length, though no names have traditions attached to them before the second half of the nineteenth century. The one *lobong* lineage that was clearly part of the chiefdom, the Rudi, also has traditions of Central Sudanic origins from Baar. But the Rudi are simultaneously acknowledged as *wegi ngom*. Given all of the seemingly ancient Eastern Nilotic lineages identified by Crazzolara in the mountain area, it is difficult to understand both Central Sudanic origins and *wegi ngom* status unless one or the other were fabricated.[66]

Evidence about a fourth Agoro chiefdom is the weakest of all. One source expressly identifies such a chiefdom, stating that its *rwodi* were rainmakers and naming its ruling lineage as Lamogi. But two other sources identify this ancient and widely used Central Sudanic name only as an Agoro lineage, with no indication that it was a royal lineage of an Agoro chiefdom.[67]

Lastly, a number of lineages in the emergent north-central zone appear to have remained outside any of the zone's chiefdoms throughout the eighteenth century. Such unattached lineages included a dozen or more in the Agoro mountains; a similar number located north of *Got* Opei; numerous lineages or lineage sections that after about 1790 become part of a new, north-central-zone Lokung chiefdom; and the Panyinga, a seemingly

65. Baar origins for Popoka *kal* are indicated in Owot A.H.T. 18; the alternative version comes from Crazzolara (1954, p. 511). These two also provide different lists of possible associated lineages.

66. The four sources indicating Central Sudanic origins are Wright (1934, pp. 19–20); additional information on the royal drum, *rwot* list, and the Rudi lineage is in Crazzolara (1954, p. 512), Pellegrini (1963, p. 5), and Owot A.H.T. 18.

67. Owot A.H.T. 18 identifies Lamogi as the rainmaking *kal* of a fourth Agoro chiefdom; Wright (1934, p. 20) and Crazzolara (1954, p. 514) merely include a Lamogi among their lists of Agoro lineages.

aggressive loner lineage finally incorporated into Padibe in the later nine-teenth century. The presence of these unattached lineages — the highest number among all the zones of Acholi — indicates the continuing coexis-tence of peoples organized on chiefly and non-chiefly principles in at least the frontier regions of emergent Acholi throughout the eighteenth century. Unfortunately, information from other frontier zones is limited, though logic alone suggests that such coexistence almost certainly marked such frontier areas for a long time.[68]

The Northeastern Zone

Reconstructing developments from about 1725 to 1790 in the northeastern zone is especially difficult because of major political restructuring and mass population movements out of the zone after the drought of the 1830s. Restructuring included the development of the Cua confederation, a pro-cess that made the pre-amalgamation history of the groups involved essen-tially part of their "absent" pasts. From the limited evidence, two or three chiefdoms developed in the emergent northeastern zone before the late-eighteenth-century drought. The first was probably Nam Okora, a break-away from the Patongo chiefdom in the southeastern zone and the likely means of introducing chiefship based on the Bunyoro/Paluo model into the eventual northeastern zone.

Patongo traditions relate that their *rwot* Lugenyi, who ruled during the mid-eighteenth century, quarreled with a brother who "went to Cua" where he founded "Lira Agonga near Nam Okora." Nam Okora texts identify Nam Okora *kal* as "Pagonga" who came from Patongo. Most also indicate a kinship with Patongo *kal*, though one source claims that the Pagonga pre-dated Patongo *kal* in the southeastern zone but lost out in a struggle with the latter over who would rule. The Pagonga/Nam Okora seem to have arrived in the *Got* Okol area during the second quarter of the eighteenth century with no *lobong* lineages, and was to remain a single lineage polity throughout its history (Map 13).[69]

68. Crazzolara (1954, pp. 508–15) has by far the most extensive listing of Agoro lineages available, numbering over twenty, with well over half not clearly associated with any of the Agoro chiefdoms. He also discusses the lineages north of *Got* Opei (pp. 516–19); the lineages and clusters of lineages that join Paloga after the drought of about 1790 (pp. 503–4), as do Wright (1934, pp. 106–9) and Owot A.H.T. 10; and the Panyinga (p. 501), as do Owot A.H.T. 16 and Owot (1976, pp. 200–201).

69. The Patongo reference to an Agonga in Cua (which also provides the chronological estimate for the move) comes from Webster A.H.T., pp. 17–18. Garry A.H.T., pp. 102, 105,

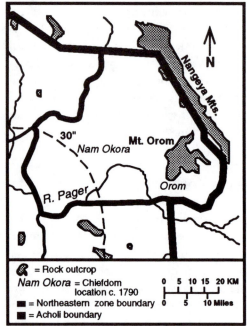

Map 13. Northeastern zone,
c. 1725-90.

The northeastern-zone chiefdom that remained most unaffected by the nineteenth-century Cua confederation was Orom. One reason for this was surely the chiefdom's favored location at the base of *Got* Orom, the second highest peak in Acholi (7,800 feet or 2,370 meters) and the richest iron-bearing site, attracting trade from far beyond the northeastern zone. The protection and the mineral resources provided by *Got* Orom must have also helped the chiefdom to remain with much of its population, when most others in the zone moved west following the 1830s drought.

Only one interview in Orom is available. It includes a *rwot* list, though it provides no indication of how the names were related. One *rwot*, Racamoi, is remembered to have suffered an attack by Patongo after a severe drought in which many Orom people were killed. As Racamoi is the fifth

112, 135, 141, and 144 note that Nam Okora *kal*, or Pagonga *kal*, broke away from Patongo. The reference to Agonga pre-dating the arrival of Patongo *kal* comes from Garry A.H.T., p. 135. The absence of associated *lobong* lineages in the formerly independent Nam Okora is noted in Garry A.H.T., pp. 102, 112, 114.

name back in the list from a twentieth-century *rwot* named Onoo, this drought was probably that occurring around 1790. There are also two remembered names before Racamoi (Lucere and Luciamoi), suggesting a founding date for the chiefdom sometime after the 1720s drought.

Orom *kal* is remembered to have come to Orom from the northeast, making Eastern Nilotic origins almost a certainty. Seven *lobong* lineages are identified, along with seven other "smaller" ones. All seem as clearly Eastern Nilotic as Orom *kal*. It is also obvious that these lineages were part of a Bunyoro/Paluo-style chiefdom, with a royal drum and all the other typical regalia.[70]

A third eighteenth-century chiefdom that may have developed in the northeastern zone is referred to as both Akara and Pajong. In traditions collected in the zone, both names are frequently linked to chiefship and a royal drum (though none of these references come from Akara/Pajong itself). Sometimes the sources read as if Akara and Pajong were separate small polities before being brought under the authority of the Cua-Bura *rwot* in the nineteenth century. More often, Akara or Pajong appear to be alternative names for the same small chiefdom, with perhaps Pajong being the name of the ruling lineage and Akara the chiefdom name. If there were an Akara/Pajong chiefdom, it was always small—consisting of two or three originally Eastern Nilotic lineages, some of whom may have been the "original inhabitants of Akara" near *Got* Okol.[71]

Conclusion

The chiefdoms that developed in the northwestern, north-central, and northeastern zones marked the furthest extension north of the new institutions and ideology of political leadership derived from Bunyoro/Paluo. The few chiefdoms founded in the northwestern and northeastern zones suggests that in these areas, we are dealing with a system approaching its geographical limits. The more protected and productive Aringa River valley

70. The one extant interview in Orom is in Garry A.H.T., pp. 129–33. Most references to former polities joined together under Cua-Bura in the nineteenth century either exclude Orom or note that Orom was not as fully incorporated as were the others. See, for example, Garry A.H.T., pp. 136, 140, 143; Crazzolara (1954, p. 522). A few sources make no such distinction, intimating a more complete integration of Orom under Cua-Bura than most evidence would support; see, for example, Garry A.H.T., 134, 146.

71. See Garry A.H.T.. pp. 103, 105, 107, 136, 138, 140, 143, 145–47; Crazzolara (1954, p. 530). The identification of the Pajong and Akara (along with a third lineage, the Palutu) as being "original inhabitants of Akara" comes from Crazzolara.

south of the Agoro range in the emergent north-central zone provided more fertile ground, not only for food crops but for the new sociopolitical order. But this order would advance no further.

In the central zone, where it had been introduced a generation or two before the 1720s drought, the new order became firmly entrenched between about 1725 and 1790. The number of chiefdoms in the zone remained small (at six), but almost all of them incorporated many more lineages than they had before. This was especially true for Payira, which by the end of the eighteenth century was the largest chiefdom in Acholi. High reliable rainfall and an insulated position at the center of an emergent Acholi — as far from the borders of divergently developing neighbors as it was possible to be — gave the central zone crucial advantages.

As we shall see in the epilogue, these advantages became especially significant after the further droughts of about 1790 and the 1830s, and after the coming of Arabic-speaking slave and ivory traders from the north after 1850. The nineteenth century saw the central zone become a dynamic growth area that was not only the geographical center, but the political and sociocultural hub of an increasingly entrenched and identifiable Acholi society and collective identity.

Epilogue

The 1720s drought marked both the dividing line between the first and second phases of chiefdom formation in north-central Uganda and the beginning of a crucial new stage in the evolution of an Acholi society and identity. When the drought struck, eleven chiefdoms based on institutions and ideology derived from Bunyoro/Paluo had established themselves. All but one of these were clustered in just two areas (the eventual central and southeastern zones of Acholi); only two had more than three or four associated *lobong* lineages; and together, all eleven chiefdoms contained no more than forty lineages. The emergence of these few, small, and scattered chiefdoms from about 1675 to 1725 had done little to mark the area of north-central Uganda apart from either its non-chiefly past or the broader region of which it was a part.

By the time of the next major drought in about 1790, a mere two generations later, dramatic changes had occurred. Instead of eleven chiefdoms, there were between sixty-five and seventy; instead of forty lineages incorporated into chiefdoms, there were over three hundred and perhaps more than three hundred fifty. No longer were chiefdoms clustered in just two areas; indeed, all of Acholi's eight zones had experienced the founding of new chiefdoms or the consolidation and growth of old ones. This vast extension and entrenchment of a new chiefly order in north-central Uganda between about 1725 and 1790 was accompanied by the spread of a new language, as Luo gradually replaced earlier dominant Central Sudanic and Eastern Nilotic tongues. Together, these developments constituted social change on a massive scale.

This social change, moreover, provided the people of north-central Uganda with a broadly common historical experience, social order, and political culture. These features in turn provided crucial foundations for the evolution of a society and a collective identity eventually called Acholi. These foundations were absent, or were at most barely present when the 1720s drought struck; by 1790 they had become securely established. Or, to shift the metaphor, the roots of Acholi ethnicity had been set.

The purpose of this epilogue is to sketch ways in which an Acholi society and identity—an Acholi ethnicity—continued to evolve over the nineteenth century from their eighteenth-century roots. This sketch is meant as a companion piece for the twentieth-century overview included in the introduction.[1]

The Continuing Evolution of an Acholi Ethnicity: The Early Nineteenth Century

By the end of the eighteenth century, north-central Uganda was occupied by a wide, virtually continuous area of people who increasingly spoke Luo and who shared the same chiefdom-based social, political, and economic order. But even as late as the mid-nineteenth century, when the first written sources on the area become available, the broad unity that characterized Acholi had not yet taken on concrete, practical forms of expression. Neither the area nor the people who inhabited it were yet perceived as a unit, either by the people themselves or by neighboring groups. One indication of this is that neither area nor people were identified (again, either from within or without) by a name that was both inclusive of the whole and exclusive of others. Both the Central Sudanic-speaking Madi and the Luo-speaking Alur and Jonam west of Acholi referred to virtually all peoples east of them as "Lango"; this included the people of Acholi. Bantu-speaking Banyoro south of Acholi used the term "Gani" to denote generally the people north of Bunyoro and west of "Kidi," the term used to identify the Langi and peoples north and east of them. Finally, the Luo-speaking Langi to the immediate south referred to the people in Acholi as either "Alira," from the name of the Acholi chiefdom nearest them, or "lo-gang," meaning "people of the village" and applied to the inhabitants of Acholi, Madi, and Alur, all of whom lived in large fenced villages.[2]

People in Acholi functioned primarily within the contexts of their individual village-lineages and chiefdoms. It was these units that were named; distinguished by recognized social, political, and economic functions; and marked by the only explicitly delimited boundaries within the area. One of the clearest indications that individual chiefdoms marked the limit of explicit group identification in Acholi is the lack of a generic term in Acholi Luo for these polities.

1. Most of what follows is an only slightly revised version of Atkinson (1989, pp. 31–39). Used by permission, Duke University Press.

2. See Crazzolara (1938, p. viii) for the first and third examples; Speke (1863, pp. 245, 329, 349, 377, and 417) for the second.

This does not mean that there were no categories of collective functioning or identity more inclusive than the individual polities. At least three were present by the middle of the nineteenth century. The earliest of these was the set of eight distinct territorial sub-regions or "zones" that developed over the eighteenth century and that have provided the principal organizing framework for this book. As noted in Chapter 1, the most dense networks of interaction and cooperation, including the crucial ties of marriage, occurred within these zones (and in some cases with immediately contiguous non-Acholi areas as well) and not between them. Most hostilities, on the other hand, took place between groups occupying different zones. These informal, unnamed zones were the only functionally meaningful groupings of people in Acholi beyond the individual chiefdoms until the nineteenth century.

Two other examples of collective functioning or identity beyond the level of the individual chiefdom developed over the first half of the nineteenth century, consequent to and largely conditioned by two major droughts and famines. The earlier of these was the drought of about 1790, which set in motion a series of population movements and social changes that transformed the geopolitical map of northern Uganda (and beyond). Then, in little more than a generation, the rains, and thus the crops, failed again. This second drought, probably in the 1830s, added its own pressures to the often stressful and still uncompleted processes of movement and change originating some forty years before.[3]

Of the many changes associated with this tumultuous period, the ones that probably had the broadest and deepest effects on Acholi were those that led to the development of much more clearly defined ethnic identities in major groups to the south and east of Acholi. At the close of the eighteenth century, present-day Karamoja and Lango districts to the east and southeast of Acholi contained a complex mixture of peoples. Except for the Jie, who were further along in the process (see Chapter 5), most of these peoples were in the early stages of developing the patterns of dense interaction and consciousness that led to the formation of the societies and ethnic groups associated with these districts today. The stresses of drought helped shape the particular form those patterns have taken into the twentieth century.

Much of the drama was played out in the dry country to the east of

---

3. For a discussion of these droughts, including chronological reconstructions, see the relevant sections of Atkinson (1978), Garry (1972b), Webster (1976b, 1976c, 1979), Herring (1979b), Lamphear (1976).

Acholi. This was cattle country, and not surprisingly the key variable in determining the fate of any particular group in this area was whether it was able to keep or augment its herds under the pressures of drought. Groups that were successful tended to remain in the area with their herds and could increasingly be identified as either mixed-farming Jie (in the north) or as part of the emergent, more pastoral Karimojong (in the south). Some less successful groups also stayed, but they were faced with the difficult task of rebuilding their herds, an absolute necessity both for survival and to become identified as either Jie or Karimojong. Many groups that were unsuccessful in maintaining their herds left the area. Some moved south and contributed to the formation of the mixed-farming Iteso. Others relocated in a more westerly direction where they either became troublesome raiders or, as destitute refugees, augmented the emergent Acholi or the mixture of peoples in Lango District south of Acholi that was beginning to develop a collective identity called Langi (Map 14).[4]

The droughts also struck Acholi, hitting the southeastern zone especially hard. The inhabitants of the zone were confronted with severe pressures, and a number of chiefdoms and even some lineages fragmented to greater or lesser degrees. Many chiefdoms, whether intact or not, left the area to settle at least temporarily near or among polities in better watered and less troubled areas to the west. At the same time, chiefdoms in Acholi (especially in the southeastern, east-central, and south-central zones) were generally forced to deal in new and more intensive ways with their eastern and southern neighbors — as raiders or potential raiders, as temporary (or not so temporary) refugees, and as more and more clearly distinct and recognizable ethnic groups. Part of the response of people in the Acholi zones that were most affected by all this seems to have been a heightened identification with similarly organized chiefdoms to their north and west and a differentiation from the increasingly identifiable and dissimilar Jie and Langi to the east and south. If during the early nineteenth century a comprehensive and clear Acholi identity had not yet evolved, people in Acholi were certainly moving in that direction. This was manifested positively in their closer identification with others who shared the same chiefly sociopolitical order, and negatively in their increased awareness that they were "not Jie" and "not Lango."[5]

4. On the situation east of Acholi, see esp. Herring (1974b, pp. 156–71; 1979b), Webster (1979, pp. 283–316), Lamphear, (1976, chap. 4), and Crazzolara (1960).

5. See Webster (1976b, 1976c), Garry (1972b, chap. 3), Atkinson (1978, pp. 409–14, 441–46).

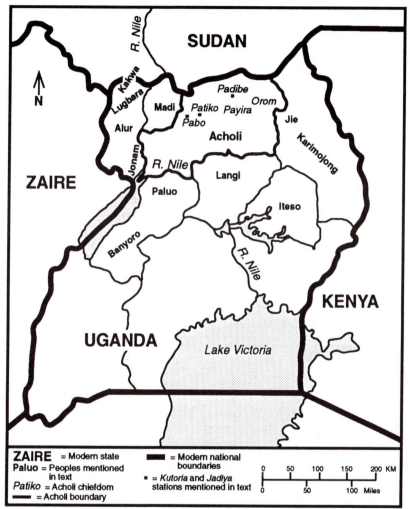

Map 14. Acholi and neighboring peoples, c. 1855-90.

The pressures of the late-eighteenth- and early-nineteenth-century droughts also promoted two more immediately tangible examples of collective functioning and identity beyond the individual chiefdom level. One of these was the emergence, especially after the 1830s drought, of a number of mainly military confederacies and alliances. Such extra-polity groupings developed in numerous zones and varied widely in size, duration, purpose, and internal structuring. The particular details and dynamics need not concern us here. What is important is simply to note the appearance, for the first time in Acholi, of these extra-polity groupings, many of them formally named and structured.[6]

A second example of extra-polity functioning promoted by the late-eighteenth and early nineteenth-century droughts resulted from the accumulation of power and influence by the central-zone chiefdom of Payira. By the late eighteenth century, as indicated above, Payira had become the largest polity in Acholi, consisting of almost thirty village-lineages and perhaps 10,000 to 15,000 people or more. Its location in the central zone near the Acaa possessed dual advantages in the turbulent and drought-stricken period of the late eighteenth and early nineteenth centuries. The first was its relatively protected position vis-à-vis the emergent Langi and Jie. While the central zone was not totally immune from Langi and Jie raids and other pressures, it was certainly much less seriously affected than areas further south and east. The second advantage was the better and more reliable rainfall than areas further east and the greater availability of ground water because of the Acaa. In addition, Payira's size may well have offered (or been perceived as offering) a greater degree of security and protection than any other polity in Acholi during this unsettled era. In any event, a large number of chiefdoms settled among or near the Payira, many of them from the especially disrupted southeastern, east-central, and south-central zones.[7]

The Payira polity then began to exert an unprecedented degree of authority and influence over many of these nominally independent chiefdoms. Payira mediated disputes among the others, enforced settlements and the payment of compensations, compelled some chiefdoms to leave the area, called on others for assistance in war, and intervened in others' purely internal affairs, perhaps even interfering with succession to the *rwot*ship. While traditions of the groups in question are adamant that no one's formal independence was lost to Payira (and this may well have been the case), there can be no doubt that Payira's influence and authority did provide for a

6. One such multi-polity grouping was the Pajule confederacy in the *Got* Okaka area of the east-central zone; see Garry (1972b, chaps. 3 and 4; 1976). Another was the Cua confederacy, which was established in the northeastern zone and then moved to the central zone. See Wright (1934, pp. 72–76); Crazzolara (1954, pp. 522–31); Garry A.H.T., pp. 121–23, 127–28, 133–37. For a discussion of a complex succession of multi-polity alliances that arose out of a series of conflicts during the 1840s and early 1850s in the area around *Got* Ato (on the border between the east-central and central zones), see Atkinson (1978, pp. 457–60). And on the Pader Paluo chiefdom or confederacy referred to above in Chap. 6, see Webster A.H.T., pp. 117–21 and A.H.T. 279.

7. Atkinson (1978, pp. 368–68).

degree of extra-polity functioning and organization that was not typical. And it would not be the last time Payira would seek power and control over others; Payira's *rwot* in the later nineteenth century would claim paramountcy over all of Acholi, and under colonial rule such paramountcy was at least temporarily recognized by Acholi's British overlords.[8]

In the end, not too much should be claimed for any of these examples of extra-polity functioning or identity. Even the largest in scale, the zones, did not come close to encompassing the whole of Acholi; most were temporary; and only a few of the confederacies or alliances referred to above were characterized, even in part, by the explicit labels, geographical definitions, or sociopolitical functions associated with the largest, established formal entities in Acholi — the individual chiefdoms.

The Further Evolution of an Acholi Ethnicity: The Second Half of the Nineteenth Century

A new stage in the development of an Acholi ethnicity began in the 1850s, when Arabic-speaking traders from the Sudan arrived seeking ivory and slaves. These traders, called *Kutoria* by the Acholi, were succeeded in 1872 by another set of outsiders remembered by the Acholi as *Jadiya*. Between 1872 and 1888, the *Jadiya* were the official representatives of an Egyptian administration on the upper Nile until 1888, though both "official" and "administration" are virtual misnomers in this case. Before exploring ways in which these outsiders and their activities — and the responses from within Acholi — contributed to the continuing evolution of an Acholi ethnicity, it will be helpful to provide some basic background information.

THE *KUTORIA* AND *JADIYA* IN ACHOLI

The *Kutoria* eventually established three stations in Acholi, which became the center of their activities in northern Uganda and the contiguous southern Sudan. The first of these stations was set up near Patiko in the central zone and was followed by others at Pabo and Padibe, in the western and north-central zones (see Map 14). Once established, these stations served two main functions. First, they were storage centers for the major commodity of trade, ivory, until it could be transported north for sale. Second, the stations were garrisons in which the outsiders and their hangers-on

8. Ibid, pp. 474–87.

could live and from which they traded and raided. Although raids were conducted both within Acholi and outside, the clear impression given in Acholi traditions is that quite quickly raiding was mainly directed against Acholi's neighbors, often with the assistance of Acholi allies. The main purpose of these raids was to acquire cattle, captives, and ivory.[9]

Due primarily to British pressure on the Egyptian government to halt slave trading by its subjects on the upper Nile, the *Kutoria* period was brought forcibly to a close in 1872. One of the leading forces behind this pressure was Samuel Baker, who had traveled through the upper Nile region, including Acholi, in 1863–65 and had written a long and popular account of his journey. Baker was even named by the Egyptian government to lead its forces against the *Kutoria* and set up an administration in their stead.[10]

The *Jadiya* administrators Baker left behind in what became known as the Equatorial Province quickly established themselves as far more troublesome and oppressive than the *Kutoria* had ever been. They established seven additional sub-stations throughout Acholi; they demanded a burdensome grain tax, which they often collected with what is remembered as excessive force and in excessive amounts; they flouted accepted Acholi codes and practices; they meted out what is remembered as harsh, unjust, and unpredictable "justice"; and they interfered frequently, and often violently, in both inter- and intra-polity affairs. This widely unpopular *Jadiya* rule in Acholi was threatened first from the outside, as insurrectionist forces of the Mahdi cut them off from Khartoum and the Egyptian government in 1883. Their hold was further weakened by increased Acholi attacks from 1885 on. Finally, in 1888, defeat at the hands of a multi-polity Acholi force prompted a final *Jadiya* withdrawal from Acholi.[11]

The links of the *Kutoria* and *Jadiya* with Khartoum, Cairo, and beyond brought Acholi into contact with a wider world than ever before. That contact was based primarily on trade, especially in ivory but also in human beings. The trade brought by the outsiders from the north and the raiding that they initiated as well introduced new wealth into Acholi. The most important forms of this new wealth were ivory, cattle, and firearms, and its

9. For general background and context on this period, see J. M. Gray (1951) and Richard Gray (1961); on the *Kutoria* in Acholi, see esp. Uma (1971); Uma A.H.T.; Baker (1866, v. 2); Atkinson (1978, pp. 507–16).

10. See references in n. 9; Baker's account of his expedition against the *Kutoria* and his establishment of an Egyptian government "administration" in the area is in Baker (1874, v. 2).

11. The most essential sources on the *Jadiya* in Acholi are Uma (1971); Uma A.H.T.; Emin Pasha (1962; 1963; 1964); Atkinson (1978, pp. 516–24).

most important feature was its extremely unequal distribution in Acholi society. The main beneficiaries belonged to one of two categories: *rwodi* and the interpreters for the outsiders. It appears that shortly after the northern traders arrived and made known their demand for ivory, *rwodi* in Acholi began to claim as a new form of tribute one tusk from every elephant killed by members of their chiefdoms. The *rwot* could exchange these for such minor trade goods as brass, copper, beads, and cloth or, if he could obtain enough tusks, for cattle or even firearms. In addition, if he helped provide either porters or men to assist in hunts or raids, he received return payment in cattle, captives, and sometimes guns. Interpreters were given the same forms of payment in return for their crucial services.[12]

The inequality in the distribution of new wealth took on special importance because, for the first time in Acholi, significant amounts of wealth began to be accumulated over time. Previously, most wealth that came into the *rwot*'s hands from tribute went back out again in the form of gift giving and entertainment. Thus, while the *rwodi* were the wealthiest members of society and used that wealth for social and political ends, neither they nor their descendants or kinsmen accumulated much of that wealth. With the new forms and quantity of wealth available during the later nineteenth century, this changed. *Rwodi* and interpreters accumulated wealth themselves and in turn passed wealth on to their sons and other kinsmen. Effects were felt throughout the society, economy, and polities of emergent Acholi.[13]

Toward an Acholi Ethnicity

The presence of the Arabic-speaking outsiders from the north played a major role in the further development of an Acholi ethnicity. When the *Kutoria* arrived in Acholi, they neither understood nor wished to bother with the intricacies of lineage and polity units and identities. Instead the outsiders identified, named, and began to define a larger entity. That entity was Acholi.

The original basis for this *Kutoria* concept was linguistic. It so happened that the Luo language spoken throughout Acholi by the nineteenth century was not completely unfamiliar to the northern traders. Their previous contact with the language enabled the *Kutoria* both to perceive the

12. References here are copious, mostly scattered throughout the collected A.H.T., esp. Uma A.H.T.; see also Atkinson (1978, pp. 524–29).

13. Again, references are numerous throughout the collected A.H.T., esp. Uma A.H.T.; and again, see Atkinson (1978, pp. 529–41).

emerging linguistic unity of Acholi and to give it a name. According to Crazzolara, when the *Kutoria* arrived in Acholi they had already

> passed through the *Collo* (Shilluk) country and evidently knew, at least to some extent, their language. When they arrived in the new country [Acholi] they soon recognized the similarity of the language of the place with the *Collo* language and started to call them *Shuuli*. At first, according to the natives, they gave the name of *Shuuli* to Obwona Awac, interpreter of Gikwiakare, *Rwoot* of Patiko [site of the first *Kutoria* station]. The name was gradually transferred to the people. As the Lwoo are unfamiliar with the sound *sh* they turned it into a *c* (*ch*) again and it became *Cuuli*; this was in due time molded into *Acooli* [or in standard spelling, Acholi].[14]

The "Shuuli" term and concept took some time in developing. The writings of European travelers through Acholi over the 1860s and early 1870s makes this quite clear. The first European to pass through Acholi was Englishman J. H. Speke. In his account of the western part of Acholi that he visited in November 1862, Speke does not mention the term Shuuli at all. Because he came from the south, was more exposed to Bantu-speakers' concepts of Acholi rather than the *Kutoria*'s, and passed rapidly through the area, however, Speke is only a peripheral source for present purposes.[15]

This is not the case with fellow Englishman Samuel Baker. Baker spent considerable time in Acholi in 1863–64 and was closely associated with the northern traders. Thus his extremely limited references to Shuuli in his book on this period suggest strongly that it was not yet a well-established term or concept. Baker uses the term (written "Sooli") only twice, both times applying it solely to the Pajok region of northernmost Acholi. The important designation for Baker in 1863–64 was "Madi." Baker uses this term to mean the entire region of northern Uganda to the north of Bunyoro. He even compiled a short Luo word list from Acholi that he classified as belonging to the "Madi language." The only identifying names that Baker consistently used for his 1863–64 stay in Acholi besides "Madi" were the names of individual chiefdoms. He usually referred to these latter as "districts," though at least three times he also called them "tribes." Since he also used "tribe" to refer to the collective Madi peoples, an entity on a quite different scale and with a very different meaning than an Acholi chiefdom, this suggests either an unawareness of such differences or an unconcern with them.[16]

14. Crazzolara (1938, pp. vii–viii).
15. Speke (1863).
16. The term "Sooli" appears in Baker (1866, v. 1, p. 237; v. 2, p. 282); "Madi" in Baker

The contrasts between Baker's account of his first visit and that of his return in 1872–73 are many and striking. By this time the Shuuli term and concept (now spelled "Shooli" by Baker) were obviously well established. Baker uses the phrase "Shooli country" throughout his book on the 1872–73 years. He also quite clearly distinguishes "Shooli country" from neighboring Madi, and applies the concept to most of the area and people now identified as Acholi. He provides a new Acholi Luo word list, and identifies it this time not as Madi but "Shooli." Finally, when Baker describes Payira's *rwot*, Rwotcamo, he notes Rwotcamo's claims to be the paramount ruler of "Shooli." Even if Rwotcamo had no basis for this assertion, it clearly suggests that there was at least some notion and utilization of the concept of an Acholi identity among Acholi themselves.[17]

After 1872–73, numerous European references confirm that the Shuuli term and concept were solidly entrenched. By the end of the nineteenth century, the people of Acholi had embraced the externally introduced Shuuli identity to the extent that they began to modify the term to fit their own needs. In 1900 an early British administrator stationed just west of Acholi reported that the "people themselves" pronounced their name "Chuuli" rather than the outsiders' "Shuuli."[18]

It seems clear then that between the 1860s and the end of the century, the designation and idea of Shuuli (then Chuuli) became established among both outsiders involved with the area and the people of Acholi themselves. For the Acholi, the Shuuli concept appears to have remained one of limited but not insignificant practical application. The primary sociopolitical unit continued to be the individual chiefdom, and the main arena of wider, less formally structured ties and activities seems to have remained the zone. There are certainly no examples from the period of Acholi-wide organization, cooperation, or other activities of any sort.

But the Acholi were clearly aware of and used the Shuuli designation and idea. The examples already noted of Rwotcamo's claim to Shuuli paramountcy and the transformation of pronunciation to Chuuli both demonstrate this. There also was an increase during the second half of the

---

(1866, v. 1, pp. 229 [which includes the Luo word list identified as "Madi"] and 237; v. 2, pp. 323, 479, 481, and end map). And for the interchangeable use of individual chiefdom names, "district," and "tribe," see Baker (1866, v. 2, pp. 481, 492, 494).

17. Baker (1874, v. 2, pp. 70, 94, 126, 528). With respect to Payira's Rwotcamo, the governor of the Equatorial Province wrote in his diaries in 1879 that Rwotcamo was "the acknowledged chief of all Acholi"; see Emin Pasha (1962, p. 128).

18. R. Macallister, subcommissioner, Nile Province (private letter to H. H. Johnson, dd. 22 October 1900; Entebbe National Archives, A.16, I, no. 8). This occurred for the reasons Crazzolara points out in the quote above.

nineteenth century in the frequency and scale of extra-polity organization and cooperation, especially within the context of the increased warfare of the period.[19]

In addition, both individuals and groups appear to have had more and more contact with more and more distant parts of Acholi than ever before, not only as a result of raiding and warfare but of new trading and hunting patterns as well. There are also indications, as noted above, that the outsiders stationed in Acholi (especially the *Kutoria*) may have raided more outside of Acholi than within. If so, it is doubtful that this was by chance or that the inhabitants of Acholi failed to notice the pattern. Finally, there are also memories that captives taken by Acholi in intra-Acholi warfare were *not* traded to the outsiders to become slaves, while this was a common practice with captives taken from elsewhere. All of this must have contributed to an increased use and meaning of the Shuuli term and concept. Throughout the period, however, surely the most common context in which the Shuuli designation was used and took on meaning for the people of Acholi was its original one: in interaction with outsiders.[20]

Conclusion

Whatever limits were associated with a Shuuli identity among the people of Acholi during the second half of the nineteenth century, it was of crucial significance that for the first time such a concept explicitly existed. Both the term and the concept were due in part to a perspective and a designation derived from outsiders. But they were also based on much longer-term developments, particularly over the late seventeenth and eighteenth centuries, that had gradually produced a common social order and political culture, as well as the broad use of the Luo language over virtually the

19. Examples include (1) the large coalition of polities that combined to fight against the Cua confederacy in the Patiko area in the 1860s (see Crazzolara [1951, pp. 241–43; 1954, pp. 524–26]); (2) the complex and shifting combination of alliances among southeastern-zone chiefdoms during a major 1880s war (see Webster A.H.T., pp. 5, 23, 89, 120; Uma A.H.T. 54–57); (3) the Payira-led coalition against Padibe in the late 1880s following the death of Rwotcamo and the withdrawal of the *Jadiya* (see Uma A.H.T. 34, 36; Owot [1976, pp. 206–7]; Anywar [1948, pp. 73–74]); (4) the continued involvement of the Koc chiefdom in south-central-zone disputes after the 1860s, long after it had moved far to the west (see Uma A.H.T. 54–56; A.H.T. 261); and (5) the large coalition of southeastern-zone chiefdoms that fought against the Jie in 1901 (see Lamphear and Webster [1971]).

20. For references to captives taken in intra-Acholi wars not being traded to the outsiders to become slaves, see in Uma A.H.T. 23, 25, 27.

whole of Acholi. This developing new order was deepened and broadened over the first half of the nineteenth century, first in response to the major droughts of about 1790 and the 1830s, and then in juxtaposition with the emergence of contrasting and sometimes competing entities and identities on Acholi's borders, particularly the Jie to the east and Langi to the south.

During the second half of the nineteenth century, the broad unity that had been emerging was explicitly recognized and named (first by outsiders) and it began to take on new uses and meanings, both for outsiders and the people of Acholi themselves. This had not been true before. Drawing upon roots that were planted about 1675, and built on foundations laid especially over the course of the eighteenth century, the development of a Shuuli identity during the second half of the nineteenth century set the stage for further evolution of an Acholi ethnicity (including the creation of an Acholi "tribe") in the twentieth century. As I have argued throughout this book, only by recognizing and investigating the deep, late-seventeenth- and eighteenth-century roots of Acholi ethnicity can we discover and begin to understand crucial components of the Acholi's always "unfinished process of coming to be."[21]

21. Lonsdale (1977, p. 132).

Appendix: Estimated Population of Acholi Chiefdoms c. 1790

This appendix is an effort to suggest very crude estimates of the population of most Acholi chiefdoms (or sometimes clusters of chiefdoms) at the end of the eighteenth century, or about 1790. These estimates have been derived mainly from early-twentieth-century poll tax figures reproduced in Wright (1934, pp. 175–81) and Okech (1953, p. 25), with additional information from Girling (1960, pp. 7, 21–44) and Langlands (1971, pp. 2, 33). In the sources, the figures given are most often listed in terms of precolonial chiefdoms and represent the number of household heads counted in that chiefdom.

The first calculation was to multiply the listed number of household heads by a factor of five to produce an estimated population in the early twentieth century, or about 1900 (column 3 below). The estimate of five persons per household is impressionistically reasonable for Acholi, if perhaps on the conservative side. Moreover, Laslett (1972, passim; including Goody [1972], which deals primarily with Africa) demonstrates a marked tendency toward constancy at this number of people per household in most societies, at most times.

It is possible that the count of household heads reported in the Acholi sources (especially in Wright and Okech) is a less reliable basis for estimating population than assessing an average of five persons per household. The British almost certainly missed a number of household heads in their count, as its purpose was to collect poll tax, and the colonial administration of Acholi was only in the process of being effectively established. Thus the method being employed here leads to a markedly conservative estimate of the Acholi population about 1900. Furthermore, the early twentieth-century population was unlikely to have been markedly larger than the population about 1790. There are no discernible reasons why the population of Acholi in general would have increased during the nineteenth century. Indeed, there are several counter-indications that (1) the major droughts of about 1790 and the 1830s, (2) the difficult years of slave and ivory trading during the second half of the nineteenth century, and (3) the major outbreak of sleeping sickness during the first decade of the twentieth century may well have caused the population in Acholi to decrease.

In order to derive a population estimate for the end of the eighteenth century that is not wholly a reading back of early twentieth-century figures, the probable number of lineages in each chiefdom is listed for both c. 1900 (column 1) and c. 1790 (column 2). In those instances where a chiefdom or cluster of chiefdoms had significantly fewer lineages about 1790 compared to about 1900, this difference is factored into the estimated population c. 1790 (column 4).

For example, the first chiefdom in the first list is Paimol. Its estimated population about 1900, based on poll tax data, is 2,700. But Paimol was then comprised of thirteen or fourteen lineages. In about 1790, Paimol consisted probably of only six lineages. Thus, Paimol's estimated population about 1790 has been calculated by dividing six by thirteen (yielding 0.462, the ratio of lineages in Paimol about 1790 compared to about 1900). Paimol's estimated population about 1900 (2,700) has then been multiplied by 0.462, resulting in an estimated population of 1,250 in about 1790.

SOUTHEASTERN ZONE

Chiefdom	No. of lineages, c. 1900	No. of lineages, c. 1790	Estimated population, c. 1900	Estimated population, c. 1790
Paimol	13–14	6	2,700	1,250
Pukor	2	2		
Umia Anyima	5–8	5–8		
Umia Pacua	3–8	3–8		
Pela	2	2	5,200	5,200*
Wol	?	7		
Parumo	?	?		
Parabongo	5	5		
Pacer	2	2		
Pader	?	2	2,750	2,750
Pabala	1	1		
Kwong	2	2		
Pacabol	3–4	3–4		
Koro	3	3	1,000	,000
Ariya	—	1		
Patongo	7–16	7–16	5,750	5,750†
Ajali	4	4		
Lira Paluo	30–34	30–34	6,300	6,300‡
Paicam	8–9	8–9		
Adilang	6–7	6–7	1,350	1,350
Puranga	12	3	6,500	1,630
Kilak	5	5	600	600
Totals§	113–138	107–131	32,150	25,830

Estimated average size of southeastern zone lineages, c. 1790:

25,830/107 = 241 persons/lineage

25,830/131 = 197 persons/lineage

25,830/119 = 217 persons/lineage (composite average)

*More than half of this estimated population would have almost surely come from Umia Anyima, placing it among the dozen largest polities in eighteenth-century Acholi.

†All the evidence indicates that Patongo was larger than Ajali, suggesting that more than half of this estimated population, perhaps 3,500 or even more, came from Patongo.

‡By far the majority of this estimated population would have been in Lira Paluo, probably in the neighborhood of 5,000.

§The southeastern-zone chiefdoms in general were greatly disrupted by the droughts of about 1790 and the 1830s; at least temporarily, many chiefdoms fragmented and many also left the zone. This makes all the totals for this zone especially tentative; see, for example, Webster (1976b and 1976c).

EAST-CENTRAL ZONE

Chiefdom	No. of lineages, c. 1900	No. of lineages, c. 1790	Estimated population, c. 1900	Estimated population, c. 1790
Lukwor	—	3		
Koyo	—	1		
Pugwenyi	—	2		
Parwec	—	2		
Lamogi	—	1	10,000	5,000
Pajule Paluo	6	3		
Painata	—	1		
Oryang	—	1		
Ngekidi	4	2		
	32*			
Pageen	9	9	3,000	3,000
Lameet	6	6	1,150	1,150
Pajimu	4	4	1,250	1,250
Lukwor	4	4	1,400	1,400
Totals	55	39	16,800	11,800

Estimated average size of east-central-zone lineages, c. 1790:

11,800/39 = 303 persons/lineage

*The Okaka-area chiefdoms were almost totally restructured following the droughts of about 1790 and the 1830s; the total number of lineages in the new chiefdoms by the end of the nineteenth century (including the Pajule Paluo and Ngekidi) was approximately 32; see Garry (1976, esp. pp. 330–33).

SOUTH-CENTRAL ZONE

Chiefdom	No. of lineages, c. 1900	No. of lineages, c. 1790	Estimated population, c. 1900	Estimated population, c. 1790
Koc	6	6	4,000	4,000*
Pokumu	1	1		
Bolo	1	2	?	?
Bwobo	4	1	1,500	380[†]
Totals	12[‡]	10	5,500	4,380

Estimated average size of south-central zone lineages, c. 1790:

4,380/10 = 438 persons/lineage

*Well over 3,000 of this total estimated population was almost surely in Koc.

[†]The estimated population c. 1790 calculated for Bwobo seems almost certainly too low for any independent polity; but that was how the numbers worked out.

[‡]A number of additional chiefdoms that came into the south-central zone only during the nineteenth century—most importantly an expanded Puranga—are not included in these totals.

WESTERN ZONE

Chiefdom	No. of lineages, c. 1900	No. of lineages, c. 1790	Estimated population, c. 1900	Estimated population, c. 1790
Pabo	12–16	12–16		
Paomo	2	2	10,000	10,000*
Pagak	6–8	6–8		
Lamogi	9	9	2,500	2,500
Papee	—	3	500	500
Pawel	1	1	1,000	1,000
Totals	30–36	33–39	14,000	14,000

Estimated average of western-zone lineages, c. 1790:

    14,000/33 = 424 persons/lineage

    14,000/39 = 359 persons/lineage

    14,000/36 = 389 persons/lineage (composite average)

*The vast majority of this estimated population would have been in Pabo, perhaps as many as 7,000; but given Paomo's acknowledged small size, that would still mean that Pagak would probably have been in or close to the 2,500 range in population.

CENTRAL ZONE

Chiefdom	No. of lineages, c. 1900	No. of lineages, c. 1790	Estimated population, c. 1900	Estimated population, c. 1790
Alero	7	7	1,500	1,500
Palaro	12	12	2,000	2,000
Payira	25–35	25–35		
Paibona	6	3	15,500	15,500*
Paico	7	7	2,500	2,500
Patiko	18	9	4,000	2,000
Totals†	75–85	63–73	25,500	23,500

Estimated average size of central-zone lineages, c. 1790:

    23,500/63 = 373 persons/lineage

    23,500/73 = 322 persons/lineage

    23,500/68 = 346 persons/lineage (composite average)

*As there is no evidence that Paibona was anything more than a small chiefdom, the vast majority of these estimated numbers, up to 14,000, were most likely in Payira, making it by far the largest of all the Acholi chiefdoms by the end of the eighteenth century.

†Lineages of Koc and Pokumu, chiefdoms which ended up in this zone in the nineteenth century, are not included here but in the south-central zone where they were for much of the eighteenth century.

NORTHWESTERN ZONE

Chiefdom	No. of lineages, c. 1900	No. of lineages, c. 1790	Estimated population, c. 1900	Estimated population, c. 1790
Atyak	12	10	3,000	2,500

Estimated average size of northwestern-zone lineages:
  2,500/10 = 250 persons/lineage

NORTH-CENTRAL ZONE

Chiefdom	No. of lineages, c. 1900	No. of lineages, c. 1790	Estimated population, c. 1900	Estimated population, c. 1790
Padibe	16–20	7–10		
Longorone	7 (?)	7 (?)		
Popoka	3–4 (?)	3–4 (?)	14,250	9,650*
Agoro	2 (?)	2 (?)		
Lamogi	1 (?)	1 (?)		
Palabek	8 (?)	10 (?)	6,500	5,200
Paloga	5–6	5–6	1,500	1,500
Lomura	—	3–4	—	?
Madi Opei	9	3	2,550	1,460
Madi Kiloc	5	5		
Totals	56–62 (?)	46–52	24,800	17,810

Estimated average size of north-central zone lineages, c. 1790:
   17,810/46 = 387 persons/lineage
   17,810/52 = 343 persons/lineage
   17,810/49 = 363 persons/lineage (composite average)
  *The estimated population figures for Padibe are combined with those for the four possible Agoro Mountain chiefdoms. Mostly because information on these Agoro chiefdoms is so limited and tentative, the population estimates for this zone need to be viewed with even more skepticism than usual. All the evidence does suggest, however, that Padibe and Palabek were among the larger chiefdoms in Acholi during both the eighteenth and nineteenth centuries.

NORTHEASTERN ZONE

Chiefdom	No. of lineages, c. 1900	No. of lineages, c. 1790	Estimated population, c. 1900	Estimated population, c. 1790
Nam Okora	1	1	1,350	1,350
Orom	8–15	8–15	2,050	2,050*
Akara (?)	2–3 (?)	2–3 (?)	?	?
Totals	11–19†	11–19	3,400	3,400

Estimated average size of northeastern zone lineages, c. 1790:

3,400/11 = 309 persons/lineage

3,400/19 = 179 persons/lineage

3,400/15 = 227 persons/lineage (composite average)

*This seems a rather low total for Orom, but is used in lieu of any alternative information.

†Neither chiefdoms that became a part of the northeastern zone only in the nineteenth century nor the lineages in them are included here.

References

COLLECTED ACHOLI TRADITIONS

TRADITIONS COLLECTED PRIOR TO THE HISTORY OF UGANDA PROJECT

The translated typescripts of sources in this section are on deposit at the Department of History, Makerere University, and in the Africana Library, Northwestern University. Page references in the footnotes come from these translated typescripts.

Anywar, R. S. 1954. *Acoli ki Ker Megi* (The Acholi and Their Chiefdoms). Kampala: Eagle Press. Trans. by N. E. Odyomo, Department of History, Makerere University.
Crazzolara, J. P. 1950, 1951, 1954. *The Lwoo*. 3 vols. Verona: Editrice Nigrizia.
Latigo, A. O. 1970a. Clan Systems in Acholi — Uganda. Unpublished ms. Trans. by J. P. M. Okulla, Department of History, Makerere University.
——. 1970b. The Koro Clan System. Unpublished ms. Trans. by J. P. M. Okulla, Department of History, Makerere University.
——. 1970c. History of Acholi Clans — Part 2. Unpublished ms. Trans. by N. P. E. Odyomo, Department of History, Makerere University.
Malandra, Alfred. 1947. *Tekwaro Acoli* (Acholi Traditions). London?: Longman. Trans. by C. A. R. Oywa, Department of History, Makerere University.
Okech, Lacito. 1953. *Tekwaro ki Ker Lobo Acholi* (The Traditions and Chiefdoms of Acholiland). Kampala: Eagle Press. Trans. by J. Nyeko, Department of History, Makerere University.
Olango, Apolo. 1970. A Collection of Traditions about Puranga. Unpublished ms. (compiled in the 1940s). Trans. by C. Okeng, Department of History, Makerere University.
Ongo, D. E. 1971a. A History of Pajule. Unpublished ms. Trans. by C. Okeng, Department of History, Makerere University.
——. 1971b. Drum Songs of Some East Acholi Kingdoms. Unpublished ms. Trans. by C. Okeng, Department of History, Makerere University.
Pellegrini, V. 1963. *Lok pa Acoli Macon* (A History of the Acholi of Long Ago). 4th ed. (orig. pub. 1949). Gulu: Catholic Press. Trans. by C. Okeng, Department of History, Makerere University.
Wright, A. C. A. 1934. Collection of Tradition from Acholi, Uganda. Unpublished ms.

ACHOLI HISTORICAL TEXTS (A.H.T.) COLLECTED AS PART OF THE HISTORY OF
UGANDA PROJECT

1. Collected by Ronald R. Atkinson

A.H.T. 201–310. Interviews conducted in western Acholi, 1970–71. Index prepared by the Department of History, Makerere University; deposited at the Department of History, Makerere, and in the Africana Library, Northwestern University. Manuscript approximately 1,200 pp. Cited simply A.H.T., with text numbers. A complete list of elders interviewed, with times and dates, is included in Atkinson (1978, pp. 641–50).

2. Collected by A. M. Garry

Interviews conducted in Chua County in east-central and northeastern Acholi, 1972. Not given general A.H.T. numbers. On deposit at the Department of History, Makerere University. Typescript 143 pp. Cited Garry A.H.T., with page numbers.

3. Collected by P. M. L. Owot

A.H.T. 1–20. Interviews conducted in Lamwo County in north-central Acholi, 1970. On deposit at the Department of History, Makerere University. Manuscript approximately 80 pp. Cited Owot A.H.T., with text numbers.

4. Collected by F. K. Uma

A.H.T. 23–40, 54–62. Interviews conducted throughout Acholi, concentrating on the late nineteenth century and the relations between Acholi and Arabic-speaking traders and administrators from the north, 1970. On deposit at the Department of History, Makerere University. Manuscript approximately 100 pp. Cited Uma A.H.T., with text numbers.

5. Collected by J. B. Webster

A.H.T. 14–18 (duplicating numbers also used by Owot), 21–22, 41–45, 47–50, 63–89. Interviews conducted in Agago County in southeastern Acholi, 1970–71. Cyclostyled, with index prepared by and deposited at the Department of History, Makerere University. Typescript 208 pp. Cited Webster A.H.T., with page numbers.

OTHER SOURCES CITED

Abrahams, R. C. 1965. Neighbourhood Organisation: A Major Sub-System among the Northern Nyamwezi. *Africa* 35: 168–86.
Adefuye, Ade. 1971. The Palwo of Northern Bunyoro: A Demographic History. Seminar paper, Department of History, Makerere University, MSP/16/71/72.
———. 1973. Political History of the Palwo, 1400–1911. Ph.D. diss., University of Ibadan.

——. 1974. Palwo Jogi: Origin and Impact upon Political History. Paper presented at the Canadian Association of African Studies annual meeting, Halifax.

——. 1976a. The Palwo: Emergence and Crisis c. 1400–1760. In *The Central Lwo during the Aconya*. Ed. by J. M. Onyango-ku-Odongo and J. B. Webster. Nairobi: East African Literature Bureau.

——. 1976b. Ethnicity and Economics: Factors of Change among the Palwo. In *The Central Lwo during the Aconya*. Ed. by J. M. Onyango-ku-Odongo and J. B. Webster. Nairobi: East African Literature Bureau.

Adimola, A. B. 1954. The Lamogi Rebellion 1911–12. *Uganda Journal* 18, 2: 166–77.

African Studies Review 30, 2. 1987. African History Research Trends and Perspectives on the Future. Guest editor D. Newbury.

Ake, Claude. 1992. Keynote Address: Ethnicity, Culture and Class Conflict in Africa. Paper presented at the Project on Contemporary Political Conflict in Natal; Conference on Ethnicity, Society and Conflict in Natal, Pietermaritzburg.

Allen, William. 1965. *The African Husbandman*. New York: Barnes and Noble.

Alpers, Edward, and Christopher Ehret. 1975. Eastern Africa. In *The Cambridge History of Africa*, vol. 4. Ed. by R. Gray. Cambridge: Cambridge University Press.

Ambler, Charles H. 1988. *Kenyan Communities in the Age of Imperialism: The Central Region in the Late Nineteenth Century*. New Haven, CT: Yale University Press.

Ambrose, Stanley H. 1982. Archaeology and Linguistic Reconstructions of History in East Africa. In *The Archaeological and Linguistic Reconstruction of African History*. Ed. by C. Ehret and M. Posnansky. Berkeley: University of California Press.

Amin, Samir. 1974. Modes of Production and Social Formation. *Ufahamu* 5, 2: 57–84.

Anderson, Benedict. 1991 (first ed. 1983). *Imagined Communities: Reflections on the Origin and Spread of Nationalism*. London and New York: Verso.

Anywar, R. S. 1948. The Life of Rwot Iburaim Awich. Trans. from Acholi by J. V. Wild. *Uganda Journal* 12, 1: 12–79.

Apoko, Anna. 1967. At Home in the Village: Growing up in Acholi. In *East African Childhood: Three Versions*. Ed. by L. K. Fox. Nairobi: Oxford University Press.

Apecu, Alex. 1972. A Pre-Colonial History of Jonam Chiefdoms. Graduating essay, Department of History, Makerere University.

Atkinson, Ronald R. 1974. Western Acholi before the Late Seventeenth Century. Paper presented at the Canadian Association of African Studies annual meeting, Halifax.

——. 1975. The Traditions of the Early Kings of Buganda: Myth, History, and Structural Analysis. *History in Africa* 2: 17–57.

——. 1976. State Formation and Development in Western Acholi. In *The Central Lwo during the Aconya*. Ed. by J. M. Onyango-ku-Odongo and J. B. Webster. Nairobi: East African Literature Bureau.

——. 1978. A History of the Western Acholi of Uganda c. 1675–1900: A Study in the Utilization and Analysis of Oral Data. Ph.D. diss. Northwestern University.

——. 1984. "State" Formation and Language Change in Westernmost Acholi in the Eighteenth Century. In *State Formation in Eastern Africa*. Ed. A. I. Salim. Nairobi: Heinemann.

——. 1989. The Evolution of Ethnicity Among the Acholi of Uganda: The Precolonial Phase. *Ethnohistory* 36, 1: 19–43.

Atlas of Uganda. 1962; 1967. Kampala: Uganda Department of Lands and Surveys.

Baker, Samuel White. 1866. *The Albert Nyanza, Great Basin of the Nile, and the Explorations of the Nile Sources*. 2 vols. London: Macmillan.

——. 1874. *Ismailia: A Narrative of the Expedition to Central Africa for the Suppression of the Slave Trade*. 2 vols. London: Macmillan.

Barth, Fredrik. 1969. Introduction to *Ethnic Groups and Boundaries*. Ed. by F. Barth. Boston: Little Brown.

Bateson, Gregory. 1979. *Mind and Nature: A Necessary Unity*. New York: Dutton.

Baxter, P. T. W., and Audrey Butt. 1953. *The Azande, and Related Peoples of the Anglo-Egyptian Sudan and Belgian Congo*. Ethnographic Survey of Africa: East Central Africa, vol. 9. London: International African Institute.

Beinart, William. 1982. *The Political Economy of Pondoland 1860 to 1930*. Cambridge: Cambridge University Press.

——. 1987. Worker Consciousness, Ethnic Particularism and Nationalism: The Experience of a South African Migrant, 1930–1960. In *The Politics of Race, Class and Nationalism in Twentieth-Century South Africa*. Ed. by S. Marks and S. Trapido. London: Longman.

Bere, R. M. 1934a. Acholi Dances (Myel). *Uganda Journal* 1, 1: 64–65.

——. 1934b. Note on the Origin of the Payera Acholi. *Uganda Journal* 1, 1: 65–67.

——. 1934c. Acholi Hunts. *Uganda Journal* 1, 2: 153–54.

——. 1946. Awich—A Biographical Note and a Chapter of Acholi History. *Uganda Journal* 10, 2: 76–78.

——. 1947. An Outline of Acholi History. *Uganda Journal* 11, 1: 1–8.

——. 1955. Land and Chieftainship among the Acholi. *Uganda Journal* 19, 1: 49–56.

——. 1960a. Acholi Methods of Hunting. Appendix D (i) in F. K. Girling, *The Acholi of Uganda*. London: Her Majesty's Stationery Office.

——. 1960b. Traditional System of Land Tenure amongst the Acholi. Appendix D (ii) in F. K. Girling, *The Acholi of Uganda*. London: Her Majesty's Stationery Office.

——. n.d. [c. 1978]. A Spear for the Rhinocerus: An African Tribe in the Early Nineteen-Thirties — The Acholi of Northern Uganda. Unpublished typescript. Colonial Records Project, MSS Afr. s1755. Rhodes House, Oxford University.

Bernstein, H., and J. Depelchin. 1978–79. The Object of African History: A Nationalized Perspective. *History in Africa* 5: 1–19.

Bloch, Marc. 1954. *The Historian's Craft*. Trans. by P. Putnam. Manchester: Manchester University Press.

Blount, Ben G. 1975. Agreeing to Agree on Genealogy: A Luo Sociology of Knowledge. In *Sociocultural Dimensions of Language Use*. Ed. by M. Sanchez and B. G. Blount. New York: Academic Press.

Blount, B. G., and R. T. Curley. 1970. The Southern Luo Languages: A Glotochronological Reconstruction. *Journal of African Languages* 9, 1: 1–18.

Boccassino, Renato. 1939. The Nature and Characteristics of the Supreme Being Worshipped among the Acholi of Uganda. *Uganda Journal* 6, 4: 195–201.

Bonner, Philip L. 1980. Classes, the Mode of Production and the State in Pre-Colonial Swaziland. In *Economy and Society in Pre-Industrial South Africa*. Ed. by S. Marks and A. Atmore. London: Longman.

———. 1983. *Kings, Commoners and Concessionaires: The Evolution and Dissolution of the Nineteenth-Century Swazi State*. Cambridge: Cambridge University Press.

Bonner, Philip L., and Tom Lodge. 1989. Introduction to *Holding Their Ground: Class, Locality and Culture in 19th and 20th Century South Africa*. Ed. by P. Bonner et al. Johannesburg: Ravan Press.

Boonzaier, Emile, and John Sharp, eds. 1988. *South African Keywords: The Uses and Abuses of Political Concepts*. Cape Town: David Philip.

Boyer, P. 1987. The Stuff "Traditions" Are Made of: On the Implicit Ontology of an Ethnographic Category. *Philosophy of the Social Sciences* 17: 49–65.

Braudel, Fernand. 1973. *Capitalism and Material Life: 1400–1800*. Trans. by S. Reynolds. New York: Harper and Row.

———. 1981. *Civilization and Capitalism, 15th–18th Century: The Structures of Everyday Life*, vol. 1. Trans. by S. Reynolds. New York: Harper and Row.

———. 1984. *Civilization and Capitalism, 15th–18th Century: The Perspective of the World*, vol. 3. Trans. by S. Reynolds. New York: Harper and Row.

Brosnahan, L. F. 1973. Some Historical Cases of Language Imposition. In *Varieties of Present-Day English*. Ed. by R. W. Bailey and J. L. Robinson. London and New York: Macmillan.

Buchanan, Carole A. 1969. The Bacwezi Cult: The Religious Revolution in Western Uganda. Seminar Paper, Department of History, Makerere University, MSP/21/1969/70.

———. 1973. The Kitara Complex: The Historical Tradition of Western Uganda to the 16th Century. Ph.D. diss., Indiana University.

———. 1978. Perceptions of Ethnic Interaction in the East African Interior: The Kitara Complex. *International Journal of African Historical Studies* 11, 3: 410–28.

Bundy, Colin. 1979. *The Rise and Fall of the South African Peasantry*. Berkeley: University of California Press.

Butt, Audrey. 1952. *The Nilotes of the Anglo-Egyptian Sudan and Uganda*. Ethnographic Survey of Africa: East Central Africa, vol. 4. London: International African Institute.

Callinicos, Luli. 1981. *Gold and Workers, 1886–1924: A People's History of South Africa*, vol. 1. Johannesburg: Ravan Press.

———. 1987. *Working Life: Factories, Townships and Popular Culture on the Rand, 1886–1940: A People's History of South Africa*, vol. 2. Johannesburg: Ravan Press.

Catford, J. R. 1951. *Katiri* Cultivation in the None District of Equatoria. *Sudan Notes and Records* 32, 1: 106–12.

Chaillee-Long, Charles. 1877. *Central Africa: Naked Truths of Naked People*. New York: Harper and Brothers.

Chapman, Malcolm, Maryon McDonald, and Elizabeth Tonkin. 1989. Introduction to *History and Ethnicity* (ASA Monographs 27). Ed. by E. Tonkin, M. McDonald, and M. Campbell. London and New York: Routledge.

Chazan, Naomi et al. 1988. *Politics and Society in Contemporary Africa.* Boulder, Colo: Lynne Reinner.

Clarence-Smith, W. G. 1977. For Braudel: A Note on the *Ecole des Annales* and the Historiography of Africa. *History in Africa* 4: 275–81.

Clignet, Remi. 1970. *Many Wives, Many Powers: Authority and Power in Polygamous Families.* Evanston, IL: Northwestern University Press.

Cohen, Anthony P. 1985. *The Symbolic Construction of Community.* London and New York: Tavistock.

Cohen, David W. 1968. The River-Lake Nilotes from the Fifteenth to the Nineteenth Century. In *Zamani: A Survey of East African History.* Ed. by B. A. Ogot and J. A. Kieran. Nairobi: East African Publishing House.

——. 1970. A Survey of Interlacustrine Chronology. *Journal of African History* 11, 2: 177–201.

——. 1972. *The Historical Tradition of Busoga: Mukama and Kintu.* Oxford: Clarendon Press.

——. 1974a. Lwo Camps in Seventeenth-Century Eastern Uganda: The Use of Migration Tradition in the Reconstruction of Culture. Paper presented at the Canadian Association of African Studies annual meeting, Halifax.

——. 1947b. A Preliminary Study of Climatic Trends in the Lakes Plateau Region of East Africa. Paper presented at the African Studies Association annual meeting, Chicago.

——. 1974c. The River-Lake Nilotes from the Fifteenth to the Nineteenth Century. In *Zamani: A Survey of East African History,* 2nd ed. Ed. by B. A. Ogot. Nairobi: East African Publishing House.

——. 1974d. Review Essay: Pre-Colonial History as the History of "Society." *African Studies Review* 17, 2: 467–72.

——. 1977. *Womanafu's Bunafu: A Study of Authority in a Nineteenth-Century African Community.* Princeton, NJ: Princeton University Press.

——. 1980. Reconstructing a Conflict in Bunafu: Seeking Evidence Outside the Narrative Tradition. In *The African Past Speaks: Essays on Oral Tradition and History.* Ed. by J. C. Miller. Hamden, CT: Archon.

——. 1983. The Face of Contact: A Model of Cultural and Linguistic Frontier in Early Eastern Uganda. In *Nilotic Studies: Proceedings of the International Symposium on Languages and History of the Nilotic Peoples,* vol. 2. Ed. by R. Vossen and M. Bechhaus-Gerst. Berlin: D. Reimer.

——. 1989. The Undefining of Oral Tradition. *Ethnohistory* 36, 1: 9–18.

Cohen, David W., and E. S. Atieno Odhiambo. 1989. *Siaya: The Historical Anthropology of an African Landscape.* London: James Currey; Athens: Ohio University Press.

Cohen, Ronald. 1978. Ethnicity: Problem and Focus in Anthropology. *Annual Review of Anthropology* 7: 379–403.

Collinwood, R. G. 1946. *The Idea of History.* Oxford: Clarendon Press.

Comaroff, John L. 1987. Of Totemism and Ethnicity: Consciousness, Practice and the Signs of Inequality. *Ethnos* 52, 3/4: 301–22.

Cooper, Robert L. 1982. *Language Spread: Studies in Diffusion and Social Change.* Bloomington, IN: Indiana University Press.

Coquery-Vidrovitch, Catherine. 1975. Research on an African Mode of Production. *Critique of Anthropology*, 4/5: 38–71.

Corrigan, Philip, and Derek Sayer. 1985. *The Great Arch: English State Formation as Cultural Revolution*. Oxford: Blackwell.

Crazzolara, J. P. 1937. The Lwoo People. *Uganda Journal* 5, 1: 1–21.

——. 1938. *A Study of the Acooli Language: Grammar and Vocabulary*. London: Oxford University Press.

——. 1950, 1951, 1954. *The Lwoo*. 3 vols. Verona: Editrice Nigrizia.

——. 1960. Notes on the Lango-Omiru and on the Labwoor and Nyakwai. *Anthropos* 55: 174–214.

——. 1969. The Hamitess — Who Are They? *Uganda Journal* 33, 1: 41–48.

——. n.d. The Madi Role in the History of Eastern Central Africa, Including Uganda. Ed. by M. Posnansky. Unpublished ms.

Crummy, Donald, and C. C. Stewart, eds. 1981a. *Modes of Production in Africa: The Precolonial Era*. Beverly Hills, CA: Sage.

——. 1981b. The Poverty of Precolonial Africa Historiography. In *Modes of Production in Africa: The Precolonial Era*. Ed. by D. Crummy and C. C. Stewart. Beverly Hills, CA: Sage.

Curley, Alberta C. 1971. Social Process: Clanship and Neighborhood in Lango District, Uganda. M.A. thesis, Sacramento State College.

Curtin, Philip D. et al., eds. 1978. *African History*. Boston: Little Brown.

Dale, I. R. 1954. Forest Spread and Climate Change in Uganda during the Christian Era. *Empire Forestry Review* 33: 23–29.

David, Nicholas. 1982. Prehistory and Historical Linguistics in Central Africa. In *The Archaeological and Linguistic Reconstruction of African History*. Ed. by C. Ehret and M. Posnansky. Berkeley: University of California Press.

——. 1983. The Archaeological Context of Nilotic Expansion: A Survey of the Holocene Archaeology of East Africa and the Southern Sudan. In *Nilotic Studies: Proceedings of the International Symposium on Languages and History of the Nilotic Peoples*, vol. 1. Ed. by R. Vossen and M. Bechhaus-Gerst. Berlin: D. Reimer.

Davidson, Basil. 1989. *Modern Africa*. 2nd ed. London: Longman.

Dawkins, H. C. 1954. The Northern Province Mountains: Speculation on Climate and Vegetation History. *Uganda Journal* 18, 1: 54–64.

Delius, Peter. 1983. *This Land Belongs to Us: The Pedi Polity, the Boers and the British in the Nineteenth Century Transvaal*. Johannesburg: Ravan Press.

Dennison, Norman. 1977. Language Death or Language Suicide? *Journal of the Sociology of Language* 12: 13–23.

Doornbos, Martin. 1988. The Uganda Crisis and the National Question. In *Uganda Now: Between Decay and Development*. Ed. by H. B. Hansen and M. Twaddle. London: James Currey; Athens: Ohio University Press.

Dorian, Nancy C. 1981. *Language Death: The Life Cycle of a Scottish Gaelic Dialect*. Philadelphia: University of Pennsylvania Press.

Driberg, J. H. 1923. *The Lango: A Nilotic Tribe of Uganda*. London: T. Fisher Unwin.

Dupre, G., and P. P. Rey. 1973. Reflections on the Pertinence of a Theory of the History of Exchange. *Economy and Society* 2, 2: 144–57.

Dwyer, John O. 1972. The Acholi of Uganda: Adjustment to Imperialism. Ph.D. diss., Columbia University.

East African Meteorological Department. 1961. *10% and 20% Probability Maps of Annual Rainfall in East Africa.* Nairobi: East African High Commission.

Eastman, Carol M., and Thomas C. Reese. 1981. Associated Language: How Language and Ethnicity Are Related. *General Linguistics* 21, 2: 109–16.

Edmonds, Keith. 1988. Crisis Management: The Lessons for Africa from Obote's Second Term. In *Uganda Now: Between Decay and Development.* Ed. by H. B. Hansen and M. Twaddle. London: James Currey; Athens: Ohio University Press.

Ehret, Christopher. 1967. Cattle-Keeping and Milking in Eastern and Southern African History: The Linguistic Evidence. *Journal of African History* 8, 1: 1–17.

——. 1968. Sheep and Central Sudanic Peoples in Southern Africa. *Journal of African History* 9, 2: 213–21.

——. 1971. *Southern Nilotic History: Linguistic Approaches to the Study of the Past.* Evanston, IL: Northwestern University Press.

——. 1973. Patterns of Bantu and Central Sudanic Settlement in Central and Southern Africa (ca. 1000 B.C.–500 A.D.). *Transafrican Journal of History* 3: 1–71.

——. 1974a. Agricultural History in Central and Southern Africa, ca. 1000 B.C. to A.D. 500. *Transafrican Journal of History* 4: 1–25.

——. 1974b. *Ethiopians and East Africans: The Problem of Contacts.* Nairobi: East African Publishing House.

Ehret, Christopher, et al. 1974. Some Thoughts on the Early History of the Nile-Congo Watershed. *Ufahamu* 5, 2: 85–112.

Elmendorf, William W. 1981. Last Speakers and Language Change: Two California Cases. *Anthropological Linguistics* 23, 1: 36–49.

Emin Pasha. 1962. The Diaries of Emin Pasha—Extracts 4. Trans. and ed. by John Gray. *Uganda Journal* 26, 2: 121–39.

——. 1963. The Diaries of Emin Pasha—Extracts 5. Trans. and ed. by John Gray. *Uganda Journal* 27, 1: 1–13.

——. 1964. The Diaries of Emin Pasha—Extracts 7. Trans. and ed. by John Gray. *Uganda Journal* 28, 1: 75–97.

Fage, John. 1978. *A History of Africa.* New York: Knopf.

Feierman, Steven. 1974. *The Shambaa Kingdom: A History.* Madison: University of Wisconsin Press.

Fischer, David H. 1970. *Historians' Fallacies: Toward a Logic of Historical Thought.* New York: Harper and Row.

Fishman, Joshua A. 1964. Language Maintenance and Language Shift as a Field of Enquiry. *Linguistics* 9: 32–70.

——. 1972a. Language Maintenance and Language Shift. In *The Sociology of Language: An Interdisciplinary Social Science Approach to Language in Society.* Ed. by J. Fishman. Rowley, MA: Newbury House.

——. 1972b. Language Maintenance and Language Shift. In *Language in Sociocultural Change.* Ed. by J. Fishman. Stanford, CA: Stanford University Press.

——. 1977. The Spread of English as a New Perspective for the Study of "Language Maintenance and Language Shift." In *The Spread of English*. Ed. by J. Fishman, R. L. Cooper, and A. W. Conrad. Rowley, MA: Newbury House.

———. 1985. Language Maintenance and Ethnicity. In *The Rise and Fall of the Ethnic Revival: Perspectives on Language and Ethnicity*. Ed. by J. Fishman. The Hague: Mouton.

Freund, Bill. 1984. *The Making of Contemporary Africa: The Development of African Society since 1800*. Bloomington: Indiana University Press.

Fried, Morton. 1966. On the Concepts of "Tribe" and "Tribal Society." *Transactions of the New York Academy of Sciences*, 28, 4: 527–40.

———. 1975. *The Notion of Tribe*. Menlo Park, CA: Cummings Publishing.

Gal, Susan. 1979. *Language Shift: Social Determinants of Linguistic Change in Bilingual Austria*. New York: Academic Press.

Garry, A. M. 1971a. The Settlement of Pajule and the Failure of Palwo Centralization. Seminar paper, Department of History, Makerere University, MSP/ 7/ 1971/ 72.

———. 1971b. Ethnicity and Change in a Group of Central Acholi Kingdoms — The Importance of Symbol and Ritual as a Key to Understanding Historical Processes. Paper presented at the Universities of East Africa Social Science Conference, Makerere University.

———. 1972a. Palace Gates — No Admission. Unpublished ms.

———. 1972b. Assimilation and Change among the People of the Okaka Plains, 1680–1930. M.A. thesis, Makerere University.

———. 1976. Pajule: The Failure of Palwo Centralization. In *The Central Lwo during the Aconya*. Ed. by J. M. Onyango-ku-Odongo and J. B. Webster. Nairobi: East African Literature Bureau.

Girling, F. K. 1960. *The Acholi of Uganda*. London: Her Majesty's Stationery Office.

Godelier, Maurice. 1977a. *Perspectives in Marxist Anthropology*. Cambridge: Cambridge University Press.

———. 1977b. The Concept of "Tribe": A Crisis Involving Merely a Concept or the Empirical Foundations of Anthropology Itself? In *Perspectives in Marxist Anthropology*. Ed. by M. Godelier. Cambridge: Cambridge University Press.

Goody, Jack. 1966. Introduction to *Succession to High Office*. Ed. by J. Goody. Cambridge: Cambridge University Press.

———. 1968. *Literacy in Traditional Societies*. Cambridge: Cambridge University Press.

———. 1971. *Technology, Tradition and the State in Africa*. London: Oxford University Press.

———. 1972. The Evolution of the Family. In *Household and Family in Past Time*. Ed. by P. Laslett with the assistance of R. Wall. Cambridge: Cambridge University Press.

Gray, J. M. 1948. Rwot Ochama of Payera. *Uganda Journal* 12, 2: 125–27.

———. 1951. Acholi History, 1860–1901, Part 1. *Uganda Journal* 15, 2: 121–43.

———. 1952. Acholi History, 1850–1901, Part 2. *Uganda Journal* 16, 1: 32–50.

Gray, Richard. 1961. *A History of the Southern Sudan, 1839–1889*. London: Oxford University Press.

Grove, E. T. N. 1919. Customs of the Acholi. *Sudan Notes and Records* 2, 3: 157–82.

Gulliver, Pamela, and P. H. Gulliver. 1953. *The Central Nilo-Hamites*. Ethnographic Survey of Africa: East Central Africa, vol. 7. London: International African Institute.

Gumperz, John J., ed. 1982. *Language and Social Identity*. Cambridge: Cambridge University Press.

Guy, Jeff. 1979. *The Destruction of the Zulu Kingdom: The Civil War in Zululand, 1879–1884*. London: Longman.

———. 1987. Analysing Pre-Capitalist Societies in Southern Africa. *Journal of Southern African Studies* 14, 1: 18–37.

———. 1992. Debating Ethnicity in South Africa. Paper presented at the Project on Contemporary Political Violence in Natal; Conference on Ethnicity, Society and Conflict in Natal, Pietermaritzburg.

Hall, Martin. 1984. The Burden of Tribalism: The Social Context of Southern African Iron Age Studies. *American Antiquity* 49: 455–67.

Hamilton, Carolyn, and John Wright. 1984. The Making of the Lala: Ethnicity, Ideology and Class-Formation in a Precolonial Context. Paper presented at the University of the Witwatersrand History Workshop.

Hammond-Tooke, W. D. 1985. Descent Groups, Chiefdoms and South African Historiography. *Journal of Southern African Studies* 11, 2: 305–19.

Hansen, Holger B. 1977. *Ethnicity and Military Rule in Uganda*. Uppsala: Scandanavian Institute of African Studies.

Hansen, Holger B., and Michael Twaddle, eds. 1988a. *Uganda Now: Between Decay and Development*. London: James Currey; Athens: Ohio University Press.

———. 1988b. Introduction to *Uganda Now: Between Decay and Development*. Ed. by H. B. Hansen and M. Twaddle. London: James Currey; Athens: Ohio University Press.

Harik, I. F. 1972. The Ethnic Revolution and Political Integration in the Middle East. *International Journal of Middle East Studies* 3: 303–23.

Harlan, J. R., J. M. J. deWet, and A. B. L. Stemler, eds. 1976. *Origins of African Plant Domestication*. The Hague: Mouton.

Harries, Patrick. 1983. History, Ethnicity and the Ingwavuma Land Deal: The Zulu Northern Frontier in the Nineteenth Century. *Journal of Natal and Zulu History* 6: 1–27.

———. 1988. The Roots of Ethnicity: Discourse and the Politics of Language Construction in Southeast Africa. *African Affairs* 346: 25–52.

———. 1989. Exclusion, Classification and Internal Colonialism: The Emergence of Ethnicity among the Tsonga-Speakers of South Africa. In *The Creation of Tribalism in Southern Africa*. Ed. by L. Vail. Berkeley: University of California Press.

Harris, Marvin. 1973. *The Rise of Anthropological Theory: A History of Theories of Culture*. New York: Crowell.

———. 1975. *Culture, People, Nature: An Introduction to General Anthropology*. 2nd ed. New York: Crowell.

Hartwig, Gerald W. 1974. Oral Data and Its Historical Function in East Africa. *International Journal of African Historical Studies* 7, 3: 468–79.

Hayes, Grahame, and Gerhard Maré. 1992. Ethnicity: Between the Real and the

Imagined. Paper presented at the Project on Contemporary Political Conflict in Natal; Conference on Ethnicity, Society and Conflict in Natal, Pietermaritzburg.

Hechter, Michael. 1975. *Internal Colonialism: The Celtic Fringe in British National Development, 1536–1966.* Berkeley: University of California Press.

Helm, June, ed. 1968. *Essays on the Problem of Tribe: Proceedings of the Annual Spring Meetings of the American Ethnological Society.* Seattle: University of Washington Press.

Henige, David P. 1972. K. W.'s Nyoro Kinglist: Oral Tradition or the Result of Applied Research? Paper presented at the African Studies Association annual meeting, Philadelphia.

———. 1974a. Reflections on Early Interlacustrine Chronology: An Essay in Source Criticism. *Journal of African History* 15, 1: 27–46.

———. 1974b. *The Chronology of Oral Tradition: Quest for a Chimera.* Oxford: Clarendon Press.

———. 1981. Review of *Chronology, Migration and Drought in Interlacustrine Africa,* ed. by J. B. Webster. *International Journal of African Historical Studies* 14, 2: 359–63.

———. 1982. *Oral Historiography.* London: Longman.

Herring, Ralph S. 1971. The Origins and Development of the Nyakwai. Seminar paper, Department of History, Makerere University, MSP/24/71/72.

———. 1973. Centralization, Stratification, and Incorporation: Case Studies from Northeastern Uganda. *Canadian Journal of African Studies* 7, 3: 497–514.

———. 1974a. Hydrology and Chronology: The Nile River as an Aid to Dating Interlacustrine Chronology. Unpublished ms.

———. 1974b. A History of the Labwor hills. Ph.D. diss., University of California, Santa Barbara.

———. 1974c. The View from Mt. Otuke: A Look at the Migrations of the Lango Omiro. Paper presented at the Canadian Association of African Studies annual meeting, Halifax.

———. 1976a. The Influence of Climate on the Migrations of the Central and Southern Luo. *Kenya Historical Review* 4, 1: 35–62.

———. 1976b. The Nyakwai: On the Borders of the "Lwo" World. In *The Central Lwo during the Aconya.* Ed. by J. M. Onyango-ku-Odongo and J. B. Webster. Nairobi: East African Literature Bureau.

———. 1978. Political Development in Eastern Africa: The Luo Case Reexamined. *Kenya Historical Review* 6, 1/2: 126–45.

———. 1979a. Hydrology and Chronology: The Rodah Nilometer as an Aid in Dating Interlacustrine History. In *Chronology, Migration and Drought in Interlacustrine Africa.* Ed. by J. B. Webster. New York: Africana.

———. 1979b. The View from Mt. Otuke: Migrations of the Lango Omiro. In *Chronology, Migration and Drought in Interlacustrine Africa.* Ed. by J. B. Webster. New York: Africana.

Herring, Ralph, David W. Cohen, and B. A. Ogot. 1984. The Construction of Dominance: The Strategies of Selected Luo Groups in Uganda and Kenya. In *State Formation in Eastern Africa.* Ed. by A. I. Salim. Nairobi: Heinemann.

d'Hertefelt, Marcel. 1971. *Les Clans du Rwanda Ancien: Elements d'Ethnosociologie et d'Ethnohistorie.* Terruren, Belgium. Musee Royal d'Afrique Centrale. Annales, 8, 70.

Hill, Jane H. 1978. Language Death, Language Contact, and Language Evolution. In *Approaches to Language: Anthropological Issues.* Ed. by W. C. McCormack and S. A. Wurm. The Hague: Mouton.

Hindess, Barry, and Paul Hirst. 1975. *Pre-Capitalist Modes of Production.* London and Boston: Routledge and Kegan Paul.

Higgins, S. 1966. Acholi Birth Customs. *Uganda Journal* 30, 2: 175–82.

Hobsbawn, Eric. 1971. From Social History to the History of Society. *Daedalus* 100: 20–45.

Hogg, Michael A., and Dominic Abrams. 1988. *Social Identifications: A Social Psychology of Intergroup Relations and Group Processes.* London: Routledge.

Horowitz, Donald L. 1985. *Ethnic Groups in Conflict.* Berkeley: University of California Press.

Iliffe, John. 1979. *A Modern History of Tanganyika.* Cambridge: Cambridge University Press.

Jameson, J. D., ed. 1970. *Agriculture in Uganda.* 2nd ed. London: Oxford University Press. (Revision of J. D. Tothill, *Agriculture in Uganda,* Oxford, 1940.)

Jenkins, Keith. 1991. *Rethinking History.* London: Routledge.

Jewsiewicki, Bogumil. 1981a. Lineage Mode of Production: Social Inequalities in Equatorial Central Africa. In *Modes of Production in Africa: The Precolonial Era.* Ed. by D. Crummey and C. C. Stewart. Beverly Hills, CA: Sage.

———. 1981b. The Product of History and Social Conscience, or How to "Civilize" the Other. *History in Africa* 8: 75–87.

———. 1989. The Formation of the Political Culture of Ethnicity in the Belgian Congo, 1920–1959. In *The Creation of Tribalism in Southern Africa.* Ed. by L. Vail. Berkeley: University of California Press.

Kamau, C. 1973. Lake Levels in the Rift Valley. Seminar paper, Department of History, University of Nairobi.

Kanyeihamba, George. 1988. Power That Rode Naked through Uganda under the Muzzle of a Gun. In *Uganda Now: Between Decay and Development.* Ed. by H. B. Hansen and M. Twaddle. London: James Currey; Athens: Ohio University Press.

Karugire, Samwiri. 1970. Institutions of Government in the Pre-Colonial Kingdom of Nkore. Seminar paper, Department of History, Makerere University, MSP/ 2/70/71.

———. 1971. *A History of the Kingdom of Nkore in Western Uganda to 1896.* Oxford: Clarendon Press.

Kellas, James G. 1991. *The Politics of Nationalism and Ethnicity.* New York: St. Martin's Press.

Kitching, Alfred L. 1912. *On the Backwaters of the Nile.* New York: C. Scribner's.

Klein, Martin. 1978. Review of *Cambridge History of Africa. Vol. 5: c. 1790 to c. 1870. Journal of African History* 19, 2: 275–77.

Kopytoff, Igor, ed. 1986a. *The African Frontier: The Reproduction of Traditional African Societies.* Bloomington: Indiana University Press.

——. 1986b. Introduction to *The African Frontier: The Reproduction of Traditional African Societies*. Ed. by I. Kopytoff. Bloomington: Indiana University Press.

Lamb, H. H. 1982. *Climate, History and the Modern World*. New York: Methuen.

Lambert, Richard, and Barbara Freed, eds. 1982. *The Loss of Language Skills*. Rowley, MA: Newbury House.

Lamphear, John E. 1970. The Inter-Relationships Which Brought about the Jie Genesis. Seminar paper, Department of History, Makerere University, MSP/5/70/71.

——. 1971. The Origin and Dispersal of the Central Paranilotes. Seminar paper, Department of History, Makerere University, MSP/19/71/72.

——. 1972. The Development of Jie Nationalism. Research seminar paper, School of Oriental and African Studies, University of London.

——. 1973. The Oral History of the Jie of Uganda. Ph.D. diss., University of London.

——. 1974. When the Ngitome Speared Their Oxen: Problems in Reconstructing the Chronology of the History of the Jie. Paper presented at the Canadian Association of African Studies annual meeting, Halifax, and the African Studies Association annual meeting, Chicago.

——. 1976. *The Oral History of the Jie of Uganda*. Oxford: Clarendon Press.

——. 1986. The Persistence of Hunting and Gathering in a "Pastoral" World. *Sprache und Geschichte in Afrika (SUGIA)* 7, 2: 227–65.

Langlands, B. W. 1968. Factors in the Changing Form, Location and Distribution of Settlements, with Particular Reference to East Acholi. In *Essays on the Settlement Geography of East Acholi*. Ed. by B. W. Langlands and L. E. C. Obol-Owit. Occasional Paper no. 7, Department of Geography, Makerere University. Kampala.

——. 1971. *The Population Geography of Acholi District*. Occasional Paper no. 30, Department of Geography, Makerere University. Kampala.

Lamphear, John E., and J. B. Webster. 1971. The Jie-Acholi War: Oral Evidence from Two Sides of the Battle Front. *Uganda Journal* 35, 1:23–42.

Langlands, B. W., and L. E. C. Obol-Owit. 1968. *Essays on the Settlement Geography of East Acholi*. Occasional Paper no. 7, Department of Geography, Makerere University. Kampala.

Laslett, Peter. 1972. *Household and Family in Past Time*. With the assistance of Richard Wall. Cambridge: Cambridge University Press.

Legesse, Asmarom. 1973. *Gada: Three Approaches to the Study of an African Society*. New York: Free Press.

Leys, Colin. 1967. *Politicians and Policies: An Essay on Politics in Acholi, Uganda, 1962–65*. Nairobi: East African Publishing House.

——. 1975. *Underdevelopment in Kenya: The Political Economy of Neo-Coloninalism*. Berkeley: University of California Press.

Lloyd, Albert B. 1907. *Uganda to Khartoum: Life and Adventure on the Upper Nile*. London: T. Unwin.

Lonsdale, John. 1977. When Did the Gusii (or any Other Group) Become a "Tribe"? — A Review Essay. *Kenya Historical Review* 5, 1: 123–33.

——. 1981. States and Social Processes in Africa: A Historiographical Survey. *African Studies Review* 24, 2/3: 139–225.

Low, D. A. 1988. The Dislocated Polity. In *Uganda Now: Between Decay and Development.* Ed. by H. B. Hansen and M. Twaddle. London: James Currey; Athens: Ohio University Press.

Low, D. A., and John Lonsdale. 1976. Introduction: Towards the New Order, 1945–1963. In *History of East Africa,* vol. 3. Ed. by D. A. Low and A. Smith. Oxford: Clarendon Press.

Lutara, W. O. 1956. Agriculture in Acholi. Unpublished paper.

MacMaster, David N. 1962. *A Subsistence Crop Geography of Uganda.* Bude, England: Geographical Publications.

Mafeje, Archie. 1971. The Ideology of "Tribalism." *Journal of Modern African Studies* 9, 2: 253–61.

Malandra, Alfred. 1939. The Ancestral Shrine of the Acholi. *Uganda Journal* 7, 1: 27–43.

Malinowski, Bronislaw. 1922. *Argonauts of the Western Pacific: An Account of Native Enterprise and Adventure in the Archipelagoes of Melanesian New Guinea.* London: Routledge and Kegan Paul; New York: Dutton.

Mamdani, Mahmood. 1976. *Politics and Class Formation in Uganda.* New York: Monthly Review Press.

——. 1983. *Imperialism and Fascism in Uganda.* Nairobi: Heinemann.

Maré, Gerhard. 1992. *Brothers Born of Warrior Blood: Politics and Ethnicity in South Africa.* Johannesburg: Ravan Press.

Marks, Shula. 1989. Patriotism, Patriarchy and Purity: Natal and the Politics of Zulu Ethnic Consciousness. In *The Creation of Tribalism in Southern Africa.* Ed. by L. Vail. Berkeley: University of California Press.

Marks, Shula, and Anthony Atmore. 1970. The Problems of the Nguni: An Examination of the Ethnic and Linguistic Situation in South Africa before the Mfecane. In *Language and History in Africa.* Ed. by D. Dalby. New York: Africana Publishing.

——, eds. 1980. *Economy and Society in Pre-Industrial South Africa.* London: Longman.

Marks, Shula, and Richard Rathbone, eds. 1982. *Industrialisation and Social Change in South Africa: African Class Formation, Culture and Consciousness, 1870–1930.* London: Longman.

Marks, Stuart A. 1976. *Large Mammals and a Brave People: Subsistence Hunters in Zambia.* Seattle: University of Washington Press.

Mauss, Marcel. 1954 (orig. pub. 1925). *The Gift: Forms and Functions of Exchange in Archaic Societies.* Glencoe, IL: Free Press.

Mayer, Philip. 1951. *Two Studies in Applied Anthropology in Kenya.* London: Her Majesty's Stationery Office.

Meillassoux, Claude. 1964. *L'anthropologie Economiques des Gouro de Cote d'Ivoire.* Paris: Mouton.

——. 1978a. "The Economy" in Agricultural Self-Sustaining Societies: A Preliminary Analysis. In *Relations of Production: Marxist Approaches to Economic Anthropology.* Ed. by D. Seddon. London: Cass.

———. 1987b. The Social Organization of the Peasantry: The Economic Basis of Kinship. In *Relations of Production: Marxist Approaches to Economic Anthropology*. Ed. by D. Seddon. London: Cass.

———. 1980. *Maidens, Meal and Money: Capitalism and the Domestic Community*. Cambridge: Cambridge University Press.

Menkhaus, Kenneth. 1989. Rural Transformation and the Roots of Underdevelopment in Somalia's Lower Jubba Valley. Ph.D. diss., University of South Carolina.

Menzies, I. R. 1954. A Pagan Harvest Thanksgiving in Acholi District. *Uganda Journal* 18, 2: 182–85.

Merrell, James H. 1989. *The Indians' New World: Catawbas and Their Neighbors from European Contact through the Era of Removal*. Chapel Hill: University of North Carolina Press.

Middleton, John. 1965. *The Lugbara of Uganda*. New York: Holt, Rinehart and Winston.

Miller, Joseph C., ed. 1980a. *The African Past Speaks: Essays in Oral Tradition and History*. Hamden, CT: Archon.

———. 1980b. Introduction: Listening for the African Past. In *The African Past Speaks: Essays in Oral Tradition and History*. Ed. by J. C. Miller. Hamden, CT: Archon.

———. 1982. The Significance of Drought, Disease and Famine in the Agriculturally Marginal Zones of West-Central Africa. *Journal of African History* 23, 1: 17–61.

Milroy, Lesley. 1980. *Language and Social Networks*. Baltimore, MD: University Park Press.

Montville, Joseph V. 1990. *Conflict and Peacemaking in Multiethnic Societies*. Toronto: D. C. Heath.

Mudoola, Dan. 1988. Political Transitions since Idi Amin: A Study in Political Pathology. In *Uganda Now: Between Decay and Development*. Ed. by H. B. Hansen and M. Twaddle. London: James Currey; Athens: Ohio University Press.

Nabudere, Dani Wadada. 1980. *Imperialism and Revolution in Uganda*. London: Onyx Press.

———. 1988. External and Internal Factors in Uganda's Continuing Crisis. In *Uganda Now: Between Decay and Development*. Ed. by H. B. Hansen and M. Twaddle. London: James Currey; Athens: Ohio University Press.

Neale, Caroline. 1985. *Writing "Independent" History: African Historiography, 1960–1980*. Westport, CT: Greenwood Press.

Newbury, Catharine. 1988. *The Cohesion of Oppression: Clientship and Ethnicity in Rwanda, 1860–1960*. New York: Columbia University Press.

Newbury, David. 1969. Dating the Acholi, Shot Down or Stood Up? Unpublished ms.

———. 1991. *Kings and Clans: Ijwi Island and the Lake Kivu Rift, 1780–1840*. Madison: University of Wisconsin Press.

Nuttall, Tim. 1992. "Segregation with Honour"? The Making of Zulu Ethnicities in Natal during the 1930s. Paper presented at the Project on Contemporary

Political Conflict in Natal; Conference on Ethnicity, Society and Conflict in Natal, Pietermaritzburg.

Nyakatura, J. W. 1973. *Anatomy of an African Kingdom: A History of Bunyoro-Kitara*. Ed. by G. N. Uzoigwe. Trans. by T. Muganwa. New York: Nok Publishers.

Nyeko, Balam. n.d. The Acholi of Northern Uganda during the Nineteenth Century. Seminar paper, Department of History, Makerere University.

Obbo, Christine. 1988. What Went Wrong in Uganda. In *Uganda Now: Between Decay and Development*. Ed. by H. B. Hansen and M. Twaddle. London: James Currey; Athens: Ohio University Press.

Obol-Owit, L. E. C. 1968. The Changing Pattern of Settlement at Omia Anyima in East Acholi. In *Essays on the Settlement Geography of East Acholi*. Ed. by B. W. Langlands and L. E. C. Obol-Owit. Occasional Paper no. 7, Department of Geography, Makerere University. Kampala.

Ocaya, A. 1959. A Study in the Geography of Atyak, Acholi. Unpublished essay, Department of Geography, Makerere University.

Ocheng, D. O. 1955. Land Tenure in Acholi. *Uganda Journal* 19, 1: 57–61.

Ochieng, William. 1975. *A Pre-Colonial History of the Gusii of Western Kenya*. Nairobi: East African Literature Bureau.

Ocholla-Ayayo, A. B. C. 1976. *Traditional Ideology and Ethics among the Southern Luo*. Uppsala: Scandanavian Institute of African Studies.

——. 1980. *The Luo Culture: A Reconstruction of the Material Culture Patterns of a Traditional African Society*. Wiesbaden: Steiner.

Odhiambo, E. S. Atieno, T. I. Owusu, and J. F. M. Williams. 1977. *A History of East Africa*. Nairobi and London: Longman.

Odongo, J. M. Onyango-ku-. n.d. [1960s]. Interrupted African Culture and Civilization. Unpublished ms.

——. 1976. The Early History of the Central Lwo. In *The Central Lwo during the Aconya*. Ed. by J. M. Onyango-ku-Odongo and J. B. Webster. Nairobi: East African Literature Bureau.

Odongo, J. M. Onyango-ku- and J. B. Webster, eds. 1976a. *The Central Lwo during the Aconya*. Nairobi: East African Literature Bureau.

——. 1976b. Chronology for the Lwo-Speaking Peoples: Introduction. In *The Central Lwo during the Aconya*. Ed. by J. M. Onyango-ku-Odongo and J. B. Webster. Nairobi: East African Literature Bureau.

Odyomo, Peter. n.d. Consensus and Leadership in the Alido Confederacy in Nineteenth Century Lango. Unpublished paper (intended for inclusion in *A History of Uganda*, vol. 2).

Ogot, B. A. 1964. Kinship and Statelessness among the Nilotes. In *The Historian in Tropical Africa*. Ed. by J. Vansina, R. Mauny, and L. V. Thomas. London: Oxford University Press.

——. 1967a. *History of the Southern Luo*. Nairobi: East African Publishing House.

——. 1967b. The Impact of the Nilotes. In *The Middle Age of African History*. Ed. by R. Oliver. London: Oxford University Press.

——, ed. 1974 (revised ed. of Ogot and Kieran, 1968). *Zamani: A Survey of East African History*. Nairobi: East African Publishing House.

Ogot, B. A., and J. A. Kieran, eds. 1968. *Zamani: A Survey of East African History.* Nairobi: East African Publishing House.

Okeny, Kenneth. 1982a. State Formation in Northern Acholi, c. 1679–1850. Seminar paper, Department of History, University of Nairobi.

———. 1982b. State Formation in Acholi: The Emergence of Obbo, Pajok, and Panyikwara States c. 1679–1914. M.A. thesis, University of Nairobi.

Okot p'Bitek. 1963. The Concept of Jok among the Acholi and Lango. *Uganda Journal* 27, 1: 15–30.

———. 1965. Acholi Concept of Fate—Woko, Wilobo and Rupiny. *Uganda Journal* 29, 1: 85–93.

———. 1971. *Religion of the Central Luo.* Nairobi: East African Literature Bureau.

———. n.d.[a]. Otole—The War Dance, and Bwola—The Chief's Dance. Unpublished ms.

———. n.d.[b]. Poetry as a Political Medium—A Study of Political Songs in Acholiland. Unpublished ms.

Oliver, Roland. 1963. Discernible Developments in the Interior c. 1500–1840. In *History of East Africa,* vol. 1. Ed. by R. Oliver and G. Mathew. Oxford: Clarendon Press.

———. 1977. The East African Interior. In *Cambridge History of Africa,* vol. 3. Ed. by R. Oliver. Cambridge: Cambridge University Press.

———. 1983. The Nilotic Contribution to Bantu Africa. In *Nilotic Studies: Proceedings of the International Symposium on Languages and History of the Nilotic Peoples,* vol. 2. Ed. by R. Vossen and M. Bechhaus-Gerst. Berlin: D. Reimer.

Olzak, Susan, and Joane Nagel. 1986. Introduction—Competitive Ethnic Relations: An Overview. In *Competitive Ethnic Relations.* Ed. by S. Olzak and J. Nagel. New York: Academic Press.

Owot, P. M. L. 1976. Padibe during the Aconya: 1400–1900. In *The Central Lwo during the Aconya.* Ed. by J. M. Onyango-ku-Odongo and J. B. Webster. Nairobi: East African Literature Bureau.

Papstein, Robert. 1989. From Ethnic Identity to Tribalism: The Upper Zambezi Region of Zambia, 1830–1981. In *The Creation of Tribalism in Southern Africa.* Ed. by L. Vail. Berkeley: University of California Press.

Parsons, D. J. 1960a. *The Systems of Agriculture Practised in Uganda. No. 1. Introduction and Teso Systems.* Uganda Protectorate, Department of Agriculture, Memoir of the Research Division, Series 3.

———. 1960b. *The Systems of Agriculture Practised in Uganda. No. 3. The Northern Systems.* Uganda Protectorate, Department of Agriculture, Memoirs of the Research Division, Series 3.

Patterson, K. David. 1969. A Revised Classification of the Central Sudanic Languages. Unpublished ms.

Peires, J. B. 1982. *The House of Phalo: A History of the Xhosa in the Days of Their Independence.* Berkeley: University of California Press.

Pender-Cudlip, Patrick. 1972. Oral Traditions and Anthropological Analysis: Some Contemporary Myths. *Azania* 7: 3–24.

———. 1973. Encyclopedic Informants and Early Interlacustrine History. *International Journal of African Historical Studies* 6, 2: 198–210.

Phillipson, D. W. 1977. *The Later Pre-History of Eastern and Southern Africa*. London: Heinemann.

Polanyi, Karl. 1944. *The Great Transformation*. New York: Farrar and Rinehart.

Polanyi, Karl, C. M. Arensberg, and H. Pearson, eds. 1957. *Trade and Market in the Early Empires: Economics in History and Theory*. Glencoe, IL: Free Press.

Portelli, Alessandro. 1981. The Peculiarities of Oral History. *History Workshop Journal* 12: 96–107.

Posnansky, Merrick. 1966. Kingship, Archaeology and Historical Myth. *Uganda Journal* 30, 1: 1–12.

Postlethwaite, J. R. P. 1947. *I Look Back*. London: T. V. Boardman.

Pumphrey, M. E. C. 1941. The Shilluk Tribe. *Sudan Notes and Records* 24, 1: 1–45.

Ra'anan, Uri. 1990. The Nation-State Fallacy. In *Conflict and Peacemaking in Multiethnic Societies*. Ed. by J. Montville. Lexington, MA: Lexington Books.

Ranger, Terrence O. 1979. European Attitudes and African Realities: The Rise and Fall of the Matola Chiefs of South-East Tanzania. *Journal of African History* 20, 1: 63–82.

——. 1983. The Invention of Tradition in Colonial Africa. In *The Invention of Tradition*. Ed. by E. Hobsbawm and T. O. Ranger. Cambridge: Cambridge University Press.

——. 1989. Missionaries, Migrants and the Manyika: The Invention of Ethnicity in Zimbabwe. In *The Creation of Tribalism in Southern Africa*. Ed. by L. Vail. Berkeley: University of California Press.

Rey, P. P. 1975. The Lineage Mode of Production. *Critique of Anthropology* 3: 27–79.

Rindler Schjerve, Rosita. 1987. Ethnolinguistic and Interpretive Concepts in Explaining Language Shift. Unpublished paper.

Ringer, Benjamin B., and Elinor R. Lawless. 1989. *Race-Ethnicity and Society*. New York: Routledge.

Roberts, Allen F. 1989. History, Ethnicity and Change in the "Christian Kingdom" of Southeastern Zaire. In *The Creation of Tribalism in Southern Africa*. Ed. by L. Vail. Berkeley: University of California Press.

Roberts, Andrew D. 1962. The Sub-Imperialism of the Baganda. *Journal of African History* 3, 3: 435–50.

Roosens, Eugene E. 1989. *Creating Ethnicity: The Process of Ethnogenesis*. London: Sage.

Rothchild, Donald, and Victor Olorunsolo, eds. 1983. *State Versus Ethnic Claims: African Political Dilemmas*. Boulder, CO: Westview.

Rowe, John A. 1988. Islam under Idi Amin: A Case of Deja Vu? In *Uganda Now: Between Decay and Development*. Ed. by H. B. Hansen and M. Twaddle. London: James Currey; Athens: Ohio University Press.

Rowley, J. V. 1940. The Madi of Equatoria Province. *Sudan Notes and Records* 23, 2: 279–94.

Sacks, Karen. 1982. *Sisters and Wives: The Past and Future of Sexual Equality*. Urbana: University of Illinois Press.

Safholm, Per. 1973. *The River-Lakes Nilotes: Politics of an African Tribal Group*. Uppsala: n.p.

Sahlins, Marshall. 1958. *Social Stratification in Polynesia*. Seattle: University of Washington Press.

———. 1968. *Tribesmen*. Englewood Cliffs, NJ: Prentice-Hall.

Sargent, R. A. The Generations of Turmoil and Stress: A Proliferation of States in the Northern Interlacustrine Region, c. 1544–1625. In *Chronology, Migration and Drought in Interlacustrine Africa*. Ed. by J. B. Webster. New York: Africana.

Schweinfurth, Georg A., ed. 1888. *Emin Pasha in Central Africa*. Trans. by R. W. Felkin. London: G. Philip and Son.

Seligman, C. G., and B. Z. Seligman. 1932. *Pagan Tribes of the Nilotic Sudan*. London: G. Routledge and Sons.

Sharp, John. 1980. Can We Study Ethnicity?: A Critique of Fields of Study in South African Anthropology. *Social Dynamics* 6, 1: 1–16.

———. 1988a. Introduction: Constructing Social Reality. In *South African Keywords: The Uses and Abuses of Political Concepts*. Ed. by E. Boonzaier and J. Sharp. Cape Town: David Philip.

———. 1988b. Ethnic Group and Nation: The Apartheid Vision in South Africa. In *South African Keywords: The Uses and Abuses of Political Concepts*. Ed. by E. Boonzaier and J. Sharp. Cape Town: David Philip.

Shaw, Timothy M. 1986. Ethnicity as the Resilient Paradigm for Africa: From the 1960s to the 1980s. *Development and Change* 17: 587–605.

Shinnie, Peter. 1960. Exacavations at Bigo, 1957. *Uganda Journal* 24, 1: 16–28.

Shiroya, J. Okete. 1970. Northwestern Uganda in the 19th Century: Inter-Ethnic Trade. Paper presented at the Universities of East Africa Social Sciences Conference, University of Dar es Salaam.

———. 1971. Inter-Ethnic Relations in Pre-Colonial Northwestern Uganda: The Lugbara and Alur as Assimilators. Seminar paper, Department of History, Makerere University, MSP/15/71/72.

———. 1978. The Lugbara States in the Eighteenth and Nineteenth Centuries. In *State Formation in Eastern Africa*. Ed. by A. I. Salim. Nairobi: Heinemann.

Skalnik, Peter. 1988. Tribe as Colonial Category. In *South African Keywords: The Uses and Abuses of Political Concepts*. Ed. by E. Boonzaier and J. Sharp. Cape Town: David Philip.

Sollors, Werner. 1989. Introduction to *The Invention of Ethnicity*. Ed. by W. Sollors. Oxford: Oxford University Press.

Southall, Aidan V. 1954. Alur Tradition and Its Historical Significance. *Uganda Journal* 18, 2: 137–65.

———. 1956. *Alur Society: A Study in Processes and Types of Domination*. Nairobi: Oxford University Press.

———. 1970. The Illusion of Tribe. In *The Passing of Tribal Man in Africa*. Ed. by P. Gutkind. Leiden: Brill.

———. 1972. Criteria for the Assessment of Lwo History. Seminar paper, Department of History, Makerere University, MSP/9/72/73.

———. 1988. The Recent Political Economy of Uganda. In *Uganda Now: Between Decay and Development*. Ed. by H. B. Hansen and M. Twaddle. London: James Currey; Athens: Ohio University Press.

Spear, Thomas. 1981a. *Kenya's Past: An Introduction to Historical Methodology in Africa*. London: Longman.

——. 1981b. Oral Traditions: Whose History? *History in Africa* 8: 165–81.

——. 1982. *Traditions of Origins and Their Interpretation: The Mijikenda of Kenya*. Athens: Ohio University Press.

——. 1993. Introduction to *Being Maasai: Ethnicity and Identity in East Africa*. Ed. by T. Spear and R. Waller. London: James Currey; Athens: Ohio University Press.

Spear, Thomas, and Richard Waller, eds. 1993. *Being Maasai: Ethnicity and Identity in East Africa*. London: James Currey; Athens: Ohio University Press.

Speke, J. H. 1863. *Journal of the Discovery of the Source of the Nile*. London: J. M. Dent and Company.

Stein, Burton. 1980. *Peasant, State and Society in Medieval South India*. Delhi and New York: Oxford University Press.

Steinhart, Edward I. 1984. The Emergence of Bunyoro: The Tributary Mode of Production and the Formation of the State, 1400–1900. In *State Formation in Eastern Africa*. Ed. by A. I. Salim. Nairobi: Heinemann.

——. 1989. Introduction. *Ethnohistory* 36, 1: 1–8 (Special Issue: Ethnohistory and Africa, ed. by E. I. Steinhart).

Stemler, A. B. L., J. R. Harlan, and J. M. J. deWet. 1975. Caudatum Sorghums and Speakers of Chari-Nile Languages in Africa." *Journal of African History* 16, 2: 161–84.

Sutton, J. E. G. 1974. The Settlement of East Africa. In *Zamani: A Survey of East African History*. 2nd ed. Ed. by B. A. Ogot. Nairobi: East African Publishing House.

Temu, A. J., and Bonaventure Swai. 1981. *Historians and Africanist History: A Critique*. London: Zed Press.

Terray, Emmanual. 1972. *Marxism and Primitive Societies*. Part 2. New York: Monthly Review Press.

——. 1975. Classes and Class Consciousness in the Abrom Kingdom of Gyaman. In *Marxist Analyses and Social Anthropology*. Ed. by M. Bloch. New York: Wiley.

Therborn, Goran. 1980. *The Ideology of Power and the Power of Ideology*. London: NLB.

Thomas, H. B., and R. Scott. 1935. *Uganda*. London: Oxford University Press.

Thompson, E. P. 1978. *The Poverty of Theory and Other Essays*. New York: Monthly Review Press.

Thompson, Richard H. 1989. *Theories of Ethnicity: A Critical Appraisal*. New York: Greenwood Press.

Tonkin, Elizabeth. 1982. Steps to the Redefinition of Oral History: Examples from Africa (Review Article). *Social History* 7, 3: 329–35.

——. 1986. Investigating Oral Tradition. *Journal of African History* 27, 2: 203–13.

——. 1992. *Narrating Our Pasts: The Social Construction of Oral History*. Cambridge: Cambridge University Press.

Tosh, John. 1973. Political Authority among the Langi of Northern Uganda, circa 1800–1939. Ph.D. diss., University of London.

——. 1978a. Lango Agriculture during the Early Colonial Period: Land and Labour in a Cash-Crop Economy. *Journal of African History* 19, 3: 415–39.

——. 1978b. *Clan Leaders and Colonial Chiefs in Lango.* Oxford: Clarendon Press.

——. 1984. *The Pursuit of History: Aims, Methods and New Directions in the Study of Modern History.* London: Longman.

Toussoun, Omar. 1925. *Memoire sur l'Histoire du Nil.* Cairo: L'Institute Francais d'Archeologie Orientale.

Tsitsipis, Lukas D. 1983. Language Shift among the Albanian Speakers of Greece. *Anthropological Linguistics* 25, 3: 288–308.

Turner, Victor W. 1969. *The Ritual Process: Structure and Anti-Structure.* Ithaca, NY: Cornell University Press.

Twaddle, Michael. 1975. Towards an Early History of the East African Interior. *History in Africa* 2: 147–84.

——. 1988. Museveni's Uganda: Notes Towards an Analysis. In *Uganda Now: Between Decay and Development.* Ed. by H. B. Hansen and M. Twaddle. London: James Currey; Athens: Ohio University Press.

——. 1993. *Semei Kakungulu and the Origins of Uganda.* London: James Currey; Athens: Ohio University Press.

Uchendu, Victor C. 1970. Traditional Work Groups in Economic Development. Paper presented at the Universities of East Africa Social Science Conference, University of Dar es Salaam.

Uganda. Lands and Surveys Department. *Atlas of Uganda.* 1st ed., 1962; 2nd ed., 1967.

Uma, F. K. 1971. Acholi-Arab Nubian Relations in the Nineteenth Century. Graduating essay, Department of History, Makerere University.

Usher-Wilson, L. C. 1947. An Acholi Hunt. *Uganda Journal* 11, 1: 30–7.

Vail, Leroy. 1981. Ethnicity, Language and National Unity: The Case of Malawi. In *Working Papers in Southern African Studies,* vol. 2. Ed. by P. Bonner. Johannesburg: African Studies Institute, University of Witwatersrand.

——, ed. 1989a. *The Creation of Tribalism in Southern Africa.* Berkeley: University of California Press.

——. 1989b. Introduction: Ethnicity in Southern African History. In *The Creation of Tribalism in Southern Africa.* Ed. by L. Vail. Berkeley: University of California Press.

Vail, Leroy, and Landeg White. 1989. Tribalism in the Political History of Malawi. In *The Creation of Tribalism in Southern Africa.* Ed. by L. Vail. Berkeley: University of California Press.

van den Berghe, Pierre. 1981. *The Ethnic Phenomenon.* New York: Elsevier.

van Gennep, Arnold. 1960 (orig. pub. 1909). *The Rites of Passage.* Chicago: University of Chicago Press.

van Onselen, Charles. 1982. *Studies in the Social and Economic History of the Witwatersrand, 1886–1914.* Vol. 1. *New Babylon.* Vol. 2. *New Nineveh.* Johannesburg: Ravan Press.

Vansina, Jan. 1965. *Oral Traditions: A Study in Historical Methodology.* Chicago: Aldine.

——. 1972. Once Upon a Time: Oral Traditions as History in Africa. In *Historical Studies Today*. Ed. by F. Gilbert and S. R. Graubard. New York: W. W. Norton.

——. 1978a. *The Children of Woot: A History of the Kuba Peoples*. Madison: University of Wisconsin Press.

——. 1978b. For Oral Tradition (But Not Against Braudel). *History in Africa* 5: 351–56.

——. 1983. Is Elegance Proof?: Structuralism and African History. *History in Africa* 10: 307–48.

——. 1985. *Oral Tradition as History*. Madison: University of Wisconsin Press.

——. 1990. *Paths in the Rainforests: Toward a History of Political Tradition in Equitorial Africa*. Madison: University of Wisconsin Press.

Veltman, Calvin. 1983. *Language Shift in the United States*. New York: Mouton.

Vossen, Rainer, and Marianne Bechhaus-Gerst, eds. 1983. *Nilotic Studies: Proceedings of the International Symposium on Languages and History of the Nilotic Peoples*. 2 vols. Berlin: D. Reimer.

Wallerstein, Immanual. 1991. The Construction of Peoplehood: Racism, Nationalism, Ethnicity. In *Race, Nation, Class: Ambiguous Identities*. Ed. by E. Balibar and I. Wallerstein. London: Routledge, Chapman and Hall.

Watson, J. M. 1952. The Agoro Systems of Irrigation. *Uganda Journal* 16, 2: 159–63.

Wayland, E. J. 1935. Past Climates and Some Future Possibilities in Uganda. *Uganda Journal* 3, 2: 93–110.

Weatherby, John M. 1979. The Raindrums of the Sor. In *Chronology, Migration and Drought in Interlacustrine Africa*. Ed. by J. B. Webster. New York: Africana.

Weber, Max. 1965 (orig. pub. 1947). Ethnic Groups. In *Theories of Society: Foundations of Modern Sociological Theory*. Ed. by T. Parsons et al. New York: Free Press of Glencoe.

Webster, J. B. 1969. The "History of Uganda" Project under the Direction of the Department of History, Makerere University College. Unpublished ms.

——. n.d. [1969]. Research Methods in Teso. Unpublished ms.

——. n.d. [1971]. A Tentative Chronology for the Lwo. Unpublished ms.

——. 1972. To the Palace Gates — And Back? Paper presented at the Dahousie African Studies Association Seminar, Halifax.

——. 1973. The Deification of Displaced Dynasties. Paper presented at the UCLA African Studies seminar, Los Angeles.

——. 1976a. The Peopling of Agago. In *The Central Lwo during the Aconya*. Ed. by J. M. Onyango-ku-Odongo and J. B. Webster. Nairobi: East African Literature Bureau.

——. 1976b. Lira Palwo: An Expanding Acholi State. In *The Central Lwo during the Aconya*. Ed. by J. M. Onyango-ku-Odongo and J. B. Webster. Nairobi: East African Literature Bureau.

——. 1976c. State Formation and Fragmentation in Agago. In *The Central Lwo during the Aconya*. Ed. by J. M. Onyango-ku-Odongo and J. B. Webster. Nairobi: East African Literature Bureau.

——, ed. 1979a. *Chronology, Migration and Drought in Interlacustrine Africa*. New York: Africana.

——. 1979b. Noi! Noi!: Famines as an Aid to Interlacustrine Chronology. In *Chronology, Migration and Drought in Interlacustrine Africa.* Ed. by J. B. Webster. New York: Africana.

——. n.d. [a]. Migration and Settlement c. 900–1900. Unpublished paper (intended for inclusion in *A History of Uganda,* vol. 1).

——. n.d. [b]. The Second Babito Dynasty in Bunyoro-Kitara and the Formation of New States c. 1650–1780. Unpublished paper (intended for inclusion in *A History of Uganda,* vol. 2).

Webster, J. B., and Ralph S. Herring. 1975. Labongo. *Kenya Historical Review* 3, 1: 97–107.

Webster, J. B. et al., eds. 1973. *The Iteso during the Aconya.* Nairobi: East African Publishing House.

Webster, J. B., and J. M. Onyango-ku-Odongo. 1971. A Tentative Chronology for the Lwo: First Revision. Paper presented at the Universities of East Africa Social Science Conference, Makerere University.

Weinreich, Peter. 1983. Emerging from Threatened Identities: Ethnicity and Gender in Redefinitions of Ethnic Identity. In *Threatened Identities.* Ed. by G. M. Breakwell. New York: Wiley.

Were, Gideon, and Francis Wilson. 1968. *East Africa through a Thousand Years.* London: Evans Brothers.

Westermann, Diedrich. 1912. *The Shilluk People: Their Language and Folklore.* Philadelphia: Board of Foreign Missions of the United Presbyterian Church.

White, Richard. 1983. *Roots of Dependency: Subsistence, Environment, and Social Change among the Choctaws, Pawnees, and Navajos.* Lincoln: University of Nebraska Press.

——. 1991a. *"It's Your Misfortune and None of My Own": A History of the American West.* Norman: University of Oklahoma Press.

——. 1991b. *The Middle Ground: Indians, Empires, and Republics in the Great Lakes Region, 1650–1815.* Cambridge: Cambridge University Press.

Wild, J. V. 1954. *Early Travellers in Acholi.* Edinburgh: Nelson.

Wilks, Ivor. 1978. Land, Labour, Capital and the Forest Kingdom of Asante: A Model of Early Change. In *The Evolution of Social Systems.* Ed. by M. Rowland and J. Friedman. Pittsburgh: University of Pittsburgh Press.

Wright A. C. A. 1936. Some Notes on Acholi Religious Ceremonies. *Uganda Journal* 3, 3: 175–202.

——. 1940. The Supreme Being among the Acholi of Uganda—Another Viewpoint. *Uganda Journal* 7, 3: 130–37.

——. 1949. Maize Names as Indicators of Economic Contacts. *Uganda Journal* 13, 1: 61–81.

Wright, John. 1986. Politics, Ideology and the Invention of "Nguni." In *Resistance and Ideology in Settler Societies.* Ed. by T. Lodge. Johannesburg: Ravan Press.

——. 1991. Ethnicity and History: Towards Discussion of the Zulu Case. Paper presented at the Critical Studies Group Seminar, University of Natal, Pietermaritzburg.

——. 1992. Notes on the Politics of Being "Zulu," 1820–1920. Paper presented at

the Project on Contemporary Political Conflict in Natal; Conference on Ethnicity, Society and Conflict in Natal, Pietermaritzburg.

Wrigley, C. C. 1958. Some Thoughts on the Bacwezi. *Uganda Journal* 22, 1: 11–17.

——. 1959. Kimera. *Uganda Journal* 23, 1: 38–43.

——. 1971. Historicism in Africa: Slavery and State Formation. *African Affairs* 70:
113–24.

——. 1973. The Story of Rukidi. *Africa* 43: 219–34.

——. 1988. Four Steps towards Disaster. In *Uganda Now: Between Decay and
Development.* Ed. by H. B. Hansen and M. Twaddle. London: James Currey;
Athens: Ohio University Press.

Yarak, Larry W. 1974. The Flemish, the Language Question and the Belgian Congo,
1942–1960. B.A. thesis, Kalamazoo College.

Index

Abi (*rwot*, Palabek), 253
abila (shrine), 87–89, 149–50
Abok (head, Parabok lineage), 245
Abona (*rwot*, Paibona), 121, 125
Abora, also Labora (*rwot*, Paico), 239
Abunga (lineage), 178
Abunga (multiple-village grouping), 178
Aburu (lineage), 172, 174, 176 n.17
Aceer (multiple-village grouping), 201 n.7
Acer (*rwot*, Pacer), 160, 171
Acholi: boundaries of, xiv, 12, 48, 58; developments, early nineteenth century, 262–67; developments, second half nineteenth century, 267–72; developments, twentieth century, 4–7, 9–11; and early Luo, 78–79; establishing chronology in, 34, 37–38, 39–40 n.40, 43–45, 80 n.5, 90 n.21, 137–38 n.1; extra-polity organization in, 263–67, 271–72; material life in, 54–61; names for (by neighboring peoples), 262; overview of sociopolitical order, 75–78; physical environment of, 46–51. *See also* Chiefdoms; Drought; Economy (precolonial); Ethnicity (in Acholi); Lineages; Oral sources (in Acholi); Rainmaking; Religion and ritual; Royal drums; Succession; Tribute; *individual zones and chiefdoms*
Acic (father, *Rwot* Alero), 108
Acoo (*rwot*, Paico), 121, 123–24
Acore (lineage), 173 n.10
Acuru (lineage), 181–82
Acut (head, Taa lineage), 147–48, 156–57 n.36
Adeng (lineage), 169 n.1
Adilang (chiefdom), 130, 145, 177–78
Adir (*rwot*, Pagak), 224–26
Adyang (lineage), 128, 169 n.1, 174
Adyang (multiple-village grouping), 128
Africanist history, 23–24, 26

Agago (modern county), 34 n.30
Agengo (multiple-village grouping; then sub-group in Lira Paluo), 172–76
Agoro (chiefdom), 256
Agoro (lineage), 69, 125, 215 n.42, 253
Agoro (multiple-village grouping), 69, 71, 125–26
Agoro mountains, 114, 245, 260; northern frontier, Bunyoro/Paluo chiefly order, 48, 255–57; source of iron, 58, 101
Agum (lineage), 159, 169 n.1, 176 n.17
Ajali (chiefdom), 127, 144, 152 n.26, 159, 159–60 n.45; and Bunyoro/Paluo, 128–29; developments, c. 1690–1725, 128–30; developments, c. 1725–90, 165–67; and drought, 129; and Paimol, 151 n.25, 165–66; and Patongo, 130–32
Ajanto (*rwot*, Patiko), 240
Ajebo (lineage), 226 n.72
Akan (southern, of Ghana), 76 n.2
Akanyi (*rwot*, Palabek), 252
Akara/Pajong (chiefdom), 241, 259
Akwang (outcrop), 129
Alano (lineage), 169 n.1
Alarapii (lineage), 245–46
Alero (chiefdom), 35 n.23, 121, 123, 229, 245; and Bunyoro/Paluo, 110–11, 232–33; developments, c. 1680–1725, 106–11; developments, c. 1725–90, 231–34; and drought, 108, 111, 231–33; and early Luo, 122; and Palaro, 109–11, 126–27
Alero (*rwot*, Alero), 106–8, 245
Alur (northwest Uganda), 33, 45, 53, 71 n.53, 262; cooperative work groups in, 60 n.32; succession disputes and consequences in, 91–92 n.23; tribute and redistribution in, 93 n.28
Amal, L., 95–97, 200 n.4, 202
Ameda (lineage), 172, 174, 176 n.17
Amin, I., 10–11, 34 n.29, 42 n.41
Amoono (wife, *Rwot* Kirya), 232

University of Pennsylvania Press
THE ETHNOHISTORY SERIES

Lee V. Cassanelli, Juan A. Villamarin, and Judith E. Villamarin, Editors

This book has been set in Linotron Galliard. Galliard was designed for Mergenthaler in 1978 by Matthew Carter. Galliard retains many of the features of a sixteenth-century typeface cut by Robert Granjon but has some modifications that give it a more contemporary look.

Printed on acid-free paper.